Twisting the Treaty

A Tribal Grab for Wealth and Power

ISBN 1 872970 33 8

Published by Tross Publishing, P.O. Box 22 143, Khandallah, Wellington, 6441, New Zealand   trosspub@gmail.com

Website: www.trosspublishing.co.nz

Printed by Print Stop, 18 Cashew Street, Grenada North, Wellington

Cover: Knox Design   www.knox-design.com.au

First Edition: February 2013
Second Edition: March 2013
Third Edition, March 2013

Tross, the publisher of this book, consists of, and is supported by, many people across the political spectrum. We specialise in publishing books on matters that New Zealanders should know about but which the authorities try to hide in a smoke of confusion, double-speak and deceit. Where other publishers shy away from certain topics, thus perpetrating a form of self-censorship, Tross is happy to fill the gap so as to keep the people informed of what is really going on in the country.
Good reading and good cheer.

From the team at Tross Publishing

ABOUT THE AUTHORS

John Robinson is a research scientist in mathematics and physics with a Ph.D. from the Massachusetts Institute of Technology. He has investigated a variety of topics, including global issues and the social statistics of Maori. His recognition of fundamental flaws in the presentation of nineteenth century Maori demographics has led him to consider the history of those times in his two recent books, *The Corruption of New Zealand Democracy* and *When two Cultures Meet; the New Zealand Experience*, where he explored the considerable shift that Maori culture went through with the coming of European civilisation, together with the important benefits of British colonisation and the falsity of claims of great harm to Maori.

Christchurch born **Bruce Moon** installed the first computer in a New Zealand university at Canterbury in 1962. Since retiring he has taught mathematics and science at a mission school in Vanuatu where, with his wife, he compiled an account of the Second World War from the memories of the local people. He has also worked in India as a volunteer at a village for disabled people at Dehra Dun and taught English and physics to Tibetan refugees in Dharamsala. He is a Fellow of the Institute of Physics and an Honorary Fellow and former National President of the New Zealand Computer Society (now the Institute of Information Technology Professionals) and served for many years as an officer of the Royal New Zealand Naval Volunteer Reserve.

David Round, a sixth generation South Islander, is a lecturer in law at the University of Canterbury. He is the author of *Truth or Treaty; Common Sense Questions about the Treaty of Waitangi* which was published in 1998. He is a keen tramper with longstanding environmental and conservation interests, and was the National Party candidate for Christchurch East at the 2005 General Election. He is a member of the Independent Constitutional Review Panel, which has been set up to counter the mischief being done by the Government's Constitutional Advisory Panel, which is stacked with Maori radicals and their supporters.

Mike Butler graduated with a B.A. in English Literature at Victoria University of Wellington and a post-graduate Diploma of Religious

Education from Unification Theological Seminary in Barrytown, New York. He worked for eighteen years as a newspaper journalist, mostly as chief sub-editor of the Hawkes Bay Herald-Tribune in Hastings. He worked as a contract writer for the New World Encyclopedia, has had a number of articles published in newspapers and magazines, and wrote *The First Colonist – Samuel Deighton, 1821-1900*, the story of his great-grandfather. Mr. Butler is also a member of the Independent Constitutional Review Panel.

Hugh Barr graduated from Auckland University with a Master of Science (Hons) degree in mathematics and, as a Commonwealth Scholar, became a Ph.D. at the University of Toronto. He worked for the D.S.I.R. as a scientist in applied mathematics from 1968 to 1996. A keen tramper he was President of the Federated Mountain Clubs of New Zealand for six years and has been Secretary of the Council of Outdoor Recreation Associations (CORANZ) since 1998. He is also one of the two co-founders of Coastal Coalition, which was formed to uphold Crown ownership of the foreshore and seabed, and he wrote the definitive book on this issue, *The Gathering Storm over the Foreshore and Seabed*. Dr. Barr was a Wellington Regional Councillor from 2001 to 2004 and he stood as the New Zealand First candidate in the Ohariu electorate at the 2011 election.

Peter Cresswell is an Auckland architect and was formerly the editor of the *Free Radical* magazine. He was a founding member of the Libertarianz Party and currently runs the "Not PC" blog. Ref: www.pc.blogspot.com

and seabed"…. His accounts of the conflicts of interest of Chris Finlayson highlight the lack of balance and fair-handedness involved since Finlayson was Ngai Tahu's treaty negotiator against government for many years….

Further, Dr. Barr points out that, under the new Act, Maori will be able to declare wahi tapu any sites they choose, with refusal of public access. This book should be carefully considered by everyone with a concern for public access to coastal areas and the need to prevent racially based legislation getting through Parliament"

- David Tranter in the Greymouth Evening Star.

Paperback. 110 pages. Price: $20.

These books are available from Tross Publishing, P.O. Box 22 143, Khandallah, Wellington 6441   trosspub@gmail.com All prices include postage to addresses in New Zealand

CHAPTERS

INTRODUCTION

This is a book whose time has come since New Zealand now stands at the crossroads of continuing as an egalitarian society with equal rights and opportunities for all regardless of race, or of becoming Apartheid Aotearoa with different rights for different races – as is already happening with the out-of-control Treaty industry and the appeasement of the small and racist Maori Party by John Key who, as we shall see, is the "Triple Traitor", having betrayed New Zealanders on three important occasions:

1. His taking the foreshore and seabed out of public ownership so that it can be handed out to iwi on a racist basis in return for Maori Party support in Parliament

2. His adoption of the U.N. Declaration of the Rights of Indigenous Peoples, allowing Maori to claim special "indigenous" rights even though they are not indigenous, having arrived in New Zealand not too many generations before Tasman.

3. His acceptance of the Maori Party's demand for a Constitutional Review Panel, stacked with Maori Party supporters and other separatists, that seeks to saddle New Zealand with an unnecessary written constitution that will put the Treaty – or, to be more precise, the recently invented misinterpretation of the wrong treaty – at the heart of our laws and national life, thereby further increasing the racial privileges of part-Maoris at the expense of the rights, resources and expectations of the rest of us.

It is worth pointing out that the first two of these Maori Party demands were made to the previous Labour government which, with courage, patriotism and common sense, dismissed them summarily.

The National Government's Marine and Coastal Area Act 2011, which took the coast and seabed (out to 12 km) from Crown (i.e. public) ownership for the first time since 1840, was the greatest swindle in New Zealand history and yet those responsible for it – the National Party, the Maori Party and that serial political opportunist, Peter Dunne - were re-elected a few months later by the victims of the theft! To paraphrase Shakespeare in *Hamlet,* "There is something rotten in the state of New Zealand" at present.

The foreshore and seabed swindle and all the rorts of the Treaty industry have been able to proceed because New Zealand is a small country lacking both a second chamber of parliament (as other

8

democracies enjoy) and an historically informed and far-sighted media that is prepared to see things in the long term and ask the hard questions. In Britain one has the choice of buying around ten daily papers whereas in Auckland, Christchurch and Wellington there is now only one daily newspaper, each of which is overseas owned and reports the news selectively and superficially. The purpose of this book is to inform the public of the harm that the Treatyists are inflicting on what was once the finest nation in the world but is now heading down the dangerous path of having important rights determined by race, with all those who are not of part-Maori blood being relegated to an inferior position.

The two main political parties have both been culpable in driving the Treaty industry but the worst of the appeasing has been done by National administrations – from former Treaty Minister Doug Graham's dodgy Ngai Tahu settlement of 1998 which, as we shall see, should never have been signed, to John Key's betrayal of both the voters and his own Party's principles. The National Party was set up in the 1930s to represent all New Zealanders equally, without giving special privileges to any one particular group. It was to provide an alternative to the then class based Labour Party. By allowing only Maoris to claim the beaches that once belonged to all of us, John Key has betrayed National's founding principle – something that National Party supporters either condone or have simply failed to understand.

Mr. Key seems more partial to rights being decided on a racial basis than other party leaders (with the exception of the Maori Party). Although this kind of apartheid formerly applied in South Africa and is to-day rife in Israel where Palestinians have far fewer legal rights than Jews, it is a concept that is alien to both British law and traditional New Zealand ways.

If New Zealand is to remain true to the democratic and egalitarian principles on which it developed, then all race based laws and funding must be abolished and what John Ansell calls a "colour blind" state must be restored. This would be of benefit to everyone, including Maoris, who would be forced to stand on their own feet like other New Zealanders and would probably be pleasantly surprised at what they are able to achieve once they take personal responsibility for their own lives (which many of them do now anyway) and are outside the backward looking and mischievous grievance industry, which is designed to keep enough Maoris in a state of poverty so that they can be used as an excuse for extracting more money from the taxpayer, which then lines the pockets of the corporate iwi interests that the Maori Party represents.

Attempts to keep part-Maoris in an artificial, re-created tribal setting, that was largely rejected by the chiefs when they signed the Treaty of Waitangi, is both unnatural and cruel. In the words of the eminent British historian, Paul Johnson, in his *History of the American People*, "In material and moral terms, assimilation was always the best option for indigenous peoples confronted with the fact of white dominance. That is the conclusion reached by the historian who studies the fate not only of the American Indians but of the Aborigines in Australia and the Maoris in New Zealand. To be preserved in amber in tribal societies with special 'rights' and 'claims' is merely a formula for continuing friction, extravagant expectations, and new forms of exploitation by white radical intellectuals." [1]

Although the grievance industry is hard on the taxpayer it is even harder on all those Maoris at the bottom of the heap who have to be kept in poverty to keep the industry going and credible. One means of retaining this cycle of inter-generational poverty is the *kohanga reo* system of "total immersion" in the Maori language for young children who, when they eventually move on to a general school, are often seriously deficient in the English language, a disability that holds them back for the rest of their lives, thereby ensuring that Maoris will always stay at the bottom of the socio-economic heap. This suits the fat cats of the Maori Party/corporate iwi very nicely as they can continue to point to "Maori poverty" as a reason to extract ever greater amounts from the taxpayer to enrich the tribal elite.

Tribalism in the 21st century is harmful not only to the integrity and unity of the state but also to those whom it engulfs, giving them a backward looking world view. And it doesn't help that Maori tribalism has been traditionally enmeshed with violence.

The first step is for the people to understand what is going on – free of government lies and media manipulation – and that is what this book seeks to achieve by its penetrating and factual accounts of the fraud on which the Treaty industry is based. The authors of this book are strongly opposed to racism and apply the word "racist" according to its true meaning (determining things racially rather than for the general good) so that, if the leaders of the Maori Party are described as "racist bullies", the reader will know exactly what is meant.

10

The authors are well aware that not all Maori are "grievers" and for that reason they refer whenever possible to "Treatyists" and "the grievance industry". Treatyists, of course, can be of any race; the common requirement is that they propagate the nonsense that the Treaty of Waitangi gave special rights to Maoris when it did not. It was simply the "entry ticket" to the world of "British subjects" for the Maoris who had previously been outside and wanted to get in. Rights for the Maoris – as for all New Zealanders – emanate from being common British subjects and not from anything in the Treaty of Waitangi. Article Two's guarantee of the ownership of their lands (until such time as they sold them) was just a restatement to Maori of the rights of all British subjects who hold freehold title.

The misuse of words has been a powerful weapon in the hands of the Treatyists, e.g. in 1975 the government's "official" Treaty translator, Professor Hugh Kawharu, defined *taonga* in the treaty as "treasure", ignoring its definition in the dictionaries and other writings at the time of the Treaty as being "property procured by the spear" (Kendall and Lee, 1820) [2], "property" [3] (William Williams, 1844), "goods" [4] (E. Wakefield, 1845), "property" [5] (Native Department translation, 1869) and "goods" [6] (Judge F.E. Maning, 1887). Furthermore, if *taonga* meant "treasure", why does the word not appear in the Maori Antiquities Act 1901? As a result of this officially condoned mistranslation (or, if you like, mischievous translation) Maori have claimed radio waves, fauna, flora, water, geothermal resources, language protection and all sorts of other intangibles that no 1840 cannibal chief would have called *taonga*.

Perhaps the most notorious and patently absurd misuse of words was when both the Waitangi Tribunal and the Maori Party's co-leader, Tariana Turia M.P., described European colonisation of New Zealand as a "holocaust". Mrs. Turia obviously doesn't know the true meaning of "holocaust" (great destruction caused by fire) just as she doesn't even know the name of the country she lives in and in whose Parliament she serves – "We refer to the signing of the treaty as the birth of this land we know as Aotearoa". The word Aotearoa was not and is not the Maori name for New Zealand. It was merely the piece of coast that, according to Maori mythology, they first saw upon their arrival here from God knows where.

The Maoris had two names for the South Island - Waipounamu (place of greenstone) and Te Waka a Maui (Maui's canoe) – and one name for the North Island, Te Ika a Maui (Maui's fish). They did not have a name for the whole country until after it was named Nova Zeelanda (later anglicised to "New Zealand") by the States-General (Parliament) of the Netherlands in 1643.

Tasman had named the country "Staten Landt" in honour of the States-General of the United Provinces (Holland) and because he thought it might prove to be continuous with Staten Landt, to the east of Tierra del Fuego at the bottom of South America. However, when in 1643 Staten Landt off South America was found to be an island, the States-General changed the name of the territory discovered by Tasman to Nova Zeelanda, naming it after Zeeland, a province in Holland which means "Sea Land" – a particularly apt name for New Zealand since so much of our beautiful country is within sight and sound of the sea.

Using transliteration (imitating the sound of the new name), the Maoris began to call the whole country Nui Tirani. It seems that Mrs. Turia is unaware of all this.

Instead of the "holocaust" of Mrs. Turia's fertile, if not hate-filled, imagination the Treaty and colonisation were, in fact, the best things that ever happened to the Maoris as they ended slavery, female infanticide, cannibalism and the inter-tribal warfare that, if left unchecked, would have driven the race to extinction. In the words of the Ngai Tahu historian, Jean Jackson, "British intervention stopped the rampant practices of *utu* (revenge) and *muru* (plunder), decisions by divination, sacrifice to appease gods, construction sacrifice [placing slaves beneath the foundation poles of meeting houses], religious cannibalism, slaves penned for cannibal consumption, slaves penned for labour, slave castration, manhood ritual tattooing, circumcision, abduction of women and children, raping of enemy women, etc." [7] Furthermore the life expectancy of Maoris, which was around 25 years at the time of first contact with Europeans, was 75.1 years for women and 70.4 years for men by 2007. The treaty also gave Maoris property rights that they had never had before; no longer could they be thrown off their lands by a bigger tribe with more powerful weapons – as Peter Cresswell explains in Chapter 3. But, instead of gratitude for saving the Maoris from themselves, all that we ever seem to get from Turia is abuse and constant demands for more money for such worthless and racist programmes as Whanau Ora. A very difficult woman to please, if not impossible.

Sometimes these politically correct activists slip off-message and reveal their true ignorance and/or bias – as happened to arch-Treatyist,

Rosslyn Noonan, who was rather inappropriately appointed New Zealand's "Chief Human Rights Commissioner" – a role that was meant to protect the human rights of all New Zealanders but which she perversely twisted into one that supported "race based policies" rather than policies based on need. During a heated exchange at a Rotorua District Council meeting, she snapped, "Go talk to Maori; it's their land". One would have thought that a person holding such a highly paid bureaucratic position would be acquainted with the Treaty of Waitangi but apparently not. Under that treaty New Zealand was ceded to the Crown and thenceforth all New Zealanders own the country and not just the Maoris. Noonan's claim that the Maoris own the country is wishful thinking and not fact.

Another who sometimes has difficulty holding his tongue, if not his temper, is National's Minister for Treaty Settlements, Christopher Finlayson who, when confronted with the new campaign for a "colour blind" state "free of all racial favouritism", damned the idea as "nuts". After all, such a concept would get in the way of his ex-client, Ngai Tahu, continuing to plunder the public purse in the name of special privileges for tribes.

Nowhere is the Treaty fraud more obvious than in the Government's adoption of an unauthorised English version of the treaty that is not the one that was signed at Waitangi by the chiefs but which includes "forests and fisheries", which the true treaty does not. This will be explained by Bruce Moon in Chapter Two. Under this false treaty nearly two billion dollars of public resources have been handed over to part-Maoris, including $170 million in the notorious Sealord fisheries deal – widely regarded as a straight out swindle of the taxpayer that was negotiated by the part-Maori, National Party minister, Douglas Graham. Mr. Graham was later convicted in a criminal court for making false statements in documents seeking money from the public and one can only wonder how much integrity, if any, he displayed during the Sealord negotiations that he conducted on behalf of the taxpayer and which resulted in him giving an unearned bonanza to his fellow Maoris on a racist basis.

Douglas Graham is the ugly face of what has now become the habit for National governments to raid the public larder and give massive, undeserved handouts to their corporate iwi friends, usually in return for political support. .

By the treaty New Zealand became British soil and all who came here subsequently (and their descendants) were to have the same rights as Maoris. However, in the last quarter of a century politicians, judges, bureaucrats and tribal leaders have distorted the treaty so as to give special privileges to part-Maoris in return for votes or for some equally grotty purpose.

High in the category of grottiness has been the behaviour of certain senior judges, starting with Robin Cooke (Lord Cooke of Thorndon), who have abused their position by delivering ideologically driven judgements resulting in confusion so that they could then step into the ensuing imbroglio and exert greater powers over Parliament, thus subverting our hard won democracy.

The current National-Maori Party coalition's push for a written constitution (the Constitutional Advisory Panel) would be the final step in this sinister process of subjecting issues of national policy not to the elected parliament as in the past but to an elite of unelected judges with their own agenda, which is certainly not that of the ordinary, taxpaying New Zealander. Have we really fought wars and shed blood for our democratic rights just to have them taken away from us by an unelected and increasingly disrespected judiciary that bizarrely gives soft sentences for violent crime, severe sentences for victimless drug "crimes", and which increasingly ignores laws passed by Parliament and long established legal precedents if they get in the way of the judges' own personal opinions?

And it's likely to get worse in the future as, since 2008, it has been Christopher Finlayson, in his capacity as Attorney-General, who has been selecting the judges and it is hard to believe that a man of such obvious bias would not have inclined towards "Treatyists" in his appointments.

The justification for government and councils to put themselves undemocratically at the mercy of local Maoris in their decision making is that these people are the *"tangata whenua"* (Maoris of a particular locality) – which is nonsense since the rather pale, part-Maoris of to-day have, in the words of Ngai Tahu historian Jean Jackson, "become genetically modified by several generations of outbreeding with Europeans". To consult *"tangata whenua"* on a local matter when most of them have intermarried with Europeans and migrated to other areas from where their ancestors lived in 1840 is just as daft as it would be to locate the descendants of the European whalers of the early nineteenth century and let them dictate whaling policy in the 21st century.

The first step in destroying the censorship of political correctness and thus regaining free speech is to use words according to their true meaning. This is one of the weapons that this book uses in order to inform the people of what is being done to them by the Treatyists who, although only a small minority, are holding the nation in a vice like grip by means of lies and intimidation of anyone who gets in their way. Intimidation is their weapon of necessity since they cannot rely on truth.

By making a frontal attack on deeply entrenched and unscrupulous interests such as the Maori Party, the Waitangi Tribunal and corporate iwi, which has been feeding off the taxpayer for decades and is now sitting on assets estimated in 2010 at \$36.9 billion,[8] this book will no doubt attract the venom of those who see it as a threat to their "right" to continue to raid the public purse through fraudulent Waitangi Tribunal claims and other similarly dodgy methods, and no doubt the usual slogans will be screamed out.

One of the labels will be "extremist" but all that denotes is the stating of a truth that lies outside the parameters of political correctness, which itself is a sterile and dishonest doctrine as well as a form of censorship imposed by the ruling elite. And, of course, there will be the usual mindless cries of "racism" from the ignorant and the mischievous. "*Twisting the Treaty*" is an attack on the racial privileges of one particular group and it calls for a "colour blind" state where there will be the same legal rights for all and no special privileges or superior funding for any one race. To label such a book as "racist" would defy both logic and truth. However, after finishing the book we are sure that the reader will be able to form his or her own opinion without the help of slogans being shouted by the representatives of corporate iwi.

The one thing that the Maori activists, radicals, "academics", smear merchants and other agents of corporate iwi will not do is engage in a meaningful debate on the issues. When tens of thousands of concerned New Zealanders from all walks of life and all political persuasions joined together in Coastal Coalition to try to prevent the theft and racialisation of the beaches, the architect of the theft, Christopher Finlayson, with his trademark arrogance and rudeness, dismissed them as "clowns" rather than discuss the issues that this greatest ever swindle in New Zealand history involved.

It is time for something better than allowing the government and the judges to destroy the hard earned racial equality of our beautiful country that the pioneers worked so hard to create. Let's not forget that it was the introduction of British sovereignty, British law and British people that was the single most positive event in New Zealand's history, transforming these promising islands from anarchy and savagery into a modern nation with rights, freedoms, a system of law, and modern amenities and infrastructure. Once people realise the extent of the harm being done to the country by the powerful minority of "Treatyists", then, if they have any spirit or interest in their future, they will react with such anger that no government could resist the call for a "colour blind state" where there will be one law for all and one flag. And no Prime Minister of questionable patriotism to allow the flying from public structures of an alternative flag to that under which our brave servicemen fought and died in two world wars. "One law for all" must be unqualified and non-negotiable if New Zealand is to have a future as good as its past. May this book be a first step in telling people the truth.

The book does not need to be read in one session. Nor do the chapters have to be read in sequence. Each chapter is a subject in itself and the authors, all with different perspectives, have been free to develop their own arguments. For this reason there is a small amount of repetition in some places which is necessary for the explanation of particular subjects.

WHY THE TREATY?

John Robinson

In the 1830s Maori society was in turmoil, and disintegrating. While many warriors continued the slaughter of intertribal warfare that had exploded with the introduction of the more effective weapon, the musket, a cultural transition was under way and others, previously warriors themselves, sought some way to put an end to the carnage.

Maori, as other Polynesian peoples, had separated from the mass of humanity some 3,000 and more years before, preserving the superstitious, Stone Age, tribal culture of that time. They had lost contact with the development of civilisation across the vast Eurasian landmass, where knowledge and thinking had evolved with the invention of writing and mathematics, with different ways of organising in nation states, with increased knowledge of the natural world and advanced technology, and new religions.

The coming of Europeans, appearing suddenly from across the seas, was an enormous culture shock. In many ways the rapid adoption of the new capabilities, with the use of new crops and tools, is proof of the resilience of Maori society. Unfortunately the one gift that most transformed Maori society over the first four decades of the nineteenth century was that efficient killing machine, the musket.

The many fortified pa on hilltops across the country showed the incoming Europeans (mostly British and French) and Americans that Maori were a warlike people. Raids and feuds were a major part of Maori life, and boys were raised to be warriors. A great warrior, successful in war, was a person of esteem. Once the capabilities of the introduced firearms were recognised, tribes competed in an arms race to build an armoury, used first by the most belligerent to attack others, then by all for self-defence and further raids.

The massive killing was evident soon after Hongi Hika returned from England, having stopped off in Sydney to purchase "three hundred muskets and a supply of powder and bullets" (other references suggest more muskets, perhaps 500 or even 1,000).[1] When he attacked the Thames tribe in the Hauraki, "the dead were variously reckoned at from two hundred to a thousand".[2] When in 1822, he assailed two pa at Auckland, "nearly all were slaughtered or taken, and Hongi left naught in their villages but bones, with such flesh on them 'as even his dogs had not required'." [3]

"Cannibalism among Maori was not arbitrary, but a devastating act of retribution. Where there had been *hara*, or offences against *mana*, there had to be *utu* (or some kind of return)." [4]

Numerous descriptions of the killing and cannibalism are found throughout the literature, from both Maori and European sources. Many are referenced in Paul Moon's *This Horrid Practice* (particularly Chapter 26), in both of my two recent books and, with reference to the activities of Te Rauparaha, in a further section of this book, "Wellington settlements and consequences".

The ravages of the subsequent fighting destroyed entire communities and displaced others. There was extensive cannibalism. Many were defeated, with survivors taken as slaves. Despite the introduction of new foods, such as the potato, the raising of crops was disrupted and pigs were increasingly exchanged for muskets. Standards of health and nutrition – and birth rates – plummeted. A lack of young people and of women (largely due to female infanticide, as young warriors were desired) was evident, both in early local counts by Europeans and in the later national census.

The fighting peaked in the five years from 1820 to 1825, but remained at a high level throughout the 1830s. According to the historian James Rutherford, there had been 506 significant battles and 36,500 casualties between 1800 and 1830. From 1831 to 1840 there were a further 96 significant battles and 7,100 casualties.[5] Since the population was declining during that decade from perhaps 90,000 to 80,000 (my estimates), those casualties account for 8-9% of the population – even after the fighting had decreased from the horrific levels of the fifteen years from 1815 to 1830. Around one-third of the Maori population perished in just forty years.

Many enjoyed that carnage. Feuds and intertribal fighting were part of the traditional Maori culture, and successful warriors enjoyed and profited from war. As in many societies, a great chief will always have many followers despite bringing death and destruction to others, as shown by the high regard for Alexander the Great, Napoleon and Te Rauparaha (the New Zealand Napoleon).

But not all gained from intertribal war. Many had been conquered, killed or were slaves. Many others despaired. Their world was falling apart. They sought a different way, a new culture. Such an alternative was at hand, presented by the British and the missionaries, a way of life with a rule of law and a religion calling for peace and coexistence rather than tribal conflict. The calls for help to the greater power, to bring a better way to deal with conflict and a strong national authority, came from many northern chiefs – those who had the greater contact and knew the British the best – and were eventually answered.

This process, consciously worked out by Maori themselves, involved enormous changes to the Maori way of life and culture. These chiefs recognised that their society was dysfunctional. The old mores no longer worked or provided a good life. The future looked grim.

Traditional Maori society had honoured the warrior chief. In that highly stratified society important men had many wives. While the loss of a chief was grounds for revenge, the lives of commoners or slaves were of little account. Slaves could be killed, and eaten, at a whim. Women did much of the hard physical labour and aged rapidly. The limited food resources after the moa became extinct by 1600 meant that nutrition was not good, and fertility levels were not high; before contact the population was growing very slowly or even static.

Then came peoples from the other ends of the earth – explorers, traders, whalers, sealers, missionaries and settlers. The newcomers were first met with traditional challenges, with intimidation and fighting to determine who was the stronger and who would dominate. Once the preliminaries were out of the way there were exchanges of goods and trade.

Much of the first contact developed where the cultures were most similar, where there were evident needs that could be readily satisfied. This included prostitution - the willing exchange of women for nails and, later, muskets. Many Maori joined the crews and showed a facility for seamanship, while learning of navigation and how to work these new vessels, along with familiarity with the cannons that were basic equipment on all ships in those uncertain times. Maori helped with the cutting of timber and flax.

New foods, tools and utensils were introduced and Maori came to value 'their pakeha', the few Europeans living among them who provided a conduit to the desired supplies. The two peoples were starting to work together, all active participants in the evolving economy.

Maori seized upon the magic of reading and writing. Many Maori and Europeans were bilingual and becoming familiar with one another's culture. For some time the unfamiliar new religion of Christianity was not popular and even those who attended missionary classes would leave Bible studies to one side to join a *taua* and take part in killing.

As well as the ongoing, traditional, intertribal wars, there were constant attacks on shipping, killing of seamen, theft of goods and destruction of ships and equipment from the times of first contact and continuing through the 1830s. Such actions had commenced at the time of the very first contact, with Tasman; they continued through the early decades of the nineteenth century and did not cease until Britain established a military presence.[6] Those who were gaining from trade acted to protect 'their pakeha' and profited by offering protection to vessels in the waters that they controlled. This was a highly profitable 'protection racket' for the chiefs of Kororareka

"Before the British flag was hoisted [Hone Heke] and his cousin Titore divided a levy of £5 on each ship entering the Bay. They collected their dues from the ships outside the anchorage, boarding them in their canoes before Tapeka Point was rounded. Many ships sailed up to the anchorages off Wahapu and Otuihu, in the passage to the Kawakawa and Waikare, and here Pomare collected his toll from each ship, for he was the paramount chief of the inner waters. Pomare also was the principal agent in the disreputable but profitable business of supplying girls as temporary wives to the crews of the whaleships during their stay in port."[7]

By the late 1830s the profits in the Bay of Islands were around £11,000 to £18,000 a year from trading, dues and prostitution to shipping.[8]

Unfortunately the new capability that was seized upon and treasured most avidly by the Maori was the musket. It was soon found that raiding parties would be more successful with a few guns, and even more so with many guns. Once Hongi Hika had recognised the value of a supply of guns, and had returned from a visit to England with sufficient funds to buy around a thousand muskets in Sydney,[9] war became universal. Warrior leaders came to dominate as fighting spread rapidly across the entire country. All production became focussed on the purchase of further arms.

The desire for *utu* and revenge, basic to Maori culture, intensified warfare as each battle left its dead and a reason for further fighting. The intertribal attacks spiralled out of control with a far greater level of killing and mass cannibalism than in the past. Tribes were destroyed and driven from their lands. Ever more captives and slaves were desired for cannibal feasts and required to raise food crops. Tribes driven from their homes were forced to settle in insalubrious places. Poor nutrition, female infanticide and the many deaths reduced fertility. The resultant shortage of women and children added to the population decline that continued throughout much of the nineteenth century. This was truly a dysfunctional society, trending towards self-annihilation.

There were 43,600 casualties in the intertribal battles of the nineteenth century – around one-third of the then population. Numbers of battles and casualties eventually declined from the peak in 1821-25, due to the eventual balance of forces (with most tribes well-armed), exhaustion and the lack of further vulnerable targets for conquest. Not that war came to an end; there were more battles and casualties in each of the two five-year periods of the 1830s than during the first three five-year periods of the century (see chart).[10]

Figure 1. Casualties in the intertribal wars.

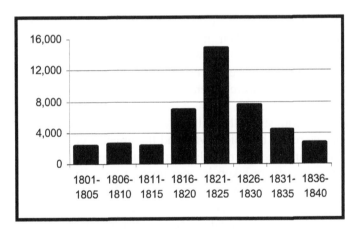

Some warriors enjoyed and profited from war and desired to continue with the traditional ways of killing and destruction, even at the much higher and more destructive level. Others were not so satisfied. Many had been conquered; their relatives had been killed, and many eaten, and they lived in fear and misery or were slaves. Others, while not under direct threat, despaired of what had happened to their society, discussed what to do and sought an alternative way, a new culture.

A new way to settle disputes, without *utu* and death, had been presented. British and American visitors had spoken of the new idea of universal equality, and the British were moving to end slavery (the slave trade was abolished in the British West Indies in 1807 and throughout the Empire in 1838). Missionaries talked of one God for all, and a religion that asks all people to live together peacefully. Maori who had travelled saw the working of the rule of law. There was a better alternative; the problem was how to end civil war and make a unified nation out of a disrupted tribal society.

The 1830s marked the watershed. "From then on, there could be no turning back." [11] Many Maori chiefs in the north were speaking of their requests and desires, for a change of direction and the assertion of a national authority. They asked the British for help, in 1831 "we pray thee to become our friend and the guardian of these islands", and in 1835 "they entreat that he [the King of England] will continue to be the parent of their infant State, and that he will become its Protector from all attempts upon its independence." [12]

These tribes agreed under the declaration of 1835 to meet once a year at Waitangi to make laws for the preservation of peace and the regulation of trade. But it soon became apparent that unity and cooperation among all Maori was absent and the steps laid down in the Declaration would not be successful. Few chiefs attended as notions of Maori nationalism were alien to tribal society, and tribal fighting continued as before.

The several steps that ultimately brought peace under a central authority were led by chiefs who had the greatest contact and exchange with Europeans and their civilisation. The meetings were in the north, and the actions were taken in coordination with British. The letter to King William in 1831 was drafted in the Bay of Islands (Northland) with assistance by missionaries, the declaration of 1835 drafted by Busby was signed at Waitangi (Northland), the Treaty of Waitangi of 1840 between Maori and British was signed at Waitangi (Northland) after debate with Captain (later Governor) Hobson, and the conference of 1860, called by Governor Gore Browne, took place at Kohimarama (Auckland).

Northern Maori had become familiar with the outside world. Their relative and leader Hongi Hika would have told of his visit to England; others had been to Sydney and worked on British and American vessels. Many Maori and Europeans were bilingual and talked together. While

22

Maori society was tribal, the whanau, hapu and iwi were not isolated. There were many family connections and much travel and visiting for meetings on the marae. They were able to learn and to compare their lifestyle with that of the developed civilisation across the world.

These chiefs who signed the various papers were warriors, successful in battle yet wanting to turn away from the slaughter. One key figure was Tamati Waka Nene (born probably in the 1780s), who rose to be one of the war leaders of the Nga Puhi and took an active part in the intertribal wars of 1818-1820. He successfully took his warriors on a rampage the whole length of the North Island, killing and plundering as he went until he reached Cook Strait. He and Patuone planned a further expedition to Waikato to avenge their relative, Taui, who had been killed there with Pomare I in 1826. But when the expedition went in 1827 they found the enemy so numerous that they returned without attacking them.

Nene became the highest-ranking chief among his own people and one of the three leaders in Hokianga. It became his responsibility, often an onerous one, to protect the Wesleyan mission (which had moved to Hokianga in 1827) and the traders (who had begun to set themselves up in the district in the mid 1820s). Nene had seen the advantages of a Pakeha presence; anxious that the district should not fall into disrepute among traders, he worked to keep the peace in the turbulent frontier society.

He was friendly with the Church Missionary Society missionaries, especially Henry Williams. By the 1830s Nene was regarded by the European community as a leader they could rely on and turn to for advice. He was among the thirteen Maori leaders who signed the 1831 petition to William IV, he signed the 1835 declaration and the Treaty of Waitangi, and he fought against Hone Heke in 1845-46. He was the first Maori speaker at the Kohimarama conference in 1860, and his name headed the list of northern leaders invited by government to set up the first Tai Tokerau *runanga* in 1862. [13]

The senior Northland warrior chiefs included the three brothers, Te Wharerahi (brother-in-law to Nene and his elder brother Patuone, both of whom came to desire peace), Rewa and Moka Kainga-mataa. Their trajectory from killer to peacemaker is reflected in the title of a chapter in a recent book, "Rewa – man of war, man of peace". [14] As their societies changed fundamentally, with the introduction of better

23

housing, carpentry and new tools, new foods, reading and writing and much more, these warriors steadily changed their attitudes.

The culture shift came to include religion, and a rejection of the old ways. Missionary William Yate told of the remarkable change in attitudes towards Christianity in the north. In 1827 "this institution was totally disregarded".[15] There was widespread indifference, with people drifting off during a sermon. Just a few years later, in 1832, Sabbath schools were well established and "our chapel was crowded to excess". [16] The many letters from Maori that Yate reports were very much personal accounts, with frequent reflections on mortality and sin, spiritualism, death and salvation. Maori were seeking, and accepting, a different way to view life and death, a new way to live.

Many Maori shared that desire for a new way, in a movement that became national in scope. The take-up of Christianity was widespread across the country during the 1830s, with reports of growing congregations from many districts.[17] It was as if a collective decision had been reached, a true social revolution. This dramatic culture shift is shown clearly in church records. Figure 2 illustrates the sudden increase in Anglican Maori churchgoers, both attendants on public worship (solid line) and scholars (dashed line).[18]

Figure 2. Maori Anglican churchgoers, 1836 to 1842

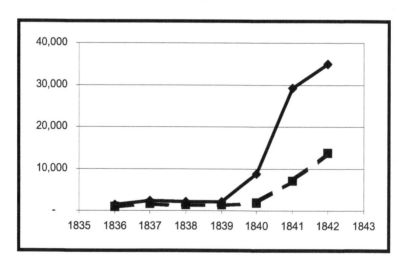

Soon after, in 1845, George Clarke, a former CMS missionary who had become Chief Protector of the Aborigines, estimated that about 64,100 Maori attended Christian services regularly, which would be 80% of the Maori population of the time.[19] Certainly a significant number of Maori were adopting the imported religion.

The British Government too was active, concerned with the developing situation and, eventually, ready to play an active part. In response to the 1831 letter, James Busby was accredited in 1833 as British Resident in New Zealand. Busby then helped chiefs to draft and forward the 1835 declaration. With the failure of that initiative, the debate continued in the British and Australian media, in the British Parliament (including a House of Lords Committee in 1837-38) and in the Colonial Office. Meanwhile Edward Gibbon Wakefield continued to press for subsidised emigration from Britain, following an idea that he first set down in *A Letter from Sydney* (1829), whereby the sale of small units of Crown land would fund colonisation.

The British recognised the potential damage of colonisation. "Whenever settlers from a people in an advanced state of civilisation come in contact with the aborigines of a barbarous country, the result is always prejudicial to both countries, and most dishonourable to the superior," declared the future Prime Minister, William Gladstone in the House of Commons during a debate on a Bill to regulate settlement in New Zealand.[20]

There was a determination to act well, and not to repeat the mistakes of the past. That widely held intention was expressed in 1842 by Charles Heaphy, who was awarded the Victoria Cross as a Major in 1864, was MP for Parnell in 1867-70 and was appointed a judge of the Native Land Court in 1878. "It may confidently be hoped that the settlement of the New Zealand islands will form an exception to the rule, that in all colonised countries the aboriginal inhabitants have suffered from their contact with Europeans, and that their extermination follows the settlement of their country." [21]

The British had a considerable experience in colonisation and were determined to protect the rights of the Maori. Instructions from the Colonial Secretary, Lord Normanby, to Hobson expressed an intention to deal with Maori fairly and to improve their situation while protecting the Maori culture.

"The establishment of schools for the education of the Aborigines in the elements of literature, will be another clear object of your solicitude; and until they can be brought within the pale of civilised life, and trained to the adoption of its habits, must be carefully defended in the observation of their own customs, so far as is compatible with the universal maxims of humanity and morals. But the savage practices of human sacrifice and cannibalism must be promptly and decisively interdicted, such atrocities, under whatever plea of religion they may take place, are not to be tolerated in any part of the dominions of the British Crown," wrote Lord Normanby in his important and humane brief to Hobson.[22]

There were further letters of instruction to Hobson as he travelled to New Zealand in 1839, and he met with Governor Gipps of New South Wales, in Sydney. Why then, after all that effort, would the British have come up with such a foolish draft as the currently accepted English version, which does not accord with the Maori version? The answer is that they did not – as explained by Bruce Moon in the next chapter. That version was a rough draft, penned by an incompetent secretary who added several pretentious expressions of his own that were soon removed before translation into Maori. It never was the official version.

It is necessary to correct a number of such fanciful stories before the real history of our country becomes clear. For example, there was no holocaust following colonisation. The decrease in Maori population during the 19th century was not the result of colonisation, the cause being the low fertility, the female infanticide and the shortage of women and young resulting from the disruptions of the intertribal wars of the first four decades of the century. The killing of the intertribal wars was by no means insignificant, as has been claimed. Indeed, the loss of one-third of the population had a considerable and lasting impact.[23]

Colonisation was not a one-sided action, forced on Maori by a devious, dictatorial power. The Treaty of Waitangi was not a poorly written piece of trickery, to form a modern basis for ongoing grievance and litigation. The call came from Maori – it could not be from all in a divided tribal society still at war – for the assertion of a central authority to put an end to bloodshed. A culture under great stress was making the transition to modernity and peace.

This was a great event for many Maori, none more so than the slaves who became free men and women. Intertribal attacks and cannibalism became unlawful. The major wishes of those chiefs were answered. We can all be truly proud of that.

26

REAL TREATY; FALSE TREATY, THE TRUE WAITANGI STORY

Bruce Moon

"The chiefs placed in the hands of the Queen of England the sovereign authority to make laws".
- Sir Apirana Ngata, M.P.

When Captain Cook arrived in New Zealand the Maoris, like all Polynesians, were a Stone Age people. They were nevertheless quick to appreciate the products of European technology. A fair-sized nail quickly became the standard price of a dusky maiden and indeed, even before getting to Tahiti, to avoid having his ship stripped entirely by randy sailors, Cook had to issue a standing order that 'No Short Iron or any thing that is made of Iron' be exchanged for anything except provisions.[1]

The Maoris were also a tribal people whose entire loyalty was to chief and tribe – which is still important to many – without a concept of a nation or country as a whole. 'Aotearoa' was sometimes used as a name for the South Island, says historian Barry Brailsford,[2] for the North Island said Michael King.[3] Take your pick. In 1840 it was 'Nu Tirani' and about a hundred years later, I recall a proclamation in Maori pasted on the wall of the Karitane Post Office in which it was 'Tominiona o Niu Tireni' (the Dominion of New Zealand).

As tribals like the Desert Arabs and Highland Scots, Maoris were a martial people and, as they were very sensitive to supposed insults, there was much fighting amongst them. The losers were usually enslaved, often mutilated, or fattened and eaten. Thus W.J. Elvy recounts the successive invasions of the northern South Island and slaughter of the inhabitants.[4] Waitaha and Katimamoe were almost exterminated by Kaitahu. The Tu-mata-kokiri who confronted Tasman were annihilated by the Ngatiapa and Kaitahu, their last stand being in the Paparoas of Westland about 1800. In their turn, two thousand Kaitahu were butchered by Te Rauparaha at Kaikoura and more at Onawe and Kaiapoi. It went on and on. Treachery was common.

In the North it was just the same. Indeed the Maoris whom Tasman had seen on the Three Kings Island had since been exterminated by raiding war parties from the mainland. It was this type of ferocity which

27

led the British government to choose Botany Bay, not somewhere in New Zealand, for their penal colony, after the loss of the American Colonies where formerly convicts were dumped.

Classic Maori warfare was entirely hand-to-hand but one example of European technology – the musket – was very quickly appreciated and its consequences for Maori society were much like that of nuclear weapons in our own time. Thus came about the 'Musket Wars' of the period 1807 – 1840 with Maori fighting Maori. The carnage was colossal. If any era in Maori history merits the name 'holocaust', this was it, and not, as is sometimes mischievously claimed, the later period of European settlement. It was Maori slaughter of Maoris.

With endemic warfare, bloody conquest, cannibalism, infanticide (especially of female children) and slavery, Maori society had become pathological. Anybody who doubts this should read the meticulously researched works of Paul Moon[5], who identifies paranoia in Maori communities.[6] They lived in "almost unbearable anxiety".[7] So anxious were southern Maoris about the prospects of murderous raids from the north that many of them eagerly sold or gave their daughters to white settlers to avoid the extinction of their race. Full-blood numbers decreased rapidly and they became predominantly a race of half-castes.[8] Ruapuke missionary, Rev. Wohlers, speaks approvingly of the southern homes of a white man and Maori woman.[9]

The consequences of this internecine Maori destruction were profound. As John Robinson shows in his 2010 book, *The Corruption of New Zealand Democracy*, the demographic effects continued for generations and not until close to 1900 were there any clear signs of recovery. The negative psychological consequences (post-traumatic stress disorder) were also profound and, as the authors quoted by Paul Moon have indicated, they may continue to the present day.

This dire behaviour ceased rapidly after 1840. It may be said with truth that the transfer of sovereignty to the British, together with the sustained efforts by the missionaries, notably Henry Williams[10], saved the Maoris from themselves.

Into the centre of the carnage, on 8th August 1823, stepped Williams with his wife, Marianne, and their three children, Edward, Marianne and Samuel. They were not the first but Henry soon became the leader of the Church of England mission and engaged in many tasks which included learning the Maori language and creating a written one. On 3rd March 1826, Henry's brother, William, and his wife, Jane, joined them. The missionaries compiled dictionaries and grammars and printed a great deal of religious and educational material.

Other Europeans were also arriving – explorers, whalers and adventurers – many lawless types amongst them. Many Maori-European interactions benefited both but, unsurprisingly, there were some misunderstandings followed by savage reprisals. At Whangaroa in 1810, all but four of the 70 aboard the *Boyd* were killed and eaten. Tragically, reprisals by English whalers led to the death of the innocent chief Te Pahi[11], not the culprit, Te Puhi. In 1772, Ngati Pou had killed and eaten French explorer, Marion du Fresne, and 26 of his crew who had apparently broken a *tapu*. In subsequent encounters, about 250 warriors were killed; most of them when about 1,500 tribesmen attacked a vastly outnumbered French force defending its hospital camp on Moturoa Island.[12]

French appearances in New Zealand waters were of concern to British and Maoris alike. The British in New South Wales feared their colonial intentions. Missionaries and Maori converts alike feared the spread of Roman Catholicism. Maoris knew that the French had not forgotten the Marion du Fresne affair – they still referred to the French as "the tribe of Marion".

The Secretary of the Church Missionary Society in New Zealand, William Yate, and Ngapuhi chiefs Rawiri Taiwhanga and Rewa in particular were anxious to have a more formal British presence in New Zealand. Yate and Rewa wrote a letter to this effect in both Maori and English versions. It was signed by thirteen Ngapuhi chiefs and sent to King William IV of Britain on 16th November 1831.

This letter was received coolly in Britain. The British were reluctant to increase their involvement in New Zealand, as British parliamentary papers of the time show clearly. For one thing, they needed plenty of effort to put into their Australian colonies (Victoria, 1834, and South Australia, 1836). The generally warlike behaviour of the Maoris also dissuaded them. However, the Yate/Rewa letter, along with continuing pleas by missionaries and others, induced British Colonial Secretary, Lord Goderich, to appoint James Busby as British Resident in the Bay of Islands.

With little authority and no means of enforcing it, Busby was in a ludicrous position. However, he did make some efforts. For instance, Maori ships trading to New South Wales didn't have a flag by which they could be recognised. In 1831 some chiefs had flown a Union Jack to warn off French ships.

Busby decided that they needed their own flag and set out to provide it. Missionary Henry Williams sketched three designs. Busby had these made up, raised them on three short poles where they hung limply, assembled fifteen chiefs and invited them to choose one. Mystified, the chiefs voted for all three. The impasse was broken by a Maori servant of Williams and one was chosen. The other two being hauled down, Busby "haughtily declared [it] the National Flag of New Zealand"[13] and rewarded all those present with a large meal. Flown occasionally and forgotten, it was rescued from oblivion by the Shaw, Savill and Albion shipping company and adopted as its house flag, serving as such as late as 1970.

Born in comic opera circumstances, it is this flag which was flown by the Tuhoe tribe in 2010 during their verbal exchanges with Prime Minister Key.

In 1835 a genuine effort was made by Busby and the northern chiefs to form some sort of government for New Zealand. "This time", wrote Michael King, "in exchange for a second cauldron of porridge, Busby persuaded the same chiefs and some additional ones [52 in total] to sign 'A Declaration of the Independence of New Zealand' by a 'Confederation of United Tribes'" [14] – a document which he himself had concocted ...

: – "a bloodless puerility", wrote Pember Reeves in 1898,
"a second and equally contrived ceremony" wrote Michael King in 2003,
"little more than a pebble" wrote Paul Moon in 2006,
"a paper pellet" said Governor Gipps in Sydney at the time,
"silly and unauthorised", said a Colonial Office official.

A congress or parliament was to meet in Waitangi each autumn but attendances soon fell to nothing and it was abandoned altogether in 1838. This was precipitated in part by the outbreak of full-scale civil war amongst Ngapuhi and two adjacent tribes. Pomare and Titore, both Ngapuhi signatories of the "Declaration of Independence" less than eighteen months previously, were openly at war. Titore attacked Pomare's pa with 800 warriors, though a little later Titore himself was killed. With efforts by the missionaries and others, the conflict simmered down after several months. "The 'Declaration' was not even acting as a regional goodwill agreement, let alone a national document of constitutional significance." [15]

It is this absurdity, this short-lived, long-dead paper tiger, the "Declaration of Independence" that Ngapuhi now seek to measure against the standing of the Treaty of Waitangi. "The hearings [of the Waitangi Tribunal]", it has been reported, "will be divided into two stages, beginning with four weeks on the issue of sovereignty, the Declaration and the Treaty." [16] By descending thus to the puerilities of Busby, the proceedings of the Waitangi Tribunal have become a Gilbert and Sullivan opera.

Indirectly the 'confederation' did have significance as it led to discussion between Maori chiefs on one hand and Busby and the missionaries on the other, of constitutional and other European political concepts, such as sovereignty, which were new to Maori thought. Even before Busby arrived it had been found necessary to invent Maori terms for some ideas unfamiliar to them. Thus in 1833, missionary William Williams coined the term 'tino rangatira' for 'high chieftain'. We may be sure that there was much discussion to clarify the meanings of such terms, no doubt conducted at times in both Maori and English.

Then in 1837, Captain William Hobson, Royal Navy, was sent to New Zealand in *HMS Rattlesnake* to protect British settlers caught between warring Maori factions. In his report on this visit he recommended that a British colony be established in the country.

The lukewarm British attitude to this idea began slowly to change. Becoming aware of the plans of Edward Gibbon Wakefield and others for large-scale, systematic, British colonisation and the need to protect existing law-abiding settlers and also the Maoris themselves from both lawless settlers and each other, the British Government decided to act. They also wanted to check the rapid expropriation of Maori land which many Maoris had been only too willing to exchange for European consumer goods.

The timing was fortunate for this country. The few decades before 1840 had seen a remarkable increase in humanitarian awareness and social conscience amongst the middle and upper classes of Britain, beyond anything elsewhere in the world ~ prison reform, reduction in the use of the death penalty, regulation of child labour, electoral reform. Perhaps the greatest of all, was the abolition of slavery throughout the British Empire, a five year process that culminated in August 1838.

The House of Lords is often criticised for being undemocratic, which it is, but it should be borne in mind that its members or their forebears were chosen for their distinguished service or achievements. It should be no surprise therefore if some of them are or were men of ability and human qualities. One such was the Marquess of Normanby, Colonial Secretary in 1839, under whose instructions James Stephen, Permanent Under-Secretary to the Colonial Office, drafted a 4,200-word brief. Stephen, an Evangelical, was a nephew of William Wilberforce, a leader of the campaign to end slavery. In fact, it was Stephen who had drafted the Act to abolish slavery.

Normanby's brief was clear, explicit, intelligent and humane. It stated for instance that New Zealand was not to become a penal settlement and 'that no convict is ever to be sent thither to undergo his punishment'. Anybody who wants to understand British intentions towards this country should read it carefully. If, in the 1980s, our politicians had bothered to look at this brief, instead of concocting their ignorant and ill-considered reference to undefined "principles of the Treaty", the situation would not have descended into its present confused and corrupted muddle.

The brief says quite explicitly that the task was: "to treat with the aborigines of New Zealand in recognition of Her Majesty's sovereign authority over the whole or any part of those Islands which they may be willing to place under Her Majesty's dominion." There was an important proviso: "The Queen ... disclaims to seize on the Islands of New Zealand ... unless the free intelligent consent of the natives, expressed according to their established usages, shall first be obtained." [17] This was the primary task in a nutshell. Free consent to the transfer of sovereignty to the Queen was the *sine qua non*.

For this task that reliable, experienced and conscientious officer - Captain William Hobson R.N., was chosen again. We may be sure that Hobson read his brief many times on his passage here and, as we shall see, he carried out his instructions faithfully and well.

Hobson proceeded to New South Wales and reported to Governor Sir George Gipps, before whom, on 14th January, 1840, he took an oath of office as Lieutenant-Governor of any territories which might be acquired. He also took the opportunity to peruse the large number of documents in the Governor's records purporting to describe land sales which had been made already in New Zealand and he had a meeting with a delegation of Sydney businessmen who had already purchased from the Maoris tracts of land in New Zealand. He needed a ship to take him there and staff to assist.

Gipps saw his chance and provided poor Hobson with "several officers, selected for their known incompetency, ... because [he] was ... anxious to get rid of them".[18] They included Willoughby Shortland, after whom Auckland's Shortland Street is named, and 3rd class clerk, James Stuart Freeman, immortalised in Freemans Bay, Auckland, a product of Eton and Oxford and a pompous ass. He was to be Hobson's private secretary.

In Sydney at the time was *HMS Herald* commanded by Captain Joseph Nias R.N., en route on an expedition which he much favoured to China. Gipps ordered him instead to convey Hobson to New Zealand. Nias was furious and, to quote a contemporary, "behaved scandalously ... offered every impediment ... and ... little respect".[19] However, they duly sailed and on 29th January 1840, dropped anchor in Kororareka Bay. Busby came aboard, his position as Resident terminating on the ship's arrival. Hobson and Nias agreed that Busby, as Resident, was entitled to a gun salute but they disagreed on the appropriate number of guns so none were fired.

Next day, 30th January, Hobson went ashore and, following his instructions from Lord Normanby, read a proclamation of his assumption of duties and another stating that all settlers' land claims would have to be ratified by the Crown in due course while any further private sales would be considered "absolutely void". That day, Busby wrote to his good friend, Tamati Waka Nene, chief of Ngapuhi, saying that on Wednesday next, 5th February, Hobson desired to meet with an assembly of Chiefs at Busby's home at Waitangi to discuss his proposals.

That gave Hobson five days to prepare. With some contribution from Freeman, he began to draft a treaty and, by the afternoon of 1st February, had eight pages of rough notes. Then that evening there was a furious row between Hobson and Nias. This and his fragile health on account of three attacks of yellow fever during his service in the West Indies, put tremendous stress on Hobson. Next day he spent in his cabin but, being confident of the support of Busby and feeling too unwell himself to leave the ship, he sent two of his staff ashore with his and Freeman's rough notes to ask Busby's advice respecting them. Busby replied that, as they stood, they would not accomplish the desired objectives and he offered to draft a treaty himself for Hobson's consideration. Hobson's men replied in turn that this was precisely what Hobson wanted. On that day and the following (2nd and 3rd) therefore, Busby made a concerted effort to prepare a draft with Hobson's rough notes as a guideline and, by the evening of the 3rd, he had a clean draft ready to show Hobson.

That evening, Hobson felt well enough to go ashore again, as Freeman's second despatch to Sir George Gipps for that day shows,[20] and Busby gave him the draft. This was probably at Busby's own cottage at Kororareka. Realising Hobson's state of health, Busby arranged for the next steps to be taken at the spacious waterfront home of Captain James Reddy Clendon, a British subject and the American consul, at Okiato, three miles south of Kororareka. Clendon, whose name is almost completely absent from New Zealand history books, had arrived in New Zealand before Busby, whose good friend he became. He was also a competent speaker of Maori. He appears to have met Hobson during the latter's visit in 1837. With the willing help of both Busby and Clendon and Busby's draft of the 3rd February in hand, Hobson was well-equipped at last to produce the final English draft on 4th February, the day before his planned meeting with the assembled Maori chiefs.

All the evidence points to the final drafting session being held at Clendon's home, the final version being penned by Busby on paper watermarked "W. Tucker 1833" from Clendon's personal stock. [Other participants had their own paper stocks from other makers which they used in writing the rough drafts which survive.] Significantly Freeman was excluded. Clendon made his own copy. For the text of this final draft in English of the Treaty of Waitangi, see the Appendix.

Following his instructions from Lord Normanby, Hobson made great efforts to ensure that the document was expressed in simple terms, using words which had close Maori equivalents insofar as was possible. Freeman's more pretentious expressions which appeared in earlier rough drafts were excluded. Thus Hobson went as far as to describe the Queen as 'Queen of England' even though she did not have such a title. (Nor does the Queen today.) [Victoria was actually the Queen of Great Britain and Ireland.]

By mid-afternoon his draft was finished and Hobson himself took it to the Mission station close by over the water, giving it at 4 p.m. to Rev. Henry Williams, Head of the Mission, with a request that he provide a translation in Maori by next morning. Hobson then returned to *HMS*

Herald. Henry Williams with his 21-year-old son Edward Marsh Williams set to work (equipped with a large pot of tea) and had it ready by morning.

Henry Williams, head of the Mission and a former naval officer, had arrived with his family seventeen years previously when Edward was just four years old. Edward, who was a bright and serious-minded young man, was therefore a native speaker of the Ngapuhi dialect of Maori which was in continual use at the mission. Henry himself had made many contributions to Maori scholarship. They were therefore very competent to do the task entrusted to them by Hobson and would certainly have known how Maoris understood the words they used, such as 'kawanatanga' and 'tino rangatiratanga'.[21]

At 9 a.m. on the morning of 5th February, Hobson landed and made his way to Busby's residence at Waitangi where the planned meeting with the chiefs was about to be held. With Busby, Henry Williams and Rev. Richard Taylor, he reviewed the Williams' translation. Busby suggested that the word 'huihuinga' for 'confederation' be substituted by 'whakaminenga' and this was accepted.

At noon the meeting got under way; Hobson read each clause from the English draft and was followed by Williams who repeated them in Maori. Quibbles over the accuracy of the translation were soon resolved – many of the chiefs were conversant with English – and all seemed satisfied that the two documents said the same thing. Hone Heke, who was said to speak and write beautiful English, said that he fully approved.[22] There can be no doubt that he understood well both Maori and English versions. No amendments were suggested. The text of the treaty as signed mirrors the Williams' translation.

As Henry Williams reported to Bishop Selwyn later, "The instruction of Captain Hobson was 'not to allow any one to sign the treaty till he fully understood it' to which instruction I did most strictly attend … That the natives to whom I explained the treaty understood the nature of the same, there can be no doubt."

Next there followed a lengthy discussion with the arguments for and against the treaty being aired fully in the Maori way. When proceedings concluded, the chiefs retired to Tii marae to discuss it amongst themselves and Williams went with them. Hobson had expected that such discussion would take several days but Rev. Richard Taylor, who was in attendance and who understood Maori practices well, predicted that they would probably want to sign the next day and then go home for a good meal. He sent a message to this effect to Hobson who had returned to *HMS Herald*, suggesting that, if Hobson sent the the Williams' original paper copy to him, he would copy it to parchment (actually dogskin) ready for the morning. Hobson agreed and Taylor did so on the evening of the 5th, keeping the original as a memento ('for his trouble').

Next morning the chiefs did as Taylor had predicted, 45 pronouncing themselves ready to sign, so early that Hobson was obliged to hasten ashore in civilian clothes (except for his hat) for the signing ceremony. (Artists' impressions of the signing with Hobson in full dress uniform, e.g. on the 1940 centennial stamp and on the base of the statue of Queen Victoria in Wellington's Cambridge Terrace, are simply imaginary)

There are somewhat variant accounts of just how many chiefs signed on that day. A list of the signatories with details in full, prepared by Carol Whyte of Auckland in 2001 gives 44. This includes some who had spoken against the treaty the previous day (though possibly as 'devil's advocates'). Hone Heke signed first. As each one did so, Hobson shook his hand and said 'He iwi tahi tatou', that is 'We are one people now'.

Hobson said of this document "This instrument I consider to be de facto the treaty, and all signatures that are subsequently obtained are merely testimonials of adherence to the terms of the original document." On Whyte's list it is stated that "signatories after 6th February, 1840, were asked to sign their allegiance to Queen Victoria". Be that as it may, the official tally of Maori signatures is 540, being men and a few women who were chiefs or asserted as much. Te Rauparaha signed twice. Whether he was counted twice, I don't know. This far surpasses the number who refused to sign (many of them being adherents of Bishop Pompallier) and the few who must have been missed in the extensive journeys of the treaty around the country. 'About one' paramount chief, Te Heu Heu, did refuse to sign,[23] Te Whero Whero being another (because, it was said, that would place him sub-ordinate to a woman – the Queen!).

Nine Europeans signed, eight including Hobson signing the original, while Joseph Thomas, living amongst Cloudy Bay Maoris, signed after his father-in-law, Nohoroa.[23]

On 17th February, William Colenso, Mission printer, fulfilled a paid government order for two hundred copies of the Treaty (i.e. the Maori language text) but no official English version was ever made.

James Clendon, in his capacity as U.S. Consul, had a duty to inform the American Government of developments. Some of Hobson's officials visited him on 17th February when he witnessed the signature of Chief Pomare II on the original Treaty document and also signed it in his own right. Probably it was that day that he received one of Colenso's newly printed copies of the Treaty which, together with printed copies of Hobson's proclamations of 30th January in his possession, he needed for his official despatch. What he needed also was an English text giving the wording of the Treaty. With none being available he had to fall back on his own devices. Fortunately he did have his own copy of the English draft made on 4th February during the final drafting session. However, being aware that Hobson might have altered this between the time he left Clendon's house on that day and the final transcription of the Treaty to dogskin just over 24 hours later, Clendon could not certify that this was a precise English equivalent.

Together with Hobson's two proclamations and a copy of the Treaty (in Maori) printed by Colenso, Clendon sent a copy of his own transcription to John Forsyth, the U. S. Secretary of State, in his despatch no.6 on 20th February, qualifying its status by saying "This Translation .. is not a copy of the Official Document in English" and saying that he would apply for an official copy in due course. What is important is that, apart from correcting Busby's two spelling mistakes, omitting Busby's crossed out word 'chiefs', somewhat more regular capitalisation and altering the date to the 6th, (since by 20th, Clendon knew the actual date of signing) the copy in the despatch is an exact copy of the final English draft from which the Treaty was translated by the Williams.[24]

Meantime, Hobson had gone south in *HMS Herald*, to the Waitemata area, to obtain signatures there. It is likely that he took his final English draft with him in order to explain to Europeans who might be present at signing proceedings what it was all about. (At least, the document as it now exists shows signs of being carried in someone's pocket and unfolded and refolded many times.) This was successful but future plans were thrown into disarray at Thames on 1st March when Hobson had a severe stroke which paralysed his right side and in this state he returned to the Bay of Islands on 6th March.

Clendon had formally acknowledged the documents he had received and requested official documents from H.M. Government. He did receive a reply with a "translation", some time before 18th March, probably from Shortland. The "translation" must have been (as we shall see) the final English draft which Hobson had given to Shortland on his return, recognising that his own days in actively seeking signatures were over.

Then, on 29th March, Charles Wilkes (later Commodore), commanding the American Antarctic Expedition, arrived in the Bay of Islands in his ship *USS Vincennes*. He wanted to "inquire into the actual state of these islands" [25] and sought Clendon's assistance to this end in order to report accurately to his superiors. This he did in his despatch Number 64 recorded in the letter book of *USS Vincennes*, now held in Topeka, Kansas, with a microfilm copy in the University of Auckland library. This despatch contains a copy of the Treaty itself, i.e. in Maori, a copy of what may have been the first actual back-translation of the Treaty to English by Captain Gordon Brown (See: Appendix 2), and a second version which can only have been copied from the final English draft, since the copyist has reproduced faithfully Busby's own mistakes (while adding a few of his own). Clearly therefore the original must have been passed over to Clendon and he never did return it!

What evidently happened is that Clendon kept the final English draft amongst his private papers which in due course (but before 1856) were passed to Henry Littlewood, his solicitor, who had practised law in Auckland since 1841. It then disappeared from sight until it was found by Beryl Needham, great-granddaughter of Henry Littlewood, in mid-March 1989 amongst domestic linen in a sideboard in the living room of her deceased mother's house. It was in a rough envelope with 'Treaty of Waitangi' scrawled on the back in ballpoint.

Thus, nearly 149 years after its disappearance, a document which is a vital link in the process of the founding of our country was rediscovered. Some civil servant decided to call it the 'Littlewood Treaty'. What it says is virtually the same as Te Tiriti, the document in Maori signed at Waitangi. It has been ignored almost entirely by officialdom which clearly does not want to know about it as it gives a severe jolt to official beliefs of which it is an indictment. Thus it was ignored on the 'Treaty 2 U' caravan which was paraded around the country in 2007, supposedly to inform the citizens (and particularly schoolchildren) about these things. The quite spurious reason given to me for this is that 'it isn't signed'. Well, one doesn't sign drafts formally!

The explanation is something like this. While the cat was away the mouse was playing. I mentioned earlier James Stuart Freeman, 3rd class clerk in the NSW Government, palmed off on Hobson by Governor Gipps as his private secretary – incompetent, pretentious, arrogant. Amongst English signatories to the Treaty he, uniquely, signed himself: 'Jas. Stuart Freeman Gentleman'.

Now, following his instructions, Hobson had been very careful to draft the Treaty in the plainest possible words. Freeman thought this was not good enough and set about drafting texts in very flowery language, as can be seen from his original rough drafts which survive, in what is now known as 'Royal Style'. After the Treaty was signed he began writing English versions the way he thought they should be and over three months produced several versions in his flowery language. Five of these were sent overseas to important people whom he seemed to think ought to get this sort of thing. Hobson did initial two of them beforehand amongst material prepared by Freeman for despatch but mostly Freeman just signed for him. Hobson was a very sick man and depended on his secretary who simply let him down.

On 13th March, 1840, a manuscript copy of the Treaty (in Maori), written by Freeman and signed by Shortland, was issued to Captain W. G. Symonds who was assigned to collect signatures on the south side of the Manukau Harbour (with the help of James Hamlin, an excellent Maori linguist), at Waikato Heads (assisted by Rev Robert Maunsell, head of the mission there) and at Kawhia. Symonds himself was said to have a vocabulary of 3,000 Maori words and was a competent army officer. However, at Manukau he found the going tough, a chief, Rewa, a disciple of Pompallier, creating a lot of opposition. By 3rd April Symonds had collected only three signatures so he decided to head south. Meanwhile, Maunsell was anxiously awaiting his arrival as he wanted to use a large gathering on 11th April, planned by the Maori chiefs themselves, as an opportunity for Treaty signing. In fact 1,100 people assembled but, as Symonds had not yet arrived, Maunsell decided to improvise. He had in his possession one of Colenso's printed copies of the Treaty (in Maori), probably sent him by Freeman about 4th March when (as recent research has revealed[26]) Freeman, unauthorised, sent him a copy on a large sheet of paper of one of his 'Royal Style' efforts which had been signed by Hobson in a very feeble hand.[27] (It is also possible that the printed copy of the Treaty was sent by Colenso on 4th March with a large consignment of printed material brought by Captain Gordon Brown.)

Maunsell, who was himself a good speaker of Maori, was very successful unaided at the meeting and many chiefs wanted to sign. The problem was that there was only room for five signatures at the bottom of the printed Maori sheet. He could perhaps have used the back but instead he put the handwritten Freeman sheet (in English) to use for a further 32 signatures. He did not bother to comment on having done this or his reason for doing so. When Symonds eventually arrived with the official document, he found that so many southern chiefs had signed Freeman's sheet that he did not ask them to sign again on the official document but sent it south by messenger for Rev. John Whiteley at Kawhia to get it signed by the few there who had not yet done so.

Rev. John Whiteley, later murdered by rebel Maoris in Taranaki in 1869, obtained nine more signatures while Symonds returned to Manukau for another attempt, taking the documents Maunsell had used and getting another seven signatures on the Freeman paper. We know this from his official report, which says that 'upwards of forty signatures were obtained' (actually 47). He did not mention the Freeman paper whose use was a unique departure from the practice of signing the Maori version, before and after. If this had been of any importance or significance beyond merely being a place to sign, he would surely have said so. In fact, the clear official intention was that Maunsell should use the copy of the real Treaty (in Maori) being brought to him by Symonds as was the case everywhere else in the country, and not one signed by mischance because the official document (in Maori) was late in arriving. There was no need at any of the meetings for an English text. Proceedings would have been conducted entirely in Maori, given the ability in it of all concerned.

Now here is the great irony of it all. In a spate of revisionist activity since 1975 this entirely spurious document has been elevated to being the "Signed Treaty in English". Its text now forms Schedule One of the Treaty of Waitangi Act 1975 and it now officially displaces the real Treaty. For a start this is contrary to international law which states that the version in the native language takes precedence. Reams of paper have been used arguing that Hobson and his helpers did a poor job by producing English and Maori texts whose meaning was so different. Gallons of ink have been used to argue that, because this false treaty is

40

so different from the real Treaty, the Williams were incompetent translators even though it has been admitted that the final English text went missing some time after the Williams had finished with it. Since three copies of that text exist in American archives, the officials concerned should have been able to find them, given that amateur investigators have done so since.

From this spurious document, spurious conclusions have been drawn by officialdom. It is claimed now that the Treaty is a "partnership between the Crown and the Maori people".[28] It is not. In Article One of the real Treaty the Maori chiefs cede the entire sovereignty of the country for ever. Article Three in return grants all Maoris the rights and privileges of British subjects and the protection of the Queen which they wanted. Now usually overlooked, this unique award to a native race was a prize to be valued. To recognise this, we need only reflect on how many people around the world today yearn for British citizenship.

Article Two makes certain guarantees to all the people of New Zealand, in effect affirming their rights as British subjects to own property, and specifies rules for the sale of Maori land. That is what the Treaty says – clear, short and succinct – and that is what it means. There was no time for deviousness and there was none. We may note that Article Three releases all Maori slaves held by other Maoris since, as already mentioned, slavery had been abolished throughout the British Empire in August, 1838. Hone Heke for one, failed to release his slaves forthwith. It also took some time for this to become effective in the Chatham Islands where the Morioris (an isolated Polynesian group) had been brutally enslaved by Ngati Tama and Ngati Mutunga from Taranaki.

Just what property was guaranteed to all the people has been widely debated, since Freeman's false treaty specifies 'forests and fisheries' which the real Treaty does not. We recall the Yate/Rewa letter of 1831 mentioned above and signed by 13 northern chiefs which says "We are people without possessions".

Geoffrey Palmer, as Attorney-General, decided to construct what he called 'The Principles of the Treaty' and legislated accordingly in 1986. This was not only based on false premises but also entirely unnecessary. Anybody wanting a fuller account of the principles on which the Treaty is based than the terse wording of the Treaty itself, need only read Lord

Normanby's brilliant, clear and humane brief to Hobson before he set out.

From the vast amount of revisionism promulgated officially since 1975 there is now widely spread a very distorted view of the foundation of our country. The nation's integrity has been gravely compromised. This must be corrected.

Given the difficulty of the circumstances (which were indeed not of Maori making), Hobson, with the able, timely and willing assistance of Busby, Clendon and Williams, father and son, did a very good job and provided a firm foundation on which to build the nation of New Zealand.

What does the Treaty mean?

In the foregoing, we have told a simple tale but one with very great consequences for New Zealand when free and untrammelled debate is permitted throughout the country. It is not the intention here to make lengthy additions to the analyses offered elsewhere, nor to discuss subsequent Maori/European relations, whether Treaty-related or otherwise. A few remarks about the Treaty itself are in order however.

Before we can decide what the Treaty means, we must ascertain what we mean by the Treaty.

Historian Claudia Orange states that "the *Southern Cross* [the Auckland newspaper, edited by S. Martin] ... printed [in August 1843] the 'official' English treaty text of 1840 alongside what it called a 'literal and true translation' – a close rendering in English of the Maori text that most chiefs had signed". [29] Then she says that there was "a government printing of both English and Maori texts in 1844, [and] sections of the document were reproduced in the colonial press from the earliest years". [30]

Treaty Consultant Brian Easton elucidates the position: "For further evidence of the low status of the various English versions after the signing of the Tiriti, consider the numerous translations made in the 1840s by those involved in land deals around Auckland.... If everyone was translating the Tiriti, then they are implying the official version in English was non-existent, unimportant, or irrelevant. In the 1840s the general view among settlers seems to have been there was no Treaty of Waitangi, but there was Te Tiriti o Waitangi which had to be translated into English....Ross reports on five versions which Hobson forwarded to his superiors in Sydney and London. There are differences between them. The main difference is that three have the Hobson-Busby preamble, two the Freeman one. One omits 'forests, fisheries'. A sixth version attributable to Hobson is in Clendon's letter to the Secretary of State on 7 July, where the preamble is again Freeman's (but "forests, fisheries" are included). What are we to make of all this? Surely it is that there was no English text of the Tiriti at the time of signing".[31] Thus Easton fully substantiates our account.

Freeman's false treaty is not the Treaty even though current legislation states that it is. We may legislate that black is white but that does not make it so. As Geoffrey Palmer has admitted since, Parliament is entirely free to change the present artificial status of the false treaty by future legislation. The Treaty, Te Tiriti, is a document in the Maori language.

Indeed, there was never an official version of the Treaty in English. We may reasonably refer for its meaning in plain language to the ungarnished translation of Captain Brown, soon after it was signed, which is presented in the Appendix, or to the translation by T.L.Young of the Native Department in 1869. Latter-day versions and in particular that of the Waitangi Tribunal's Hugh Kawharu, are so overlain with their authors' agendas or changes in the meaning of words to be well-nigh worthless.

We have however, the so-called "Littlewood Treaty" which is concluded here to be beyond reasonable doubt, the final draft in English of 4th February, 1840, from which Te Tiriti was translated by Williams, father and son. Since its discovery, officialdom, with support from authoritarian historians, has done all it can to discount the worth of this document and obscure its existence from the public view. Thus Orange calls it "just another copy of the Maori translation by an unknown author". Seventeen years after its discovery, the official Treaty of Waitangi Information Unit at last got round to commissioning a chosen historian, Donald Loveridge, to "investigate" it. And guess what! He did the hatchet job that the government so desperately wanted.

The phrase in the treaty "all the people of New Zealand" does not imply that the treaty is with existing British subjects in New Zealand which is a legal nonsense and impossibility since they were already British. In the second paragraph of the important preamble, it quite clearly states that "her Majesty...proposes to the chiefs...to agree to the following articles." Then the second article begins with "The Queen of

43

England confirms and guarantees to the chiefs and tribes and all the people of New Zealand the possession of their lands, dwellings and all their property." This is unequivocal. It was important to make such a guarantee to all the people but the Queen negotiated (through her representative) with the chiefs who were the highest authorities in the country at the time.

Only one British signature was required since Great Britain was a unitary power with a single head of state. (In fact, as we have noted, actually nine Britons did sign) By contrast there were very many tribal heads in New Zealand and 540 of them did sign but the common Maori people did not sign.

The second article of Freeman's false treaty (except in one of its many variant versions) guarantees to the Chiefs and Tribes the full possession of their fisheries and forests. It is reasoned below that 1840 Maori would have had a very different idea of who were the owners of the forests and fisheries than most of their modern counterparts. One may pause here to consider what I mean by "my property". I speak naturally of "my country" and "my children" and I certainly do not mean nor imply that I own them in the sense that I own "my car" or "my old boots". What is "mine" has two different meanings and "my property" embraces just one of them. In 1840 a Maori would not have thought of owning the forests, fisheries and foreshore in this sense. If they were thought of as belonging in any general sense to the tangata whenua, the word which expresses that concept is "sovereignty" and that is just what Maoris were yielding. Property to them would have meant things like their canoes and domestic goods.

That is far from the case at present. As David Round has said "It is impossible to avoid the conclusion that the ignoring of the Littlewood document is motivated by political considerations. There is no scholarly searching after truth, whatever the consequences, here. Treatyist 'scholars' are clearly avoiding the document for fear of where it might lead them.

All versions of the Treaty promise equality before the law, when Maori are given the rights and privileges of British subjects. Partnership is entirely a modern political invention. It is pernicious, but it is to be found nowhere in any version of the Treaty.

... The problem is not any particular form of what was signed in 1840, but improper modern interpretations of that – and the whole irrational dangerous mania concerning the Treaty which has held this country in thrall for the last [thirty] years. It is there we should direct our concerns."

Having clarified what is said in the final draft, the next step is to ascertain how accurately the Williams' translation reflects it. We dismiss the claims of Orange and others, based on faulty evidence, that they were incompetent translators. We dismiss likewise the disgraceful remarks attributed to Constitutional Advisory Panel member Deborah Coddington that they deliberately mistranslated Hobson's final English draft with which, in fact, it corresponds almost exactly.

Hobson's primary task, as clearly stated in Normanby's brief, was to secure "the recognition of Her Majesty's sovereign authority over the whole or any part of the country", not, be it noted, by any means but with "the free intelligent consent of the natives."

Thus Article First of the Treaty, addressed to the chiefs, states that they "cede to the Queen of England for ever the entire Sovreignty [sic] of their country". This is totally clear. Williams, father and son, translated "sovereignty" as "kawanatanga". Of course, this was not a word in the pre-European Maori language. It was devised by the British for a concept new to Maoris but it was not unknown to them in 1840 owing to their discussions of the preceding years. The Maori text was checked for Hobson next morning by Busby and missionary Taylor with Henry Williams. It is inconceivable that Hobson would have accepted "kawanatanga" had they expressed any doubts that it was the right word.

Ignoring all this, the revisionist historian, Anne Salmond, has weighed in recently with a statement to the Waitangi Tribunal that "kawanatanga was not a plausible stand-in for sovereignty." Now this is based on the fundamental mistake that translation is the same as derivation. It is not. "Kete Wananga" is a modern Maori term for "library" ~ another concept unknown to pre-European Maoris but its derivation is "wisdom basket".

By Article Third of the Treaty all Maoris become British subjects. This was a prize, yearned for to this day by millions of people. It was a prize to 1840 Maoris and they knew it. It freed all Maoris who were slaves to other Maoris. It is said that a cause of Hone Heke's rebellion in 1844 was the behaviour of one of his slave women. If he were continuing to regard her as such, he was infringing on her rights as a free British subject.

Article Second of the final draft "guarantees to the chiefs & tribes and to all the people of New Zealand the possession of their lands, dwellings and all their property". "Possession" was rendered by the Williams as "te tino rangitiratanga". The 1869 back-translation by T.E. Young of the Native Department is "the full chieftainship of their lands, their settlements and their property". This merely stated the common law right of British subjects to own property and, strictly speaking, was redundant.

"Te tino rangitiratanga" is based on another missionary-coined expression, "tino rangitira". It was used by William Williams when he informed the chiefs of the appointment of Busby, to describe Lord Goderich, British Colonial Secretary at the time ~ a high official indeed but in no sense a sovereign. As the historian, Phil Parkinson, has said, "Kawharu's [modern] mistranslation of "te tino rangitiratanga" as 'the unqualified exercise of chieftainship' is not merely erroneous but preposterous." [32]   As stated in Normanby's brief, the British were not going to tolerate cannibalism or slavery or other arbitrary exercise of chiefly practice which in any case infringed the rights of other Maoris as British subjects. Again, it is absurd to suggest that the first provision of the Treaty having been for the cession of sovereignty, Hobson and his advisors would have contradicted themselves a few lines later to allow sovereignty to continue to reside with the chiefs. In no fair or reasonable way can the 1840 meaning of "tino rangitiratanga" be said to be "sovereignty". Recent posturing by Ngapuhi claiming that it does is nonsense.

Property was translated as "taonga" which is its meaning given in William Williams' 1844 Maori dictionary. It is also Brown's back-translation of "taonga" in March, 1840, as well as Young's in 1869. Whatever it may be claimed that "taonga" means today, emphatically it did not mean "treasure" in 1840. David Round has noted that "it certainly would not have included language and other cultural manifestations; but, as Mr Denis Hampton has so ably pointed out, neither would the word 'taonga' in 1840 either". It is an utter farce that such claims as that to the radio spectrum, based on "taonga", can be taken seriously by our politicians.

Even more revealing is the meaning for "taonga" given in *A Grammar and Vocabulary of the Language of New Zealand*, by Kendall & Lee, 1820, compiled by Professor Samuel Lee of Cambridge University and lay missionary in New Zealand, Thomas Kendall, who visited Lee there with Shungie Ika (Hongi Hika) that year during the latter's arms-gathering expedition. Not only did Shungie return with a

46

suit of armour and more than 300 muskets to resume his slaughter of other Maoris; he also rendered considerable assistance in compilimg the dictionary. The entry is: "Taónga, s [noun] Property procured by the spear."

This entry gives clear insight into the nature of Maori (and, in particular, Ngapuhi) society of the times. Property was what one possessed by force of arms. As John Ansell, the leader of Together New Zealand, has remarked, "A bit hard to procure an electromagnetic spectrum with a spear, I'd have thought." [33]

We may thus assert in plain English that all transactions that have given assets to any Maori tribe on the basis of a claim to the Waitangi Tribunal that such assets were "treasure" are fraudulent and should be returned to the Crown forthwith.

In summary, we have the Treaty, devoid of gloss. The Maori chiefs ceded sovereignty. In return, Maoris became British subjects and all the people of New Zealand kept their land, dwellings and property. Revisionist claims to the contrary should be rejected firmly, fully, forthwith and forever.

The Sequel

As copies of the Treaty were taken around the country, Maori chiefs, with few exceptions, signed with enthusiasm and more than five hundred did so. They did not have second thoughts later. In 1860, at Kohimarama, Auckland, Governor Gore Browne convened the greatest gathering of chiefs that has ever occurred. He wanted to find out their opinion on the tangled mess of land claims in Taranaki, with conflicting tribal Maori groups claiming the right to sell to settlers. Discussions took more than a month and were minuted meticulously.[34] Of immediate interest are the emphatic assertions, made repeatedly by those present, of loyalty to the Queen, their sovereign and to her law and it is particularly striking how many chiefs of Ngapuhi spoke thus. As Treaty veteran, Tamati Waka Nene, said: 'I know no sovereign but the Queen, and I shall never know any other." Te Taurau spoke: "I am from Ngapuhi. ... there [is] but one name upon earth – the Queen. Let us then rest under the [Queen's] Government." Said Wi Te Tete "Let me have the last word! We have now become one people under the Queen." It was a chorus.

Anne Salmond has responded: "No professional historian would take that as definitive evidence of Maori understandings in 1840." [35] That is both paternalistic and ridiculous. Maori memories were well-trained and there can be no reasonable doubt that an event as significant as the Treaty signing would have remained vividly in their memories twenty years later.

Observations of some other authors

We have the testimony of Rev. Samuel Warren writing in 1863: "I was present at the great meeting at Waitangi when the celebrated treaty was signed, and also at a meeting which took place subsequently on the same subject at Hokianga. There was a great deal of talk by the natives, principally on the subject of securing their proprietary right to the land, and their personal liberty. Everything else they were only too happy to yield to the Queen, as they said repeatedly, because they knew they could only be saved from the rule of other nations by sitting under the shadow of the Queen of England. In my hearing they frequently remarked, 'Let us be one people. We had the gospel from England, let us have the law from England'."

"My impression at the time was that the natives perfectly understood that, by signing the treaty, they became British subjects, and though I lived amongst them more than fifteen years after the event, and often conversed with them on the subject, I never saw the slightest reason to change my opinion. The natives were at the time in mortal fear of the French, and justly thought they had done a pretty good stroke of business when they placed the British lion between themselves and the French eagle." [36]

The way that the Treaty has been manipulated for political ends was examined by Stuart C. Scott, LLB in his 1995 book *The Travesty of Waitangi*. It is important to note that Scott must have been unaware that the final English draft of the Treaty had been found in 1989, since he would almost certainly have referred to it if he had known about it. This says a lot about the effectiveness of official suppression of information about the final English draft.

Scott explodes many modern myths on which the arguments of Maori revisionists have been based.

One significant observation by Scott is that the Ngai Tahu Annual Report of 1991 (p.224) records P.B. Temm Q.C. counsel for Ngai Tahu (later Mr Justice Temm), "as submitting to the [Waitangi] Tribunal that 'there is a new development taking place in our constitutional law ... triggered by the Treaty of Waitangi Act [1975].' Mr Temm submitted that the absolute power of parliament would be curbed by its obligation in respect of the Treaty".[37] Scott later describes an example with respect to the disposal of surplus Crown land about which he says "Here we have vindication of P.B. Temm's comment to the Tribunal." [38]

That any legislative act should be held to curb the absolute power of Parliament is a grave situation indeed. Bearing in mind that the Treaty actually says "The Chiefs...give absolutely to the Queen of England for ever the complete government of their lands",[39] we see clearly just how much the Treaty of Waitangi Act of 1975 (as interpreted) has perverted the constitutional position in New Zealand.

Michael King in his *Penguin History of New Zealand* gave a generally well-received account of the history of these islands but makes no mention of the final English draft of the Treaty. His discussion of Treaty issues is therefore inevitably one-sided. It is beyond reasonable belief that King did not know that this draft had been found fourteen years before he wrote. We shall probably never know now why he did not mention it. We may ask however, what were the pressures put upon him not to do so?

It is relevant to quote the following from King "The modern Maori concept of *tino rangatira*, which we would recognise as corporate tribal authority, developed because the Westminster parliamentary system of one person – one vote could not co-exist with the mid-nineteenth century concept of chiefly authority which was what Henry Williams had in mind when he formulated the term *tino rangatira* for the text of the Treaty of Waitangi. This of course means that the *tino rangatiratanga* which the Treaty promised to protect is not the *tino rangatiratanga* modern Maori seek to have delivered. But there is nothing extraordinary in that: all cultures that are alive, change over time and their words change their meaning. The Maori culture of the twenty-first century is not Maori culture frozen at 1769, nor at 1840." [40] What this means is that whatever the legitimacy or otherwise of claims for "the *tino rangatiratanga* modern Maori seek to have delivered", it is false to appeal to the Treaty to justify them.

It is even more specious to appeal to the false treaty for justification. This has been done now in numerous cases before the Waitangi Tribunal or settled by it. The false treaty refers to "forests and fisheries" which the real Treaty does not. We may be assured that Hobson fully intended that Maoris' customary rights to the areas in which they fished for food be wholly protected since they were important sources of nourishment. It is beyond belief, however, that he envisaged any Maori rights (as distinct from the rights of all New Zealanders) to thousands of square miles of ocean waters in New Zealand's quite recently extended economic zone in which they had never cast a line. As a result of manipulations based on Freeman's false treaty all New Zealanders have borne the cost of the Treaty of Waitangi (Fisheries Claims) Settlement Act 1992 which resulted in $150,000,000 of taxpayers' money being used to purchase half of Sealord Products Ltd, which has been given to Maori interests or, if you like, the tribal elite.[41] The integrity of governments and all others concerned in such shoddy deals must be seriously questioned.

Indeed it may be asked whether 1840 Maoris considered that they owned any forests and fisheries. As I was taught at school, before cutting down a tree to make a canoe or a meeting house, Maoris would perform extensive rituals asking permission from Tane, god of forests to do so. When they fished, the first fish caught was tossed back to Tangaroa, god of the sea, in acknowledgment that they were intending to take his fish, a practice which still exists in the Chatham Islands.

In further discussion, Parkinson notes that the phrase "*tino rangatira*" never really became common usage, "a single late and remarkable exception" being its use amongst many others as a title for Queen Victoria in a petition by some Rotorua residents. He continues: "That the Queen herself could be addressed as 'the tino rangatira' by Maori tends to show that activist appropriation of the term in the 1980s and following rests on unstable ground."

Durie (quoted by Parkinson) also acknowledges that "there is, then, no single definition of *tino rangatiratanga* and little comfort can be derived from linguistic origins or simplistic notions about an 1840 understanding of sovereignty". We may thus dismiss claims of latter-day activists for 'Maori autonomy'.

In the words of Sir Apirana Ngata: "the chiefs placed in the hands of the Queen of England, the Sovereignty and authority to make laws." The Maori Battalion, too, knew where they stood: "For God! For King! And for Country! AU − E! Ake, ake, kia kaha e!"

50

Conclusion

1. The Treaty is a document in Maori – "Te Tiriti o Waitangi" – and there is only one Treaty.
2. There can be no reasonable doubt that the so-called "Littlewood Treaty" is Hobson's long lost, final draft in English of 4th February, 1840, of the Treaty of Waitangi.
3. Freeman's bogus "Treaty in English" is not and cannot be either a draft of the Treaty in English nor a translation of it.
4. All the chiefs who signed Te Tiriti knew that they were surrendering sovereignty completely and forever. This was confirmed by the many chiefs at the Kohimarama conference in 1860.
5. By The Treaty, all Maoris became British subjects, including the thousands who were held in slavery by other Maoris. This was an unprecedented privilege granted by the most powerful empire on earth.
6. The Treaty does not say anything else. "Partnership" is a false recent invention.
7. There is one and only one so-called "Principle of the Treaty" – Hobson's word to each chief as he signed, at very birth of our nation – *He iwi tahi tatou* – "We are one people now".
8. It is time for all New Zealanders of every creed and race to speak up. Let not be damned all those who cry "enough".

PROPERTY RIGHTS - A BLESSING FOR MAORI NEW ZEALAND

Peter Cresswell

"If history could teach us anything, it would be that private property is inextricably linked with civilisation."
– Ludwig von Mises, Human Action

"Nothing is ours, which another may deprive us of."
-- Thomas Jefferson, Letter to Maria Cosway

The intellectually lazy inflexibly assume that, before Europeans arrived, all of the New Zealand land mass was owned by the Maori who inhabited some parts of the country. This is the thinking that concludes that some four hundred tribesmen somehow "owned" every piece of land, stone and forest in the South Island. This cannot be true.

It simply cannot be said that "the Maori people" ever "owned" New Zealand in any meaningful sense of the word. Before Europeans arrived Maori at best only owned what they used and inhabited; those bits of the place that, in the words of John Locke, they "mixed their labour with." They did not own all of New Zealand; they only owned what they used and inhabited.

On that basis there are large tracts of the country that to this day have never been owned by Maori, nor by anyone else.

However, in reality Maori actually owned nothing at all before Europeans arrived. Not New Zealand, not the lands on which they lived or hunted, not even the things with which they had mixed their labour. How can this be so?

Let's begin by examining Maori culture, and the notion of culture itself. It should be understood immediately that "culture" is not racially determined—it is the product of all the thinking of those who subscribe to it—a product of the brain, not the blood. In Ayn Rand's words, it "is the sum of the intellectual achievements of individual men, which their fellow-citizens have accepted in whole or in part, and which have influenced [a people's] way of life." [1]

"Cultures are not merely customs to which people have a sentimental attachment," writes Thomas Sowell, "or badges of 'identity' which permit them to engage in breast-beating. Cultures are particular ways of accomplishing the things that make life possible ... Cultures transcend race... When cultures are seen as more than group differentiations, their role as vast accumulations of human capital can be better appreciated." [2]

Not all cultures are equal. Some are vastly better than others. So how do we judge one culture against another? Well, as Thomas Sowell once pointed out, "Cultures are not museum-pieces. They are the working machinery of everyday life. Unlike objects of aesthetic contemplation, working machinery is judged by how well it works..." [3]

How then did pre-European Maori culture work for those living within it? For the individual Maori the answer is "bloody poorly."

When Europeans began arriving on New Zealand's shores Taranaki was empty, Auckland was largely deserted, and Maori living elsewhere were part of a culture that enthusiastically embraced tribalism and its concomitant warfare, slavery and cannibalism.

And it was a dying culture – dying because, to use to-day's jargon, it was unsustainable. When Europeans arrived, the Maori population had flattened out at approximately 115,000[4] and Maori were living a subsistence lifestyle with short life spans, a limited diet, limited food resources, and constant battling over the few resources still remaining. "By 600 years [before the present] many animals had been driven to extinction or close to it, and very large areas of the country, even in remote inland South Island valleys, were being burnt regularly." [5]

The country's natural resources had been all but stripped bare by slash and burn agriculture—stripped bare because, without secure property rights, there was no incentive to maintain those resources; the Tragedy of the Commons was in operation, and the result was desperation, starvation and constant fighting over scarce means of survival. "The characteristic pattern of warfare and fortification in New Zealand in the late prehistoric period is intimately linked with an overshoot of population with regard to wild food resources – and hence conflict." [6] In other words, they were hungry and fought over the few wild foods left, and they couldn't grow new food because they were constantly fighting. Without security, domestic cultivation was extremely difficult—and this was a warlike culture utterly bereft of security.

So why, when there was so much pressure on resources, were Taranaki and Auckland so empty? One very good reason: these places were simply too dangerous to live in!

53

Taranaki was too dangerous because of constant utu wars with Waikato Maoris. As historian Keith Sinclair explains, "Taranaki was almost unpopulated because in the 1820s, after many of the local Maoris had migrated to Otaki and Cook's Strait, the Waikato tribes had killed or enslaved all the rest." [7]

Those Taranaki Maoris who fled the slaughter – and who had thereby avoided being killed, eaten or enslaved – only began to arrive back in Taranaki once it was safe to do so. What made it safe was the rule of law – the protection of individual rights that British law once did so well. The rule of law was a great gift to Taranaki Maoris; it quite literally saved their lives. One would like to think that those Taranaki Maoris alive to-day who are un-enslaved, uneaten and flourishing under the remnants of that rule of law would sometimes give thanks to its inception.

Ironically, having escaped the Taranaki slaughter himself, Te Rauparaha embarked upon on an eighteen-year rampage that only concluded – temporarily – with his signing of the Treaty of Waitangi on 14th May, 1840. Says historian Steven Oliver, "He believed that the treaty would guarantee him and his allies the possession of territories gained by conquest over the previous eighteen years." [8] It did, but he still broke it when he reverted to the old ways of war rather than law.

And what about Auckland? Auckland was too dangerous because, then as now, it was so damned attractive. These days, properties on Mount Eden are some of the most expensive in the country – expensive precisely because they are so desirable. When you have secure property rights, the value of a property is a reflection of its desirability, of how many want to live in such a place, and how much they are prepared to pay to live there. In those pre-European days the Mount Eden slopes were equally desirable. However, because they were so highly desired, they were empty.

Imagine! Empty because they were desirable. Why so? Because of the absence of property rights. Without secure property rights it just wasn't safe to be in a place where everyone wanted to be!

A place that everyone would quite literally kill for is a place for which you could give your right arm, or even your life. Consequently "when Europeans came to Auckland, they saw only a wilderness of scrub, for all the isthmus had been gardens and was in various stages of regeneration." [9]

It hadn't been empty for long. Kiwi Tamaki's Waiohua tribe had spent the seventeenth and eighteenth centuries living and "slash and burn" gardening around Mount Eden (Maungawhau) and One Tree Hill (Maungakiekie). These hills had everything a seventeenth century estate agent could dream of – they offered great defensive positions, fantastic northern slopes for kumara pits, and a delightful location between two sparkling harbours. But in a culture where ownership is held by conquest rather than by right, having everything means that you very soon have nothing – because someone else wants it, and who gets to keep it is he who has the biggest friends.

At that time the Auckland isthmus was a war zone that Thomas Hobbes would have recognised. In Auckland's war of all against all, Waiohua, Kawerau, Ngati Maru, Ngati Huarere and Ngati Whatua fought, re-fought and fought again across this narrow strip of land hung between two magnificent harbours. Ngati Paoa from Thames eventually took Mount Eden and many of Auckland's other volcanic cones from Kiwi Tamaki, only to be ejected themselves about 1780 by Ngati Whatua.

But the wars were not yet over. In 1818 Ngapuhi swept down from Northland with their guns, and over the next few years slaughtered or enslaved all who remained. Mount Eden and One Tree Hill remained empty. In 1835 Ngati Whatua crept timidly back to Okahu Bay and Greenhithe. "During the Ngapuhi wars Tamaki-makau-rau was almost deserted, and remained so until 1835 when Ngati Whatua returned....In March, 1840, three Ngati Whatua chiefs met Governor Hobson and signed the Treaty of Waitangi.....These men saw the pakeha as a possible insurance against further raids." [10]

Neither Te Rauparaha nor the Ngati Whatua chiefs were stupid. Te Rauparaha wanted to secure the land he had taken by conquest. Ngati Whatua wanted to secure land they had only recently taken by conquest and from which they had then been ejected. It seems abundantly clear that their concept of "ownership" to which they subscribed was based not on right, but on conquest.

So, did Maori actually own land then, in the full meaning of the term "own"? The Cassells Dictionary defines "own" to mean "to have as property by right." Note that phrase "by right." Contrast that meaning with that of the word *taonga*, often translated as "treasured possessions or cultural items, anything precious." This is an important word, especially since the Treaty of Waitangi guarantees to Maoris "full, exclusive and undisturbed possession of their lands, dwellings and other properties...." translating "properties" as *taonga*. But is that translation strictly true if the concepts defined by the two words are different?

Examining the etymology of the word *taonga* suggests they are very different, and throws light on how pre-European Maori culture viewed property: tao means 'a lance, or spear', nga is simply the definite article. So by 1840 *taonga* meant "things that you could take and hold by use of the spear." In other words: loot, booty or plunder – things you take by conquest. Like the plunder of a pirate, not the treasure of a trader. Things you only "own" until someone bigger than you takes them from you.

This is "ownership" not by right, but by force. Maori culture in 1840 did not recognise the concept of "right," and had no concept of ownership beyond the playground notion of grabbing what you can when you can.

I hasten to point out there is no shame in this. The concept of rights - a "moral principle defining and sanctioning man's freedom of action in a social context" [11] - integrates a tremendous number of sub-principles and concrete facts. The identification of this moral principle represented an enormous intellectual advance that took thousands of years of and dozens of thinkers to identify. Indeed, the discovery and understanding of rights by Enlightenment-era thinkers was still being developed and understood by Europeans themselves in 1840, the discovery being instrumental in helping Europeans shake off their own savage past. (Indeed, while I know very little about them, it is virtually certain that my own Scottish ancestors were, only a few short generations before 1840, little more than warring tribal savages themselves, totally illiterate, highly superstitious and primitive in every way - yet the culture of which they would have been a part was so radically transformed by the freedom, peace and prosperity produced by secure property rights that Voltaire could say 250 years ago, "We look to Scotland for all our ideas of civilization.")

European thinkers had access to what Edmund Burke called "the great bank and capital of nations and ages." [12] Maori did not. That rights underpin the peaceful, secure ownership that many Europeans were already beginning to take for granted was a fact only slowly understood by Enlightenment thinkers cashing a cheque on that bank. Their coming to New Zealand re-connected Maori to that great bank of ideas and human capital from which they had been cut off for at least a millennium - at a time when the principle of property rights was still (just) in full flower.

Hernando De Soto documents the difficulties faced by cultures in the modern world that are cut off from any legal property systems. "Much behaviour that is today attributed to cultural heritage is not the inevitable result of people's ethnic or idiosyncratic traits," he says, "but of their rational evaluation of the relative costs and benefits of entering the legal property system." [13]

He might have been writing of Maori in 1840. Because what even Maori leaders seemed to realise by then is that "ownership" by conquest, rather than by right, was imposing tremendous costs.

Taranaki Maori and the Ngati Whatua chiefs began to realise that Pakeha law might protect them better and provide them with a better long-term platform for prosperity than they could ever achieve with their spears. But whether they ever "owned" the land by right to which they now lay claim is severely problematic. It is beyond doubt, however, that they could not fully utilise even the land they did lay claim to until protected by law, however imperfect that protection might have been since.

Ownership is a crucial need of human life – only ghosts can survive without material sustenance. But human beings need to produce the material sustenance they require to survive – so the concept of property rights was thus a crucial step in advancing human civilisation. It was a gift from Enlightenment thinkers like Hugo Grotius and John Locke. Man is not born with the material needs to ensure his survival; he must instead produce for himself the goods he needs in order to survive and prosper. Further, in order to plan ahead, he must be able to keep the goods he has produced and the means by which he has produced them – which means he requires the security of ownership, of right.

"Formal property is more than a system for titling, recording and mapping assets," observes De Soto[14], "it is an instrument of thought, representing assets in such a way that people's minds can work in them to generate surplus value… Well-crafted property [systems] enable us to pinpoint the economic potential of resources so as to enhance what we can do with them. They are not 'mere paper': they are mediating devices that give us knowledge about things that are not manifestly present… The capacity of property to reveal the capital that is latent in the assets we accumulate is borne out of the best intellectual tradition of controlling our environment in order to prosper."

In his invaluable book describing the history of property rights, Tom Bethell enumerates what he calls the "four great blessings that cannot be easily realised in a society that lacks the secure, decentralised private ownership of goods. These are: liberty, justice, peace and prosperity." [15] These were amongst the blessings that Europeans brought to New Zealand as part of their Enlightenment culture.

Consider the histories of Mount Eden and One Tree Hill. These two volcanic cones offer a compelling contrast between how land is used with property rights and without. With property rights, land is used to its maximum potential; the most valuable land is highly prized, and highly priced, ending up in the hands of those who value it the most. However, when land is owned not by right but by conquest, then land use becomes quite unrelated to its value – land ends up in the hands of anyone or no-one, and the most valuable land is often unused because its very desirability leads to the potential danger of re-conquest, and the risk of being killed and eaten, or enslaved yourself.

In the absence of any conception of property rights then, Maori culture had stripped bare the environmental resources that sustained their survival and left valuable land bare precisely because it was valuable. It was a culture on its knees. It was the tragedy of the commons. It was starvation, slavery and warfare. It was a culture whose machinery was killing those trapped within. What saved them were the "rights and privileges of British subjects" guaranteed to them by Article Three of the treaty. Chief among these rights and privileges were property rights, bringing blessings previously unknown to this warrior culture.

Ayn Rand observed, "The right to life is the source of all rights – and the right to property is their only implementation. Without property rights, no other rights are possible. Since man has to sustain his life by his own efforts the man who has no right to the product of his effort has no means to sustain his life. The man who produces while others dispose of his product is a slave." [16] The absence of secure property rights in Maori New Zealand shows us the literal truth of her observation.

Captain Hobson R.N. With diligence and integrity this Royal Navy captain made the Treaty of Waitangi with the Maori chiefs – the first time that Great Britain had extended all the rights of British subjects to a native race. After each chief signed Hobson said, "*He iwi tahi tatou*" (We are now one people) – a noble concept that survived until the separatism of the modern treaty industry began to drive a sword through the unity of the country.

Te Rauparaha, cannibal chief of Ngati-Toa, would lead his canoes across Cook Strait to kill, cook and eat South Island tribes. In the Ngati-Toa settlement 2012 Treaty Minister, Christopher Finlayson, threw in an extra $10 million "in compensation for Ngati-Toa's loss of its maritime empire in Cook Strait" (the right of its warriors to cross the Strait on missions of bloody conquest).

Te Kooti carried out the worst massacre in our post-1840 history when, on 9th November, 1868, he and his henchmen butchered 70 settlers and friendly Maoris (including babies) at Matawhero, Poverty Bay, In 2012 Finlayson rewarded Te Kooti's tribe, Rongowhakaata, with $250,000 of public money and control of the Matawhero Reserve as compensation "for the stigmatisation of Te Kooti".

TRUE PATRIOTS ALL

Don Brash. His courageous speech at Orewa outlined a promising and non-racial future that has been destroyed by the (inverted) racism and political opportunism of his successor, the less principled and less patriotic John Key.

Winston Peters gave his Party's support to help Labour pass the Foreshore and Seabed Act 2004, which affirmed the long held position that the Crown (i.e. the public) owned the foreshore and seabed. In this, as in his opposition to the harmful "Free Trade" Agreement with Communist China, Peters was being true to his party's principle and name – New Zealand First.

Dr. Hugh Barr, co-founder of Coastal Coalition, a co-author of this book and Secretary of the Council of Outdoor Recreation Associations of New Zealand, has been a long time advocate for outdoor recreation rights.

Sir Apirana Ngata, scholar, Member of Parliament and, unlike the separatists of to-day, a strong advocate of Maori interests within a unified nation. In his *The Treaty of Waitangi, An Explanation*, he declared, among other things, that the confiscations after the wars of the 1860s were not a breach of the treaty and that they were, in fact, a Maori custom, viz. revenge. He described the treaty as "a gentleman's agreement which, on the whole, has been not badly observed".

HALL OF SHAME

Geoffrey Palmer started much of the modern Treaty industry when, as Labour's Attorney-General, he foolishly allowed claims to go back all the way to 1840. Then, after leaving Parliament, he set up a private law practice which dealt with the very claims that his complicated and unnecessary law change had brought about. Very nice for him but his legacy is not good for the country.

Lord Cooke of Thorndon. This over-promoted judge started the unfortunate movement of judges into the realm of politics where they don't belong. His motive was a dirty one – to create confusion with his loose language so that self-opinionated judges like him could then step into the ensuing imbroglio and exert greater powers over the elected Parliament, thus subverting our hard won democracy.

John Key. The "Triple Traitor". By stealing the beaches off the public, by adopting the U.N.'s mischievous Declaration of the Rights of Indigenous Peoples, and by setting up the Constitutional Advisory Panel with the apparent intention of entrenching Maori privilege into an unnecessary written constitution, John Key has three times betrayed the general public so as to appease the Maori Party.

Christopher Finlayson was the master-mind behind the theft of New Zealand's priceless foreshore and seabed from public ownership so as to make it available for his iwi friends and ex-clients to claim. Deeply compromised by being Ngai Tahu's lawyer in its aggressive and dubious Treaty claim, Finlayson is the last person who should be entrusted with handing over the foreshore and seabed to tribes. The deceit, bias and secrecy that he has shown during his term as Treaty Minister suggest that he is unfit to hold any public office – political, judicial or otherwise.

Michael Cullen, Labour's Treaty Minister who, in the final months of the Clark government (2008), gave approximately $1 billion of Crown forests (the "Treelords" deal) to nine tribes, one of which was Tuwharetoa. Then lo and behold, after leaving Parliament, Cullen took the position of Principal Treaty Claims Negotiator for Tuwharetoa, the very tribe that he had recently enriched with so much formerly publicly owned and valuable forests. Cullen is also a member of the government's Constitutional Advisory Panel, thus suggesting a conflict of interest as his Tuwharetoa masters have a strong interest in inflicting a written, Treaty based constitution on the rest of us so as to entrench Maori privilege forever.

THE LAW MADE SIMPLE

David Round

We are constantly lectured about our "obligations" under the Treaty. Plausible members of the grievance industry and their comfortably-off supporters among the caring classes drone on about the Treaty and its "principles", and the solemn obligations which these things impose upon us. These obligations are, of course, to enrich "Maori", whoever exactly they are, with gifts of money and land, well-paid jobs with only light duties, and racially-entrenched political and social privilege to elevate them for ever above the rest of us.

These obligations are presented to us as just that - as things which we are somehow obliged to do. Beyond an airy reference to the Treaty, these people never explain ~ and are never asked to explain - the precise basis of our dutiful self-sacrifice. But their fluent and self-assured manner gives the ordinary citizen the distinct impression that their case is an open and shut one. And, without actually saying so in so many words, they certainly contrive to give the impression that the law is on their side.

This chapter is about the law. When you have finished it you will realise that, although several statutes certainly refer to Treaty "principles", and several judges have made some disgraceful political judgments, yet nevertheless the case in law - not to mention in justice and common sense - for any sort of Maori privilege is patent nonsense and special pleading.

Everything I write here about the law is absolutely orthodox. It is difficult to get Treatyists to admit as much. They twist and turn in argument and, unless one is well-informed and listening carefully, they can get away with some preposterous statements. But the nonsense comes from the Treatyists. The academic exploration of the implications of the Treaty and its principles is now, like the indoctrination and intimidation of the young with the same, a significant professional occupation. For the present, however, although you would hardly know it, the legal situation with regard to the Treaty is still mostly satisfactory and, if accompanied by a little gumption and intelligence on our leaders' part, would still be able to serve as the basis for a just and colour-blind state.

That situation may not, however, last much longer. In 2012 a 'Constitutional Advisory Panel', established as part of the National Party's coalition agreement with the Maori Party, began "educating" and hearing the views of the public on a number of constitutional issues, including, most notably, the meaning and place of the Treaty in our constitutional arrangements. The Panel's own constitution is carefully racially defined. Five of its twelve members are New Zealanders of European descent, and five are of Maori descent, including the angry extremist Professor Ranginui Walker and several other persons whose views are likely to be of similar radical hue. Most of the European New Zealanders on the Panel are not notable for their doubts about Treatyism and its fallacies and perilous consequences. (Sir Michael Cullen, for example, currently has connections with the Tuwharetoa tribe as a consultant.) Then the Panel has one New Zealander of Asian descent, Peter Chin, ex-mayor of Dunedin, and one of Pacific Island ancestry, Bernice Mene, television host and netballer - a lovely lady, doubtless, but one does wonder, with all respect, precisely what insights she will be able to bring to the Panel's deliberations. The Panel's very terms of reference presume the existence of a "Treaty relationship" and require that New Zealanders' views be sought "in ways that reflect the partnership model and are responsive to Maori consultation preferences".

The Panel's recently-announced "Engagement Strategy" [1] stacks the procedures and prefers certain participants at every step of its journey. We can already see all too easily what the general direction of its recommendations is likely to be. But if the Treaty and its "principles" are in any way "enshrined" or even mentioned in a new written constitution, it is virtually certain that even their slightest mention will be used by politically motivated judges as a licence for them to sit in judgment upon Acts of Parliament and strike down laws if they were considered to "breach" Treaty "principles". To have the Treaty in our constitution would end up by the replacement of the democratic expression of the people's will with rule by the opinion of a tiny handful of unelected, highly-paid officials who, lurking under the benign name of "judges", are already pursuing a highly political programme which is tearing our nation apart.

For centuries the most fundamental principle of our constitution has been the supremacy of Parliament - the legal principle that Parliament's "Acts" ("statutes" as they are also called) are our highest law, and prevail over everything else. This Parliamentary supremacy is, of course, the constitutional expression of the democratic principle. It is one of our most important rights, won slowly and painfully only in the course of centuries of struggle against would-be tyrants. As we will see, Treaty "principles" are so vague that they can be used to justify practically any conclusion one might want to come to and that is why they are so dangerous.

No-one would assert that Parliament is perfect. But given a choice between the robust, if occasionally foolish, decisions of a popularly elected assembly - decisions which may of course be reversed after an election - and the unalterable, unappealable, divisive, racist agenda of a handful of cloistered appointed officials - judges - unanswerable to anyone - which would we prefer?

But I am getting ahead of myself. Let us look at the law. It is all perfectly straightforward and comprehensible, and the lay person need not be afraid of being confused. It is only the enemies of accountable democracy who are keen to claim that the whole matter is so complicated that only really clever, trained people like themselves are qualified to act as High Priests, equipped to approach the Holy of Holies and then return to announce the will of the sacred Treaty to the waiting nation.

Firstly, we should look at what is, surely, a very basic question -

What the Treaty Actually Says

All the talk we hear now is of the "principles" of the Treaty. As we will see shortly, Parliament, since 1975, has mentioned the "principles" in a number of statutes, without offering any guidance at all as to what the "principles" are. It has been left to others - judges, and Maori themselves - to "discover" what these principles are. "Principles" are the fundamental ideas, propositions or assumptions which underlie something, and so inevitably the "principles of the Treaty" are either meaningless platitudes (which are still very dangerous, because they can be used to justify absolutely any decision) or politically-charged opinion. We will look at the principles in a little while. But let us start at the beginning, and look at the actual words. What does the Treaty actually say? Surely this has to be the most important question of all. The words, after all, have to be paramount. They must form the basis of any "principles" that can be extracted from them. But, to our great

61

surprise, we discover that the Treaty's actual words are generally neglected.

Really, this is not surprising at all, for the Treaty's actual words - its terms - provide no foundation at all for racial privilege and the modern Treaty industry.

Nearly all the chiefs signed either the original, used at Waitangi, or copies of it, and written in Maori. The actual real treaty then is the Maori treaty. It is sometimes spoken of as the Maori "version" or "translation", but it is in fact the original. The singular exception was at the Waikato Heads, where some chiefs signed on a copy of Freeman's "Royal style" text written in English, because the document in Maori, which had been intended to be used, had not arrived. This sequence of events has been described by Bruce Moon in Chapter Two.

Freeman's version is most certainly an expansion of the Maori original. As explained below, an overwhelming case can be made that any alleged fundamental differences between the two are completely illusory. But to begin, let us ask, what does the treaty - the real Maori treaty - actually say?

After a preamble dwelling on the British desire to protect the Maori and secure to them the blessings of peace and good order (as opposed to the genocide of the preceding couple of generations) - after speaking of the continuing and increasing (and unstoppable) number of British settlers and the necessity of settled government and its laws and institutions (which only Britain could provide) and describing Captain Hobson's appointment as emissary -

By Article I, the chiefs cede all their rights and powers of sovereignty to the Queen ~ that is to say, to the British government and people.

By Article III, the Queen's government extends its protection to the people of New Zealand and grants Maori the status of British subjects - no less than that, and no more. This is, obviously, just the other side of Article I's coin. The British could not so protect Maori unless they had the jurisdiction, arising out of sovereignty, to do so.

And by Article II, the Queen - the British - confirmed and guaranteed to the chiefs and tribes and all the people of New Zealand the possession of their lands, dwellings, and all their property. Their rights to these, like the rights of all other British subjects, were to be respected by the Crown and the law.

Article II continued that the chiefs granted to the Queen the exclusive right of purchasing such land as the proprietors thereof might be disposed to sell at agreed prices. This ceased to be the case in 1862, when the Native Lands Act first established a land court with jurisdiction to determine ownership. Once that ownership was determined, that land could then be on-sold by its Maori owners directly to European purchasers. The proceedings of these Native Land Courts, as they were originally known, are sometimes condemned, usually without much or any justification, for they were scrupulous in their operations and operated only at the requests of Maori themselves. But that aside, let us note that this particular part of the sacred Treaty disappeared long ago without any suggestion that that disappearance was improper.

So this must be our starting point – all that the Treaty promised was that Maori were to live as British subjects. They were to enjoy their property, as all subjects do, and were to enjoy the protection of the Queen's law. But that was all. There were no promises of special rights, no suggestion that government was to be a "partnership" between Maori and the Crown. There can be no special rights when all that is promised is the equality of British citizenship. There can be no "partnership" between the Queen and some of her subjects.

Today, we all undoubtedly live under the Queen's sovereignty, enjoying our property and the protection of the law. The terms of the Treaty have nothing to add to this. Its promise has been fulfilled. The Treaty's terms are excellent - a colour-blind state of free and equal citizens. But needless to say, this is not a conclusion which Treatyists and radical Maori find satisfactory. For that reason, they contrive to discover Treaty "principles" which are the opposite of what the Treaty actually says. But before we look at those "principles" let us examine another attempt to avoid the clear and obvious meaning of the Treaty - and that is by

Alleged Differences Between the English and Maori Versions; Sovereignty and "Taonga"

Some Treatyists argue that the Treaty's terms - its actual words, which we have been thinking about - are not what has just been described here, because there are (so they allege) differences between the English and Maori versions.

Nearly all chiefs signed the Treaty in its Maori form. It was to those words, and not to any later English translation, that they committed themselves. There are principles of law which say the same thing, but it is surely both justice and commonsense that people are to be bound only by what they have heard and understood and agreed to, rather than someone else's version of the transaction.

No-one could object to that principle. It remains only to ask if there are any vital differences between the English and Maori versions - if the English version we are familiar with, which expresses our understanding of the agreement on that 6th of February 1840, is fundamentally different from what the chiefs understood themselves to be signing.

This question is, as lawyers would say, a question of fact rather than one of law. What do the Maori words mean? In the circumstances of the time, what did the chiefs understand them to mean?

It is only comparatively recently that this has become an issue. For most of the time since 1840, there has been not the slightest suggestion of any significant difference between English and Maori versions. It has been quite clear that Maori themselves saw no difference. That fact is in itself important evidence. If there had been such differences, the matter would have been raised long ago.

The arguments are over two related matters. The first is sovereignty itself. Did the chiefs understand that they were yielding up whatever sovereign rights they may have had to the Queen, or did they believe that they were remaining sovereign while granting Her Majesty only some lesser position? The second point disputes exactly what it was which the Queen guaranteed to Maori in return. In the English translation the Queen guaranteed them the possession of their property. The Freeman version uses the grand phrase 'lands and estates, forests fisheries and other properties', but this is merely an amplification with the same essential meaning. Whether one says simply "property" or "lands and estates, etc", one is speaking of the same thing. Both refer to what Maori actually owned at the time the Treaty was signed. But it is now alleged that the Maori version, which simply used the word "taonga" to refer to all these things, actually promised the protection of much more.

Sovereignty

Let us turn first to the argument over sovereignty itself. This is not just a dusty tiff amongst antiquarians. It is highly relevant to our future because, as noted above, in 2012 a "Constitutional Advisory Panel" began to consider, among other things, what place the Treaty should have in our constitutional arrangements, and there can be no doubt but that some Maori will be making very vigorous representations alleging that they never "signed their sovereignty away". Nga Puhi's current claim before the Waitangi Tribunal alleges precisely that. So it is important to get the record straight.

In the English version the chiefs cede to the Crown "all the rights and powers of sovereignty" which they possessed. This sovereignty is expressed in the Maori version by the word "kawanatanga". In return, the Queen guarantees the chiefs full, exclusive and undisturbed possession of their property. The Maori words used for this full possession are "te tino rangatiratanga".

The Treatyist argument is that the Queen's kawanatanga is less than full sovereignty, and that sovereignty is actually better expressed by te tino rangatiratanga, which Maori therefore still retained, and still do retain to this day.

For various reasons this argument simply will not hold water. It is quite clear, as Bruce Moon explains in Chapter Two, that these words cannot bear these alleged new meanings. Even the Waitangi Tribunal has accepted that "the essentials of sovereignty were not lost on Maoris in the debate at Waitangi…From the Treaty as a whole, it is obvious that it does not purport to describe a continuing relationship between sovereign states. Its purpose and effect was the reverse: to provide for the relinquishment by Maori of their sovereign status and to guarantee their protection upon becoming subjects of the Crown. In any event, on reading the Maori text in the light of contemporary statements, we are satisfied that sovereignty was ceded." The Tribunal suggested that "te tino rangatiratanga" was merely "tribal self-management…similar to what we understand by local government" - but which, of course, could not survive the disappearance of tribes as living entities.

Both *kawanatanga* and *rangatiratanga* are missionary words, coined by the missionaries and having no general currency in the Maori language. Kawana, in fact, is simply the Maori pronunciation of 'governor', and the word appears in the Maori New Testament to describe Pontius Pilate, the kawana of Judaea. Rangatira is certainly a

Maori word, but *rangatiratanga* - the nature or quality of being a *rangatira* - is not. Nor could the word *rangatira* be strictly interpreted as "chieftain". A rangatira is rather a nobleman or gentleman. It would include chieftains - *ariki* - but it also includes others. By 1840 most Maori were familiar with the Bible, and would have known that the Judaea of Pilate's time was a province of the Roman Empire, and they would have had a fair idea of what that entailed - a Roman governor with very great power, and yet still the servant of a distant absolute authority. Judaea was in fact only the tributary of a foreign occupying power, and a power, as readers of the New Testament would know, resented by many Jews. By 1840, too, many Maori had visited Australia, some even England, and they would have acquired a fair idea of what the Queen's law meant in practice. They would also have come to understand Britain's actual immense physical power which, through the Royal Navy, extended across the world.

The Tribunal, in the quotation above, referred to "contemporary statements". This is indeed the proper approach; to listen to what people said at the time - and also to give words the meanings which they had at the time. That Maori present at Waitangi understood what was meant by *kawanatanga* is evident from the remark of one chief that if *kawanatanga* were ceded, he would thereafter have to ask the permission of the British authorities to paddle his canoe across the river. He would not see such restrictions in his day - but he clearly knew what authority *kawanatanga* involved. By 1860, when any possible misunderstandings about what sovereignty meant in practice would have been long dispelled, the Kohimarama Conference, attended by many chiefs who had signed the Treaty, was notable for repeated emphatic assertions by those present of loyalty to their sovereign queen and her law.

From books such as R.D.Crosby's *The Musket Wars: A History of Inter-Iwi Conflict 1806-1845*, John Robinson's *When Two Cultures Meet; The New Zealand Experience* , Ian Wishart's *The Great Divide* and Paul Moon's *This Horrid Practice: The Myth and Reality of Traditional Maori Cannibalism*, it is clear that living in pre-European Maori society was, in Paul Moon's words, "an anxious or nervous experience". R.D.Crosby considers that, of an estimated 100,000 – 150,000 Maori living in New Zealand at or around 1810, by 1840 probably somewhere between 50,000 and 60,000 had been killed, enslaved or forced to migrate as a result of the wars. "Not only was death widespread," Paul Moon writes, "so too was violence associated with war, killing and the threat of being killed. ...The gentle reposes of Maori figures in the paintings of George Angas belie the stratum of fearful anticipation that afflicted life in almost all Maori communities".[2] We can easily see, then, why many Maori in 1840 coveted - as many people still do to this day - the membership of a great and powerful polity which would bring peace, law and many material comforts to a dark and war-torn land.

We may safely say, then, that assertions that Maori did not agree to the surrender of their sovereignty at Waitangi are patent nonsense, a modern invention and a lie.

Remember, too, that sovereignty, even as a matter of law, is not just an abstract idea but an actual brute fact. It is a century and a half too late to deny the sovereignty of the Queen, or "Crown". There comes a time when the most intractable of us must face facts and give up attempting to live in the past.

An example: In 1688 the undoubted lawful king of England and Scotland, James II, was overthrown in a revolution. It was a revolution. It was a break in legal continuity. By the law of 1687, those occupying that throne in 1689 had no right to it, and neither ever since have any who claim through them. By the same token, since only the rightful king can summon a parliament, there has not been a valid parliament since the rightful king was toppled. Now it would be absurd to maintain that today. Shortly after those events, and until the exiled dynasty's final hope was extinguished on the tragic moor of Culloden in 1746 - perhaps even just a little longer - one could have maintained with some degree of seriousness that the rightful king was in exile, and that a usurper sat on the throne - but one cannot say it now. Reality, the harsh light of day, has, however sadly, ended the beautiful dream.

So it must be with Maori sovereignty. At Waitangi Maori did agree that it should pass to the Queen; but even if they did not, sovereignty has passed to the Queen since. New Zealand's constitutional arrangements are as they are now. Get used to it.

Moreover, what might Maori sovereignty look like if we were somehow determined to put it into practice? If we gave it to them, what exactly would we be giving them? What exactly is being asked for here?

That is a good question. The Treaty was with "chiefs and tribes". But they are gone. Most of those of Maori descent live lives indistinguishable from the rest of us. They may be able to name their tribe - and it is a fine thing to know ones ancestry, and where and how one stands on the earth - but their tribes are not their lives, any more than clans, say, are a living force for most of us of Scots descent. If anyone wants to see re-created ancient tribal structures and way of life, and the absolute power of life and death which chiefs and *tohungas* wielded over their people, it is only those planning to be with the chiefs and *tohungas*. So really, the restoration of ancient tribalism would not please even radical Treatyists. For all their rhetoric, Treatyists know very well which side their bread is buttered on. Actual secession would be more trouble than it was worth.

So what would "Maori sovereignty" mean in practice? After all the threats used as bargaining counters, it would end up in practice meaning special privileges for Maori for ever in relation to the constitution and the law. This is much cheaper and easier for a financially desperate and not particularly scrupulous government. Members of the present National-led government will be well retired before the worst of the chickens come home to roost. So why not betray democracy, and gerrymander the electoral system so that Maori will enjoy disproportionately large representation in Parliament?

Some Treatyists claim a separate Maori House of Parliament - some even claim that Maori must have sole rule. Very well, it is hard to imagine that at present, and one can only wonder how seriously these people believe in it themselves. But they keep straight faces as they say it, and clearly they will take as much as they can get. Why not jack up some exciting new constitutional development - a written constitution, perhaps, or just a ruling from the exalted upper judiciary - something to justify Treatyist judges in overruling Acts of Parliament and imposing an unalterable, unappealable, politically correct and eternal tyranny of "Treaty principles"? At the very least why not pay "Maori" increasingly outrageous amounts of compensation as some pathetic attempt on our part to silence the song of writhing guilt they are playing on our poor, stupid, gullible heartstrings?

Do not think, by the way, that only young fire-eaters argue for Maori "sovereignty". Hekia Parata, National's unimpressive Minister of Education, has attempted to rewrite the Treaty unilaterally by saying that *te tino rangatiratanga* "does not have to be territorial sovereignty; it can be cultural or political sovereignty". A current National Party Cabinet Minister – and one unfortunately in charge of the education (indoctrination?) of our children - then, believes in Maori "political sovereignty". What might that mean exactly? Her husband, Sir Wira Gardiner, former chief executive of the Ministry of Maori Development, former Maori Vice-President of the National Party, now head of Te Papa – "Our Place", as it is called with a fine sense of sarcasm - is also an advocate of tribalism. He rejects "the common criticism that tribalism is divisive and is holding Maori back...what we are seeing in Bosnia is a desire by Bosnians to return to ethnic roots. The Bosnians, Croats, Serbs and Muslims were forcibly placed together...The break-up of Yugoslavia shows that tribalism is not dead. Of course it is going to cause trouble. But just because it creates problems doesn't mean that it's wrong".[3]

I would have thought that, if the break-up of Yugoslavia had any lesson for us, it was not to go down that path. But this knight of the realm, former head of a government department and ethnic fat-cat is not too concerned at all about atrocities and bloodshed. They are no more than "problems", a price worth paying for realising the dream of the new tribal Aotearoa.

How many more people like this "power couple" are there? What are they doing? Should anyone with ideas remotely like these be in charge of a school bus, let alone our education system?

Taonga

The other alleged difference in meaning between English and Maori versions of the Treaty concerns "taonga", a word rendered in the familiar Freeman English version as "lands and estates, forests, fisheries and other properties". As explained in Chapter Two, it is now regularly claimed that this English translation is too narrow; that *taonga* meant a treasure, anything treasured; and so the Maori language is a *taonga*, and so is Maori "culture", and so the poor old taxpayer is obliged to fund Maori Television and umpteen other means of cultural indoctrination. Old people are a *taonga*, as explained later. The Waitangi Tribunal has held - I am not making this up - that Maori are entitled to a share, at least, in the allocation of the radio spectrum, because Maori navigation was guided by the stars, and starlight is part of the electro-magnetic spectrum, and so the spectrum is a *taonga*, and Maori therefore have rights to the radio waves in another part of the spectrum. That is what the Tribunal solemnly found that Treaty principles require. Treaty principles will take you anywhere. Why do we take these people seriously?

This entire argument is nonsense. It is absolutely clear, from dictionaries scrupulously compiled by scholarly missionaries with every reason to be absolutely accurate, that in 1840 *taonga* meant no more than "property" or "possessions". It had no metaphorical or extended meanings. Sometimes it was defined simply as "property acquired at the point of the spear". It did not include language or culture. Who, in 1840, ever thought that Maori "culture" would need saving? Were not many Maori very eager to partake of the white man's culture, even to the extent of forsaking their old gods, the god of war prominent among them, for the Christians' gentle Saviour? If told that their language would die out within a couple of centuries, what would they have said? Very possibly, that they got a better one in exchange. At the least, they would have laughed at the idea that laws and government can save a culture. Cultures survive if they want to, and only if they want to. A language will not survive unless people want to speak it. If not enough people want to do so, then that's that. What can a law do? Even if the wish of Mr Tim Groser, the current Minister of Trade, were to come true, and Maori were to be made compulsory in schools, it would fare worse than the Gaelic of Ireland, which, despite almost a century of pious labour and compulsion (now considerably relaxed after the policy's complete failure became evident to all) and some valiant rearguard actions, is now - sadly - continuing to decline slowly but surely towards eventual extinction. The mere fact that Mr Groser believes that New Zealanders would tolerate such an imposition must cast serious doubt on his grip on reality. What would be dropped from the curriculum to make way for pandering to this useless fad? What of the cost? Where, for that matter, are the teachers?

People always have a "culture". But culture is simply how we live. It is not the fancy-dress which we put on when we go to the marae or the opera or some grand or solemn event; it is the language we actually speak, the food we actually eat, the clothes we actually wear, the work we do, the games we play, the television we watch. We cherish our ancestral inheritance, whatever it may be, and we would be sad if it were to disappear completely; but it is only a part of our culture. When people complain about the disappearance of Maori culture they are talking about the disappearance of old things that no longer have meaning or purpose. Cultures evolve and cross-pollinate, and separate and merge. Culture is how we actually live, and the way of life and significant mainspring of most New Zealanders, of whatever race, is much the same. Differences have more to do with geography, employment and income than with race.

You will notice that these two claims - the one for sovereignty, and the one that says that everything is a *taonga* - are not all that unlike each other under the skin. They both want everything, they just demand it in different ways. And both are nonsense.

In another way, of course, these two claims contradict each other. If Maori still have sovereignty, whatever exactly that means, and the Crown is in some inferior position, then the Crown is not going to be in any position to guarantee the enjoyment of *taonga*. That is the right and duty of the person with sovereignty, surely. One cannot have it both ways.

Aboriginal Title

This is a very simple matter, and you must not be put off by a slightly intimidating name. This legal situation has nothing to do with the Aboriginal peoples of Australia. But the meaning of the word is certainly connected. *Ab origine* is Latin for "from the beginning". The principle of aboriginal title is simply that, when the Crown acquires sovereignty over a new territory, its sovereign rights are subject to the continued ownership by the local inhabitants of their territory and territorial rights. The Crown is sovereign; but the native inhabitants are not thereby dispossessed and thrown out onto the street. That would go against justice and common sense. (Dispossession, if not worse, was however the lot of Maori conquered by other Maori.) No, the owners of the land continue to own it. Their ownership is ab origine - it existed from the beginning of Crown sovereignty, and before that, and continues to exist. It is just that that ownership is now subject to the Crown's lordship.

This aboriginal title can of course be extinguished. The Crown may purchase the land, most obviously, or Parliament may enact a statute of confiscation. The various Native Land and Maori Land Acts provided a different means of ending it. A Land Court would hear evidence about ownership, and then record certain claimants as the owners. This converted the status of the land from "Maori customary land" (customary title and aboriginal title are the same thing) to "Maori freehold land". When we now speak of "Maori land" we are speaking of this Maori freehold land, the titles to which are kept in the Maori Land

Court. Very possibly there is no Maori customary land left in the country. Perhaps some tiny parcel lurks unnoticed somewhere.

It is important to note that this principle of aboriginal title has nothing to do with the Treaty. It would exist if the Treaty had never been entered into. It does not exist because of the Treaty, and it does not derive its force from it. It is not necessary to claim some independent legal force for the Treaty in order to establish aboriginal title. Aboriginal title is a principle of the English common law, which has long applied wherever English law travels. The Treaty, however, is consistent with the principle. Its second clause, whereby the Queen promises Maori the continued enjoyment of their lands, dwellings and other property, expresses the same thing.

Just how far aboriginal title can take Maori remains to be seen. Even after the latest round of full and final settlements of historic Treaty claims, Maori are still attempting to claim water, and that claim may involve some aboriginal element. The current Maori Land Act (1993) gives the Maori Land Court, among other things, a general jurisdiction[4] to declare if any land is held by any person in a fiduciary capacity (i.e. similar to the relationship of trustee and beneficiary) to Maori. If so, the Court may make an appropriate order vesting the land in Maori. The Court recently held that a legal road - unformed, certainly, but that is legally irrelevant - running between blocks of Maori land was held by the local district council in a fiduciary capacity, and therefore ordered the land to be vested in the Maori plaintiffs. The somewhat elusive idea of "non-territorial aboriginal title" has been claimed recently - a situation where the alleged Maori interest is not ownership of land or water, but some lesser right, such as the right to continue to enter for the gathering of food.

Further discussion of this matter can easily become detailed, tangled and lengthy. Let us end by reminding ourselves of the main points; that aboriginal title does not owe its existence to the Treaty, but rather to English common law; and that such title can be extinguished by lawful means. A valid purchase is such an extinction.

The Disappearance of the Parties

One final matter remains before we look at the actual legal status of the Treaty, and that is to look at the identity of the parties to the Treaty. Who were they? And do they still exist, at least in anything more than name? They may still have legal form, but do they have anything more?

This question is one of justice and common sense rather than strict law, but if one party or the other, or both, no longer exist in recognisable form, then surely it becomes absurd to speak of the Waitangi agreement between them as having any moral force.

1. The Crown

The agreement was between Queen Victoria and Maori chiefs. Maori continue to speak of the Queen and the "Crown" in an outdated way which, if anyone else were to use it, would invite only laughter. They speak of a 'special relationship' they allegedly have with the monarch. When Maori claimants are negotiating with the Crown over the use of publicly-owned resources in Treaty settlements - conservation lands, for example - those claimants regularly object to allowing members of the public, representing the present public owners and users, to be involved in the negotiations, on the ground that the Treaty was not with any ordinary citizens, but with "the Crown". This was the basis of Sir Tipene O'Regan's refusal to countenance Federated Mountain Clubs (FMC) and the Royal Forest and Bird Protection Society participating in negotiations over Ngai Tahu's claim to national parks and other public conservation lands at the time of the most recent of Ngai Tahu's procession of claims.

But this is absurd. It is now quite impossible, under our constitution, to draw any distinct clear line between "the Crown" and the people. Government is the Queen's but, as we all know, she has no actual control over the Ministers who theoretically serve her. She must do as they advise her; she "reigns but does not rule". The "Crown" therefore means not Her Majesty herself, but the Queen's government - all the public service, with the Queen's Ministers at their head. Her Ministers - a "minister" is simply an appointed servant - are chosen from Members of Parliament, and enjoy the support of a parliamentary majority. The public service obeys the laws Parliament enacts. Parliament is elected by the people. The "Crown" then is the totality of our government, ultimately chosen by and responsible to the people. It is not a person or institution in its own right. When "the Crown" settles a Treaty claim, the money and assets it uses do not come from some secret special hoard of gold and jewels which Her Majesty has hidden away in a castle somewhere. No, the assets used in Treaty settlements are the assets of the New Zealand people. Any money which the government chooses to give to anyone is not the Crown's, the government's or the state's. It is the money of taxpayers, taken from them and given to someone else; and we are therefore entitled to be fully consulted in the process. Every secret Treaty negotiation, then, every exclusion from the public, every shoving of a settlement agreement through Parliament without any opportunity for public input, justified on the ground that it is a private matter between "the Queen" and a tribe - every such dealing is based on a nonsensical lie.

2. 'Maori' - tribes? Or what?

So much for "the Crown". What of the descendants of the Maori signatories of 1840? In most cases, their claims of entitlement are equally absurd. Many of those demanding compensation for alleged historic wrongs, and perpetual privilege in the future, have never suffered disadvantage in their own lives, nor are they in any meaningful sense "Maori" at all .

Giving compensation to their fifth and sixth generation descendants of mixed blood is both bizarre and dishonest. There are many New Zealanders who are descended from the clans who were "cleared' off their ancestral lands in the Scottish Highlands in the period 1790-1840 by both the authorities and lairds who wanted the green straths and glens, where the clansmen lived and grew their small crops, for grazing sheep. These displaced clansfolk moved on – often to the colonies – and made successes of their lives in new environments. But we don't see their fifth and sixth generation descendants jumping up and down in front of the Scottish Parliament in Edinburgh and demasnding compensation from the Scottish taxpayer of the 21st century for the alleged wrongs that were done to their forebears.

The Maori chieftains who signed the Treaty were, like their tribesmen, full-blooded Maoris. Their descendants are not. New Zealand law no longer requires any particular proportion of Maori ancestry before one can claim to be Maori. The 1993 Maori Land Act and Electoral Act, for example, now define a Maori simply as "a person of the Maori race of New Zealand; and includes any descendant of such a person". Other statutes use the same definition.[5] No particular proportion of Maori ancestry, then, is necessary before one can enrol on the Maori electoral roll or do anything else, e.g. accept special racial privileges available only to "Maori". One may have only the tiniest, merest fraction of Maori blood and still be legally entitled to call oneself "Maori", allege that one has suffered from ancestral wrongs, and enjoy the benefits of taxpayer generosity. Ngai Tahu has tribal members on its books who have only one two-hundred-and-fifty-sixth Ngai Tahu ancestry. We all know very well that most "Maori" have European names, complexions and lives just like everyone else's. On what basis, then, should they enjoy special enrichment from the taxpayer or any special privileges in our law?

Most of us would say that it is only just that any claims we have for the remedying of an injustice we have suffered should pass to our heirs and successors. But the point is that there are no longer, in New Zealand, two distinct groups whom we can label Maori and Settler. We have been marrying each other for two centuries. All Maoris are only "part-Maori"; they are of mixed Maori and European descent. We hear statements that the number or proportion of Maori is increasing. The number of people who so describe themselves may be, but the figure is meaningless. All these people also have European blood, and it would be just as accurate to say that the number of Europeans with some Maori blood is increasing.

When any modern "Maori", then, claims for an injustice allegedly done to his ancestors, he is actually claiming for a wrong done to some of his ancestors by others of his ancestors. If his Maori ancestors suffered from the injustice, very possibly his European ancestors benefited.

Certainly, if an injustice were done in the past, and people today do suffer because of it, then it is reasonable to make redress. But - leaving aside the questions of whether injustices were actually done, and whether (if they were) they have already been remedied - leaving those issues aside, the question must be asked whether today's living claimant has in fact been injured. The mere fact that one of a claimant's sixteen great-great-grandparents, say, suffered an injustice is no proof at all - indeed, is hardly evidence at all - that today's claimant has been injured. It is surely unlikely that someone with only that slender strain of Maori blood has ever suffered.

The remedying of injustice should, surely, benefit only the victims of injustice. For our government to bestow special benefits and privileges on those who have not suffered and are not entitled to them is an actual injustice to the rest of the population. Our government and public service have for some years, then, been engaged in such a programme of creating racial injustice.

75

It is interesting to note a strong difference of opinion even among "Maori" themselves as to the precise party with whom the Crown made its promises under the Treaty. Was the Treaty with all Maori, or was the Treaty only with "tribes"? If the Treaty were only with tribes, then all settlements would also have to be with tribes; anyone of Maori descent wishing to benefit from a settlement would have to apply to his or her tribe, and any Maori without tribal connections would simply miss out. If that were so, then many Maori would indeed miss out on any benefits since they, especially those at the bottom of the heap and most in need of a little assistance, have little or no connection with their ancestral tribes. They may hardly know what their tribes are. Even for those Maori who do retain some link with their ancestral tribes, that link is usually a purely formal one. Tribes are not genuine living entities as they were in 1840. Professor Elizabeth Rata maintains that there is a great historical discontinuity between nineteenth century Maori tribes and their self-styled present-day successors. She considers that "the real character of contemporary *iwi* is that of an economic corporation concealed by neotraditionalist ideology".[6]

Any settlements that are just with tribes, then, would benefit only those people retaining tribal connections; and, indeed, not even all of them, but all too often, only a privileged few. Many poor and disadvantaged Maori would miss out altogether. Such an approach would completely contradict a common justification for Treaty settlements, that they are part of a process to restore all Maori to prosperity and dignity. But needless to say, "pan-Maori" settlements bypassing tribes are bitterly opposed by tribal Maori. Sir Tipene O'Regan, for example, has condemned proposed settlements of fisheries claims on a non-tribal basis as "suntanned welfarism".

The matter has been fought out in the courts, with immense benefits to lawyers, in several cases concerning the Treaty of Waitangi Fisheries Commission and its proposals for the distribution of benefits. Various judges were inclined to think that people of Maori descent unable to establish tribal affiliations should still be entitled to benefit from a settlement intended to benefit all Maori, and the proceedings were often described by the judges as futile and doomed to failure as an attempt to resolve underlying and deep-seated divisions.[7] The eventual arrangement was something of a compromise. But we note the existence of the dispute.

Indigenous?

The archaeological evidence is clear that the ancestors of the Maori arrived in New Zealand only somewhere about 1200 A.D., if not slightly later. Maori settlement certainly preceded European, but Maori had been living here for little more than four hundred years before Tasman in his turn reached our coasts, and it is not impossible that Spanish and Tamil vessels - perhaps, so some suggest, even Chinese - had earlier touched our shores. Nevertheless, certain Maori spokespeople are often pleased to describe Maori as "indigenous". What does this word mean? And why should we be concerned about the classification? There is no doubt about the fact or dates of Maori settlement; why should a little label concern us?

The issue is of particular concern because in 2007 the United Nations adopted a Declaration on the Rights of Indigenous Peoples.[8] This document declares that certain human beings, simply because of their (completely undefined) status as "indigenous", have special rights, which appear to take priority over the universal human rights which we thought everyone enjoyed. Contrary to reasonable expectations, the Declaration nowhere contains any definition of who or what an indigenous person is. It would not be unreasonable, surely, to expect a definition. It is surely essential. We do not need one in the case of the 1948 Universal Declaration of Human Rights, because that deals with absolutely all human beings, and we know what they are. But who is indigenous?

According to the dictionaries, there are only two things that the word may mean. In the first place, "indigenous" may mean simply "born or produced naturally in a land or region; native to that soil, region, etc." In that sense, all native-born New Zealanders are indigenous. We may speak a language and have a culture that developed elsewhere, but so, for that matter, did the first Maori when they arrived from Hawaiki.

Secondly, "indigenous" may mean "not introduced; belonging naturally to a region". So the moa and the kiwi are indigenous; they were not introduced, they belong here naturally. In that sense, though, if we are speaking of a people whose ancestors have lived in a place from time immemorial, then New Zealand has no indigenous inhabitants, for human beings first set foot on these islands a mere eight centuries ago.

Those are the only two things this English word can mean. Yet it is clear (although only by implication) that the Declaration takes

77

"indigenous" to mean something completely different - to mean, in fact, "having ancestors who arrived somewhere first". The Lapps of Lapland - the Sami, as they are now to be known - are alleged by commentators to be the only indigenous people left in Europe. No other Europeans are "indigenous" to the lands they may have occupied for thousands of years. The Anglo-Saxons are not; neither are the Gaels of the Celtic fringe, descendants of the Ancient Britons driven to those fringes by the invading Saxons. In Japan, only a few thousand Ainu, an ancient people, are said to be indigenous; other Japanese, despite 5,000 years of occupation, are not.

But if Japanese and Britons, despite thousands of years of occupation, are not indigenous, how can Maori be indigenous after a mere eight hundred?

Moreover, by what part of the law of nature does arriving somewhere before anyone else confer a completely new and extra set of inherent and indefeasible "human rights"? Many New Zealand descendants of the European pioneers would rather like the idea that, because their ancestors arrived here some generations ago, they now have more rights than more recent immigrants. There will be no prizes for guessing the reaction of human rights advocates to that suggestion. But if the descendants of earlier immigrants who arrived by sailing ship may not have special rights, why should the descendants of those who arrived by canoe?

Why? Simply because "indigenous rights" are part of a political programme. "Indigenous" peoples are generally considered to be pre-colonial, primitive and oppressed. That might well, in other parts of the world, very often be the case. The best way to remedy that oppression, though, would surely be by respecting basic principles of non-discrimination and agreed universal human rights, rather than by inventing an entire category of completely new rights enjoyed only by the nebulous category of indigenous persons. To speak of "rights" which only these people have is to debase the whole idea of rights, and will inevitably give rise to the suspicion that all human rights, even the best of them, are nothing but a political platform. That is not good for anyone.

The United Nations Declaration on the Rights of Indigenous People is not merely an amplification of our universal human rights. Its forty-six articles very clearly declare that some human beings, simply because they are "indigenous", have more rights than anyone else. Many of these indigenous rights are ones held by "indigenous people" collectively, rather than by individuals; they are completely incompatible with rights, as we understand them, for individuals and families. They are "rights", then, for indigenous communities to be left alone and run by traditional leaders on traditional lines, resisting any changes the humbler indigenous might desire. If an indigenous "people" running its own affairs wanted to maintain a sexually oppressive traditional practice - the burqa, say, or genital mutilation, which is to prevail: indigenous rights or universal human rights? One or the other must go. Under the guise of a declaration of rights, the United Nations is actually depriving human beings of the right to develop and change. This is paternalism of the most oppressive kind.

The rights the Declaration lists are, as we might expect, rights to just about everything. After a preamble of twenty-four headings which sets the general tone (and also, incredibly, condemns any assumed superiority on the basis of ethnic or cultural differences, and recognises that the rights of the indigenous vary from place to place!) the Declaration recognises rights to self-determination, autonomy and self-government, to equality and freedom from discrimination, the maintenance of their own identity, the inviolability of their culture, the freedom to develop their culture, the recognition of customary law, their rights to keep and control (and to recover completely) their ancestral lands, their rights to autonomy and self-government in internal and local affairs, the right to redress for takings of their property (including cultural, religious and intellectual property) and the duty of states not just to consult them but actually to obtain their consent before adopting measures that might affect them.....All this and much more.

This is simply not compatible with the Treaty's declaration that Maori are British subjects like any others and equal before the law. It is not compatible with the integrity of the state of New Zealand. The Declaration's final article declares that nothing in it may authorise or encourage any action which would dismember or impair, totally or in part, the territorial integrity or political unity of states, but this is in plain contradiction to everything that has gone before. If, in our own country, the descendants of Maori might run their own affairs according to their own customary law and develop their lands and laws as they please, and the Crown must seek their consent before doing anything which affects them, then at once we have separate racially-defined communities on their own territories and exempt from the ordinary laws of the land. (In

79

South Africa, these used to be called Bantustans ("homelands"), and were generally considered to be a bad thing. It is remarkable that advanced "anti-racist" thought now embraces the "separate but equal" formula which American and South African blacks long struggled against.) If this is not at least partial dismemberment of our nation, what is it?

The final article also states that the Declaration shall be interpreted in accordance with the principles of "justice, democracy, respect for human rights (!), equality and non-discrimination", among other wonderful things. But to apply these would mean that the Declaration should not be applied at all.

Incredibly, it was a National Party-led government that signed New Zealand up to this Declaration. To its great credit, Helen Clark's Labour government had refused to do so. Labour was particularly concerned about clauses which a) would guarantee Maori rights to "lands, territories and resources which they have traditionally owned" - in other words, the entire country; b) required that all lands "taken" be replaced by others of equal size and quality - which is impossible, because it ignores the legitimate claims of everyone else, and also ignores full and final settlements of historic claims; c) would effectively grant Maori a veto over all laws and decisions which might affect them, including plans for national resource management. It was the National Party, under John Key, which committed our country to this mischievous Declaration, not in the interests of the country but to buy the parliamentary votes of the small, racist Maori Party.

It may be a minor comfort that international law draws a distinction between declarations and treaties. Treaties bind states which ratify them, whereas declarations are more "aspirational", "a standard of achievement to be pursued in a spirit of partnership and mutual respect".[9] That is not much help, though. The United Nations, all its agencies and all states are obliged to work towards the Declaration's full realisation. Here in our own country, the Declaration is already being called in aid as an argument for racial preference. Merely because it is a declaration and not a fully-binding treaty does not mean that it will not be used to reproach and belabour us for any reluctance we might evince to make further concessions to a small, greedy group of Maori separatists.

Moreover, as a simple matter of fact, we must repeat the question we considered before. Even if the Maori of 1840 could be considered "indigenous", in what sense can someone whose racial inheritance is more non-Maori than Maori be considered indigenous now? Dr Peter Sharples, the current Minister of Maori Affairs, has a white father of British-born parents, and a part-Maori mother. How is he "indigenous"? Someone who is only one eighth or one sixteenth Maori cannot really be described as being, in any meaningful sense, Maori at all. Genetically they are not; their cultural milieu is unlikely to be Maori; it is unlikely that they have ever experienced any racial prejudice or any misfortune in their own lives because of the Maori strand in their ancestry. In a free country, of course, people are entitled to describe themselves as they please, and if someone with only a tiny drop of Maori blood wishes to describe him or her self as Maori, and ignore or even deny all other ancestry, then he or she should be free to do so - even though such a denial of most of what he is might well be thought to be unhealthy or even weird. But it is another thing altogether when that is followed by a claim to special treatment and special legal and economic status and privilege under the Treaty, or as an "indigenous" person. Such claims must be justified. It is not enough for someone with only a fraction of "indigenous" blood to hang a fish-hook around his neck and claim that we owe him. We are entitled to demand evidence that he deserves this special treatment and our taxpayer dollars.

Treatyists are always very evasive when this question of blood and identity comes up. They usually say that the issue of who is a Maori is one "for Maori to decide" - that no-one else is entitled to examine the credentials of those wishing to enrich themselves at the public expense. All must be accepted at face value. That is hardly a surprising answer, but it is entirely unacceptable to taxpayers and honest people of common sense.

A definition of who is Maori would not be impossible, and, as noted above, our own laws once contained a minimum requirement of at least 50% Maori ancestry. The Alaska Native Claims Settlement Act 1971 imposes a test of at least "one-fourth degree or more Alaskan Indian, Eskimo or Aleut blood", or, in the absence of proof of a minimum blood quantum, anyone "regarded as a native by the native village or group of which he claims to be a member and whose father or mother is regarded as native.." Village and groups are defined also. Membership of them must be vital and living, not a mere matter of tracing descent from a remote tribal ancestor.

The Indigenous Declaration may be appropriate to countries whose simple pre-colonial populations are still comparatively discrete and distinct entities. There are very few such communities here ~ one or two remote settlements in Northland, the East Coast and Ureweras might possibly qualify, but few others.

The time is long overdue for a careful definition, not just of what "indigenous" might mean, but of what "Maori" itself means, for without such a definition the number of opportunists on a very lucrative gravy-train will only continue to increase.

Everything comes at a cost. The undoubted civil freedoms which we take for granted come at the cost of weakening the social cohesion and sense of community present in more traditional societies, including older European ones. Most of us would be reluctant to return to that more limiting and oppressive past (as we might well consider it) unless it was absolutely necessary. Many New Zealanders of Maori descent are, not surprisingly, attracted by the promises of privilege and riches which can be extracted from their alleged status as an indigenous and distinct Maori people. But they cannot have it both ways. If they wish to live free and comfortable lives integrated into a caring modern society, they cannot at the same time claim to be living in traditional structures of authority and custom. Few Maori live that way now, and few, I suspect, would want to.

The Treaty of Waitangi in International Law

Having cleared the decks of all this preliminary clutter, let us now consider the status of the Treaty in law ~ both in international law and the law of New Zealand. We have already made it clear that the Treaty's actual terms - the sovereignty of the Crown and the equality of Maori as the Queen's subjects, just like everyone else - cannot give Maori any of the special rights and riches which they seek, and so in a way the question of the Treaty's legal status could almost be said to be unimportant. But let us take no chances!

In both cases - both international and New Zealand law ("domestic law", as lawyers often speak of the law of a particular country, to distinguish it from international law) - the situation is perfectly simple.

As to international law, first of all -

The Treaty of Waitangi is not a valid international treaty.

That is correct. For the sake of emphasis, and just in case you missed the point of that sentence, I shall repeat it in slightly different words. In international law the Treaty of Waitangi is a nullity. It has no legal standing as a Treaty in international law. It does not exist in any official treaty list.

This has long been generally accepted. The reason is that treaties can be made only between states, and Maori, not formed into an organised state but living in much smaller and far less sophisticated societies (and indeed, ones in a constant state of flux, given the intensely war-torn nature of the times) were simply incapable of entering into such an agreement in 1840. Maori were tribes of warring Stone Age cannibals. They lived in a horrifyingly violent society, in squalid conditions in rough, smoky huts, without metal, without pottery, without reading and writing, with art traditional and rudimentary, and music and oral literature more primitive than that of the age of Homer. It was preposterous to regard every microscopic agreement with a handful of such primitive people, without even the wheel or a written language, as having as solemn a status as the Treaty of Westphalia, or Utrecht, or Vienna. Such, at least, was the analysis of international lawyers of the time and later. It is not an unreasonable attitude. Lines must be drawn. The Treaty of Waitangi was something, but it was not an actual treaty - just a necessary preliminary political proceeding whereby the colonising power had a preliminary meeting with the native inhabitants to make sure that they knew what was going on and had no serious objections.

That would surely be a sensible thing for a would-be colonising power to do, would it not? It would be wise to check that everything was going to be fine before one finally committed oneself. And so one makes soundings; one enters into negotiations. And understandings are reached. But that does not make them "treaties". Do not be misled by the label "treaty". The "Treaty" of Waitangi was in effect merely a memorandum of the general amiable preliminary understanding reached under the pohutukawas above the beach in early February, 1840, before the official business of colonisation went ahead - the official proclamation of sovereignty on the 21st of May, 1840, and the rest. (A proclamation of sovereignty, of course, was completely unnecessary unless the international law of the times considered February's agreement to have no legal standing.)

Some revisionists now condemn this approach, saying that it is "Eurocentric" in its refusal to recognise small primitive tribes as the equals of great modern nations. It is not Eurocentric at all. It is merely commonsense and plain eyesight to see differences between the two parties. Do not forget that the Treaty's actual words are no more than a very general statement of intent and benevolence.

But even if the view were considered "Eurocentric", the fact is that international law is a creation of the western nation-state system that emerged from the wreckage of Christendom after the Reformation and Wars of Religion. We are not arguing here about whether we should be nice to each other, we are considering the simple legal question - according to western-based international law, is the "Treaty" of Waitangi a valid international treaty?

The answer is "no".

To repeat: No.

One must make another point also, arguing in the alternative, as lawyers do - which is that the Treaty was an agreement whereby one of the two parties agreed that sovereignty was the Queen's. Even if Maori had the "political pen" of the Western nation-state, and the ability to enter into binding international treaties, nevertheless the agreement would still only be a valid treaty by which Maori agreed to lay down that political pen, and extinguish themselves as a sovereign entity. That being so, how can they be anything now but the Queen's subjects?[10]

The Treaty of Waitangi in the Law of New Zealand

The Treaty of Waitangi has of itself no legal standing as part of the law of New Zealand. I shall illustrate this point at some length but, before we go there, let us just say this again, and pause for a moment to absorb some of the implications of this statement. Without wishing to be condescending about the Treaty knowledge of my fellow-citizens - and you have good reason to be ill-informed, given the general messages and implications we are all force-fed every day about our "obligations" - I imagine that this simple fact may come as something of a surprise to many of you, so let me say it again. The Treaty of Waitangi, in and of itself, does not form part of the law of New Zealand.

Given, as I say, that all the Treaty does is amiably to establish the Queen's sovereignty and the status of Maori as her property-owning subjects, it would not make any difference if the Treaty's terms were part of our law; but, as it happens, the Treaty is not part of our domestic law at all. There are various reasons for this, all of them reasonable and indeed obvious.

For one thing, the Treaty was regarded as a mere preliminary political proceeding and memorandum of good intent. How could this vague mutual expression of future co-operation become the law of the land? And why should it? All it is is a statement of general goodwill. It is not a treaty in international law.

Moreover, even if it were a valid international treaty - which it is not - there is an ancient principle of English law which says that no treaty or other international agreement can become part of our law until it is ratified and put into our law by a normal Act of Parliament. This is very wise. Treaties are entered into by Our Sovereign Lady the Queen, but they are of course, actually arranged by the Queen's Ministers, the government. Would we want to see the situation where our Prime Minister, whoever he or she may be - not necessarily someone we approve of - is free to go overseas, sign a secret deal with a foreign power, and that deal's provisions automatically become part of our law? I do not think so. So treaties enter our law only when Parliament adopts them; and they then owe their force in our law to that adoption. An international treaty does not become part of our law until Parliament says so.

Furthermore, since all the Treaty actually does is to declare British sovereignty, and Maori as British subjects, what possible point would there be in a parliament ratifying it? The establishment of the New Zealand Parliament itself was an expression of British sovereignty. To ratify the Treaty would add nothing at all to what was already the clear legal situation.

The Treaty has absolutely no independent legal standing in New Zealand law. This is absolutely clear. It has been regularly stated and repeated in recent Court of Appeal judgments. The Treaty is, of course, along with so much else, part of the social background and situation in which law is made, "part of the context in which legislation is interpreted", but that is all.[11]

It follows, therefore, that British sovereignty over New Zealand was not, as a matter of law, acquired by the Treaty; and it follows also that the question of whether or not a particular chief or tribe assented to the Treaty is completely irrelevant to the sovereignty of the Crown, which exists everywhere.

If the Treaty has any place in our law (and it does have some), that is only because some statute or other refers to it in some way or another. And then its legal efficacy is only by virtue of that statute and only to the extent that that statute requires. In other words, it is still the statute that is the law, not the Treaty. A statute can refer to the Treaty in the same way that it can refer to any other document.[13]

Various statutes do refer to the Treaty. One is the Treaty of Waitangi Act 1975, which, despite its perhaps slightly misleading name, merely establishes the Waitangi Tribunal. We will look at the Tribunal later.

There are other statutes, also, which refer to the Treaty, and to these we now turn. There are not many. As of 2002, anyway, a mere thirteen other Acts of Parliament contained clauses imposing any obligations in respect of the Treaty. None of these statutes, however, refers to the Treaty itself, or to the terms of the Treaty. The general approach of all of these statutes is, rather, to require that in their administration some degree or other of respect must be paid to "the principles of the Treaty".

The principles. Not the terms, the principles, the underlying ideas. And what those principles are, to be perfectly frank, is entirely a matter of personal opinion. Parliament, for whatever reason, has never seen fit to enlighten us as to what the principles are. The courts have therefore been forced to make their own list, which we shall examine shortly. That list, of course, has a certain legal standing. But anyone else is also free to have an opinion and compile a list of "principles". The Waitangi Tribunal has always been obliged to base its recommendations on "Treaty principles", and so it must identify them. The Maori Council, which brought the big case on the Treaty (seen shortly) in 1987, proposed its own list to the court, as did the Crown. The 1988 Royal Commission on Social Policy found three principles.[12] The Justice Department has proposed five "Principles for Crown Action on the Treaty". And there is nothing to stop any private person from compiling his own list and then to go around insisting that that list is the genuine article and should be respected. This is the first thing to remember about Treaty "principles" - that they are entirely a matter of opinion; opinion which is, obviously, highly politically-charged, and usually in the service of some private agenda.

There are other things to remember also, but before we get there it may be of interest to look at the 1987 "Maori Lands Case", as it is often

86

known, which first made Treaty principles a central matter of public interest and importance. After describing this case I shall then go on to speak more generally of the principles, so the impatient reader may, if he so desires, skip the following section on the case without fatally wounding his or her understanding.

New Zealand Maori Council v Attorney-General [1987] 1 NZLR 641 ('The Maori Lands case')

The State-Owned Enterprises Act 1986, made as part of the then Labour government's major shake-up of our country, established a considerable number of new state-owned enterprises (SOEs). These enterprises were to carry on commercial or semi-commercial operations which had previously been performed by government departments such as the Forest Service and the Lands and Survey Department. The SOEs' principal objective was to operate as successful businesses. Crown assets, including lands owned by the Crown, could be transferred to them. Obviously many of these enterprises, such as the Forestry Corporation and the Lands Corporation, would have to own some of the lands of the old government departments in order to operate.

What if some of this land, which was to be transferred to a new enterprise, were the subject of an historic Treaty claim? That situation was provided for. Section 27 of the Act said that in that situation the SOE took the land subject to the claim; that it could not transfer the land to anyone else and that, if the Waitangi Tribunal made a recommendation for the land's return to the Maori claimants and the government concurred, then the land would have to be handed over to the successful claimant.

So far so good. Nowhere in the Act, though, was there any provision dealing with future claims; with claims which might be lodged in future over lands transferred to these enterprises.

When the Bill was proceeding through Parliament, however, the Labour government had (at the Maori Council's suggestion) inserted a new clause into it, which eventually became section 9. This section says: "Nothing in this Act shall permit the Crown to act in a manner that is inconsistent with the principles of the Treaty of Waitangi".

A very good case can be made that this clause was intended to be no more than a pious and meaningless piece of lip-service. In his book *I've Been Writing* Mr. Richard Prebble, a Cabinet Minister at the time, described the consternation in the Beehive, even among well-known

87

constitutional experts, when the court made its decision in this Maori Lands case. In later years Sir Geoffrey Palmer claimed that he foresaw the court's decision and approved section 9's insertion in the legislation with that decision in mind. That might well be making a virtue out of necessity. Bear in mind that in this Maori Lands case the Crown argued, as explained below, that it had never been intended that section 9 was to apply to land at all.

But section 9 became law, along with the rest of the Act, and the Crown then prepared to transfer large areas of land to the new SOEs. At that point the Maori Council sought judicial review of the Crown's plans. The Council sought to stop these land transfers. It argued that to transfer any lands to the SOEs without more ado would be in breach of Treaty principles, which (by section 9) the Crown was obliged to respect. This was because it might be that land not subject to a claim at present might nevertheless be subject to a claim in future - and, obviously, the Crown would be less able to settle that claim if the land concerned were no longer available to it, but had instead been transferred to an SOE. It might be, also, even if that particular land were never claimed, that that land could still be used by the Crown in settling a claim, in substitution for other land which was no longer available.

The Crown, in its argument before the court, said that this could not have been Parliament's intention. If section 9 were to prevent transfers of land, then the new enterprises would, in the Solicitor-General's words, be able to operate only "in a withered and crippled way". The purpose of the Act would be frustrated, and Parliament could never have intended that. Land was not the only Crown asset to be transferred, but it was certainly the main one. Parliament had intended, the Crown argued, that section 27 (dealing with land already the subject of claims) was to be the only section dealing with land. Section 9 applied to other matters, and there were indeed other matters to which it could apply, but as far as land went section 27 was a complete code, which excluded the more general words in section 9.

Those are very reasonable arguments, and indeed even Sir Robin Cooke, the President of the Court of Appeal, agreed that Parliament "thought the Act would have the effect now contended for by the Crown". Nevertheless, even though Parliament had that intention, and even though the words of the Act could be interpreted to achieve that intention, five judges in the Court of Appeal chose to ignore the words and intentions of Parliament, our supreme lawmaker, and to hold instead that such land transfers were improper. This is a clear example, and by no means the only one, of "judicial activism" - of judges deliberately abandoning their proper role as the judges of disputes and instead making quite improper political decisions. Yes, I am sorry to say it, but we cannot trust some of our judges, who are only too ready to behave as politicians pursuing a policy, rather than to apply clear and established law. I shall return to this point later.

Leaving that aside for the moment - in this case the judges held that section 9 did apply to transfers of land, and they made a declaration that land transfers would be unlawful unless some system were established to allow compliance with Treaty principles. They did this because they decided that a transfer would breach the "Treaty principles" which section 9 spoke of. After much negotiation several amending statutes were passed which were considered acceptable to all parties.So - what were

The 'principles'?

Many trees have died in explaining the "principles" of the Treaty. The judgments in the Lands case alone run to seventy-nine pages, and many of those pages are about the principles. There have been quite a few other cases since, and enough commentary to sink a ship. But it will be safe to summarise these "principles" as follows:

The judgments generally considered the Treaty to be a "solemn compact". The Crown - politically, if not by strict law - obtained sovereignty by it in return for promising protection to Maori. The parties must act towards each other reasonably and in good faith. It is a partnership between races. The Crown would behave honourably. A duly elected government must be free to follow its chosen policies, and to make laws for the whole community. The Crown has a duty of active protection of Maori in the use of their lands and waters. The Crown should grant redress where the Waitangi Tribunal recommends it. (In later cases the Court rapidly came to change its mind about that particular blank cheque.) Maori have a duty of loyalty to the Queen, full acceptance of her government and reasonable co-operation. In certain circumstances the Crown may have a duty to consult Maori.

That is a fair summary of the "principles" and, as I have observed elsewhere, few of us would find fault with most of the items on that list. They seem perfectly reasonable. So what possible objection can there be?

89

There are several objections. The first, in fact, lies in what I have just written, that it is hard to find fault with the list. That is because the list is only a vague list of pleasant generalities, which can mean everything and nothing. It could be used to justify any decision that any court ever wanted to come to. In this particular case, the court chose several items on the list which led it to declare that the Crown's actions were unlawful. But the court could just as easily have chosen other items on the list - the freedom of the Crown to govern, the Maori duty of loyalty - and have come to the opposite conclusion. A list of platitudes is not a helpful guide to anyone. It detracts from the age-old axiom that there must be certainty in the law. Indeed, without certainty there cannot be law in the first place. Where wide discretion exists, there is an end of the Rule of Law. No-one would ever know, in any particular situation, what Treaty principles required until the matter had been submitted, at crippling expenditure of time, money and vexation, to judges who would be able to find in the list of principles a justification for any decision they wanted to come to. References to Treaty principles are an open invitation to judges to make political decisions, and some judges, including our highest ones, are only too keen to accept the invitation. There is an old legal saying that the interest of the state (and of the parties!) lies in an end to litigation; but Treaty principles are a guarantee of litigation.

But that is not all. Here is a shorter summary of the principles, made by Sir Robin Cooke in a later case:[13] "An enduring relationship of a fiduciary nature akin to a partnership, each party accepting a positive duty to act in good faith, fairly, reasonably and honourably towards the other."

Now according to Cooke this is the description of the relationship, implied by the Treaty's principles, between Maori and the Crown and, when put just in those terms, it is not unreasonable. But should it not also be the relationship existing between the Crown and all New Zealanders? Surely the Crown should act towards all of us (and we towards the Crown) in good faith, fairly, reasonably and honourably? Should that not be the case? So what are the judges saying when they say that this is what Treaty principles require? Are they implying that non-Maori New Zealanders are not entitled to the same degree of fair dealing from their own government? That Crown actions are to be judged by two different standards, depending on the race of the citizen? To hell with that.

But if, on the contrary, the judges were to agree that "Yes, non-Maori New Zealanders may also expect the same relationship with the Crown" - well, in that case, there is no difference at all between Maori and non-Maori New Zealanders in their relationship with the Crown, and we are all absolutely equal, as we should be.

Let us hope that the judges will get around to saying this one day. It is a little worrying that they have not bothered to make the point yet. But any talk of a "special relationship" between the Crown and Maori automatically implies that non-Maori are not entitled to the same degree of fair dealing. A special relationship between the Crown and one class of citizens automatically puts all other citizens into a second inferior class.

We might say one little word in the Court of Appeal's defence. Its judgment has, in one important respect, been constantly misrepresented, until it is now difficult for the most careful speaker to avoid repeating the same error. That error concerns "partnership". The Court of Appeal never spoke of a specific partnership between Maori and the Crown. We hear such talk every day, but it has absolutely no legal basis. It is impossible for there to be a "partnership" between the Crown and any of its subjects. If any citizens were to be the Crown's "partners" in government, then they would not be the Crown's subjects at all. They would be equal to the Crown - and the rest of us would therefore be subject to them as we are subject to the Crown. If Maori were the Crown's partner, then the rest of us would be subject to Maori just as we are subject to the Crown.

But, as I say, the Court of Appeal did not say that. It did certainly use the words "partners" and "partnership" but it used these words with deplorable looseness, and interchangeably with the word "parties". The arrangement between Maori and the Crown was not a precise legal partnership, such as we find in marriage or a business partnership; it was "something in the nature of" or "a relationship akin to" a partnership. Later Sir Robin Cooke wrote of "an analogy" of partnership.[14] Something which is analogous is similar, comparable, a metaphor - but it is not the same thing. He also later emphasised that even genuine partnerships can have partners with greater or lesser interests, and that use of the partnership word did not mean "that every asset or resource in which Maori have some justifiable claim to share should be divided equally".[15]

The court spoke also of a partnership between races. And, of course, the court also made it quite clear that Maori are subjects who owe duties of loyalty and obedience to the Queen's government.

This very sloppy use of the word "partnership" has caused immeasureable harm. The judges in 1987 may not have foreseen the monstrous distortions which the "Treaty partnership" has since undergone. But they must still be blamed for it because judges are supposed to be cautious and careful and to use words properly so that what they say can not later be distorted.

A "partner" and a "party" are quite different things. The buyer and seller of a house are parties to a contract just as the signatories at Waitangi were parties to an agreement. But that does not make any of them partners.

The judges' sloppiness is all the less excusable because "partners" and "partnership" are words with a special and very precise legal meaning. Both the common law and the Partnership Act deal with the special status of business partners. Once the Court of Appeal used the word "partner" at all, it was inevitable that that expression would be taken up and interpreted as indicating some more or less precise legal relationship of equals. Cooke's later remarks indicate that he subsequently realised the problem caused by his own political ambitions or stupidity.

But by then the horse had well and truly bolted. The word has taken on a life of its own. Every day it is spoken of and referred to, with the implication that the partnership is an actual one, and one of equals. Words are powerful things, and this one is very dangerous. It is important to remember, then, that "partnership" is impossible to reconcile with the clear words of the Treaty or with the declared "principles" of the Treaty, that Maori are the Queen's subjects like everyone else.

Something else which Sir Robin Cooke said, however, must alarm us. He said that the interpretation of the State-Owned Enterprises Act "should not be approached with the austerity of tabulated legalism. A broad, unquibbling and practical interpretation is demanded..." He later said that "the Treaty has to be seen as an embryo rather than a fully developed and integrated set of ideas".

An embryo is something in an early and rudimentary stage, a creature still growing in the womb and not yet brought to birth, a seed full of potential. But this is not what the Treaty was. Nor is it true that it was not "a fully developed and integrated set of ideas". It has one idea in it, a very simple and clear one - that the Queen is sovereign, and Maori are her subjects. But to claim an obscurity gives judges the chance to clear the obscurity up. To claim that the Treaty is only an embryo, with a lot of development ahead of it, gives judges the opportunity to develop it into whatever social and political views they please.

Any extraction of "principles" from the Treaty is an entirely speculative personal exercise. The Treaty means what it says, and anything more than that is just your opinion and invention against my opinion and invention. To discover partnership or a special relationship in the Treaty is not done by simple provable logic. The Ministry for the Environment has written that the concept of partnership "cannot be found in the words of the Treaty".[16] Sir Geoffrey Palmer has written that "some of the scholarship surrounding the Treaty is highly suspect, fuelled as it is by political motivation rather than detached analysis".[17] Paul McHugh has written that "no-one pretends that the language of partnership and fiduciary obligation was exchanged....at Waitangi in 1840".[18] Instead, he speaks of the courts of to-day "construct[ing] what amounts to a contemporary mythology of the Treaty". That is not something, though, that courts should be engaged in.

If we need any further evidence about the completely arbitrary and personal nature of Treaty principles, we need look no further than the multiplicity of views as to what the principles are. I have already mentioned some lists - the Court of Appeal's, the Maori Council's, the Crown's, the Royal Commission on Social Policy's. The Anglican Church thinks that Treaty principles require separate legislative institutions for different races.[19] (This is the same Anglican church which has already established three legislative chambers of its own on racial lines - Maori, Pakeha and Pacific Islander - and which, incredibly, also condemns racism as a heresy)

By this time we are approaching seriously weird territory. Let us look at no more crazy lists of principles. Just remember that everyone has his or her own list, and each list is a matter of personal opinion. The only list with any sort of legal standing at all is the Court of Appeal's - even that is constantly misunderstood and misrepresented - and, even at the best of times, that list is a very biddable horse which any ingenious rider can get to ride in any direction he pleases.

Judicial Activism

All recent decisions about the Treaty have to be understood as having been made in a certain climate of judicial attitudes and opinion. It may horrify us to think that judges let their opinions and attitudes influence their decisions, but so it is. To a certain extent it is always inevitable, but judges at least once fought against the tendency. Now, sadly, it is often openly declared and celebrated, and some judges deliberately choose to go beyond their proper role of only applying and, where necessary, interpreting the law.

We have long had a wise legal tradition which says that judges should not interfere in politics. Politics is one thing, and judicial decisions are another. Our judges, it has long been thought, should confine themselves to deciding particular disputes according to law, not engaging in political adventures. Judges will only soil and stain and discredit themselves if they descend into the dust of the arena. We have politicians to listen to the people, weigh up practicalities and public and private interests and, if need be, change the law. That is not the judges' job. Judges only hear the evidence about this or that particular dispute; they do not receive public petitions and listen to lobbyists and special interest groups, or commission investigations and reports and what have you. Nor do they have any better political knowledge or ability than you and I. Nor, for that matter, should litigants in any particular case have to provide anything more than the facts and law of their particular case; they should not have to provide enormous amounts of research and information free of charge to enable judges to base changes to the law on the best possible grounds. Yet without such research, judges are no better informed than anyone else as to how laws might be altered.

Such has always been our tradition, the tradition of the "separation of powers". In essence, this idea is generally taken to require that judges should be free from political interference when they carry out their functions. We would all agree that that is highly desirable. Yet this good thing, like all good things, comes at a price. Some of our judges, regrettably, have forgotten what that price is. A certain amount of self-flattery assists them. Their analysis, and that of many lawyers, seems to be simply - and simple-mindedly - that the separation of powers merely requires that judges (who are of course good) must be protected from interference from politicians - who are, of course, evil. But that is only half the story. Yes, the separation of powers does indeed require that politicians should stick to politics, and not interfere in judicial matters.

But the other side of the coin, the other part of the bargain, is that judges, likewise, should also stick to their core business - that they should confine themselves to their proper role in judging disputes according to law - as they promise to do by their oaths of office - and not engage in politics.

This is quite different from the situation in the United States of America, for example, where the Supreme Court has the power to strike down legislation as being "unconstitutional". Unlike New Zealand, the United States has a written constitution, which, among other things, defines the powers of the president and Congress. If an action of the president or an Act of Congress is held to breach those constitutional rules, then it can be declared null and void. Needless to say, arguments can easily arise over whether some modern law or action complies with a constitution originally written over two centuries ago in very different circumstances – even though there have been some amendments over the years.. Most recently, for example, there has been immense debate over whether the health insurance reforms, the Affordable Care Act, of President Obama and the Democrat Party are allowed by the constitution. Of course, the gentlemen who framed the American constitution in the eighteenth century never turned their minds to this question.

Today's constitutional arguments, then, have to be fitted into the concepts and language of two and a half centuries ago; and no fit can be exact. A better approach, surely, would be to say - as we in New Zealand can still say - that it serves little purpose to try to fit a twenty-first century statute into eighteenth century terms. Every generation, we have long held, should be the master of its own law. But that cannot be done in the United States; or at least, as I say, it can be done only to the extent to which the law of the present day can be presented in terms of a constitution written in the eighteenth century. Needless to say, there is much learned and abstruse debate about the proprieties of different approaches to interpreting the constitution - all of it, of course, ultimately in the service of particular political philosophies. But we could surely argue that all these arguments are artificial and undesirable. If the elected representatives of the people wish to make a law about health care, to take that recent example, they should be free to do so. That is how democracy works or, at least, how it should work. The drafters of the American constitution never turned their minds to the health care issue; what they might have thought about it is entirely a matter of speculation. It would be quite unsatisfactory that a perfectly reasonable present-day law could be struck down as "unconstitutional" by judges who are, in effect, behaving as politicians.

For this is an inevitable result of the United States system. Judges of the Supreme Court and other superior courts become, in fact, a species of politician. After they are nominated by the president, they must be approved by the Senate, and senators of all political persuasions examine their records and careers very carefully in order to detect desirable or undesirable political attitudes. We may tut-tut about judges undergoing a political examination. But these judges are not our judges ~ not yet, at any rate. Once appointed, judges of the American Supreme Court are not only there for life (as are ours) but they wield far greater power than ours do - yet. They could have struck down President Obama's health-care reforms, one of the major achievements of his first term as president; and they clearly base many of their decisions very much on their political attitudes. In those circumstances, a political examination of nominee judges is entirely reasonable.

There is no such parliamentary political examination of judicial nominees in New Zealand because until recently judges confined themselves to judicial business and studiously avoided making political decisions. They have traditionally kept their side of the bargain of the separation of powers. Regrettably, and incredibly, some judges are no longer inclined to abide by the terms of this bargain. Recall for a moment the penultimate paragraph above concerning the 1987 Lands case. Sir Robin Cooke, the President of the Court of Appeal, agreed that the State-Owned Enterprises Act was capable of being interpreted as the Crown contended, and he agreed that that interpretation was probably Parliament's intention. That being so, his duty as a judge was clear. It was to give effect to the intentions of Parliament, which is, under our constitution, our supreme lawmaker. Yet he did not. He chose, in fact, to ignore Parliament's words and intentions and impose his own political agenda on the government and our country.

This is, alas, not the only example of judges in Treaty cases trespassing on matters well beyond their proper constitutional role. The trespass has often been stealthy, but it is now being done with increasing impudence.[20] Sir Robin Cooke established the trend. Remarks that "Treaty obligations are ongoing" and "will evolve from generation to generation as conditions change", like his calls for a "broad, unquibbling and practical interpretation" of legislation, set the scene for

96

regular future political intervention by judges. Indeed, Cooke declared his admiration for North American courts (even though operating in an entirely different political, social, constitutional and legal setting) which have "so exercised their jurisdiction as to bring about or encourage changes with deliberate speed." It is no business of a court to "encourage change". That has, hitherto, never been any part of a judge's proper role. But many of Cooke's judgments had a distinctly political flavour to them. He spoke of the courts following a "middle path". But it is not for judges to follow any path other than the legal one. If the law leads them to one side of the middle, then that is where the judges should go. The middle path is for politicians, not judges.

There was some hope, at the end of Cooke's career, that judges were beginning to come to their senses and realise that their decisions would never settle the political and economic arguments being pursued under the guise of "the Treaty debate". But it was not to be. Our current Chief Justice, Dame Sian Elias, has been notable for her cavalier, if not downright contemptuous, treatment of established law. At the time of her appointment the then Leader of the Opposition described her as being "prepared to push the boundaries of case law", and she has indeed dealt most injudiciously with not a few well-established judicial decisions. It is not just Treaty decisions of the new Supreme Court, in which she now sits, that have been criticised to an "unprecedented" extent by senior lawyers;[21] the quality of decisions on a wide range of issues has been criticised here and overseas, and concerns have been expressed about the effects on our case law and our international reputation. Many commercial litigants are turning to mediation and arbitration because of disenchantment with the courts; disputes raising important issues are settled out of court because of the fears of all parties that the Supreme Court will engage in some fantastic and quite unorthodox adventure of its own. In fairness, Elias cannot be criticised for the quality of her fellow judges; but she must take her fair share of the blame for the way her court is run. She is, after all, the Chief Justice.

But on the subject of the Treaty, Maanu Paul, of the New Zealand Maori Council, described her at the time of her appointment as "our best weapon", and her attitudes to Treaty issues strongly indicate that he may not have been wrong. In an article in the *New Zealand Herald* on 22nd December, 2012, Fran O'Sullivan wrote, "Cabinet Ministers are understood to have asked Crown Law to look at whether grounds…exist for a challenge" to the Chief Justice's presence on the bench to hear the

Maori water rights claim. The column comments that "Elias's prior connections with the Maori Council were so deep that it is surprising that the issue has not come up in a considered way before. She successfully acted for the Council on several high-profile Treaty claims against the Crown", and "made her name" in the 1987 Lands case.

Two examples of Elias's attitude will suffice. One concerns the foreshore and seabed. Dr Hugh Barr describes this issue much more fully in his book *The Gathering Storm over the Foreshore and Seabed*. The point to make here is that the entire matter of the foreshore and seabed had been settled by a 1963 decision of the New Zealand Court of Appeal, the *Ninety Mile Beach* case.[22] That case held that, once the Maori Land Court had made a decision about who owned the dry land above the high tide mark, then the Maori Land Court's jurisdiction came to an end, and it simply did not have any authority to adjudicate over who might own the foreshore below the high tide mark. The question could no longer arise. The 1963 Court of Appeal asked the very reasonable question, "if...there may have been Maori owners of the foreshore different from the Maori owners of the land above high water mark...in what direction did these Maoris retire when the tide came in..?" The only possible owners of the foreshore had to be the owners of the land above; and since the Maori Land Court had just adjudicated on their claim, and drawn a boundary line, there was no more to be said.

In 2003, in the *Ngati Apa* case,[23] the New Zealand Court of Appeal, presided over by Elias C.J. (who was, it must be admitted in fairness, only one of the judges, the others being Gault, Tipping, Anderson and Keith) overturned that decision, and ignited the whole sorry train of controversy - leading even to the foundation of the Maori Party, among other things - which has bedevilled our country from that time to this, and shows no signs of fading away in the near future.

Now there is a general rule, long accepted by the Court of Appeal, that it should usually follow its own previous decisions[24]. It is an aspect of the wise general approach of the law that precedents are to be respected. Without a respect for precedent, without deciding similar cases in a similar way, we can hardly speak of a system of law at all. More specifically, the rule in relation to previous decisions of the New Zealand Court of Appeal was that a later Court of Appeal might depart from them if it saw fit, but its approach should always be "cautious". The textbooks list the circumstances when the Court might be more inclined to overrule its own past decisions. Here, drawn from the textbooks, is the list, with point by point commentary.

1. The present court will be readier to overrule an earlier decision if the present court is a full one of five judges (as opposed to the three who usually sit). This was so in *Ngati Apa*.

2. The present Court will be more likely to overrule if the earlier court was divided in its opinion. This was not so in *Ninety Mile Beach*. Indeed, those 1963 judges are generally regarded as being learned and sound - a "strong court".

3. The present court will be less likely to overrule an earlier decision often relied on as a precedent. The *Ninety Mile Beach* decision had been relied on for forty years, not just by other judges but by Parliament itself, as being an accurate statement of the law. Statutes had been made relying on it.

4. "The nature of the issue will be relevant." Presumably, this means that, where the issue is one of personal liberty or social importance, the present court will be readier to overrule the earlier case to achieve a just result. It might perhaps be argued, then, that the nature of this social issue requires greater generosity to Maori. It could well be replied, however, that certainty of title to land, and public ownership of and access to the seacoast are every bit as important. This point must also be read in the light of point 9 (below) that where an issue is a contentious political one - as this surely is - it is best left to Parliament.

5. Conflicting overseas decisions may encourage overruling. This issue was not raised in *Ngati Apa*.

6. "Changing social conditions may make old decisions inappropriate to modern conditions." But New Zealanders' commitment to public ownership of the seacoast is as strong as ever. A small minority of Treatyists is more vocal than in 1963, but that is all; and courts should hardly alter their decisions according to the whim of the mob.

7. A present-day court will be readier to overrule if the case concerns some matter which courts are particularly able to deal with - technical matters of evidence and procedure, for example. This was most certainly not the case here.

8. The relevant standard for reviewing earlier decisions is the community values prevalent at that time, not the values now. On the matter of the foreshore and seabed, it could well be argued that the

community's general sense has not changed since 1963; but most certainly, the 1963 court was not out of touch with the values of its time.

9. "It is relevant whether the direction of the law is appropriately decided by the courts or whether legislation was a more desirable method of change. Questions heavily influenced by public policy should be left to Parliament." It could surely not have escaped the notice of even the most cloistered judge that Maori and Treaty issues are highly contentious and politically charged. So are questions of the public ownership of the coastline. The obvious and proper course to be followed by any prudent court - any court not composed of would-be politicians or utter fools - would be to say that change to long-established law on such matters of high policy is best left to Parliament.

The learned authors of these surveys of our legal system conclude their summaries of the following of precedent by observing that "perhaps the most important point to note is that the Court of Appeal would not overrule an earlier decision simply because it preferred a different view of the law. The Court recognised the importance of certainty in the law and held that there must be a compelling reason for creating a degree of uncertainty by overruling a previous decision". By that approach, *Ninety Mile Beach* should very clearly have been affirmed.

Law students are marked down if they do not know this. They have more knowledge of, or at least more respect for the law, than highly paid judges sworn to serve it but who instead leap boots and all into a blatant political adventure, which has already promoted immeasurable acrimony and division, and which threatens to cause much more.[25]

But even more brazen has been Elias's attitude to our highest and most ancient constitutional principle, the supremacy of Parliament. On at least two occasions (in a public lecture and an article in the Public Law Review) she has implied that she and her fellow judges are entitled - right now - to strike down Acts of Parliament if they conflict with her interpretation of "Treaty principles" or international law.[26] She couches these claims in grandiose and windy terms, of course, but she maintains that Parliament "legislates under the law of the constitution",[27] which is determined by the courts - that "an untrammelled freedom of parliament does not exist",[28] and that Parliament's restraint from making laws which she disapproves of is not a matter of grace - of self-imposed voluntary restraint - but a "matter of obligation".[29]

Underneath this deliberately opaque language she is apparently claiming the right to frustrate the community's will, for no better reason, essentially, than that she does not like it. She has no ability to do more than frustrate; courts cannot research and develop policy, or make whole detailed statutory arrangements, and indeed in her arrogant person she exemplifies the reasons why judges should be kept well away from government.

She is not the only one to entertain these dreams of power without responsibility; former judge Sir Edward Thomas, now mercifully retired, has also publicly "postulated the possibility that Parliament's legislative supremacy is not absolute".[30]

This is a would-be power grab that is fundamentally anti-democratic in its nature. The phenomenon of judicial activism is not confined to New Zealand, and is indeed part of a wider anti-democratic movement. The West's caring liberal class has been dismayed to discover that not everyone in their own countries agrees with everything they propose. The common people, heavens above, have doubts about many parts of the liberal agenda! So now there are regular attempts to remove such matters from public scrutiny altogether, in particular by handing final adjudication on these matters to courts, which very often are staffed by politically-correct liberals very ready to declare "unconstitutional" any law they find unpalatable. That is a very good part of the reason why many members of the New Zealand caring classes want a written constitution – because, when we have one, the final decision on lots of matters - race, immigration, multiculturalism, social welfare, abortion, euthanasia, the death penalty and a hundred other things - will be decided not by the representatives of the nasty, dirty, stupid citizen voters, who cannot be trusted to do the right thing, but will be decided instead by their friends among the judges, who are very certain that they know what is best for everyone right now. Democracy? That is just so "old hat" and "nineteenth century". We have moved on! Written constitutions, activist judges, a greater role for international agreements, an entrenched Treaty and "partnership" - all would have the effect of removing power for ever from the people and their elected representatives and giving it to their enlightened friends who know best. That is the fundamental reason why a written constitution for New Zealand - at present, at least, knowing what would undoubtedly be put into it - is a disastrous suggestion.

How might any possible future supremacy of Treaty principles be worked out in practice? The opportunities are endless, for the "principles of the Treaty" by now simply mean Maori privilege. The Treaty, as its admirers now interpret it, means essentially that Maori have first dibs at everything and are entitled to be waited on hand and foot by everyone else for ever.[31] So just about any statute could be considered to be in breach of Treaty principles. Here is a genuine example. About fifteen years ago an old Maori man in Northland was refused kidney dialysis treatment by the local health care provider. He was not refused on racial grounds, but on purely clinical ones. There simply was not enough dialysis available for everyone who needed it, and so some people, the least able to profit from the treatment, just had to fall off the bottom of the list. This particular patient was not only quite old, but had several other medical conditions which meant that he would not benefit from dialysis as much as others would.

This news caused a stir - prompted chiefly, I suspect, merely from the realisation that our country could not afford every medical treatment for everyone, and that rationing was necessary, and some people (of whatever race) would just have to miss out. But the Maori Council objected to this man losing out, and maintained that to do so was against the principles of the Treaty. Why? Because old people were a "taonga", guaranteed under the Treaty. Therefore, Treaty principles required that old Maori people took priority in the distribution of health care. Not to treat him was "to sacrifice Treaty rights to financially driven policies", and a "clear sign of a lack of faith on the part of the Crown Treaty partner". But by the same token, young Maori people are also, surely, a taonga. Surely, by the same token, all Maori people are. And so, hey presto - Treaty principles require across-the-board pro-Maori racial discrimination in health care. The Maori Council has already said so. Now, if a judge were able to strike down legal arrangements that failed to respect that Treaty principle, where would we be?

That same argument could be used to strike down every legal and administrative arrangement in the country, and replace it, if judges were so minded (and some of them clearly are), with a principle of racial preference. There would be no reason in principle why even Parliament's allocation of public funds could not be struck down by judges as showing insufficient regard for Treaty principles. The poor old

102

taxpayers would still pay, but their representatives would not have the final say on how the money was spent. Since ancient times our cry has been "no taxation without representation". Treaty principles in a constitution would put an end to that.

The supremacy of Parliament is the most fundamental principle of our constitution. For centuries our ancestors fought proud and haughty kings, would-be despots, to establish this vital principle of freedom. Parliament manifests the democratic principle we cherish and esteem. For this freedom to rule ourselves many of our forefathers struggled, lived in hardship and died on bloody fields. We would all agree that Parliaments are not perfect - indeed, our present Parliament cuts a very sorry figure in comparison with what parliaments could be and have been - and we could all probably come up with suggestions for improvements in our system of government. The answer to unsatisfactory Parliaments, though, is to improve our democracy, not to undermine it. Although democracy may not be a satisfactory system of government, all the alternatives are worse.

Yet here we have New Zealand judges, sworn to do justice according to law, who ignore precedent and the established law and custom of centuries and imply that they have the right to sit in judgment on Acts of Parliament and, it necessarily follows, to declare them to be invalid if they breach the judges' very pro-Maori understanding of "Treaty principles" or international law, including, of course, the indigenous rights bits. A handful of arrogant, appointed officials - judges are, after all, just appointed officials, not infallible gods, who want to impose their own political views about the Treaty on the whole country (and, we may be sure, impose other views as well later on) - consider it a positive and wonderful advance for us all if they were to become the absolute masters of our laws and indeed of our lives. If judges ever were to make such a judgment, it would be every bit as much a coup d'etat as if armed men were to enter Parliament and drive the Members from it at gunpoint. It would be treason,[32] and it would be tyranny. Yet some of our judges are already openly implying it.

Heaven help us. The law will not, at this rate. If judges purport to strike down statutes and thereby, in effect, depose Parliament, how could we restore our ancient rights and liberties? It would be no use for Parliament to make a statute reasserting its powers, because the courts would just strike that down also. And, obviously, it would be no use appealing to the judges who committed that treason in the first place.

103

The only way would be by the same method we used against kings who sought to impose a tyranny in the past.

Historically the ultimate fate of tyrants has been that they have been deposed and even put to death. It is vital to the whole community that incipient tyranny should be nipped in the bud as soon as it becomes manifest - in the interests of all of us, including the would-be tyrants themselves.

But even if things never become quite that dire, let us reflect on this: Some of our highest judges now appear ready, quite unconstitutionally, to strike down statutes if they offend against the judges' own interpretation of Treaty "principles". That being so, how would they behave if any written constitution were to give the Treaty even the slightest mention? There can be little doubt but that any mention of the Treaty, even the tiniest, would be taken, on one legal pretext or another, as an excuse for justifying a judicial power to sit in judgment on all of the people's laws.

For that reason alone, it is absolutely vital that any future written constitution we might receive must not mention the Treaty.

But, given the times in which we live, and more particularly the stacking of the Constitutional Advisory Panel with Treatyists and their shaping of the whole "conversation", it is out of the question that we could have a new constitution which did *not* mention the Treaty.

The conclusion we are forced to, therefore, is that we must not have a new written constitution.

Hilaire Belloc's advice, as the motto of one of his Cautionary Tales, was to

> Always hold on tight to Nurse
> For fear of finding something worse.

The Waitangi Tribunal

The Waitangi Tribunal was established by the Treaty of Waitangi Act 1975. It was given the right to consider laws, policies and actions of the Crown which were "inconsistent with the principles of the Treaty". In doing this it had to make its own decisions as to what those principles were, for Parliament offered no guidance on the matter.

It is particularly important to realise that the Tribunal is not a court of law. Courts make binding declarations as to what the law is. With one small exception, however, all the Tribunal can do, if it discerns a breach of "Treaty principles", is to make "recommendations", which a government is free to act on or ignore as it pleases. Some people have attempted to argue that there actually is some obligation to act on Tribunal recommendations. This is nonsense, as a moment's thought about the meaning of the word "recommendation" would make clear. Some interested parties have recently taken to speaking of the Tribunal's "rulings". Its findings are not "rulings", any more than they are "decisions". There is nothing binding about them. They are recommendations. The brief generous suggestion by the Court of Appeal in the 1987 Lands case that Treaty principles may involve some sort of obligation to act on those recommendations has no basis in the statute. In fact, it directly contradicts the statute; and even Sir Robin Cooke was very careful to retract that suggestion in a later case,[33] and emphasise that Tribunal recommendations "are not binding on the Crown of their own force. They may have the effect of contributing to the working out of the content of customary or Treaty rights, but if and when such rights are recognised by law it is not because of the principles relating to the finality of litigation". In other words, claims to the Tribunal are not actions at law - they are not "litigation" - and the Tribunal's recommendations are only that, and are not binding.

Since the Tribunal can only make recommendations, it follows that it has never had the power to order anything, and certainly not to order that any private land be given to Maori. That is not to say, though, that its recommendations could not affect private land. The moment the Tribunal made some recommendation, or even observation, concerning private land, the owner of that land, and any potential buyers, are entitled to expect trouble ahead. Land occupations become possible. The land could very easily drop greatly in value. Who would be prepared to buy it, and thereby buy so much trouble for himself? So, following the very public occupation of Mr Allan Titford's privately-owned farm in Northland, a 1993 amendment to the Act[34] declared that (subject to the exception in the next paragraph) "the Tribunal shall not recommend....the return to Maori ownership of any private land or the acquisition by the Crown of any private land". This does not necessarily stop the Tribunal from making remarks, however and declaring that in its opinion the land was originally acquired unjustly, and such remarks might well lead to a drop in the land's value as any would-be owners might fear trouble ahead; but short of doing away with the Tribunal altogether it is difficult to see what more Parliament could have done.

105

There is only one situation where the Tribunal may make binding recommendations. That is in the case of land transferred to SOEs following the 1987 Lands decision. Parliament enacted, as part of the negotiated agreement following that decision, that in the case of lands transferred to SOEs at that time - but in no other case - the Tribunal could direct that appropriate parts of those lands (whether still owned by the SOE or on-sold to another) should be returned to claimants.

When the Tribunal was first established, it did not have any "retrospective jurisdiction". When established in 1975 it was only authorised to investigate alleged breaches of Treaty principles which had occurred since 1975. It could not investigate any actions earlier in our history. And so, of the eight major reports it had issued by 1989, only two were concerned with land; one was about the Maori language, one with sea fisheries, and four were concerned with broad environmental questions of present day pollution and contamination, where the Tribunal's reports did the whole public a service in challenging unhealthy practices.

But that was changed by Labour in 1985, when the Tribunal was given the power to investigate *any* alleged wrong since 1840. It was that change in the law that opened the floodgates to the abundance of historical claims which have so preoccupied the nation ever since. Many of those claims, of course, as explained elsewhere in this book,[35] were already the subject of earlier amicable "full and final" settlements.

What of the Tribunal's actual findings and reports? It simply cannot be expected to write scholarly and impartial history, and it does not. The Tribunal does not merely look at what happened in the past, describing and analysing it and setting it in the context of its own time and place. The Tribunal inevitably looks at the past in the light of the present; it regards the past as lawyers would, as a resource from which material can be quarried suitable for a desired conclusion. The Tribunal does not approach the past as an historian would, but rather in the pursuit of present day objectives. If the claimants before it are to succeed - and that is the general expectation - then the Tribunal must find fault in the past. That fault is judged by the standards of the present day - the "principles of the Treaty" - rather than by the standards of the time. The Tribunal then makes proposals for the future. This is no basis for impartial history.

"Waitangi Tribunal history," writes Associate Professor Richard Boast, is "Whig history with a vengeance, in that the actions of people

106

in the past are being judged not by their standards but by ours." Mr Boast observes that "in determining the 'principles' of the Treaty, the Tribunal's stance has been determinedly present-minded. There has been no attempt to search for, say, a nineteenth century understanding of what the 'principles' of the Treaty may have been, and to judge the actions of the Crown in the past by such an historically-relativist understanding. Rather, the Tribunal has preferred to construct a set of standards which it perceives as valid and relevant at the present day, and to judge the Crown's actions in the past by those standards...Historians involved in the...process are therefore engaged in a process which is in a fundamental respect profoundly unhistorical." [36]

Likewise, Dr Giselle Byrnes, the author of *The Waitangi Tribunal and New Zealand History*, suggests that Tribunal reports should be regarded "not just as quasi-judicial findings, or as the recommendations of a commission of inquiry, but as a new genre of history..." She argues that the Tribunal writes a "post-colonial" history, which is "by definition, more concerned with the present (and possibly even the future) than the past".

But a "history" that is more concerned with the present and future than the past is not history at all as that word is commonly understood. A body that produces reports more concerned with the present than the past could be better described as a special interest group than as one merely engaged in a "new genre" of history. Talk of being engaged in "post-colonial history" is nothing but a fancy way of saying that the Tribunal is not much more than an impressively-named Maori lobby group.

The Tribunal found in its Ngai Tahu report that Stewart Island and its outlying islands were acquired without any breach of Treaty principles, but nevertheless made a recommendation that certain of those islands desired by Ngai Tahu be "returned" to them. Would we consider a judge unbiased if he found that a plaintiff's claim was without foundation but nevertheless recommended that the defendant pay compensation anyway? The Tribunal hearing the Ngai Tahu claim reprimanded a Crown witness who had given evidence of pre-European Maori environmental destruction, because his evidence was hurtful to the claimants. What faith can we have in a tribunal which expects to hear only evidence supporting one side of the case?

Likewise, the Tribunal produced the first "interim" volume of its Taranaki report without actually hearing the evidence of the Crown "on many matters". It was in that volume that it described Taranaki history as an "ongoing holocaust", evidently to be compared to Europe under the Nazis. Any holocaust, however, preceded the arrival of British settlers, as invading tribes from the Waikato slaughtered and scattered the locals, leaving the land empty as the settlers found it.

The Tribunal has decided that, because Maori used the stars for navigation and "incorporated them in their own philosophical world view", therefore the electromagnetic spectrum (of which the light of the stars forms a part) is a "*taonga*" guaranteed by the Treaty, and there is a Treaty principle giving a "right to the development of that *taonga* through technology that has subsequently become available".[37] In other words, navigating a canoe by the stars entitles Maori to radio waves. One commentator wrote that this decision may "come to be seen as a watershed in Waitangi jurisprudence and the credibility of the Tribunal...the logic...is elusive. Some [may] see the Tribunal's report as confirmation of the intellectual and political bankruptcy of the Waitangi process. But we should always appreciate those who contribute significantly to the sum of the local human comedy." [38]

Just as this book was going to press, news arrived of a Nga Puhi sub-tribe which is making a Waitangi Tribunal claim for Maori to earn a dividend for the use of wind for commercial electricity generation. This is so preposterous a claim that one cannot help but wonder if it is a joke; but it appears to be entirely serious. That is not to say that the Waitangi Tribunal will endorse it, but I would not stake a very large sum of money that they will not. If the wind, the very air, can be found to be the valid subject of a Tribunal claim, then there is no reason why that claim should be limited to commercial users of air such as wind farms. There is no reason on principle why we should not all have to pay for our share in this precious Maori-owned resource. And so, for the breath of life and therefore our very lives, we will owe a debt to the *tangata whenua*. Although in one way that might seem a far-fetched conclusion, in another way it would only be the logical end of the direction we have been taking for a generation.

But given that this generation's round, anyway, of historic claims has been more or less dealt with (the Tribunal, of course, then getting on to other things), Parliament in 2006 made another amendment to the Treaty of Waitangi Act. Section 6AA of the Act now declares that, after 1st September 2008, "no Maori may submit a claim to the Tribunal that is, or includes, a historical Treaty claim". That would be a small mercy;

108

but the Tribunal seems hardly to be aware of the section's existence. In 2012, at the time of a planned sale by the government of shares in state-owned electricity companies, the Maori Council lodged a claim with the Tribunal that Maori had a Treaty claim to water - some sort of proprietary interest in water that should be recognised by law. Now in 1967 the Water and Soil Conservation Act declared that "the sole right to dam any river or stream, or to divert or take natural water, or discharge natural water or waste into any natural water, is hereby vested in the Crown". Anyone who wished to use natural water had to obtain what was then called a "water right", and which now, under the Resource Management Act 1991, which continues the same arrangements, is called a water permit. Current rights to use water to generate electricity were granted under those two statutes. Even if some Maori proprietary right in water could be identified, therefore, and even if it had survived the arrival of the English common law of water in New Zealand - highly dubious propositions - any such rights were finally extinguished in 1967, if not before. 1967 is forty-one years before 1st September, 2008, the date on which no Tribunal claim may have an historical element. Yet the Tribunal has just entertained a water claim which is complaining about a state of affairs over forty years old.

This unsurprising finding of the Tribunal led the Maori Council to apply to the High Court for a declaration that the government's proposed sale of shares in the state-owned electricity companies would be in breach of section 9 of the State-Owned Enterprises Act, which, you will recall, declared that "nothing in this Act shall permit the Crown to act in a manner inconsistent with the principles of the Treaty". The Crown, be it noted, was not proposing to sell the water itself, but merely shares in electricity generation companies which currently held valid water permits. The water permits themselves will not be affected by the sale; the holders of the permits – the companies - will also remain the same. It is just that some of the shares in those holder companies would in future be privately owned. The Maori Council's challenge excited mixed emotions for, although Maori claims to water were resented by most New Zealanders, further sales of public assets, our "family silver", were almost equally disliked – especially in the depths of a recession when prices would be at their lowest - and for that reason the Maori Council's challenge was less disliked than might have otherwise been expected. Be that as it may, Justice Ronald Young, in December, 2012, upheld the Crown's proposed actions. He did not have to come to any conclusions about water ownership to do so; the basis of his judgment was simply that Parliament itself had removed these companies from the State-Owned Enterprises Act by a recent amendment, and that the Maori Council was essentially asking the court to review a decision of Parliament - which, under our constitution, is still, quite rightly, impossible.

Incredibly, some people still seem to take the Tribunal seriously. Let us ask ourselves - suppose that some persons calling themselves Maori felt aggrieved about something, or saw an opportunity for enrichment somewhere by playing the Treaty card - what would they do? The issue might be radio waves, or a television channel; it might be native plants and animals; it might be traditional art; it might be fisheries, or fresh water, or even the wind. What would these people do? They would go to the Waitangi Tribunal, saying that this particular thing is guaranteed to us under the Treaty. It is a *taonga*! The word *taonga* is now wide enough to cover absolutely everything. Everything is a *taonga*, and so this is. And what will the Tribunal do? It cannot seriously be supposed that the Tribunal would reject such a claim. That is not why it was set up, and there would be the devil to pay if ever it said "no" to a claimant. And as Dr Byrnes points out, it is making its recommendations for the present and the future. So the Tribunal, in each and every case, will say "yes". Yes, Maori, primitive people that they were, they had their own language, and the starlight, and art, they ate fish, and plants and animals, they used water...and so of course, in every case, the Tribunal will act simply as a semi-official lobby group saying "Maori should have this too - preferably all of it, or at least a big share". And this for no better reason than that once, when living here by themselves two hundred years ago, they knew and used the rivers, say, and breathed air, to take the most topical examples. It matters not that there have been various full and final settlements, including very recent ones, where no-one thought of raising the issue of water and air. They've just thought of something else, and so they want that too. And so they go to the Tribunal asking for this new thing - let us call it x - and what will the Tribunal say? We can predict that with our eyes closed. Yes, the Tribunal will say, Maori did live in a close relationship with x - a spiritual relationship with x - x has its own life-force, and is part of the whole Maori world view - the relationship with x may not be "ownership", as Europeans understand it, but in any case, there was a relationship, and Maori deserve a share of x, at least....

110

We have certainly reached the stage by now where the participation of the Tribunal in an argument contributes nothing to the debate.

He Iwi Tahi tatou

The debates over the Treaty which now convulse our national life are not primarily legal debates. The Treaty is not part of our law, and never has been. Even if it were, though, its terms would not do Treatyists any good, because all it actually says is that Maori are the Queen's subjects like everyone else. Captain Hobson expressed its true meaning perfectly in 1840 - *He iwi tahi tatou* - "Now we are one people".

"The extraordinary fact of the past forty years of our history," Chris Trotter has written, "is the manner in which this bold rejection of Captain Hobson's famous declaration...has become the official policy of the New Zealand state. Not, I hasten to add, the policy of the New Zealand people, who have never been given the opportunity to formally endorse, or reject, the separatist 'two nations in one state' orthodoxy which now prevails in our universities and throughout the public service." [39]

Nevertheless mention of "Treaty principles" in statutes has enabled lawyers to become involved and to transform much of the debate into legal forms and forums. This of itself is bizarre. The Treaty issue has been allowed to become an immense and growing political problem, with many social and economic ramifications. It has the potential to, quite literally, destroy our country. In what other area of our national life, faced with such a problem, would we think that the solution was to get the lawyers in? Lawyers' skills are in quarrels and contention. A good argument has been made that the English Civil War might not have happened had it not been for lawyers on both sides insisting that their parties stand on their rights. But we need reconciliation. We cannot find that in arguments in the courts, nor in further announcements by the Waitangi Tribunal of Maori entitlements.

Despite several decades of unparalleled openmindedness, patience and generosity on New Zealanders' part, race relations have seriously deteriorated. We have now reached the stage in our national life when the division of our country into "us" and "them" is taken for granted. We have not just one but two political parties represented in Parliament openly dedicated to promoting the interests of the Maori "race". As

111

usual, these Maori race-based parties, like many other exclusively Maori-oriented programmes and practices, seem somehow to have escaped the racist label, although if any equivalent White Party were ever established it would instantly be condemned by every concerned right-thinking liberal person as racist, neo-Nazi, etc. As perhaps it might be. Or it might not. But what is sauce for the goose is surely sauce for the gander.

But the division into them and us was not always thus. And our race relations have become increasingly bitter and polarised at precisely the same time as we have been following the policies of the last several decades deplored in these pages. Surely the evidence of these decades is that those policies have been completely unsuccessful in promoting our racial brotherhood, national unity, prosperity and happiness. Yet, illogically, the failure of these policies will be used as an argument that they should be applied with redoubled vigour, since it will be claimed that they have failed hitherto only because they were applied with insufficient determination. As they say, there is nothing that succeeds like failure. Those policies have been promoted by well-meaning and kind-hearted men and women, although ones not without the usual mixture of less worthy motivations - gullibility, stupidity, ignorance of the past, cowardice and strange inferiority complexes among them. But the kind hearts of the promoters do not guarantee the policies' success; all it proves, once again, is that the road to hell is paved with good intentions.

The Treaty mythology is now firmly entrenched not just among many Maori but also in universities, teachers' colleges, theological colleges and the public service. It is characterised by an increasing conviction that alleged past wrongs and "Treaty principles" must entitle Maori to wealth and privilege, and that any failure of those to appear must be the fault of white oppressors. But it must also be obvious by this time, surely, that Maori demands will never end. When the latest round of "full and final" settlements was in full swing we were assured by such luminaries as the recently-convicted Sir Douglas Graham, sometime Minister of Treaty Settlements, who enjoyed nothing more than displaying his own nobility and superiority of character to his benighted countrymen, that after those settlements were achieved we could all put the past finally behind us and move forward together as one nation. That has not happened. It is obvious that it never will. Indeed, Maori are already explaining that there will be a fresh round of

112

historical claims in the next generation, because binding future generations by a full and final settlement is "not the Maori way". But in the meantime, we have seen the foreshore and seabed issue, the United Nations Declaration on the Rights of Indigenous Peoples, and now claims to fresh water and a very determined move to have the Treaty put into a written constitution. If that last thing were ever to happen, then New Zealand is irrevocably doomed to poverty and the eternal strife of a racially divided society.

But in any event our chances of happiness are fast receding. No-one among our leaders, not even any hard-headed lawyer, seems to be asking what are surely the most basic and obvious questions - where are our present policies leading? Is the separatism and division of the last generation, justified by radical misinterpretations of the Treaty, a good thing? We would laugh aloud at the suggestion that giving greater influence and public assets to farmers or manufacturers, say, or the elderly, the poor, the Business Roundtable or the trade union movement, would be certain to have only beneficial affects on the nation as a whole. We would say, quite rightly, that such groups will just be furthering their own interests at the expense of the rest of us. Why do we assume that Maori are any different? Continuing demands for Maori entitlement are nothing but the demands of con-men. The Treaty industry is now a gigantic racket, which will continue for as long as gullible New Zealanders accept everything that every plausible rogue tells them. How have we forgotten so easily the lesson of human history and human nature as depicted by Kipling -

And that is called paying the Dane-geld;
But we've proved it again and again,
That if once you have paid him the Dane-geld
You never get rid of the Dane.

At the least, the Treaty industry will continue until the public cupboard is absolutely bare, which, at the rate our country and the whole world are going, will not be that far off. And what happens then, when we have nothing left with which to continue to appease this increasingly aggressive and demanding faction, which will of a certainty consider that our generosity hitherto has been quite inadequate to set them up in their desired lifestyle? What happens when they still demand more, and there is no more to give? Even if we were to grant them some "sovereign" rights of some sort or another, it would not satisfy them. When have we ever heard one word of thanks, however grudging, for the generosity of the past generation? When do we hear Maori leaders express any hint of a desire for reconciliation? If they do ever whisper such a thought, it will only be grudgingly, and on the condition that it is possible only after the rest of us - another group of people entirely, note - have made full and adequate restitution. Yet nothing we do will ever be enough.

The last generation has been one of continuing and accelerating demands. We are already some considerable distance down an increasingly slippery slope. We are not quite, but almost, at the point of no return. We are so bewitched by the Treaty and its misinterpretations that it seems never to have occurred to us that anything but good could result. We have for so long been a peaceful and prosperous nation that we seem to imagine that that is the inevitable and unalterable way of things - that no matter what we do, no bad things can ever happen to us. But little, good, innocent New Zealand is not exempt from the laws of history. We have long prided ourselves on being the "social laboratory of the world". We seem to have forgotten that laboratory experiments do not always succeed.

Douglas Graham, National's former Treaty Minister. "Doug Graham won't go down in history as the man who did so much to settle the long-standing Maori grievances. Instead he'll be remembered as the white man who sold out his fellow New Zealanders, Maori and non-Maori, to a bunch of brown gangsters and their pale brown thugs". (Allan Duff in the Rotorua Review, 17th June, 1997)

Joe Williams presides over the biased and racist Waitangi Tribunal that, looking backwards to magnify grievances rather than forward to the future, has no place in a modern democracy. He seems to deny the nation's sovereignty by saying, "Aotearoa and New Zealand must be able to co-exist in the same space". Is a man with such an apparently warped view of our constitution fit to be a High Court judge?

Stephen Gerard O'Regan (sculptured) This Irish New Zealander changed his name to Tipene - apparently to reinforce his slight Maori credentials (he is believed to be one-sixteenth Maori). Thus "validated", he became Ngai Tahu's highly paid "Treaty negotiator". O'Regan is reputed to be a multi-millionaire and that is what Treaty settlements are all about – enriching the pale-faced fat cats of corporate iwi while doing very little for ordinary Maoris.

Leonie Pihama. This tattooed advocate of "indigenous rights" (special rights for part-Maoris) is a member of the Constitutional Advisory Panel. It is hard to see how someone so steeped in racial rights for one group can possibly bring an open mind to something as important as imposing a written constitution for all New Zealanders. The Panel has been stacked with "Treatyists" and is not representative of New Zealanders in any way. For that reason any recommendations it makes should be regarded with the greatest suspicion.

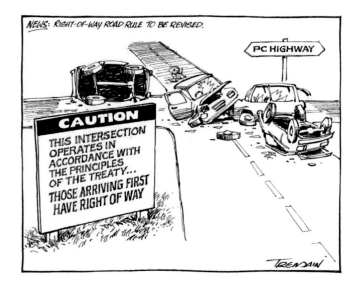

When **Sian Elias, Mrs. Hugh Fletcher,** was appointed Chief Justice Maanu Paul of the Maori Council described her as "our best weapon" and her subsequent behaviour suggests he was not wrong. But judges should not be "weapons" for a particular cause – especially a racist one - and the sad truth is that, on Elias' watch, the reputation of the judiciary has sunk to an all time low as she and certain other senior judges have used their position to push their own political agenda, playing their "Treaty tricks" on the rest of us.

PARIHAKA – THE FACTS

For a minority to swindle a majority to the extent that the Treatyists have cheated the rest of us a huge dose of lies, misinformation and indoctrination is necessary to achieve such a fantastic outcome. And, as Hitler and Goebbels so amply proved in the 1930s, the greater the lie, the more likely it is to be believed.

Probably the biggest whopper that the Treatyists have used to justify their false position is the Waitangi Tribunal's 1996 interim Taranaki report, which stated, "The invasion and sacking of Parihaka must rank with the most heinous actions of any government in the last century" (the 1800s) [including Tsarist Russia's pogroms and Prussia's brutal and unprovoked wars against Denmark, Austria and France, not forgetting the slavery that lasted for so long in the United States and Brazil]. The Tribunal called it "the holocaust of Taranaki history."

This ignorant and gross distortion of the truth has been repeated by several Treatyists, including Tariana Turia M.P., and a language teacher in New Plymouth, who was described as a "Maori academic" (as they all are), Keri Opai, who backed his ridiculous claim of "holocaust" by citing "the pillaging of Parihaka".

The name of this place is starting to enter the lexicon of the grievance industry in a big way with the Human Rights Commission making the silly statement, "The events that took place in and around Parihaka.....have affected the political, cultural and spiritual dynamics of the entire country." There have even been calls to have a special national day celebrated as "Parihaka Day" as well as a recent propaganda film called "Tatarakihi". So, it is time to look at the facts.

Fact No. 1 By the time of the Treaty of Waitangi there were only about a hundred and fifty Maoris left in the whole of the Taranaki. Roughly a third of the population had been massacred by invading tribes from the Waikato, around another third had been taken back to the Waikato as slaves, while the remaining third had fled to the Wellington area.

Nine hundred members of this last third then invaded the Chatham Islands in 1835 where they killed, ate and all but exterminated the peaceful Moriori who lived there. A hundred or more Moriori women were laid out on the beach and stakes were driven through their bodies, the men being treated similarly. They were then eaten by Taranaki

Maori.[1] The Moriori population of about 1,600 was reduced to 101 survivors.

These were the Taranaki "holocausts" – Waikato Maori slaughtering Taranaki Maori, and Taranaki tribes butchering the peaceful Moriori.

Fact No. 2 In 1840 the authorities began purchasing land in Taranaki from very willing sellers.

Fact No. 3 With the arrival of settlers at New Plymouth in 1841, coupled with the general peace and ending of slavery that flowed from the Treaty of Waitangi, many of those who had fled Taranaki during the intertribal wars took the opportunity of returning so as to reclaim the lands which, under Maori custom, they had forfeited when conquered by the stronger Waikato tribes.

Fact No. 4 These returning tribesmen quarreled among themselves over who owned the land and who had the right to sell it. This created great confusion with the result that, in some cases, the British paid for the same piece of land four times to satisfy conflicting Maori claims and sharp practices.

Fact No. 5 Wiremu Kingi and some of his fellow Taranaki tribesmen violated the Treaty of Waitangi when they made armed rebellion against the Crown. In the ensuing mayhem numerous settler families were murdered and their houses and barns burned to the ground. In one twelve month period (1860-61) 177 settler farms were destroyed. The mass slaughter and burning of the settlers' livestock was indeed a "holocaust" of farm animals.[2]

Fact No. 6 When hostilities ended some Maoris had their lands confiscated by the Crown for having rebelled against the State as they had been warned would be the case and in accordance with their own practice in the Chatham Islands and elsewhere. Confiscations did not cause the rebellion; they were punishments for it. According to the great Maori scholar, Sir Apirana Ngata, these confiscations were not a breach of the Treaty of Waitangi and they were understood as being fair enough under the old Maori law of *utu* (revenge). Under pre-1840 Maori custom there would have been a far worse fate for the losing Maori side than mere confiscation of some land.

Fact No. 7 In 1864 the self-appointed "prophet" Te Whiti – more accurately a "cult leader" - adopted what he said was a policy of "pacifism", taking as his symbol the white feather. The white feather was, in fact, a symbol of the genuinely pacifist Moriori of the Chatham

Islands before they were all but exterminated by Te Whiti's fellow Taranaki tribesmen. In 1867 Te Whiti squatted on some Crown land at Parihaka that had been confiscated as punishment for the rebellion. On this land he proceeded to build a settlement which housed his followers as well as being a haven for Maori fugitives from the law – people like Hiroki, who on 19th September, 1878, murdered John McLean, a cook to the survey party at Moumahaki. In defiance of the law Te Whiti refused all requests to hand him over to the authorities.

In September, 1881, Titokawaru, the apostle of ritual cannibalism, and about two hundred of his fellow Hauhaus left their settlement at Ngawhitiwhiti with their chattels and moved in to Parihaka.[3] Such was the company that Te Whiti was keeping.

Fact No. 8 During the next fourteen years the authorities repeatedly warned him that he would pay dearly if he did not give up his illegal occupation. The Premier, Sir John Hall, made several efforts to talk with Te Whiti but, like so many "prophets", he proved not only evasive but downright obstructive, sending out parties of natives to plough up the lands of European settlers at several places between Hawera and White Cliffs.

These Parihaka people also harassed storekeepers. "Yesterday a party of twelve Maoris, when returning from Parihaka, entered Loveridge's store at Oakura, commenced pulling the things about, and were very bounceable. The Constabulary had to be called in to eject them," wrote the *Auckland Star* on 24th June, 1879.

They also stole horses from settlers' farms,[4] pulled down a newly built stockyard at Ngakumikumi[5] and extracted a one pound toll from passing travellers. "Such incidences indicate the belligerent nature behind the façade of passive resistance that the settlers had to long endure," wrote Dr. Kerry Bolton in his recent work *The Parihaka Cult*. Far from being a genuine pacifist, Te Whiti's ploy was to provoke conflict with the government.

Fact No. 9 In this "republic of peace" more than a thousand Maoris were huddled together in most unhygienic conditions. "In Parihaka there are nearly two hundred cases (of measles) and there have been about twelve deaths," wrote the *Auckland Star* on 22nd September, 1875.

By early 1881 Parihaka was in a bad way with a scarcity of food that compelled the digging up of half-ripened potatoes and people were deserting the place. On 12th September, 1881, the *Taranaki Herald*

117

reported that Parihaka was infected by vermin and "was absolutely filthy through lack of sanitary precautions".

Fact No. 10 After all diplomatic efforts to resolve the stand-off had failed the government decided that, to dissuade others from taking the law into their own hands, the time had come to end the illegal occupation of this attention seeker who was so publicly thumbing his nose at the government. On 5th November, 1881, fourteen years after the occupation began, 959 members of the Volunteers and 630 of the Armed Constabulary rode in to reclaim Parihaka – which they did without firing a single shot. The death toll was zero and the only injury was to a boy's foot which was accidentally trodden on by a trooper's horse. Some Treatyists have claimed that the soldiers "violated" the women but there is not a shred of evidence for this allegation.

During the ensuing occupation there might have been some consensual sex between members of the government forces and the Maori women – as had been going on since the earliest contact with Europeans – but dates, places and names have always been absent from these vague "rape" allegations. In the words of Doctor Bolton, "The Constabulary and Volunteers were under close scrutiny, with the presence of several reporters" while James Cowan, the leading authority on the native wars, wrote that the Armed Constabulary was "officered by a splendid set of frontier soldiers".[6]

Among the things discovered in this "republic of peace" was a stockpile of around 250 weapons,[7] including breechloaders, Enfields, revolvers and a variety of ammunition. It has been said that the only reason they were not used was the overwhelming numbers (about 1,600 men) in the government's force.

Conclusions:

There was indeed a "holocaust" in Taranaki during the intertribal fighting in the years before 1840 when the local Maoris were either killed or enslaved by Waikato tribes or fled to Wellington.

Taranaki tribesmen then invaded the Chatham Islands and all but wiped out the peaceful Moriori in what could conceivably be called a "holocaust.

There was also a "holocaust" of settlers' farm animals, instigated by Wiremu Kingi.

There was no holocaust at Parihaka and nobody was injured except the poor boy whose foot was accidentally stepped on by a horse.

118

TWISTED MORALITY – THE MATAWHERO MASSACRE

So much for Parihaka, which the Treatyists are trying to elevate into the greatest "injustice" in our history. We shall now go east to Matawhero, a small settlement of hard working pioneer families a few miles inland from the present city of Gisborne.

It was shortly before midnight on Monday, 9th November, 1868, when Te Kooti and about a hundred of his fellow Hauhau savages, all mounted, crossed a ford on the Waipaoa River at Patutahi and rode into Matawhero to slaughter seventy of its sleeping inhabitants – 33 Europeans and 37 friendly Maoris.[1]

Among those murdered by rifle, bayonet, tomahawk and *patu* (a sharp-edged stone club) were Major Biggs, his wife and child and their servant, Mrs. Farrell; Lieutenant Wilson, his wife and four children and their servant, John Morren, who was cut into three pieces; two sheepfarmers, Messrs. Dodd and Peppard; James Walsh, his wife and their three week old baby; Mr. Cadell, the Matawhero storekeeper; Mr. and Mrs. McCulloch and their baby who died at its mother's bloody breast as well as Mary McDonald, the seven year old niece of Mrs. McCulloch; Mr. and Mrs. Newnham and their infant child; Mr. J. Mann, his wife and their one year old child; Maria Goldsmith (a half-caste) and her brother; and Messrs. Padbury, Rathbone and William Brown

Among the friendly natives who were killed on that terrible night were Paora Matuakore and "a staunch and loyal friend of the settlers", Piripi, as well as his wife and three sons.

In the words of James Cowan, "The place (Matawhero) was ablaze with burning homes, and the blood-maddened Hauhaus were galloping over the country, shooting indiscriminately, looting and destroying......The various raiding parties united at Patutahi, after sweeping out all life from Matawhero, Makaraka, Repongaere, Makauri and other settlements".[2]

In the words of Lieutenant Gascoyne, who saw the horrors a few hours after they occurred and while the fires were still burning and the stench of dead flesh filled the air, "Men and women were eagerly enquiring of every newcomer for information of their missing friends, mothers were weeping alone for their children, wives for their husbands, and husbands for their wives." [3]

Pretty gruesome, this worst ever massacre in our post-1840 history. But the Treatyists do their best to ensure that it is kept hidden, yapping on instead about the so-called "outrage" at Parihaka where, as we have seen, the sole injury was to one boy's foot and that accidentally.

And what about Mr. Finlayson, that self-appointed crusader whose mission in life seems to be to raid the public purse for the purpose of righting every conceivable wrong in our history? In Finlayson's eyes this brutal massacre of seventy settlers and friendly Maoris does not seem to have touched any instincts of humanity as, by the Rongowhakaata Claims Settlement Act that he steered through a compliant Parliamernt, he rewarded the descendants/tribe of Te Kooti, the architect of this atrocity, with a Crown "apology" for the "stigmatization of Te Kooti" as well as vesting the Matawhero Reserve in the tribe's name and giving them $250,000 of taxpayers' money. We are not making this up!

However, when it is coupled with Finlayson chucking in an extra $10 million of public funds to Ngati Toa for the "loss" of Te Rauparaha's right to lead his war canoes across Cook Strait to murder and eat the inhabitants of Marlborough, it starts to fit a rather warped pattern.

Finlayson's "morals" – or lack of them – are his own affair but to use taxpayers' money a century and a half later to enrich the descendants of these cannibals and murderers is more than most principled New Zealanders can stomach and it is not surprising that questions are being asked whether Finlayson understands right from wrong.

The Crown apology for the "stigmatisation" of Te Kooti is laughable, if not perverted. Peter Sharples, co-leader of the Maori Party, said in Parliament, "This redress is a significant step towards rehabilitating the reputation of Te Kooti". How can the reputation of such a callous brute be rehabilitated? He has no reputation to rehabilitate. Te Kooti was an evil, bloodthirsty savage who slaughtered and chopped up numerous innocent people, including babies. He is the second worst murderer in our history – after Te Rauparaha.

And Matawhero wasn't his only massacre in the district. Five months later, on 10th April, 1869, he attacked another Poverty Bay settlement, Mohaka, killing seven Europeans – Mr. and Mrs. Lavin and their three young sons aged from three to eleven, as well as a sheepfarmer, John Cooper, and an elderly man, Richard Wilkinson, who was lame. According to Ben Biddle, a veteran scout in the Armed Constabulary who found the bodies, the two oldest of the Lavin boys

120

had only bayonet marks on them – from being thrown up in the air to land on the sharp points of the bayonets – a trick of the equally cruel and sadistic Japanese soldiers in the Second World War. "Mr. Lavin's children were playing by a pond in Mr. Cooper's garden at the time of the massacre, and the youngest was found with a toy boat in his hand. The two eldest had received several bayonet wounds," wrote the *Nelson Colonist* in its issue of 11th May, 1869.[4]

About forty Maoris were also massacred in the same raid.[5] "Those in the small out-settlements who were surprised by the invading force were mercilessly killed. Many were shut up in a wool-shed and, as they were brought out one by one, they were tomahawked and bayoneted," wrote James Cowan.[6]

For Finlayson – and the craven, unprincipled National Party that he manipulates – to use our money and a Crown "apology" to reward Te Kooti's descendants/tribe for the old savage having "a bad name" is an affront to both decency and historical reality. It suggests that this particular minister is either historically ignorant of such things as the Matawhero massacre – possible in view of the Treatyists' efforts to keep it quiet – or else he is seriously lacking in morality. He seems to regard the bloody slaughter of Te Kooti and the cannibalism of Te Rauparaha as mere details of history that can be ignored if they get in the way of the supreme need of appeasing the corporate iwi interests that are driving the extreme and unjustified treaty settlements.

Of course, Finlayson's defenders – and he does have one or two of them, notably the *New Zealand Herald* – would argue that it is Parliament that passed this reward to the Te Kooti mob for the "stigmatisation" of his name and that Finlayson is only one vote in that "Chamber of Chamberlains". This, however, ignores the reality that in Treaty matters Mr. Finlayson seems to reign supreme. John Key is putty in the hands of Finlayson and the National Party caucus is putty in the hands of John Key. And so, what Mr. Finlayson decides to give to Maori out of the public purse is exactly what they get. And the most repulsive thing of all is that Finlayson, as mentioned elsewhere, has been heavily defeated on all three occasions on which he has stood for Parliament in an electorate. The voters of Wellington have consistently rejected him and yet he seems to have the powers of a virtual dictator - powers that, as we shall see in the later chapters, he is using (or "abusing") to steal vast resources from the public so as to enrich his iwi friends and to undermine the sovereignty of the nation.

And as for Sharples – by him taking up the cudgels for Te Kooti he has stuck the knife into the respected memory of those thirty-seven Maoris whom Te Kooti butchered on that terrible night as well as all those who were so brutally executed at Mohaka. But, of course, the Maori Party is not about standing up for the ordinary Maori – people like the murdered Paora Matuakore and Piripi – but about enriching the tribal elite which seems to be the Maori Party's sole reason for existence.

TWISTED HISTORY, TREATY SETTLEMENTS CRITICISED

Mike Butler

The year is 1834. Whaler Jacky Guard took his young wife Elizabeth and their children from New Zealand to Sydney. In April, while returning, their barque *Harriet* hit a southerly gale, and was driven ashore near Cape Egmont, Taranaki. All managed to reach the shore and in true shipwreck story style rigged up tents made of the ship's sails. On Wednesday, May 7, about 200 Taranaki Maori armed with muskets, spears, clubs and tomahawks surround them. "They told us with the greatest indifference that they intended to kill us all," Jacky Guard wrote in his diary. The next day Guard offered gifts to ward off attack. On May 9, "they ... appeared in greater numbers ... and ... said they would eat our hearts". The attack came on May 10.

"At eight, a m.... the natives rushed upon us and killed two of our men. ...During the skirmish, Mrs Guard was twice knocked down by the savages, with a child at her breast, and but for her comb would have been instantly killed; she was, however, taken prisoner ... with her two babies. We were now reduced from 28 to 14; ...those who were wounded...were soon despatched by the savages, and cut up into small portions convenient for cooking, ...for they consider it a luxury to feast on their enemies." [1]

Jacky Guard and several others were released on the understanding that they would return with a cask of gunpowder as ransom. Escaping to Cloudy Bay, Guard reports that twelve of his crew were killed and eaten and he names some of them, including his wife's brother whose flesh was offered to her. They made it to Sydney. He returned in August with two ships, *HMS Alligator* and the New South Wales government vessel, *Isabella*, and 65 armed men and rescued his wife, children, and eight surviving sailors.[2]

Fast-forward to 2012. The Nelson Provincial Museum hosts an exhibition titled "The Taranaki War 1860-2012 Our Legacy - Our Challenge". On display near the entrance is a video showing an unnamed couple standing in front of what appears to be a Maori meetinghouse. The woman speaks about the *Harriet* shipwreck of 1834 and starts by saying quite flatly that there was no cannibalism of the ship's crew. Why would a museum exhibition include a barefaced lie? When challenged, historian Kelvin Day, who created the exhibit, said

123

"the content attempts to recognise that there is no such thing as one true history and we believe it offers the best overall representation of the events of this period".[3] NZ History Online records cannibalism at the *Harriet* shipwreck, reporting that "Betty Guard also described how she 'saw the Natives cut up and eat those they killed belonging to the *Harriet*'".[4]

The *Harriet* shipwreck is just one of countless unfortunate events that occurred in the past and there is little that can be done about them now. But we do have a problem in that our brief history is being scrutinised, sifted, and weighed, to create accounts that have been twisted to justify multi-million dollar payouts to tribal trusts for grievances. Therefore, deleting aspects of the past that show Maori in a bad light, such as the cannibalism after the *Harriet* shipwreck, creates a false picture of Maori as innocent victims at the hands of the "wicked coloniser". This creates a black and white version of history that is simply wrong.

Sadly, the Waitangi Tribunal, which is sifting through our history, is not impartial. Tribunal reports look at the various actions of the Crown, in the light of its treaty obligations, as they affected the various districts and tribes. The reports seek to appraise aspects of British colonisation as it affected the control and possession of lands and waters. They do not deal with the various actions of chiefs, tribes, and other Maori individuals from 1840 to 1975. They do not deal with the inter-tribal wars from 1820 to 1840. The Waitangi Tribunal can only hear claims from Maori concerning Maori grievances. The tribunal cannot hear grievances from non-Maori, of which there are many. The reports therefore cover a fragment of New Zealand history in a one-sided manner.

What made me interested in our history? Research into the life of one of my great-grandparents who was the first New Zealand Company colonist to step ashore at Petone, Wellington, on January 22, 1840, made me read a lot of 19th century New Zealand history -- both that written close to the period, and the substantial re-writing done by the Waitangi Tribunal from the late 20th century on. *The First Colonist - Samuel Deighton 1821-1900*[5] draws upon his letters and other primary sources, early settler histories, biographies, more recent histories, and Waitangi Tribunal reports. I expected Tribunal reports to deal with history; I did not expect them to be finely crafted arguments in support of the claims they purport to investigate. Taxpayers should be outraged that a government-funded body is writing a new history in which the Crown is depicted as deceitful, settlers rapacious, and Maori as helpless victims in need of compensation.

A lot of money is at stake. Between 1989 and 2012, a total of 47 settlements transferred cash and assets worth nearly $1.8 billion from all the taxpayers of New Zealand to a number of recently created, private tribal organisations ostensibly to settle an array of grievances. No government asked the paying public whether they agreed or disagreed; therefore there is no clear mandate for a process that costs around $170 million a year (excluding settlement cash and assets),[6] and which continues without genuine public scrutiny. As the payouts grow bigger the claims become more tenuous. Each settlement brings an abject apology from the government and tearful claimant statements that the settlement is far from the actual losses endured over the previous 172 years. Each signing is heralded with Maori culture theatre combining menacing war dances, singing, wailing, prayers, the waving of Stone Age weapons, and the wearing of feather cloaks and grass skirts. This chapter will take you on a quick journey through some of the past 200 years to show how history has been twisted almost beyond recognition in this tribal grab for money and power.

The treaty

Treatyists - those who seek to measure everything by the Treaty of Waitangi - argue that the transfer of sovereignty and colonisation of New Zealand started with the treaty. The details of history show that this is not true. That treaty, which is discussed in detail in Chapters Two and Four, is a simple, three-paragraph text with a preamble and postscript. The treaty says that the chiefs cede sovereignty to the Queen; the Queen confirms to chiefs and the people of New Zealand the rights of subjects, including possession of property, with the Queen and her agents having sole right to buy land. Since then the Queen and her successors have exercised sovereignty for over 173 years.

At the time of the first signing of the treaty, on February 6, 1840, the first shipload of colonists, on the *Aurora*, had already arrived at Petone, on January 22, my great-grandfather being among them. The New Zealand Company's colonisation scheme goaded the British Colonial Office into sending Hobson to negotiate the cession of sovereignty. Treatyist historians would have us believe that the nation was founded when the Treaty of Waitangi was signed on February 6,

1840. But the treaty was one step of the process whereby Britain acquired sovereignty over New Zealand that included proclamations, occupation by settlers, and conquest through the 1860s wars.

Hobson asserted sovereignty over the North Island on 21st May, 1840, on the grounds of cession by treaty. Thomas Bunbury, acting for the stricken Hobson, proclaimed sovereignty over Stewart Island based on discovery, and over the South Island on 17th June on the grounds of cession. Hobson's assertion of a Crown monopoly on land sales and purchases seriously undermined the New Zealand Company's grand scheme of buying land from chiefs for very little and selling it for £1 an acre. By 1858, 59,000 settlers outnumbered the Maori population of 56,409.[7]

Armed conflict accompanied British settlement

Sporadic armed conflict accompanied British settlement. There was a clash of attitudes to land ownership. Settlers came with a clearly established view of private property rights in which a block of land was described on a title deed, and changed hands with signatures on a sale and purchase agreement in return for money or goods. Maori held land communally, often with different rights to the same piece of land, and held the area until a stronger group pushed them out. One group may have the right to catch birds in bush and in an area, another to fish in the area's river, and yet another to grow crops there. Exclusive boundaries were rare; rights were under constant negotiation. A British buyer might do a deal with only some of the owners, and soon face claims from further owners, leading to serious clashes and bloodshed. Chiefs could sell land to establish prestige. They could also sell land that others had rights over as a way of getting revenge against the other party.

A dispute over land erupted at the Tuamarina Stream in the Wairau valley, 25 km from the one-year-old settlement of Nelson, on June 17, 1843, between New Zealand Company settlers and Ngati Toa chiefs. This was the first serious armed clash between Maori and settlers after the treaty was signed. In a bungled attempt to arrest Ngati Toa chief,Te Rauparaha, and his nephew Te Rangihaeata, four Maori fighters died and three were wounded, while among the British the toll was 22 dead, including a New Zealand Company official, Captain Arthur Wakefield, and five wounded. Moreover, twelve settlers were shot or clubbed to death after surrendering to Maori fighters who chased them. Ngati Toa said this was revenge, or "utu", for the inadvertent death of Te

Rangihaeata's wife, who was at the scene. After the clash, Maori fled the area fearing a prompt crackdown by the British. News of the killings reached Britain, all but destroying the New Zealand Company's grand immigration scheme. But the new governor, Robert FitzRoy, upset settlers when he seemed to side with the Maori killers and severely criticised the actions of the New Zealand Company. Fitzroy, who was recommended by the Church Missionary Society and who began his term in December, 1843, had to deal with the consequences of the killings.

Nearly two years later, a simmering dispute in the far north erupted into the Flagstaff War. Nga Puhi chief Hone Heke, the first to sign the Treaty of Waitangi, and his ally, Kawiti, fought the British in a series of clashes between March 11, 1845, and January 11, 1846, in and around the Bay of Islands. The conflict is best remembered for Hone Heke's challenge to the authority of the British by cutting down the flagstaff at Kororareka (later Russell), four times, first on July 8, 1844. Hone Heke took exception to the relocation of the capital to Auckland and the imposition of a tariff, two initiatives by the settler government that reduced his income. He was also responding to an insult from a former slave who lived with an English husband, the Kororareka butcher.

The next year, in early 1846, discontent boiled over in the Wellington region when Te Rangihaeata's warriors threatened and stripped 13 Hutt Valley settler families of their possessions. Six hundred troops moved to Wellington from the Bay of Islands on February 3, 1846, creating a total force of 800. Troops destroyed the principal Hutt Maori village on February 27, the inhabitants of which agreed to leave the area. The trouble continued. FitzRoy was recalled and a new governor, George Grey, declared martial law on June 18, 1846, for the lower North Island excluding Wellington. A patrol clashed with a war party personally led by Te Rangihaeata on the early morning of July 17.

In violation of the new sovereignty established under the Treaty of Waitangi but perhaps inspired by FitzRoy's wimpish response to the Wairau massacre, Te Rauparaha called on the disaffected upper Wanganui and inland tribes to join with chiefs Mamaku and Rangihaeata to raid the Hutt Valley, but a letter making this call was intercepted by my great, great-uncle, Richard Deighton, who passed it on to Grey. This prompted Grey to have Te Rauparaha arrested on July 23, 1846. The old warrior was held under supervision for the following two years, ending his ability to lead an armed challenge.On July, 29,

127

1846, British troops attacked Pauatahanui Pa, which Rangihaeata evacuated, and on August 6 they attacked his pa at Horokiwi, the defence of which was abandoned on August 13, thus ending the war in Wellington.

Why go through this old history? There is widespread ignorance of New Zealand's history because little is taught in the schools. In fact, New Zealand is unique in that history is not explicitly taught to all students. Into this void the treatyists make their outrageous claims and no one, not even politicians at the highest level, have enough knowledge to counter these claims. The following shows how the history of the settlement of Taranaki, Waikato, and the South Island has been re-written to justify multi-million dollar payouts.

Who was to blame for Taranaki troubles?

The Waitangi Tribunal's Taranaki Report blames European settlement in 1841[9] but missionary Samuel Ironside, who lived in Taranaki from 1855 to 1858, and wrote a detailed account of the events that led up to the first Taranaki war in 1860, disagreed.[10] Taranaki was deserted in 1839, Ironside wrote. A large force of Taranaki fighters left the area in 1830 to support Te Rauparaha, while subsequent raids by Waikato fighters meant "hundreds upon hundreds of its people were killed and eaten by the savage conquerors, and hundreds more were driven into the Waikato, and held in hopeless slavery there," Ironside wrote. Just nine years before the Treaty of Waitangi was signed, a Waikato war party of about 4,000 fighters butchered and ate 1,000 Taranaki Maori at the second siege of Pukerangiora Pa at Waitara, in 1831. It was there that the Waikato chief, Te Wherowhero, later to become the first Maori "king" (Potatau I), personally clubbed 150 unarmed captives to death.[11]

When Colonel William Wakefield of the New Zealand Company visited the Cook Strait area in 1839, Taranaki chiefly exile, Wiremu Kingi Te Rangitake, of Te Atiawa, urged him to buy the then deserted Taranaki. The New Zealand Company was a private British company that planned to profit from colonising New Zealand by buying land cheaply direct from Maori and selling land orders to colonists. Ironside described the New Plymouth scheme as £200 for a land order, which gave them a quarter acre (1011.7m2) of town land, 50 acres (20.23 hectares) of suburban land, and 150 acres (60.7ha) of country land.

128

Wakefield entered into three transactions that involved Taranaki. In October, 1839, after concluding transactions involving land around Wellington, Wakefield claimed to have bought 20 million acres (eight million hectares) from Aotea Harbour near Waikato in the north to the Hurunui River in the South Island. A later transaction known as the Nga Motu deed covered all the coastal lands north of New Plymouth, including Waitara. A further deed involved land immediately south of New Plymouth.[12]

Ironside noted that, "These natives willingly signed the deed of sale, and agreed to put up large temporary houses for the expected settlers from Plymouth, Devonshire, and Cornwall. This New Plymouth settlement was hailed by the trembling remnants (of Taranaki Maori), and also by the exiles in Cook Strait, as likely to prove a wall of defence for them against their ancient foes, the Waikato. They judged that Waikato would never venture to molest them if they had a white man's town at hand." [13]

Waikato Maori, hearing of the sale of Taranaki by their former slaves were angry, and resolved to come down in force and destroy them, so missionary Ironside travelled with the Waikato people to negotiate peace. The Waikato Maori were happy once they received a large portion of the purchase money, and Governor Hobson further satisfied Waikato claims by paying the captive-killer, Te Wherowhero, the sum of £400.[14]

In January, 1841, New Zealand Company surveyors laid out New Plymouth town over 550 acres (222 ha), and farms were to be laid out in over 68,500 acres (27,720 ha) from New Plymouth to beyond Waitara. Sections were sold in England. By 1843 there were over a thousand settlers there.[15] However, the returned Maori exiles, finding freedom and safety, began to threaten and claim the ownership of the land that they had been happy to sell three or four years earlier.[16] In July, 1842, a party of natives drove off settlers who had taken up land north of the Waitara River. In 1843 there was a further confrontation when a hundred men, women, and children sat in the surveyors' path.

In June, 1844, a lawyer named William Spain was commissioned to investigate the New Zealand Company's New Plymouth purchase since it took place before the treaty was signed. All land sales and purchases entered into before 1840 were to be investigated. Between 1815 and 1840, chiefs sold at least 314,414 ha (776,935 acres) throughout New Zealand, with some areas sold multiple times.[17] (The total land area of

New Zealand is 26.8 million hectares.) Spain awarded 60,500 acres (24,483 ha) to the company and their settlers. There was an immediate Maori protest, and a group was formed to drive out the settlers. The new Governor, Robert FitzRoy, stunned settlers and Maori alike when he rejected Spain's recommendation because he considered that it would be an injustice to a large number of Te Atiawa who had fled the area more than ten years earlier.[18]

FitzRoy allotted to settlers a small block of 3,500 acres (1,416 ha) around the township of New Plymouth and told them to leave their farms in the outlying areas. The New Zealand Company complained in London, and the Colonial Secretary, Lord Stanley, disapproved. FitzRoy was recalled and his replacement, the more resolute George Grey, was instructed to buy back for settlers the area that Spain had proposed.[19] Ironside said that from that time New Plymouth was virtually under Maori control, and noted: "The mischief was already done [by FitzRoy]. The natives had found out that, by assuming a threatening attitude, they could obtain any exorbitant demands and it was with great difficulty that first the Grey Block, then the Tataraimaka Block, and afterwards the Bell Block were so acquired, in all about 60,000 acres, for which a heavy price had to be paid the natives." [20]

Some united Maori opposition to land sales appeared at a large meeting of 2,000 at Manawapou near Hawera in May, 1854. The "land leaguers" as they were called were willing to kill to prevent land sales. Wiremu Kingi, who had sold the whole district to the New Zealand Company fifteen years earlier, was by that time chief of the land league.

One chief who wished to sell a block of his land was Maori magistrate, Rawiri Waiaka, of the Puketapu *hapu* of Te Atiawa. A land purchase commissioner asked Waiaka to mark out the boundaries of the block. Rawiri, his brother Paora, and three other family members were doing this on August 3, 1854, when a group of fellow Puketapu men, acting on behalf of a vehement land league activist named Katatore, murdered them. Ironside stressed that Rawiri was head chief of his tribe and he, and his people, owned the land offered for sale.

Ironside wrote: "Their friends at once rose to arms, and would have executed summary vengeance on the murderers. But Mr. Turton, the Wesleyan missionary, dissuaded them from their purpose - told them to leave the matter with his Excellency the Governor, who would surely punish the guilty. But a delay of several months occurred, and when at length, Colonel Wynyard, the officer administrating the Government, visited the place, the land leaguers from the south, of whom the notorious Titokowaru springs, had rallied round Katatore, and the Governor found himself face to face with a native war.

He refused to undertake the responsibility, as he was only administering the Government until his successor was appointed. So he shook hands with the murderer, and desired him and the rest of the natives to keep the peace in future. But the friends of the murdered Rawiri, finding the governor would not punish the guilty, at once took the offensive, and for five long years the province was the scene of a bloody, disastrous war between rival sections of the natives."

The opposition raised was that of the land league. There were fears for New Plymouth's longer-term prospects if opponents to land sales gained support. A feud with murders and counter murders between those who wanted to sell and those who didn't continued until 1860.[22]

When Bishop Selwyn in August, 1855, issued a pastoral letter in which the allegation that settlers were coveting Maori land first appeared, Ironside, as the resident minister of the English settlers, felt it his duty to protest. In a letter to the local newspaper, dated September 22, 1855, he wrote: "A large and intelligent section of the native population was, from the very first anxious to sell. The reluctance of the governor to purchase land was a great source of grievance to all the well-disposed natives of the province; clearly it was not the settlers' greed for land which had originated the war." [23]

Anarchy continued until March, 1859, when Governor Thomas Gore Browne called a large meeting to end the fighting. He said that murderers should be punished according to law, that he, as Governor, did not want to buy their lands nor did the white people; they would prefer trading with them. But he did say that, if any chief wished to sell his land and could prove his title, he would buy that land and protect the vendor in the sale of it. Waitara chief Te Teira Manuka sprang up and shouted, "Governor, will you buy my land?" Gore Browne said: "Yes, Teira, if you can prove your title, I will buy your land" [24] Wiremu Kingi was at this meeting. A significant detail was that Te Teira laid down his *parawai* (mat) at Gore Browne's feet as a customary sign that the deal was sealed. If another disagreed, it was customary for him to withdraw the mat as a sign of dispute. Wiremu Kingi did not withdraw the mat to demonstrate his disagreement at that time. He simply told the gathering that "Waitara shall not go".

The mat issue prompted significant discussion among chiefs attending the meeting. Ngati Raukawa chief, Hukiki, told a gathering of Waikato tribes at Ngaruawahia, which was attended by chief land purchase officer Donald McLean, that he questioned Wiremu Kingi, who said: "I did not take up the mat, but I spoke my word. The *pakeha* wants our land, but this war is about your Maori king. Don't listen to the *pakeha*, but bring your flag to Waitara. Go back and clear them out, send them all back to England." [25]   In other words, Wiremu Kingi was clear that the contested issue in Taranaki was sovereignty, not land.

After two commissioners spent ten months investigating ownership of Te Teira Manuka's 980-acre (396 ha) block of land known as Pekapeka, at Waitara near New Plymouth, the government's chief land purchase officer accepted the offer. A £100 deposit was paid with the balance to be paid as soon as the survey was completed. Chief land leaguer, Wiremu Kingi, purported to forbid the sale. The government tried to survey some of the land in February, 1860, and found the block occupied by protestors. This was considered an act of rebellion. Martial law was declared, troops occupied part of the block and attacked Wiremu Kingi's fortified pa there on March 17, 1860.

That was how the first Taranaki war started. That war was fought until March, 1861, by more than 3,500 imperial troops brought in from Australia, as well as volunteer soldiers, militia, and pro-government Maori, against rebel Maori forces that fluctuated between a few hundred and about 1,500. By the time peace was agreed on April 8, 1861, total losses of colonial troops, settlers, and pro-government Maori were 64, while anti-government Maori casualties totalled 196.[26] Compared to the pre-1840 Musket Wars these were small numbers. The fighting caused economic hardship, with migration all but coming to a stop and the destruction of three-quarters of the farmhouses at Omata, Bell Block, Tataraimaka, and settlements nearer the town. Wiremu Kingi retreated to Waikato and did not submit until 1872. Spot the treaty breaches by Maori in that sequence of events.

During 1865, some 1,199,622 acres (485,469 ha) of Taranaki land were confiscated under the New Zealand Settlements Act 1863, which aimed to settle trained soldiers upon confiscated land so as to bring peace to disaffected areas. A compensation court made 518 rulings entitling pro-government Maori to 79,238 acres (32,066 ha). The final total of confiscated land in the area was 462,000 acres (186,964 ha).

Sporadic armed resistance flared up later. From 1864 a number of Taranaki Maori became fanatical followers of the Pai Marire Hau Hau cult that blended Maori beliefs with stories from the Old Testament. Cultists decapitated enemies and drank their blood. Another anti-government chief, Titokowaru, waged a campaign in Taranaki from June, 1867, to February, 1869. More followed the self-styled prophet, Te Whiti o Rongomai, who waged a campaign of passive resistance in Taranaki from 1867 from a village he built on confiscated land at Parihaka. In December 1879, the government launched an inquiry known as the West Coast Commission into grievances over Taranaki land confiscations. Te Whiti boycotted the inquiry and faced a government crackdown at Parihaka in 1881, in which nobody died or was killed.

So there you have it. Savage inter-tribal conflict meant that Taranaki was deserted in 1839. It was the arrival of white settlers that made it safe for Maori, who had either fled the area or had been taken away in slavery, to return. Those returnees played a duplicitous game with the settlers and their government so that the area descended into anarchy with settlers losing rights to land they had bought, losing farms they had established and, in some cases, losing their lives. Ignorance of this creates the knowledge void into which Tariana Turia, as Associate Minister of Maori Affairs for the Clark Labour Government, could make outrageous claims about "post colonial stress disorder" resulting from the "holocaust suffered by many Maori tribes during the land wars".[27]

The Waikato war

The 1863 Waikato war was connected to the 1860 Taranaki war, involving a number of the same people. Waikato tribes regarded northern Taranaki as part of their domain. Chief Te Wherowhero extracted a payment from the colonial government before white settlement proceeded. Waikato fighters were involved in Taranaki fighting from 1860. There is no Waitangi Tribunal report on Waikato grievances, because the 1995 Waikato-Tainui settlement was negotiated directly with the government. The only official history is contained in an agreed summary in the Waikato-Tainui Deed of Settlement, which creates the illusion that government forces unexpectedly set upon innocent Waikato Maori because they wanted the land. This deliberately distorted summary says:

1. In 1863-1864, the Crown engaged in a war against Maori in the Waikato, causing suffering to the people there.

2. After the war in the Waikato, large areas of land . . . were unjustly confiscated by the Crown under the New Zealand Settlements Act 1863.

3. In 1926, a Royal Commission chaired by Sir William Sim (the Sim Commission) was appointed to consider whether confiscations under the New Zealand Settlement Act 1863 had been excessive. In its report, the Sim Commission found that the general confiscations of land in the Waikato were "excessive". The Sim Commission was precluded by its terms of reference from inquiring into the consistency of the confiscations with the Treaty of Waitangi. The Sim Commission also reported that the confiscation of lands from tribes driven from their *kainga* north of the Mangatawhiri before it's crossing by General Cameron in July 1863 was a "grave injustice".

4. The Crown acknowledges that grave injustice was also done to tribes south of the Mangatawhiri, their lands being invaded and confiscated.

5. The Waitangi Tribunal wrote in the Manukau Report (Wai 8) in 1985: "It can simply be said from the contemporary record of Sir John Gorst in 1864, from the report of the Royal Commission sixty years after that, and from historical research almost a century removed from the event, all sources agree that the Tainui people never rebelled but were attacked by British troops in direct violation of Article 2 of the Treaty of Waitangi."

6. The war caused loss of life among Waikato *iwi* and the effect of the *raupatu* [confiscations] both immediately and over time has had a crippling effect on the welfare, economy, and development of Waikato.

7. The injustice of the *raupatu* is felt as keenly by Waikato today as in the past, as has been testified to the Crown by *kaumatua* and *kuia* as expressed in the affidavits filed by the plaintiffs in *R.T. Mahuta and the Tainui Maori Trust Board* v *Attorney General* [1989] 2 NZLR 513.

8. Waikato have pursued compensation on the basis of the principle of "land for land" – "*I riro whenua atu, me hoki whenua mai*" (as land was taken land must be returned), and "*ko te moni hei utu mo te hara*" (the money is the acknowledgement of the Crown of their crime)

9. On 16 March, 1987, Robert Te Kotahi Mahuta on behalf of himself and on behalf of the members of Waikato-Tainui, and of the Tainui Maori Trust Board and Nga Marae Toopu filed a claim with the Waitangi Tribunal concerning Crown actions to the Waikato Claim Area, and certain other matters. That claim was registered with the Waitangi Tribunal as Wai 30. Those parts of the Wai 30 claim dealing with the *raupatu* have been the subject of petitions to the Crown since 1865 and direct negotiations with the Crown since 1989.

10. Having reviewed these longstanding claims in relation to *raupatu*, the Crown has concluded that the confiscations of land in the Waikato since 1863 were both unjust and a breach of the Treaty of Waitangi.

11. The Crown and claimants have negotiated with each other in good faith in an endeavour to settle the Waikato claim and to remove the sense of grievance over time felt by Waikato. They recorded their agreement in principle to the matters required to effect a settlement of the Raupatu Claims in the Heads of Agreement.

12. In 1993, the Crown vested in Potatau Te Wherowhero for the benefit of Waikato the Hopuhopu Military Base as a goodwill gesture.

13. As contemplated by the Heads of Agreement, the parties now wish to record the basis on which they will settle the Waikato Claim and the overlapping claims will be settled.[28]

Several chiefs in the Waikato signed the Treaty of Waitangi, but the main chief, Potatau Te Wherowhero, refused even though he was asked on several occasions. Because Waikato-Tainui had conquered Taranaki by 1831, they regarded Mokau in north Taranaki as the southern border of their realm. Te Wherowhero had received payment from the government to end his claim over north Taranaki. During the 23 years after the treaty was signed, settlement had developed around the coast so

Waikato Maori, residing mainly up the river, remained largely untouched. What follows are the details, missing from the Waikato-Tainui Settlement Deed, of how Waikato tribes were involved in the first Taranaki war and what led to warfare in the Waikato area.

Waikato-Tainui had set up its own "kingdom" in opposition to the colonial government which had Queen Victoria as sovereign. Wiremu Tamehana, a leader of Waikato tribe Ngati Haua, persuaded Waikato chief Te Wherowhero (the captive-killer) to become the first Maori "king", installed as Potatau I in April, 1858. Tamehana aimed to create solidarity among Waikato, Ngati Maniapoto and adjacent tribes through the leadership of a chief with the prestige of Te Wherowhero.

Tamehana sided with the Taranaki land leaguers since he sought to resist further land sales and settler encroachment. After fighting erupted at Waitara, on March 17, 1860, war parties from Waikato, Maniapoto, and Ngati Haua provided the main opposition to colonial government forces in Taranaki.[29] Ngati Maniapoto from Waikato fought beside Taranaki people to defeat imperial troops at Puke-ta-kauere, near Waitara, on June 27, 1860, and in January, 1861, Rewi Maniapoto led an unsuccessful attack on a redoubt at Huirangi. Fighting at Waitara provided young Waikato men, bored with the settler peace, the chance to roam, fight, kill, and plunder.

The involvement of Waikato fighters in the Taranaki war demonstrated to the government the danger of a large body of hostile Maori occupying the centre of the North Island with the ability to attack isolated coastal settlements at any time. To gain support for the Waitara war and isolate supporters of the Maori "king", Governor Thomas Gore Brown convened a month-long conference of about 200 chiefs whom he considered loyal at Kohimarama, Auckland, starting on July 10, 1860. The first Maori "king", Potatau I, died shortly after on June 25, to be succeeded by his son, Tawhiao. This second Maori "king" did not command the respect that Te Wherowhero had, which meant that tribes in the Waikato became disunited and spun out of control from 1860 to 1864.

John Gorst arrived in Waikato in October, 1860, to teach at a mission school. Upon his arrival at Taupiri, about 75km south of Auckland, he encountered a war party threatening to declare war unless the government turned over a settler alleged to have killed a Maori. Gorst warned them against war. He later noticed that Waikato Maori stopped wearing settler clothes and pulled their children out of settler schools – which he took as signs that they had turned against the government.

Wiremu Tamehana sought peace in the Waitara war in March of 1861 in the hope that he could negotiate a realm for the new Maori "king", Tawhiao, in Waikato. Fighting ceased on April 8, 1861. Sir George Grey returned for his second term as governor in September, 1861. Grey distributed £6,000 to Waikato chiefs, as well as flour and sugar, since farming had been neglected during the Waitara fighting and hunger was an issue.[30] To introduce British law in Maori districts, Grey appointed civil commissioners and resident magistrates to represent the government and to co-operate with local *runanga*.

Lawlessness prevailed in Waikato, rendering Grey's efforts ineffective. Waikato chiefs ignored Tawhiao, who lacked the respect needed to unite tribes in his area. Auckland settlers feared an attack from Waikato. Grey had work begun on the Great South Road in 1861, from Auckland to the Mangatawhiri River, which is just north of Meremere. Approximately 12,000 soldiers were involved in the construction over two years. The Waikato tribes saw the proximity of soldiers and the road as a threat. Gorst was appointed resident magistrate for Waikato in January of 1862. He was nominal head of the school, supervised the building of a police station at Kihikihi, and published a newsletter to counter Tawhiao's newspaper "Hikoi".

Waikato king maker, Wiremu Tamehana, and later Maniapoto chief, Rewi, became involved in a dispute over the Tataraimaka block 15 km south of New Plymouth. This was European land seized in retaliation for Waitara fighting by Ngati Ruanui. Grey was overheard to say, while meeting Tamehana at Taupiri, "I shall not fight with your king, but I shall dig around him with spades until he falls of his own accord". News of this statement spread like wildfire through Waikato. Maniapoto warriors seized Gorst's printing press on March 25, 1863. Gorst and his family were driven out of the area on April 18, an event that showed that Rewi had gained control over king movement politics. Waikato chiefs said they would fight if the military road crossed the Mangatawhiri River

Supporters of the Maori "king" subsequently developed two plans of attack on Auckland, one involving a night attack when the town would be set on fire in a number of places by Maori living there for that purpose. This plan was recorded in the 1926 Sim Commission report. The attacks did not eventuate. An intercepted letter from Tawhiao to

137

Wellington's Te Ati Awa leader, Wi Tako Ngatata, written before troops crossed the Waikato border river, the Mangatawhiri, promised war and called on him to be ready.[31] Letters from Waikato chiefs Taati Te Waru and Porokuru Titipa to tribes in the southern part of the North Island, also written before troops crossed the Mangatawhiri, called for a general war.[32]

Before any such uprising could occur, the government issued an order on July 9, 1863, requiring all Maori living north of the Mangatawhiri River, to take an oath of allegiance to the Queen and give up their weapons. Those refusing to do so were required to retire to the Waikato. A further proclamation dated July 11, 1863, warned that those who wage war against the government would have their lands confiscated.[33]

Colonial government soldiers crossed the Mangatawhiri River on July 12, 1863. Maori unwilling to take the oath were evicted as the colonial force advanced. Fighting occurred at Meremere, Ngaruawahia, Rangiaowhia (southwest of Cambridge) and at Orakau (near Te Awamutu) during 1863 and 1864. Historian James Cowan, whose father fought in that war, wrote in the 1920s that: "It was a racial war; the Maori aim was to sweep the *pakeha* to the sea, as the *pakeha* government's object was to teach the Maori his subjection to British authority. The Europeans were not without warning that the sharp and barbarous old methods of warfare were to be revived." [34]

The Waikato war killed 619 anti-government Maori and 162 Europeans and pro-government Maori. Wiremu Tamehana made peace in 1865.[35] Although the final action in the Waikato war was on April 2, 1864, at Orakau, the colonial government had yet to fight the fanatical Pai Marire, also known as Hau Haus, who beheaded their victims and carried those heads around for use in religious rites. The Hau Hau war spread from Taranaki, through Waikato, to Opotiki, down the East Coast to Napier, and back into the Ureweras, where the guerrilla fighter, Te Kooti, another self-styled prophet who created the Ringatu religion, and his followers fled. Shots fired at the retreating Te Kooti on February 14, 1872, are regarded as the last shots of the New Zealand wars. "King" Tawhiao did not submit until 1881.

A proclamation confiscating land was issued in December, 1864 under the New Zealand Settlements Act 1863, following the earlier warning on July 11, 1863, which said "a large number of the inhabitants in several districts of the colony have entered into combinations and

138

taken up arms with the object of the extermination or expulsion of the European settlers and are now engaged in open rebellion against Her Majesty's authority." Proposed confiscations were contentious at the time. Former chief justice, Sir William Martin, argued that the confiscation of New Zealand private land would only result in a "brooding sense of wrong". Native Minister Donald McLean said the confiscations were an expensive mistake.

The confiscated Waikato territory initially comprised 1,202,172 acres (486,501 ha), including virtually all of Waikato north of a line drawn from Raglan to Tauranga. Approximately 314,364 acres (127,218 ha) were returned to those Waikato Maori who were judged not to have rebelled. The area finally confiscated totalled 887,808 acres (359,283 ha).[36]

If there is any doubt about what took place in New Zealand during the 1860s, there are numerous letters, statements, and news reports from the time that show it was a struggle between supporters of the Maori king against supporters of the British Queen. Missionary Reverend Morgan summed up the struggle when he wrote to parliament at the time saying:

"The vital question with the Maori Kingites now, is whether the King or the Queen shall possess the *mana* of New Zealand. Hence the frequent expression of the Waikatos now in arms, 'we are going to fight for New Zealand. We sent the king's flag to Taranaki, and it is our duty to follow the king's flag. We are fighting for the mana of our island'." [37]

The British government acquired sovereignty over New Zealand by treaty of cession, by proclamation, by occupation, and by conquest. After more than twenty years of settler occupation and government, the wars of the 1860s meant that the issue of sovereignty finally was decided with unwilling tribes on the battlefield by conquest.

Ngai Tahu's never-ending South Island complaints
South Island tribes continue to nurse a grievance that goes back to 1848 even though the island was untouched by war or confiscation. What was that grievance that has generated five settlements, the latest in 1998, with additional top-ups forthcoming? The initial complaint related to a purchase of 20 million acres (8,093,712 ha) in 1848 known as the Kemp purchase, and was about boundaries and allegedly insufficient reserves. As property values increased over time, the argument developed into one of insufficient payment and grievances spread to

139

other transactions. Here are the details of the 10 deals in which a handful of Ngai Tahu chiefs sold most of the 37.366 million acre (15,121,483 ha) South Island for a total of £14,750:

1. An estimated 400,000 acres (161,874 ha) of Otago were sold to the New Zealand Company for £2,400 on July 31, 1844.

2. Twenty million acres from Otago to Nelson spanning both coasts were sold to the colonial government represented by native secretary, Henry Tacy Kemp for £2,000 on June 12, 1848 (the Kemp purchase).

3. A total of 59,000 acres (23,876 ha) at Lyttelton (then known as Port Cooper) were sold to the government in August, 1849 for £200.

4. A total of 104,000 acres (42,087 ha) at Port Levy on Banks Peninsula were sold in September, 1849 for £300.

5. In 1856 almost all the remaining land on Banks Peninsula, approximately 67,000 acres (27,113 ha), was sold via the Akaroa deed for £150.

6. Over seven million acres (2,832,799 ha) of Southland were sold for £2,600 on August 17, 1853 (the Murihiku deed).

7. One million acres (404,685 ha) of North Canterbury were sold for £500 on February 5, 1857.

8. A total of 2.8 million acres (1,133,119 ha) of Kaikoura for £300 on March 29, 1859.

9. Seven million acres (2,832,799 ha) on the west coast for £300 on May 21, 1860.

10. Stewart Island for £6,000 on June 29, 1864.[38]

The total of £14,750 in 1864 would be the equivalent of about one year's pay for 164 people, based on wages for a government court interpreter who at that time was paid around £90 a year. According to the Reserve Bank inflation calculator, that amount would be worth around $1.5 million in 2012.

How Ngai Tahu, with a population of fewer than 2,000 people in the 1840s, came to be regarded as owners of the South Island is an interesting debate that apparently government agencies have conceded to Ngai Tahu. Originally from Poverty Bay and Hawke's Bay, Whatua Mamoe and others arrived in the South Island in the 16th and 17th centuries when they merged with another former North Island tribe Waitaha to become Ngai Tahu. Te Rauparaha's Ngati Toa tribe invaded from the Wellington region in 1828, inflicting heavy casualties, forcing Ngai Tahu to retreat south. Ngati Toa incursions meant that Ngai Tahu were ready to welcome European settlers to avoid further attacks.

New Zealand was short of many things in the 1840s but land was not one of them. The Treaty of Waitangi gave the Crown the sole right to buy land from Maori. The land had no commercial value before the introduction of capital and effort, which came with the settlers. Government land purchase officers reminded vendor chiefs that the value of any land retained by Maori as reserves would increase as settlers developed farms and towns.

The few Ngai Tahu, who lived in tiny, isolated settlements dotted around the coast of the expansive and mostly uninhabited South Island, had been selling plots of land to sealers and whalers since 1800. In five transactions in the 1830s Ngai Tahu sold 15 5-million acres. A French whaler named Captain Langlois thought he bought Banks Peninsula in 1838 with a down payment of £6. He returned with a boatload of Nanto-Bordelaise Company colonists in August, 1840, and paid the balance of £234. But when they arrived at Akaroa, they were told that the vendors had no right to sell, so a further purchase was arranged. This became the subject of a land commissioner's court hearing in Akaroa in 1843, where Ngai Tahu representatives denied the 1838 sale and claimed that the 1840 sale involved only portions of the harbours there, not the entire peninsula. The court acknowledged the French right to 30,000 acres (12,140 ha). North Island tribe Ngati Toa sold northern South Island land to the New Zealand Company from 1839.[40]

A dispute over the 20 million acre (8,093,712 ha) Kemp purchase was the earliest Ngai Tahu complaint. Land purchase officer Henry Tacy Kemp did not mark out reserves before signing the deed in June, 1848, as he had been told to, because it was winter; the rivers were high, and surveying impossible. The lack of settled reserves and the fact that

141

Kemp had accepted that the handful of Ngai Tahu living there had ownership of and could sell such a huge tract of land incurred the ire of his superior, Lieutenant Governor Edward Eyre, who dismissed Kemp. Eyre, who was the immediate subordinate of Governor George Grey, sent a novice Native Land Purchase Department officer, Walter Mantell, in August, 1848, to finish the job. Mantell made 15 different reserves totalling 6,356 acres (2,572 ha) for 637 people.[41]

When Eyre and Mantell were in Akaroa in 1848, they were told that Ngai Tuahuriri wished to reserve a large strip of land running right across the island to the west coast from the Waimakariri River on the east coast. Kaiapoi Ngai Tahu claimed that a large tract was not included in the sale, and demanded that the southern limit of the North Island tribe, Ngati Toa's, purchase be moved from Kaiapoi to Kaikoura. A number of Ngai Tahu complained they had received nothing from the first instalment of £500 paid to chiefs Taiaroa and Tikao on June 12, 1848, and chief Taiaroa asked for £40 to make that problem go away. Mantell refused to budge.[42]

The complaint resurfaced in the 1860s, when Ngai Tahu began to subdivide reserves into individual 14-acre (5.6 ha) lots, starting with the Kaiapoi reserve, with entitlement based on a list of residents compiled in June, 1848, by Mantell. A Native Land Court judge noticed the provision in Kemp's deed allowing for future reserves, without connecting this provision with the fact that Mantell had provided them later in 1848. Grey promised, in 1867, to have Ngai Tahu's grievance examined, and the following year Mantell told the Native Land Court in Christchurch that he had not fulfilled the terms of the deed. Therefore, Judge Francis Dart Fenton reserved a further 4,930 acres (1,995 ha) in Canterbury and Otago, and set aside a number of small fisheries easements. This was Ngai Tahu's first settlement.

Complaints continued. H.K. Taiaroa as Southern Maori M.P. told a parliamentary select committee in September, 1872 that the 1868 award should not be regarded as final. He cited an 1862 speech by his father, Taiaroa, the chief involved in the Kemp purchase, that the purchase price was a down payment and that Ngai Tahu only signed because Kemp threatened to send soldiers to take the land. Although Taiaroa offered no evidence, the select committee urged further inquiry.

Judge Fenton, who conducted the inquiry, reported in 1876 that: Ngai Tahu were not promised tenths in 1844; that Kemp did not intimidate Ngai Tahu; that the boundaries (which were disputed) were part of the deeds and could not be questioned; that Mantell did not use threats against Ngai Tahu; and that the Native Land Court in 1868 (over which Fenton presided) had given *mahinga kai* a most extensive interpretation and made appropriate orders for reserves; that the court increased the reserves to 14 acres (5.6 ha) per head and, had the government suggested a much larger quantity he, Fenton, would gladly have sanctioned it.[43]

Despite this clear statement that the claim had no merit, Taiaroa persevered, calling the Fenton report deceitful and repeating the complaint in parliament. Prime Minister Sir George Grey relented and in February, 1879, set up a Royal Commission under T.H. Smith and F.E. Nairn, which recommended reserves of one acre (0.4 ha) reserved for every 10 acres (4 ha) sold to European settlers. That commission consulted Ngai Tahu widely and took no evidence from the Crown.[44]

The government took no action so Taiaroa and Ihaia Tainui petitioned parliament, citing the Smith-Nairn commission, seeking relief for their grievances. The Native Affairs Committee reported on August 25, 1882, that the reserves made at a Native Land Court sitting on May 7, 1868, were given in final settlement of all claims. The Ngaitahu Reference Validation Act 1868 was invoked as confirmation of this. A select committee report in September, 1884, on the petitions of Te Maiharoa, Te Wetere, and others, endorsed this finding. At a further select committee in 1888 Taiaroa conceded that a majority of chiefs had signed the 1848 sale. That select committee heard a past secretary of Native Affairs, William Rolleston, who had been involved in the 1868 land court hearing, challenge Taiaroa's assertion that not all claims were submitted.

In May, 1886, Native Land Court Judge Alexander Mackay was hired to head a second Royal Commission to inquire into all cases where Maori alleged that land had not been provided. He said that land awarded as reserves in 1868 was not allotted equally. He recommended a further 130,700 acres (52,892 ha) for the Kemp purchase, a further 55,412 acres (22,424 ha) for the Southland Murihiku purchase, and for Otago a total, including the area already allowed, of 14,460 acres or 5,851 ha (one-tenth of the 144,600 acres contemplated for the settlement)[45].

Ngai Tahu cried poverty but who was to blame? "The poverty of the people (at a reserve at Otago Heads) is entirely attributable to their own indolence and apathy," Judge Mackay wrote in 1872. "They have plenty of land of good quality and might live in comparative comfort if they would only exert themselves." Instead the tribe leased out its reserves to settler farmers.[46] Mackay criticised Ngai Tahu even though he advocated for their concerns. Rolleston noted that Ngai Tahu people were "not fully or profitably occupying the reserves they already have. They are simply letting the land and not occupying or cultivating more than a portion of it; and the tendency of the enlargement of these reserves is to create a people living in idleness".[47] Joint committees in 1888, 1889, and 1890 considered Mackay's recommendations. The 1889 committee concluded that promises made in regard to residences and cultivations were fulfilled, while the 1890 committee recommended further inquiry.

Mackay was appointed again in December, 1890, as a Royal Commissioner to ascertain if any Ngai Tahu had insufficient land for their support by working it. His investigation covered the Otago, Kemp, Banks Peninsula and Southland Murihiku blocks. Mackay found no cases of entire destitution, but noted that 90 per cent possessed either no land (44 per cent) or insufficient land (46 per cent), and seasonal work was limited. In December, 1893, Cabinet appointed Mackay and Percy Smith, the surveyor-general, to complete a list of landless Maori and assign sections to them. The South Island Landless Natives Act 1906, which granted 142,463 acres (57,652 ha) of land to settle 4,063 "landless" Maori constituted Ngai Tahu's second settlement.

This settlement did not stop complaints. Ngai Tahu criticised the land offered as remote, covered in uneconomic stands of timber, unsuitable, and mostly not surveyed. By 1910 Ngai Tahu restated its claim to the Native Affairs Select Committee for more land. Michael Gilfedder and Henry Douglas Morpeth Haszard were appointed in 1914 to inquire into reserves for landless Maori, and recommended vesting all landless native reserves, for which the titles had not been uplifted, in the Commissioner of Crown Lands for the district in which such reserves were situated, in trust for the Maori owners. They also recommended that the Native Land Act 1909 be extended to enable Maori occupying their own sections to borrow money to improve their land.[48] By then, Ngai Tahu had achieved two settlements, but the complaints continued.

What were the grievances in 1882?

A "grievance", according to the Concise Oxford Dictionary, is "a real or fancied ground of complaint". Resentment is the anger, spite, or

144

bitterness caused by a perceived wrongdoing, injustice, or humiliation. The complex nature of overlapping customary land ownership is a recipe for conflict, and conflict over land predated British settlement. Because the Waitangi Tribunal looks solely at the interaction between the Crown and Maori, the widespread injustice and humiliation that resulted from the turmoil of the inter-tribal musket wars that started around 1800 is ignored. Those wars reduced the Maori population by around 40 percent, from around 120,000 to 70,000, and the associated cruelty, cannibalism, and chaos not only intensified fear and loathing between some tribes, but also dispersed many from their traditional territories.[49] Tensions were rekindled as missionaries persuaded chiefs to free their slaves, as chiefs sold land, as settlers arrived, and as the peace brought by settlement enabled tribes to return to land from which they had been driven in the inter-tribal wars, bringing further land disputes.

As already mentioned, the treaty enabled pre-1840 land sales to be investigated, so in many cases chiefs were able to get back land that they had sold and for which they had been paid. From 1840 chiefs found out that, if they complained, they could get compensation. In some cases land that had been sold was returned to chiefs to sell again. A more organised effort seeking redress occurred in 1882, when chiefs took just nine grievances to England. By comparison, by June, 2009, a total of 2,034 claims were registered with the Waitangi Tribunal, and that was after 23 major claims had been settled, some on numerous occasions. The 1882 grievances were:

1. The greed of the New Zealand Company which caused conflict in Wairau (on June 17, 1843, near what was to become Blenheim, when in a bungled attempt to arrest Te Rauparaha and his nephew Te Rangihaeata, four Maori and 22 settlers were killed)
2. The war against Te Rangihaeata in 1842-3 and the unlawful execution of his followers.
3. The war in the north against Heke and Kawiti (1845).
4. The divisive fight between Te Hapuku and Te Moananui (in Hawke's Bay in 1857) caused by government land buying in 1848.
5. The war against Wiremu Kingi at Waitara.
6. The Waikato war in 1863.

7. The tribal fight among Ngati Tautahi in which four people were killed because of corrupt land-buying practices by government agents who expended £700,000 in the process.

8. The imprisonment of 200 of Te Whiti's men in 1879.

9. The imprisonment of Te Whiti in 1881. The deputation asked for the release of Te Whiti.[50]

That deputation, from a tribal gathering at Waitangi in March, 1881, assembled grievances from the Far North, Hawke's Bay, Waikato, Taranaki, Wellington, and the top of the South Island. Not included was the single grievance from South Island tribe Ngai Tahu, which at that time was complaining about the extent of the fulfilment of one condition of one deed of sale – the Kemp purchase. The list was by no means exhaustive but stands in dramatic contrast to the number of late 20th century claims.

The 1920 native land commission

By 1920, when the Native Land Claims Commission sat, 11 petitions and claims from Maori in different parts of New Zealand were reviewed to assess redress.[51] Grievances of the 1940s could be seen in a series of final settlements between 1944 and 1958 that dealt with claims from Ngai Tahu, Taranaki tribes, Waikato-Maniapoto, Whakatohea, and Urewera people. Commission chair, Judge Robert N. Jones, found substantially in favour of all Maori claimants in different regions.

For Ngai Tahu, this commission calculated compensation by working out that the Kemp purchase involved 12.5 million acres of commercially viable land once the Arahura block, the Banks Peninsula block, the reserves actually provided, and "absolutely valueless land", such as snowy mountain tops, waste beds of rivers, and precipitous cliffs, were deducted. They subtracted the purchase price paid of £2,000 to give £76,125 and to this was added 72 years interest at 5 per cent (£274,050) to give a total amount of £350,175. A sum was added to recognise Ngai Tahu expenses, bringing the total sum to £354,000. This commission recommended a lump sum payment of £354,000.[52]

The Sim inquiry 1926

A further commission chaired by Supreme Court Judge William Sim was set up in 1926 to consider whether confiscations in Taranaki,

146

Waikato, Tauranga, Whakatane, Opotiki, Urewera, Gisborne, and Hawke's Bay exceeded in quantity what was fair and just. At that stage the inquiry was not linked to Treaty of Waitangi obligations because the government held that Maori who fought against the government had repudiated the treaty. That commission recommended a £5,000 annual payment to Taranaki tribes for land unjustly confiscated.[53] Sim found that confiscations in Waikato were excessive and recommended an annual payment of £3,000. Waikato initially wanted the land returned, but received annual payments from that year, although they became intermittent during the 1930s.

Communist Party's Maori self-determination policy 1935
The term "Maori self-determination" was introduced into New Zealand politics in the 1935 general election by the Communist Party of New Zealand. This was a strategy used at the time of the Russian revolution by Bolsheviks to expand their support base by promising the 80 formerly tribal subject peoples of Czarist Russia "the right to manage their own affairs," "the right to self-determination," "the right to speak, read, write, use, and be taught in their own language". The strategy was used to stir up the multi-ethnic empire of Austro-Hungary, and later to undermine the hold of European nations over their colonial possessions, so as to deprive them of their sources of cheap labour, raw materials, and markets for finished goods. Communists around the world were told to promote the independence aspirations of minority ethnic groups to bring them into violent conflict with the status quo, thus splintering the nation and bringing about socialist control. This strategy did not take hold in 1935 because Maori lived in rural areas and had no contact with urban communists.

Full and final settlements 1944-58
Southern Maori M.P. Eruera Tirikatene, of Ngai Tahu, elected to Parliament on May 26, 1943, urged final settlement of grievances that had remained unresolved since the 1920s, starting, of course, with those of his own tribe. The Ngai Tahu Claim Settlement Act 1944 awarded £300,000, payable at a rate of £10,000 a year for 30 years. This was Ngai Tahu's third settlement of complaints that initially arose from reserves claims and boundary disagreements over the 1848 Kemp purchase.

The 1944 Taranaki Maori Claims Settlement Act was intended as a final settlement of claims in that area. The Taranaki Maori Trust Board had received a £5,000 annuity since the Sim commission recommendation, plus a £300 lump sum payment for loss of property at Parihaka in 1881. The 1944 Act described it as a "full settlement and discharge of the aforesaid claims".[54]

The Waikato-Maniapoto Maori Claims Settlement Act 1946 was a final settlement of grievances over the confiscation of Maori lands in the Waikato and provided for the establishment of the Tainui Maori Trust Board to receive £5,000 a year in perpetuity plus a further £5,000 a year for 45 years, to cover arrears since 1936, when negotiations with the Labour government began. Tainui received £4,155 in 1948 as part of a surplus lands settlement.

In the Finance No. 2 Act, on October 12, 1946, the government settled with Whakatohea, a tribe located in the eastern Bay of Plenty region that had sustained land confiscation, for a lump sum payment of £20,000. In 1958, Urewera claims were settled with a lump sum payment of £100,000. A claim relating to Rotorua Township Pukeroa Oruawhata land in Waiariki district was settled in 1954 for £16,500. Earlier, the 1922 Arawa lakes settlement agreed that the government controlled the lakebeds and had the right to use the water, while the tribe had title to all islands not already sold, and right to access them, as well as use, management and control of parts of lake beds, and any Crown lands on the border could be vested in Arawa. Tribe members could catch any indigenous fish. Arawa District Trust Board would receive an annual grant of £6,000.

The Maori Affairs Amendment Act 1967

The Maori Affairs Amendment Act 1967 jump-started the latest round of complaints. That Act introduced compulsory conversion of Maori freehold land with four or fewer owners into general land, and increased the powers of the Maori Trustee to acquire by compulsion and sell so-called uneconomic interests in Maori land. A Maori Council member slammed the move as "the last land-grab". The Act was passed at a time when it was fashionable to protest. Civil rights protests in the United States influenced Maori protest that coalesced into a Maori nationalist movement. New Zealanders went out on the streets to join the world-wide protest against the Vietnam War, as they did against

148

rugby tours with apartheid South Africa, that culminated in street battles between baton-wielding police and crash-helmeted protesters.

Ngai Tahu's fourth settlement

Ngai Tahu's fourth settlement came soon after 1969, when the Ngai Tahu Trust Board petitioned Parliament asking that the 1944 Act be revoked and new legislation enacted providing for an in-perpetuity payment of $20,000 a year as a full and final settlement of the tribe's claim. At that stage the tribe's spokesman, Frank Winter, argued that the 1944 settlement had never been accepted as full and final. The Maori Affairs select committee heard the petition and rejected it. To address claims that alleged insufficient consultation, Southern Maori M.P. Whetu Tirikatene-Sullivan, the daughter of Eruera Tirikatene, said there were 109 movers and seconders of formal resolutions at as many as 80 meetings accepting the compensation. The petitioners asked to present an amended petition in the hope of receiving a payout of $600,000 but were rebuffed since they could offer no further evidence. However, the Labour government in 1973 introduced a Bill to facilitate payments of $20,000 a year with Maori Affairs Minister, Matiu Rata, arguing that the 1944 settlement was accepted only on the basis that more was to come in the future.

Maori nationalist protest

A specifically Maori-issues activist group known as Nga Tamatoa (The Young Warriors) emerged in 1970 out of a conference at Auckland University organised by the above-mentioned Ranginui Walker, a primary school teacher turned Maori studies professor. The group consisted of mainly urban and university educated Maori who took inspiration from Marxist liberation and indigenous rights movements across the world, including the gun-carrying Maoist American Black Panthers. The group called for the Treaty of Waitangi to be "ratified". It organised nationwide petitions to have the Maori language taught in schools, and made submissions on government policy. Some may remember the "Honour the treaty" and "Te reo" graffiti daubed around university towns at that time.

Nga Tamatoa disrupted the 1971 Waitangi Day ceremony, and in the following year it staged a walkout. In 1973 Nga Tamatoa protested at the ceremony by wearing black armbands to mourn the loss of 25.2 million hectares (the entire land area of New Zealand) of "Maori land".

149

When questioned by the government, the Auckland Maori Council supported Nga Tamatoa by citing 14 statutes that it said contravened Article 2 of the treaty, including the Public Works Act, Mining Act, Petroleum Act, Rating Act, and Town and Country Planning Act.

The Kirk Labour government was shocked that members of a government-created body should agree with fringe activists, but duly accommodated the activists' views. Maori Affairs Minister, Matiu Rata, pushed through legislation to give Maori greater control over administration of their land, gave official recognition to the Maori language, relaxed the definition of who was Maori by dropping the requirement for a fixed degree of Maori blood, and created training programmes for Maori. That legislation was the Maori Affairs Amendment Act of 1974. The lesson for Maori protestors was that protest brings concessions.

An 80-year-old activist named Whina Cooper literally took the land protest to the streets when she led a march to Parliament, organised by Nga Tamatoa, from Te Hapua in the Far North, starting on September 14, 1975, demanding that no more Maori land would be sold. The march brought about 5,000 Maori and supporters to Parliament on October 13 of that year. A petition signed by 60,000 people was presented to Prime Minister Bill Rowling. The marchers arrived on a Monday, three days after the Treaty of Waitangi Act 1975 was passed.

Discovering grievances

Geoffrey Palmer, who was also justice minister and Attorney-General in the Lange administration, described the steps he took regarding Maori grievances in his 1992 book *New Zealand's Constitution in Crisis*. As a Nelson boy, Palmer grew up believing there were no racial problems in New Zealand. But east coast Maori students he met at university acquainted him with an alleged "history of oppression". Later, as a student in Chicago, he lived in a ghetto during the civil rights protest era, with whites on one side of the street and blacks on the other. There he became aquainted with the United States political system, in which the Supreme Court interprets a written constitution, and where there was a mass of case law on civil rights. He concluded – undemocratically -- that courts "were more reliable in providing racial minorities with true equality than legislatures were".[58] Because addressing Maori grievances was politically unpopular, legislation to address grievances ran the risk of being outvoted. So he

150

set up "processes, and procedures and the principles on which decisions should be based".[59] He appeared to want to ensure that his drive to implement race-based affirmative action would not be derailed by Parliament or voters who (not surprisingly) did not agree with this form of racial discrimination.

The Treaty of Waitangi Act 1975 and the Waitangi Tribunal

The Treaty of Waitangi Act 1975 provided a legal process by which Maori Treaty claims could be investigated, and was the first legal recognition of the treaty. That Act established the Waitangi Tribunal as a permanent commission of inquiry, which means it is set up to be a part of the New Zealand socio-political scene forever, and rather foolishly gave a handful of unelected tribunal members the exclusive authority to interpret the treaty. It aimed to examine current policies and practices against the yet-to-be-defined so-called "principles" of the treaty but it did not allow the tribunal to investigate historical breaches. The tribunal can order witnesses to come before it, it can order material or documents to be produced before it, and it can actively search out material and facts to help it decide on a claim (courts are limited in their ability to do this). The Waitangi Tribunal is an "expert" forum, with its own business unit, and operates independently from the Justice Department's Tribunals Unit, although other tribunals are usually under the direction of the district court.

While other tribunals have specific legislation that marks out exactly how to take every step, the Waitangi Tribunal exists under the Treaty of Waitangi Act 1975 and its amendments, and other statutes, which give only general guidelines, thereby allowing judges to create the rules as they go along, not unlike a kangaroo court. The Waitangi Tribunal is free to receive whatever evidence it pleases: anecdote, reminiscence, hearsay are acceptable. There was a situation that prompted Waitangi Tribunal chairman, Eddie Durie, to say that some claimants had asked researchers to alter findings that were unhelpful to their cases. Others had made payment to researchers conditional upon findings being altered in the claimants' favour, according to a *New Zealand Herald* report on November 17, 1999, and as outlined from personal experience by John Robinson in his book *The Corruption of New Zealand Democracy*.

The tribunal attracted dramatic public attention in 1983 when it ruled in favour of Te Atiawa claimants over the discharge of untreated

151

sewage and industrial waste through the Motunui outfall in Taranaki. Deputy Prime Minister Geoffrey Palmer, who did extensive treaty and Maori issues work as a minister in the Lange Labour Government, noted that the Motunui report rediscovered "the Maori language version of the treaty, especially the words *taonga*, *kawanatanga* and *rangatiratanga* from which has flowed a new political vocabulary".[60] Palmer also wrote that: "The tribunal had created (through the Muriwhenua claim) a new legal approach to the treaty by removing the shackles of past precedent".[61] For those unversed in law, a respect for precedent or, if you like, the wisdom of the courts over the centuries, is the foundation of the rule of law and it is both surprising and disturbing that Palmer would show so little respect for it.

Claims back to 1840 allowed

Palmer enabled the Waitangi Tribunal to investigate claims all the way back to 1840, although the idea was born at a *hui* at Turangawaewae marae, Ngaruawahia, during September, 1984. A workshop lecture on the establishment of the Waitangi Tribunal explained how its architect, Matiu Rata, failed to make it retrospective to 1900. As a motion to recommend making the tribunal retrospective to that date was put, the workshop chairman, Turoa Royal, asked where the motion put his Thames-Coromandel goldfield complaint dated at 1867. The lecturer recommended the motion should therefore ask for claims back to 1840 be investigated. The motion was passed, and the *hui* general assembly put the recommendation to the Lange Labour Government.[62] Palmer, who was then deputy prime minister, said with an amazing lack of prescience that he "did some research on the outstanding grievances and it did not appear that looking into them would open a can of worms, which many feared. I took the view that the claims may take a decade to deal with, that it would cause some anguish but would be worth it in the end." [63]

Palmer thought that the tribunal would give Maori an outlet for their grievances, ending protest action. When the policy was announced, I recall tearing the story off the teleprinter where I worked as a newspaper sub-editor. I remarked: "that will open a Pandora's Box". The Treaty of Waitangi Amendment Act was passed in 1985. At that stage there was no hint of cash compensation for a complicated history, which would show a lack of common sense and foresight, but that was to follow.

Claims trickle becomes flood

Claims started to trickle in, then multiplied, and became more complex. For example, Ngai Tahu filed a general claim dated August 26, 1986, which challenged the Crown's move to transfer Crown pastoral leases and Crown land generally out of Crown ownership. This claim was amended in November of that year to include a general complaint about actions of Crown officials in the acquisition of Ngai Tahu lands from 1844, as well as specific complaints about the Crown failing to honour allocation of tenths in respect of the Otago purchase and a reference to improper alienation of reserves. Ngai Tahu on December 16, 1986, identified the Crown freehold and leasehold interests to which it laid claim. A request from the Waitangi Tribunal for specific details of the acts and omissions of the Crown prompted a further amended claim from Ngai Tahu on June 2, 1987. An amended claim of September 5, 1987, related to the granting of perpetual leases of Maori lands reserved from the West Coast purchase and administered under the Maori Reserved Land Act 1955. The Ngai Tahu claim to sea fisheries was detailed in a claim dated September 25, 1987. Ngai Tahu rights to inland waters comprising lakes, rivers and streams that were within the area of the Kemp purchase were asserted in a claim dated April 13, 1988. Ngai Tahu reformulated their marine fishing claim on June 25, 1988.[64] There seemed to be no limit to what they thought they could claim.

Treaty principles created

Treaty "principles", that are not explicitly stated in the three articles, preamble, and postscript of the treaty, were "discovered" in 1986 after the Maori Council took the government to court over a planned transfer of assets to State-owned enterprises. Palmer wrote that the Maori Council could not have taken that case to court if the government had not allowed the investigation of grievances back to 1840,[65] which, of course, was his own doing. By enabling claims back to 1840 Palmer had indirectly enabled the Maori Council to take this case to court.

As mentioned in Chapter Four the government had decided to change most of its trading departments into corporations run for profit. Much Crown property and extensive tracts of Crown land were to be transferred to these corporations. Palmer was responsible for the design and passage of legislation to do this, the State-Owned Enterprises Act

1986. Section 27 of the Act said that land subject to a treaty claim could not be transferred to another enterprise and could be recovered after a Waitangi Tribunal recommendation. But Section 27 did not provide for land subject to claims after the Act came into force. To ease concerns, as the Bill was going through Parliament, the Labour government inserted what was to become the notorious Section 9, which said: "Nothing in this Act shall permit the Crown to act in a manner that was inconsistent with the principles of the treaty." At that stage the "principles" were undefined. These principles and Section 9 of the State-Owned Enterprises Act 1986 were to become a veritable "can of worms" which would plague the Key government through 2012-13 in its efforts to partly privatise some State-owned power generating companies.

Maori, who in 1986 had only just gained the right to take to the tribunal claims dating back to 1840, were concerned that Crown land passed to a State-owned enterprise could not be returned under the treaty to claimants. After the State-Owned Enterprises Act 1986 was passed, but before land and assets were transferred, the Maori Council sought a declaration to stop the transfer until arrangements were made to deal with Maori claims related to those assets. Contrary to Palmer's opinion, in *New Zealand Maori Council v Attorney-General* in 1987 the Court of Appeal held that the "principles" overrode everything else in the Act. Palmer said that the decision set government policy back. Subsequent legislation, known as the Treaty of Waitangi (State Enterprises) Act 1988, provided a solution, or partial solution, by enabling asset transfers to State-owned enterprises subject to claims before the tribunal.

In this case the president of the Court of Appeal, Justice Robin Cooke, gave a summary of what he said were the "principles" of the Treaty of Waitangi. His principles are related neither to the treaty's preamble, nor to instructions given by Lord Normanby, the Secretary of State for the Colonies when the British relationship with New Zealand was being finalised. Cooke's summary appears to be little more than a personal opinion given legitimacy by the position he held. Here are his principles in somewhat greater detail than was given in Chapter Four.

(a) 'The Queen was to govern and the Maoris were to be her subjects; in return their chieftainship and possessions were to be protected, but . . . sales of land to the Crown could be negotiated.'

154

(b) Because there was some inevitable potential conflict between those principles, both parties had a duty 'to act reasonably and with the utmost good faith' towards one another.

(c) The principles of the treaty do not authorise unreasonable restrictions on the right of a duly elected government to follow its chosen policy.

(d) The Crown assumed a duty of protection towards Maori: 'the duty is not passive but extends to active protection of Maori people in the use of their lands and waters to the fullest extent practicable.'

(e) The Crown has a duty to remedy past breaches: 'the Crown should grant at least some form of redress, unless there are good grounds justifying a reasonable Treaty partner in withholding it – which would only be in very special circumstances, if ever.'

(f) The Crown had an obligation to consult with Maori in the exercise of *kawanatanga*. Cooke was guarded, however, as to the practical extent of that obligation.[66]

Principles of Crown action
What was the government's response to the appearance of the treaty "principles" 147 years after the treaty was signed? Palmer had already noted that there was no adequate advice within the executive on treaty matters and, in a bid to get the civil service to centre decisions on the treaty, he got Cabinet to agree to his Maori "wish list" in June, 1986. These were:

1. All future legislation referred to Cabinet at the policy approval stage should draw attention to any implications for recognition of the principles of the Treaty of Waitangi.
2. Departments should consult with appropriate Maori people on all significant matters affecting the application of the treaty, the Minister of Maori Affairs to provide assistance in identifying such people if necessary.

3. The financial and resource implications of recognising the treaty could be considerable and should be assessed wherever possible in future reports.[67]

So about a year after saying that allowing claims back to 1840 would not open a "can of worms", Palmer was now saying that the financial and resource implications could be "considerable". References to the treaty began to appear in statutes. Palmer set up a unit within the Justice Department to deal with the Crown's response to treaty negotiations and claims. This unit would generate policy, co-ordinate other departments on the treaty, and negotiate with Maori on claims. That unit wrote a 15-page booklet titled *The Principles for Crown Action on the Treaty of Waitangi*. The booklet was adopted by Cabinet and published on July 4, 1989. Included was an introductory statement by Prime Minister David Lange and the "official" English and Maori texts of the Treaty of Waitangi without preamble or postscript. The government's five principles are:

1. The Kawanatanga Principle -- The Principle of Government
The first article of the treaty gives expression to the right of the Crown to make laws and its obligation to govern in accordance with constitutional process. This (Article 1) sovereignty is qualified by the promise to accord the Maori interests specified in the second article an appropriate priority.

2. The Rangatiratanga Principle -- The Principle of Self-Management
The second article of the treaty guarantees to Maori the control and enjoyment of those resources and *taonga* which it is their wish to retain. The preservation of a resource base, the restoration of *iwi* self-management, and the active protection of *taonga*, both material and cultural, are necessary elements of the Crown's policy of recognising *rangatiratanga*.

3. The Principle of Equality
The third article of the treaty constitutes a guarantee of legal equality between Maori and other citizens of New Zealand. This means that all New Zealand citizens are equal before the law. Furthermore, the common law system is selected by the treaty as the basis for that

equality although human rights accepted under international law are incorporated also.

The third article also has an important social significance in the implicit assurance that social rights would be enjoyed equally by Maori with all New Zealand citizens of whatever origin. Special measures to attain that equal enjoyment of social benefits are allowed by international law.

4. The Principle of Cooperation
The treaty is regarded by the Crown as establishing a fair basis for two peoples in one country. Duality and unity are both significant. Duality implies distinctive cultural development and unity implies common purpose and community. The relationship between community and distinctive development is governed by the requirement for cooperation which is an obligation placed on both parties to the treaty.

Reasonable cooperation can only take place if there is consultation on major issues of common concern and if good faith, balance, and common sense are shown on all sides. The outcome of reasonable cooperation will be partnership.

5. The Principle of Redress
The Crown accepts a responsibility to provide a process for the resolution of grievances arising from the treaty. This process may involve courts, the Waitangi Tribunal, or direct negotiation. The provision of redress, where entitlement is established, must take account of its practical impact and of the need to avoid fresh injustice. If the Crown demonstrates commitment to this process of redress, then it will expect reconciliation to result.[68]

Race-based affirmative action begins
These "principles" with all their inconsistencies, contradictions, and high-sounding nonsense, appear to have been the blueprint for government policy since 1989. Palmer, who introduced these five principles when he was deputy Prime Minister, Minister of Justice, and Attorney-General, said that they were based on the material available at the time, including the "estates, forests and fisheries" official English text of the treaty, the Maori text, Waitangi Tribunal findings, and

judicial decisions to that time - in other words, the faulty interpretation of the treaty as already explained in the second chapter of this book. The Crown "response principles" were published four months after the discovery of the Busby February 4th document (Littlewood text of the treaty), without acknowledging either the existence or the contents of that vitally important text.

Palmer said that these principles were not intended to rewrite the treaty but, by ignoring the preamble and postscript, he removed the treaty from its 1840 context and obscured its intent. His "kawanatanga" principle watered down sovereignty by linking it to a requirement to give priority to Maori interests. The "rangatiratanga" principle puts an obligation on the government to preserve for Maori a resource base and actively protect "taonga", whatever they are. His principle of "equality" introduces race-based affirmative action to redress what he thought were serious imbalances in health, education and housing. His principle of cooperation imposes on the government the requirement to consult with Maori. On this point Palmer shows no sign of realising that the partnership requirement gives Maori an extra and special consultation privilege that non-Maori New Zealanders do not have. His principle of redress imposes on the government the responsibility of setting up a process for resolving grievances to bring about reconciliation. Palmer shows his ignorance of the pattern shown through our brief history in which, once Maori learned that the "wicked white coloniser" would pay compensation, numerous issues to compensate proliferated.

Once the principles of Crown action on the Treaty of Waitangi began to influence legislation, race-based affirmative action initiatives sprouted. Historian Michael Bassett, a former Waitangi Tribunal member who earlier was a Cabinet Minister in the Lange Labour Government, said: "The push for special privileges, separate agencies, quotas, commissions and departments took off. Nepotism, tribalism and racism reared their ugly heads. The most-able Maori were embraced by the professions. Others chased the treaty gravy train, or found places in well-paid organisations like the Crown Forest Rental Trust or the Fisheries Commission. Lower-paid departments and agencies, however, face a constant struggle to identify able Maori managers. Some promote young people too quickly." [69]

Tribunal member re-translates treaty

Over the years, while it was apparent that there were discrepancies between the English and Maori texts, it was not an issue. The Treaty of Waitangi Act, the creation of the Waitangi Tribunal, and the creation of the treaty principles put the treaty under scrutiny. A professor of social anthropology and Maori Studies and Waitangi Tribunal member, Sir Hugh Kawharu, in 1989 re-translated the Maori text of the treaty. He may be blamed for the *rangatiratanga kawanatanga* confusion.

Although it should be blindingly obvious that, to understand the meaning and intent of an agreement that is in two languages, one simply has to look at the source text, in this case, the English (from which Te Tiriti was translated), and look at the words used in the other language (Maori) to convey the meanings. Kawharu did not do this. He looked at the words used in Maori and imagined what chiefs in 1840 may have understood those words to mean, and he used those imagined meanings to translate the Maori text. His imaginings are detailed in the footnotes to his translation, as shown in a few key words – "sovereignty", "kawanatanga", "possession" and "rangatiratanga"

Where the English source text uses the word "sovereignty" in article 1, the Maori text uses the word kawanatanga. Kawharu said "There could be no possibility of the Maori signatories having any understanding of government in the sense of 'sovereignty' i.e. any understanding on the basis of experience or cultural precedent" so he translated "kawanatanga" back to English as "complete government".

We have already shown in Chapter 2 that the Maoris who signed the treaty knew very well that they were ceding sovereignty to the Queen. Fuller versions of their speeches at the time are extensively quoted in two recently published books *When Two Cultures Meet; the New Zealand Experience* by John Robinson and *The Great Divide* by Ian Wishart.

Where the English text uses the word "possession" in article 2, the Maori text uses the phrase "tino rangatiratanga". Kawharu notes that "unqualified exercise" of the chieftainship would emphasise to a chief the Queen's intention to give them complete control according to their customs" adding that "'tino' has the connotation of 'quintessential'" He translates "tino rangatiratanga" in Article 2 as "unqualified exercise of their chieftainship over their lands".

This was how the Treaty of Waitangi, in which the chiefs cede sovereignty to the Queen; the Queen confirms to chiefs and the people of New Zealand the rights of subjects, including possession of property, with the Queen and her agents having sole right to buy land, was twisted into the nonsense of the newly invented "Cooke-Palmer Treaty", in which chiefs agreed that the British governor could govern settlers while chiefs could carry on with the "unqualified exercise of their chieftainship".

Everything becomes a grievance

As already mentioned, a whole new generation of grievances appeared when the Fourth Labour Government's Treaty of Waitangi Amendment Act 1985 allowed the Waitangi Tribunal to investigate claims back to 1840. Once it became apparent that the government would pay significant amounts of money, the grievances multiplied. Working for the Waitangi Tribunal, historian Professor Alan Ward analysed the 650 or so historical claims lodged between 1985 and 1997 and sorted them to match the tribunal's interpretation of the treaty and the 1986 treaty principles. Ward's seven categories were:

1. The "loss of *rangatiratanga*", which includes the loss of resources, and the exclusion of Maori from the decision-making institutions.

2. Purchases under the Native Land Acts, which extended well into the 20th century, particularly the "individualisation of title", which the colonial government promoted partly to encourage Maori to develop their land.

3. Crown purchases from 1840 to 1865, which were manipulative and which denied or discouraged Maori leasehold and joint venture arrangements and the coexistence of aboriginal title rights.

4. Confiscation or forced cession after military occupation, in particular districts, although the area of land and the number of people affected were much less than were subject to manipulative land purchasing.

5. The colonial government's failure to ensure that adequate reserves of land remained in Maori ownership, or in trust, to fund Maori welfare.

6. The loss of ownership or control of rights in foreshores and inland waterways.

9. Public works takings disproportionately imposed upon Maori land, the rating of Maori land, and the good and bad consequences of development schemes.[70]

Ward's seven categories show that the scope for grievance had been greatly extended so that everything that occurred since 1840 became potential grounds for a complaint, no matter how much the colonial government had bent over backwards to accommodate Maori concerns. In 1882 the complaints involved armed conflict and imprisonment. In 1997 the complaints had moved on from those already raised and included issues that only appeared after the treaty was re-interpreted from 1985 and after the various treaty "principles" were created. The biggest, chart-topping grievance that applied to all of Maori ancestry, irrespective of how fortunate or unfortunate they may be, is that they were suffering under the yoke of no longer having the right of "unqualified exercise of their chieftainship". That required generous compensation for everyone.

History and bias
Waitangi Tribunal reports contain thousands of pages of "history", but they are nevertheless carefully constructed, persuasive arguments in which the history is woven around the tribunal's flawed interpretation of the treaty, so-called treaty principles, and seven broadly defined grievances to justify the payment of compensation. Historian Dr Giselle Byrnes called the tribunal's efforts a "noble, but ultimately flawed experiment". In her 2004 book *The Waitangi Tribunal and New Zealand History* she writes that tribunal reports "are deeply political and overwhelmingly focused on the present. It commits the ultimate faux pas of judging the past by the standards of the present." [71] While she supports the claims process, she pointed to the 1996 Taranaki report that said: "that this claim is just going to blow (the Government's fiscal-envelope policy) kind of thinking apart. It really tried to challenge that mentality that there should be a cap on treaty settlements." [72] Dr Byrnes, who left the Waitangi Tribunal after two years, warned that the tribunal

should make overtly clear its inherent bias, otherwise lay people reading tribunal reports will be misled.

Byrnes quoted criticism from historian W.H. Oliver who labelled the tribunal's use and misuse of the historical method as "presentist".

"The reports exemplify an instrumental but – because never explicitly avowed – elusive way of writing and using history [with] a historical mentality less concerned to recapture past reality than to embody present aspiration. [Thus there is] an instrumental presentism which is remarkably evidence free . . . shaped by a current political agenda." [73]

Joe Williams, who was Waitangi Tribunal chief judge in 2004, disagreed with the view that judging the past by the standards of the present was a flaw. He said the tribunal must assess the past by the standards of today, saying "as a truth and reconciliation body, the tribunal is required not merely to describe and understand the past, but also to judge it . . . We are there to describe, to understand and then judge. And it's from judgement that reconciliation comes." [74] His comment carried the implication that he was describing a kind of historical group process encounter session of the sort found in mental health counselling sessions even though nowhere in the Treaty of Waitangi Act is there reference to the tribunal being a "truth and reconciliation" body. But, as has already been stated, it is a type of kangaroo court that makes the rules as it goes.

An example of how history is woven around the tribunal's interpretation of the treaty, treaty principles, and seven broadly defined grievances to justify the payment of compensation may be seen in Chapter 16 of the Ngai Tahu Report 1991, in the analysis of eight Crown purchases of South Island land. The introduction to that chapter says:

"By 1864 Ngai Tahu were in a parlous, some might say pitiable condition. They were now an impoverished people largely confined on uneconomic patches of land, almost entirely isolated from mainstream European development, neglected by government at both central and provincial level, marginalised and struggling to survive both individually and as a people. Their *rangatiratanga* greatly diminished, their communal way of life and the cultural and spiritual values associated with it seriously undermined. As settlement steadily encroached on them from all sides, as land was progressively fenced and drained, as their access to *mahinga kai* steadily decreased, Ngai Tahu eked out a bare subsistence on land incapable of sustaining them. No wonder their voices came to be heard more and more in protest. Why did this happen? The short answer, as must by now be abundantly clear, is that the Crown failed, time and time again, to honour *the principles of the Treaty of Waitangi.*" [75]

A Native Land Court judge observed earlier in this chapter that Ngai Tahu people put themselves into poverty because they preferred to lease out their reserves rather than work on them and develop them and, when cash ran out, they went back to the government for more. The terms *"rangatiratanga"* and "principles of the Treaty of Waitangi" are reproduced in italic type to show how the argument has been wrapped around these concepts to justify compensation. The issue here is how the tribunal report writer has connected their poverty in 1864 with diminished "rangatiratanga" which uses the tribunal's post-1985 definition of "rangatiratanga" as meaning "chiefly authority" rather than "possession". The report also links Ngai Tahu's 1864 situation with the Crown's alleged failure "to honour the principles of the Treaty of Waitangi" that were dreamed up 122 years later, in 1986!!!

The fiscal envelope
In 1995 the Bolger National Government developed a "fiscal envelope" proposal that set a limit of $1 billion for the settlement of all historical claims. At a series of consultation meetings around the country Maori vehemently rejected such a limitation in advance of the extent of claims being fully known. The fiscal envelope concept was dropped after the 1996 general election.

Waikato's second settlement: money acknowledges the "crime"
Settlements began in a small way with the Waitomo Caves settlement in 1989. The Crown transferred land at the Waitomo Caves to the claimant group, subject to a lease, and provided a loan of $1 million. Next up was the 1992 commercial fisheries settlement of $170 million, discussed in Chapter 12. The Waikato-Tainui settlement of $170 million was the next biggie, and that included the "write the apology on a cheque" attitude where "the money is the acknowledgement by the Crown of their crime". This involved a substantial amount of land and a number of buildings, commercial properties, and leases. It included about 200 unimproved properties, plus another 200 improved properties. The list includes a polytech campus, Waikato University campus,

163

railway land, courthouses, Department of Corrections property, police stations, power stations, Crown forests, CoalCorp property, Electricity Corporation property, Ruakura AgResearch, Welfare properties, NZ Post properties and so on, that are leased by Crown entities for 31 years. Details of the ongoing rental income are not available, so we do not know the extent of the guaranteed and continuous flow of rent from the government. But isn't it nice in a time of recession to have a guaranteed rental income when there are so many commercial buildings unleased?

There was no reference to the earlier settlement of these grievances through the Waikato-Maniapoto Maori Claims Settlement Act 1946, which provided for the establishment of the Tainui Maori Trust Board to receive £5,000 a year in perpetuity plus a further £5,000 and £1,000 a year for 45 years. Having the Queen apologise in person riled royalists, who said that Prime Minister Jim Bolger should never have put the reigning monarch, as head of the Commonwealth, in the position of having to apologise to the descendants of those who fought against the Crown.

Clause 5 of the agreed history in the 1995 Waikato-Tainui settlement deed asserts that "all sources agree that the Tainui people never rebelled but were attacked by British troops in direct violation of Article 2 of the treaty". None of those claimed sources are cited. This is a blanket attribution disallowed even by Wikipedia and has no place in scholarly research yet there it remains, in a government deed of settlement, funded by the taxpayer. The Waitangi Tribunal argues that the Maori king movement was an authentic expression of "tino rangatiratanga" and not a challenge to the Queen's authority. These assertions appear to be latter-day fabrications apparently to justify the $170 million settlement.

Despite the fact that the main Waikato chief had not signed the treaty, the Maori and English official texts of the treaty are printed at the top of the Waikato-Tainui settlement deed, apparently to bring the settlement under the treaty. There is no consideration of the fact that Maori taking up arms against the government would be a breach of the treaty, if Waikato-Tainui in 1863 were under the terms of the treaty. There is no acceptance that the war led to loss of life on both sides. In the demand that the land taken must be returned and that money would be the acknowledgement of the "crime", there is no indication of whether taking up arms against the government would be considered a crime.

The Waikato-Tainui deed argues that the confiscations were a breach of the treaty, but Sir Apirana Ngata, a Ngati Porou leader who was the first Maori to graduate from a New Zealand university and who became M.P. for Eastern Maori, was clear that the land confiscations could not be objected to in light of the treaty. He wrote in 1922, "Some have said that these confiscations were wrong and that they contravened the articles of the Treaty of Waitangi. The Government placed in the hands of the Queen of England, the sovereignty and the authority to make laws. Some sections of the Maori people violated that authority. War arose from this and blood was spilled. The law came into operation and land was taken in payment. This itself is a Maori custom - revenge, plunder to avenge a wrong. It was their own chiefs who ceded that right to the Queen. The confiscations cannot therefore be objected to in the light of the Treaty." [76]

Ngai Tahu's fifth settlement

Ngai Tahu's fifth settlement in 1998 was based on 65 grievances: 11 for the Kemp purchase, 18 for the Banks Peninsula purchases, 10 for the Southland purchase, while six covered both the North Canterbury and Kaikoura purchases. Eleven grievances concerned the West Coast purchase, three involved Stewart Island, and a further three related to the Princes Street reserve in Dunedin. There was a grievance about perpetual leases, and one about access to resources, or *mahinga kai*. A single claim was filed and rejected for the Otago purchase. After sifting through Ngai Tahu's proliferating complaints detailed earlier, the Waitangi Tribunal concluded:

> "Ngai Tahu have certainly a sense of grievance about the paucity of payment they received for their land but then Ngai Tahu have always regarded the purchase price not as a properly assessed market value consideration in the European concept but rather as a deposit; a token, a gratuity.
> The Tribunal found that, in acquiring more than half the land mass of New Zealand from the tribe for £14,750, which left Ngai Tahu only 35,757 acres (14,470 ha), the Crown had acted unconscionably and in repeated breach of the Treaty, and its subsequent efforts to make good the loss were found to be 'few, extremely dilatory, and largely ineffectual'." [77]

Ngai Tahu's $170 million 1998 settlement included 63 commercial properties, 116 farms totalling 96,426 ha, 34 forests totalling 174,930 ha, the sale and leaseback of seven commercial properties, the right of first refusal to buy four major South Island airports and Timberlands West Coast, plus other properties. Because Ngai Tahu selected 34 forests as part of its settlement, it was eligible for Crown Forests Rental Trust rent from 1989, which led to a further $35 million payout in 2000. [78] I saw no mention of the earlier settlements in the deed.

"Cultural redress" appeared in the Ngai Tahu settlement, especially the vesting of Mount Cook in Ngai Tahu, that gifted it back to the Crown. Seventeen cultural redress sites were transferred to Ngai Tahu, "runanga" were appointed to hold and administer seven areas, historic reserves were created at seven areas, statutory acknowledgements and deeds of recognition were extended over 64 mountains, lakes, rivers, wetlands, and lagoons, 14 *"topuni"* (overlay of Ngai Tahu values) were created, as were 72 *"nohoanga"* camping areas, which are one-hectare sites on public land adjacent to rivers and lakes for use by Ngai Tahu members for 210 days each year, and from which, in a reversed version of the former whites-only policies of the southern United States and South Africa, non-Maori are excluded.

In the words of Dave Witherow, a trustee of Public Access New Zealand, writing in the *Otago Daily Times* at the time in an article entitled "Ngai Tahu deal is a swindle", the Department of Conservation have been "kneecapped through the imposition of 'protocols' designed to ensure maximum tribal interference at every point. The obvious intent is to provide Ngai Tahu with a degree of manipulation of public land far beyond its democratic entitlement." [79]

Ngai Tahu were also given ownership of effectively all of the country's greenstone. The Ngai Tahu (Pounamu) Vesting Act 1997 gave Ngai Tahu all greenstone (pounmau) in "their traditional area" and in parts of the sea adjacent to that area. [80] Pounamu includes bowenite, nephrite, and serpentine. The tribe vigorously assert their rights over this formerly publicly owned asset.

Thirty-nine pieces of distinctive tahutahi (snowflake) jade seized by police from a Franz Josef bookshop in 2011 had to be returned to Ngai Tahu. [81] David Saxton and his son, Morgan, who later died in a helicopter crash, were convicted of stealing "Ngai Tahu's" pounamu and were ordered to pay $300,000 in reparation. [82] This is the type of thing that happens when, as is so often the case in Treaty settlements, an asset that has been owned and enjoyed by the public since 1840 is privatised to a small group of people on a racial basis – in Ngai Tahu's case largely people of only one-eight and one-sixteenth Maori blood who have not lived in a tribal structure for several generations.

Ngai Tahu opted for forestry ownership as a part of their settlement, and in 2009 this created another opportunity for the tribe when the National Party led government wanted the Maori Party's five votes to pass its amended Emissions Trading Scheme. Ngai Tahu claimed that the scheme would reduce the value of their forests and, in their usual bullying way, threatened court action. Despite legal advice that the government should reject a bid for compensation, the government gave Ngai Tahu and four other tribes the right to carbon credits for forestry on more than 35,000 hectares of Crown conservation land for 70 years.

$126.5 million more for Taranaki tribes

Re-opening the Taranaki claims, the Waitangi Tribunal argued that the Taranaki grievance stood "on two major foundations, land deprivation and disempowerment, with the latter being the main." [83] Despite a warning by Maori in 1860 that "the war is not a struggle of the Maori with the pakeha; it is not a war with the missionary; it is not a war with the magistrate; it is a war of the King with the Queen" [84] - in other words a war of sovereignty, the tribunal in the Taranaki Report blatantly sides with those who chose to resist British sovereignty and blames the colonial government for confiscations of Taranaki land and all subsequent woes. The report fails to give sufficient weight to the numerous attempts by the colonial government to meet anti-government Maori demands, and fails to call to account Wiremu Kingi's duplicity and his campaign to wage war on the white settlers using Taranaki as the battleground.

Since 1985 five Taranaki tribes have received at least $126.5million in financial redress.

Ngati Tama is a northern Taranaki tribe claiming 1,000 members, some of whose ancestors devastated the Chatham Islands Moriori people in 1835. The tribe, which had 74,000 acres (29,946 ha) of land confiscated and later supported Te Whiti's campaign of passive resistance at Parihaka, received $14.5 million in cash in 2003.

Ngati Ruanui of Taranaki claim 4,000 members, whose ancestors resisted selling land, particularly the blocks at Waitara and Waitotara, and fought against the government, received $41 million in 2003.

Ngaa Rauru Kiitahi, a tribe claiming 3,000 members, whose district in 1840 was at the mouth of the Wanganui River and whose claims relate to lands sold to the New Zealand Company in 1839 and to land confiscated in 1863, received $31 million in 2005.

Ngati Mutunga (1,300 members, some of whose ancestors also devastated the Chatham Islands Moriori in 1835 while others fought against the government at Waitara) received $14.9 million in 2006.

Taranaki Whanui ki Te Upoko o Te Ika, a Wellington-based collective claiming 17,000 members that comprises people of a number of Taranaki iwi, received $25,025,000 cash plus interest in 2009.

Deadline set for historical claims

The Clark Labour-led government set a deadline for historical claims for midnight September 1, 2008 - already 24 years after the "clever" Geoffrey Palmer opined that the whole process would be over in ten years. The pace of claims rose from five or six a month in the first part of 2008, to 800 in August, with 600 in the 48 hours preceding the deadline. People filing a claim needed only to show that they were of Maori descent and note the historical grievance allegedly suffered. More than 1,100 new historical claims or amendments to claims were registered by the deadline, bringing the total to 2,034 by June 2009. [85]

Settlement cash a mixed blessing

Unfortunately for Waikato-Tainui, internal bickering followed the sudden influx of prosperity in 1995, between the revered 155-year-old Kingitanga movement, embodied by the then Maori "queen", Dame Te Atairangikaahu, and new democratic forces within the tribe. In five years the tribe's $245 million asset base had been eroded by 16 per cent, and the tribe struggled with a $24 million debt. Details of the tribe's woes came with news of an $8.6 million debt that forced the sale of the Auckland Warriors rugby league club into which Tainui had invested $6.27 million. [86]

Bickering continued between the new Maori "king", Tuheitia Paki, the eldest son of the late Dame Te Atairangikaahu, and members of the tribe's parliament, Te Kauhanganui, who questioned his use of tribal funds and his choice of company directors.

Otherwise, the tribe's legal entity, Waikato-Tainui Te Kauhanganui Incorporated, manages and distributes income for the collective benefit of approximately 57,000 registered Waikato-Tainui tribal members, for education, health and well-being, marae, social and cultural development. Waikato-Tainui's tribal parliament, Te Kauhanganui, is

168

the sole trustee of the tribal group and has over 190 members - representing 68 marae associated with the Waikato Raupatu Claims settlement. In the tribe's 2010-2011 report, Tainui Group Holdings and Waikato Tainui Fisheries appear to have shaken off past financial woes since the tribe's companies reported a 24 per cent growth in those holdings and stated aims to have assets worth $1 billion by the start of the next decade.[87]

Fears were expressed that treaty settlement money was being frittered away. Wellington Maori were split over Port Nicholson block money after $3 million was lost in 2011.[88] Taranaki tribe Ngati Tama did worse when it lost all of its $14.5 million payout in failed investments, the biggest of which was more than $12.5 million with Australian based computer software company My Virtual Home Ltd, which went into liquidation with no assets. Other investments included $4.39 million with Tu Ere Fishing Ltd that was dissolved, and $1.19 million with property investment company Open Group Ltd which had no estimated value when Ngati Tama reported the loss.[89]

A grievance industry

The settlements process has created a new and distinct industry. Not only are there more than 120 government workers operating the Waitangi Tribunal and Office of Treaty Settlements, there is a whole host of others contracted to perform various tasks. Lawyers, researchers, *iwi* representatives, and meeting organisers for the 2008 "Treelords" deal racked up $57 million in fees and expenses in the deal, masterminded by the then Treaty Minster Michael Cullen, which transferred ownership of central North Island forests to nine tribes. Of this, an incredible $20 million went to tribal representatives to meet and negotiate among themselves! Part of the $57 million went to lawyers and consultants. Up to $10 million was paid in fees to finalise the deal. The amounts involved prompted Maori rights lawyer, Annette Sykes, to say "The brown bureaucracy of the Maori world should be held accountable for the sort of money the Central North Island deal facilitators earned. . . . We're not talking about money from the Crown here either. This is purely Crown Forestry Rental Trust money".[90]

More proof that treaty claims have become a multi-million dollar industry for lawyers appeared in a *Dominion Post* report on 9th January, 2013, which said that claims generated $79 million in legal aid since 2006. Justice Department figures detailed the millions of dollars of

169

taxpayer money paid out each year to help Maori groups seek compensation for alleged historical treaty breaches. Unlike civil or criminal cases, claimants can obtain legal aid regardless of their financial circumstances. Dame Margaret Bazley's review of legal aid found that, of the 75 most expensive cases in the 2008-09 year, 41 percent were for treaty claims.[91]

Tribunal inquiry bias alleged

Ngai Tahu became the paragon of commercial expertise but remains dogged by criticism of the legitimacy of its settlement. Christchurch researcher, Denis Hampton, submitted in 1998 that the Crown, representing the taxpayers of New Zealand, was at best half-hearted in presenting its case before the Waitangi Tribunal. The Crown had difficulty attracting historians to research the case while the well-financed claimants' historians had expertise and were well-prepared, he wrote. The evidence of the Crown's first witness was withdrawn. Another Crown witness involved claimants in his research. At least two Crown witnesses had inappropriate expertise. Crown witnesses failed to submit important evidence, mostly to do with allegations that Ngai Tahu preferred to lease out rather than work their land. Crown witnesses inexplicably were instructed to refrain from acting as advocates for the Crown! Ngai Tahu troubles were wholly blamed on Crown misdeeds without reference to the economic depression before 1900 that made life difficult for Maori and non-Maori alike. Journalist Brian Priestley, hired to do publicity for Ngai Tahu, commented that "it would be hard to imagine any public body less well organised to get at the truth."[92]

Treaty issues commentator, Amy Brooke, stressed that Justice Minister Doug Graham told the Maori Affairs select committee virtually to ignore the nearly 400 submissions on the Ngai Tahu settlement Bill since it had already been signed! The public appears unaware that once a treaty negotiations minister signs a settlement with tribal claimants, a binding contract is created, and the subsequent passage of legislation to release funding is a rubber-stamping exercise. Crown lawyers at the Ngai Tahu tribunal hearing were kneecapped by being told that Ngai Tahu would not be cross-examined because confrontation "was not the Maori way".[93] In fact, Ngai Tahu mastered the art of aggressive litigation, according to the tribe's former chief counsel Christopher Finlayson, now the Treaty Negotiations Minister. In an interview with the *Sunday Star-Times*, Finlayson said: "I used to love going to the

170

office in the morning when we were suing the Crown. . . .Ngai Tahu mastered the art of aggressive litigation, whether it was suing the Waitangi Tribunal and Doug Graham or the Director-General of Conservation. It was 'take no prisoners'." [94]

Ngai Tahu leaders appear to feel the need to justify their settlement since they continue to argue that they settled cheaply. Chairman Mark Solomon told Q&A television current affairs programme on June 6, 2010, that: "There was an exercise done by Treasury which took the lands that Ngai Tahu had been dispossessed of or hadn't been awarded in reserves like they should have, and they gave it a 1988 value. Treasury stood before the Waitangi Tribunal and stated that Ngai Tahu's loss was between 12 and 15 billion dollars. We used the same documentation with our external advisors, Credit Suisse First Boston, who stood in front of the tribunal and said we absolutely disagree, the figure of loss to Ngai Tahu is between 18 and 20 billion." [95] Please remember that, when the Crown bought land from Ngai Tahu, the South Island was virtually empty waste lands with fewer than 2,000 people. In fact, its chiefs, the so-called "owners", had tried to sell most of it prior to 1840 for much less than the Crown paid for it.

Treasury confirmed there were confidential discussions with Ngai Tahu about land lost but said that details were too sensitive for release since they may have an impact on other negotiations. Upon receiving his knighthood in December, 2012, Solomon's first comment was that Ngai Tahu's settlement "accounted for about 1.5 percent of what the tribe had lost".[96] Does this mean that, despite the final settlements and top-ups, the Ngai Tahu grievance remains not settled? Why does Solomon persist in lamenting the land the tribe lost when his forebears sold it, in some cases on several occasions? Well, if you have scored a settlement on dodgy grounds, you would have to keep defending it with apparently preposterous statements, wouldn't you?

Relativity clauses (Top-ups)

The government agreed to make further payments to maintain the real value of Ngai Tahu's and Waikato-Tainui's settlements as a proportion of all treaty settlements. The $1 billion is in 1994 dollars and that equates to around $1.5 billion in 2012 dollars. The 1995 Waikato-Tainui $170 million settlement was described as "17 percent" of the theoretical $1 billion, and the Ngai Tahu deal 16.1 percent. Persistent questioning got the Crown and Ngai Tahu to confirm that the relativity clause was triggered for the year ended June 30, 2012. The government calculated that the amount payable to Ngai Tahu was $45.6 million, or $68.5 million when adjusted for inflation. And the amount for Waikato Tainui would be $70 million.[94] Who expected Waikato-Tainui spokesman Tukoroirangi Morgan to say that the tribe would accept the $70 million cash payment while adding that the tribe would demand a significantly larger sum, believed to be in excess of $120 million?[97] These top-ups are nothing more than an undeserved and unearned bonus for these two greedy and opportunistic tribes. They have already been compensated in every possible way and yet still have their hand out for more – based on the total of what other tribes might get.

In the interests of taxpayer integrity an enquiry is needed into these unnecessary "top-ups". Although the Crown has agreed to them that doesn't mean to say that they must be paid. Why not have an enquiry and link these top-ups to the non-payment of tax by the business arms of these two tribes? Ask them to forfeit the "top-up" at this time of record government deficits and, upon their (almost certain) refusal, take away their tax-free status, making it retrospective to the time of their original settlements so that the amount of tax that they would have to pay on their profits of the previous twenty or so years would exceed their top-up. That way the taxpayer would get back the amount of the top-up and probably more. There is a general presumption against retrospective taxation but in this case it would seem eminently appropriate.

Conclusion

This chapter provides evidence that claimants in a number of major settlements have, with help from the Waitangi Tribunal, twisted history to justify further multi-million dollar payments. Ignorance of our brief history, even at the highest levels of government, has enabled these claims to slide through without scrutiny or question. Nine grievances listed in 1882 ballooned to 2,034 in 2009, after a decision by the Lange Labour government that allowed investigation of claims all the way back to 1840. It is repugnant that in a democracy a handful of unelected Waitangi Tribunal members should have the exclusive authority to interpret the treaty, and that they continue to do so in a way that undermines the meaning and intent of the treaty so as to justify the division of assets and power along racial lines. Tribunal reports blame the colonial government for every conceivable difficulty that Maori experienced since 1840, despite overwhelming evidence that points to

172

Maori organised and armed resistance. Far from being innocent victims, Waikato tribes fought in Taranaki, drove settlers from the King Country, and refused to acknowledge the sovereignty that was ceded at Waitangi some 20 years earlier. In the South Island, there was neither armed conflict nor confiscation. Nevertheless, Ngai Tahu complained for 150 years and achieved five settlements with top-ups agreed. Their complaints may be traced to disagreements over boundaries and reserves in one transaction between a willing buyer and an equally willing seller. The evidence shows considerable effort by the colonial government to honour agreements. Were Ngai Tahu wronged or did they find that it was more profitable to keep asking for more?

The current round of settlements started with an attempt to get Maori protest off the streets and became mixed up with race-based affirmative action. The fact that Maori activists still regularly take protests to the street, to the marae at Waitangi, and to beaches in the Far North, shows that generous treaty settlements have not stopped protest, and possibly may have encouraged more. Although it was claimed that the settlements would promote reconciliation, racial ill-feeling appears higher now than it was before the Fourth Labour Government so foolishly allowed claims back to 1840. Treaty settlements have re-written history, the factual basis of which is open to serious challenge. Most grievances had been settled by 1960 on a full-and-final basis and that should have been the end of the story.

Waitangi Tribunal reports spin the details of history into finely crafted arguments supporting compensation. In 2004, historian Michael Bassett, then a sitting Waitangi Tribunal member who earlier was a Cabinet Minister in the Lange Labour Government that set the course for the latest round of treaty settlements, wrote in the *Dominion*r: "It is surely time to re-examine the tribunal's usefulness. The captivity of crusading historians and those who have built careers out of sowing, then farming, grievances, the current body has passed its sell-by date. There is enough evidence to settle all outstanding historical grievances quickly. That process should be completed. What the future relevance of the treaty might then be requires further public debate. That issue involves all of us, not just the Waitangi industry's vested interests." [98]

WELLINGTON SETTLEMENTS AND CONSEQUENCES

John Robinson

From time to time we read of a Treaty settlement somewhere across the country with large sums handed over to a Maori group, supposedly for some past wrong. The process that started some years ago with the intention of settling the few remaining genuine property claims, with no thought of alienation of the commons (beaches and seas, national parks, and the like), has spiralled out of control. Maori now lay claim to the water and air, to special control of local government and separate government in a break-up of the nation. This is an application of the mantra of Animal Farm, "all animals are equal but some animals are more equal than others".

At a national hui at Tuarangawaewae in Ngaruawahia united groups, including the Iwi Leaders Group, the New Zealand Maori Council, the Kingitanga, and *iwi* from around the nation, heard Maori "King" Tuheitia declare "We have always owned the water!" [1] In addition to the well-advanced desire for beaches and seas, rivers and lakes, Ngati Kahungunu have extended the wish list with a claim over underground water in the Hawkes Bay aquifer[2]. Ngati Puhi have launched a claim over the commercial use of wind.[3] The Ngati Uenukukopako iwi has claimed the airspace over Rotorua Airport, which "could give them control over operating hours, or the power to impose a curfew".[4] Claims cover all parts of the natural world, all of creation.

National parks are going. A deal with Tuhoe will "wrest the pristine Te Urewera National Park out of Crown ownership", to be governed initially by "a board comprising Crown and Ngai Tuhoe nominees". After a five-year review, Tuhoe hope that full control will be handed over to them – as will no doubt happen. The deal also includes *mana motuhake*, or self government – including a target of Tuhoe control "over the delivery of government and iwi services to its communities and peoples." [5] The suggestion for a separate Maori justice system has been on the table since 1988.[6] Here is the recipe for a Bantustan-style break-up of the nation.

The settlement process is there to service only Maori; the Waitangi Tribunal may only consider a claim by a Maori and not a "pakeha" who may have a legitimate historical or modern claim. One such case is that of Allan Titford from Northland who was run off his legitimately purchased and owned farm by local Maori. He applied to the Tribunal, but was denied the opportunity of taking his case, because he is not a Maori.[7]

There was no talk in the Treaty of Waitangi of such separation or of partnership but rather an expression of unity and equality, an expression of Hobson's proclamation, "Now we are one people." The chiefs had promised to "cede absolutely to the Queen of England for ever the Government of all of their lands" and in return all Maori were promised "all the rights and privileges of British subjects", equally with all other New Zealanders.[8] British law was to apply to all.

Surely this division of the nation, in contradiction to the Treaty, is our business. These are our commons, our coast and rivers, our town belt and national parks, our councils, our moneys paid in taxes to our government. The very form of our governance that is challenged is our affair. Yet so often it is only when it comes to our neighbourhood and we have direct experience of the consequences that we realise what is going on and think to ask how this spreading division of our country and racial differentiation could be coming about. I live in Wellington, in Island Bay. I walk the Town Belt, I walk and swim the coast and have rowed, canoed and swum to the island in the bay, Taputeranga. This is my land and my community. I have taken an interest in local history and written an article for the South Coast Historical Society about the 1821 and 1827 battles on Taputeranga (the island in the Bay) when the permanent residents, Ngati Ira, were killed and driven out by Ngati Toa and their allies.

When in 2009 I learned that Ngati Toa claimed ownership and control over this public estate, I decided to find out what was going on, and how such an outrageous claim could be taken seriously. I have subsequently dealt with aspects of this local claim in two recent publications, in chapters "A case study: Ngati Toa" [9] and "The new apartheid society".[10]

The settlement process was developed in discussions involving Maori only – twelve regional *hui*, each on a marae, and a national hui in the Beehive. Other New Zealanders played no part, with only Maori invited to send representatives to the national *hui*.[11] Other New Zealanders were shut out from the first.

The written guidelines require that the first step, to be completed before negotiations proper begin, must be to establish the facts and

175

ascertain the historical basis for the claim. That "further historical research" is often funded by the Crown Forestry Trust for the claimants, and is strongly biased in their favour – neither open nor balanced. This is no way to establish historical facts, and a number of historians have been highly critical of that legalistic approach to the rewriting of history, creating "counterfactual" history, "a type of history created in an atmosphere ... clouded with retrospective recrimination." [12] History is now written to support grievance and to force payments from a willing government.

In the local settlement that affects my community even that basic requirement was broken. The verification and the historical account were not completed when an offer was made to Ngati Toa, in 2009. It still did not exist as late as March, 2012, when the Minister, Christopher Finlayson, informed me that this was still "under negotiation".

During the years when my local commons were negotiated off into private hands, along with much property and public funds, I remained in the dark and ignorant of the grievances claimed in the non-existent historical account. The affair was said to be between the iwi and the Crown alone. It actually has nothing to do with the Crown – with the Queen or the Governor General. It is the Government, elected by us all and supposedly representing us all, acting through one man alone, the Minister of Treaty Settlements. Once Cabinet agrees with a draft settlement, it is rubber-stamped by a subservient Parliamentary majority, in a Government dependent on the votes of its Maori Party allies. Thus iwi "negotiate" with a body that they control, dividing up our land as if we don't belong here any more, as if our existence is irrelevant. It is only when a Treaty settlement Bill is introduced into Parliament, and referred to a select committee – here the Maori Affairs Committee, for this is considered a matter for Maori only and not all New Zealanders – does the public have an opportunity to make submissions. [13] The manner in which such submissions are treated is so derisory that in 2011 Finlayson suggested changes to Parliament's rules to fast-track more than 20 settlements, "because they stem from legal agreements which are already entered into". [14]

A fox is in charge of the hen house. Christopher Finlayson is a rogue minister apparently totally committed to the cause of separate identity. When he was a lawyer (at Bell Gully) acting for Ngai Tahu in their Treaty claim, he spent years fighting for Ngai Tahu against the government through a series of high-profile court battles. Since becoming Minister of Treaty Settlements, Finlayson has enthusiastically set about making a name for himself by handing out the national family silver to his mates, so as to be remembered as the man who signed a multitude of costly Treaty settlements.

The government is thus trying to reverse the outcome of the nineteenth century fighting (between 1840 and 1885) in which so many New Zealanders – colonial militia, settlers murdered in their homes and kaupapa (friendly Maori) – shed their blood in defence of both the Treaty of Waitangi and a united, non-racial New Zealand. They have no mandate to do this.

In September, 2012, the agreement with Ngati Toa was initialled and at last the Deed of Settlement, containing the Historical Account that should have preceded the settlement, was available.[15]

Ngati Toa claim *whenua* (rights to the land) over a considerable area.

"Following their migrations south from Kawhia in the 1820s Ngati Toa Rangatira had established a powerful position in the Cook Strait region. Their position was based on military victories and relationships with other tribal groups, and also on trade with Europeans."[16]

Their *rohe* (territory) covered much of the south of the North Island and the northern part of the South Island.

"According to Ngati Toa Rangatira tradition the northern most point of the Ngati Toa Rangatira *rohe* is Whangaehu; in the North Island it extends eastwards to Turakirae Heads and encompasses Te Moana o Raukawa. In the South Island, the Ngati Toa Rangatira *rohe* includes all of Te Tau Ihu; its southernmost point on the West Coast is the outlet of the Arahura River and Kaikoura on the Eastern Coast."[17]

This *rohe* was gained by the military victories of *taua* (war parties), for the most part in the two decades before the Treaty of Waitangi brought a promise of peace. The claim was based on *take raupatu* – the conquest, subjugation and displacement of the original occupants. Since those rights are to be honoured today, and any loss is to be recompensed, they must be considered carefully, and not just passed over lightly as in the historic account, which glosses over awkward questions, thus committing a lie of omission.

What were they like, those *taua*, the conquest on which Ngati Toa base their *rohe* and many claims? The answer is found in the writings of Te Rauparaha's son, Tamihana Te Rauparaha.[18]

177

• At Mokau: "The Ngati Tama cut up the bodies of the slain and carried them to their *pa* to be cooked, as was the Maori custom." (page 19).

• At Wairau: "About 500 were killed in the battle, four *pas* were captured and a thousand women and children were slain." (pages 30, 32)

• At Rangitikei: "Three *pas* were captured and 200 men and 800 women and children were killed, while others were brought to Kapiti for slaves." (page 33)

• At Akaroa: "Two hundred men were killed and perhaps 300 or 400 women and children; many were also brought aboard the ships as slaves. Heaps of men were left dead ashore." (page 41)

• At Whakapuaka, near Kaiawa: "Some of the men were spared but about 200 were killed, as well as 600 women and children. The killing continued as they moved along the coast to Whakatu (Nelson), Waimea, Motueka and Taitapu. The people were decimated, with the remnants being left as slaves ..." (page 44)

• At Kaikoura: "What a wonderful war party! Everywhere lay dead Ngai Tahu. About 500 men were killed and 800 women and children." (page 49)

• At Wanganui: "The *pa* was captured and its people killed as they tried to escape. The survivors slept out in the bush and were hunted and killed by the war party for the next four days. Probably a thousand people were killed and many were taken prisoner." (page 56)

The killing in my neighbourhood at Taputeranga does not even warrant a mention, being just one of a multitude of attacks on Maori across the whole area. In these accounts the focus is on chiefs while slaves, women and children are numbers only, of lesser account in Maori culture. Ngati Toa wish to inherit grievance but refuse to acknowledge the inheritance of responsibility for that widespread mayhem.

One grievance was that "the Crown's actions were in breach of the Treaty of Waitangi in respect of ... Crown policies, to weaken the influence of Ngati Toa Rangatira and their chiefs".[19] In fact the reduction of the power of chiefs was a promise of the Treaty. The wish of the northern chiefs who wrote to the British Crown in 1831 and 1835, and who signed the Treaty in 1840, was for a central authority to put an end to the bloodshed by war parties led by independent warrior chiefs.[20]

The principal chief of Ngati Toa, and the most feared warrior chief of them all, was Te Rauparaha, who had led the many *taua* in the killing

178

described above. He was undoubtedly a bloodthirsty warrior, a great general and a master tactician. Yet the removal of this key warrior chief from the scene at a crucial time, when Governor Grey was endeavouring to bring peace to the Wellington region, is also made a "grievance" and is said to be in breach of the Treaty of Waitangi, with the claim that "this campaign included an unjustified and spurious declaration of martial law, the illegal capture of Te Rauparaha and others ..." [21]

Te Rauparaha was a wily warrior, following the rule that "all's fair in love and war", and not to be trusted. After all, trickery and deceit are a part of warfare. Here are two examples of his deceptions.

At Akaroa Te Rauparaha had the captain invite the Ngai Tahu chief Tamaiharanui on board the *Elizabeth*, where he was taken captive, while the 30 men who were with him were killed. Tamaiharanui and his wife killed their daughter to prevent her being made a slave. On arrival at Kapiti, "they were cut open and their blood drunk" in a horrible death. [22]

At the *pa* of Onawe at Akaroa, "Te Rauparaha thought of a cunning scheme that might bring about a speedy capture. He would send prisoners into the *pa* to tell the defenders that they would not be killed if they made peace. When Te Rauparaha explained his idea to the other chiefs most of them agreed, so chiefs of rank who had been captured at Kaiapohia were sent into the *pa* to tell the people that all was well.... Then someone called out the pre-arranged signal, and grimaces were made and eyes rolled in defiance as the whole war party charged into the *pa*, which was soon captured. Only those who resisted were killed; all the others were taken prisoner." [23]

Although he had twice signed the Treaty of Waitangi, Te Rauparaha had no intention of keeping his word, as shown in these comments made in June and July 1843, shortly after the killing at Wairau. [24]

He said, "I am the king of all this land. I have lived a king, and I will die a king, with my *meri* in my hand. Go! I am no beggar! Rauperaha will fight the soldiers of the Queen when they come, with his own hands and his own name. . .. As for Wikitoria, never mind that woman. ...Who is she that she should send her books and her constables after me? What have I to do with her? She may be Queen over the White people; I am the king of the Maori! If she chooses to have war, let her send me word, and I will stand up against her soldiers."

Wakefield then reported "I asked him, whether he had not signed a paper to say the Queen was his chief, when Mr Williams brought it to him, and also on board the man-of-war? He turned round sharply and said, 'Yes! what of that? They gave me a blanket for it. I am still a chief just the same. I am Rauperaha! Give me another blanket tomorrow, and I will sign it again. What is there in writing?'

Thus one of the most powerful of the 512 chiefs spoke of the much vaunted Treaty of Waitangi, which he had signed twice according to all accounts."

In 1846, when fighting had broken out in the Hutt, Governor Grey received a report of a letter bearing Te Rauparaha's signature, addressed to the inland and up-river natives of the Wanganui tribes, urgently inviting them to join their chief Te Mamaku and his ally Te Rangihaeata in the campaign against the European settlements. Grey then ordered the capture of Te Rauparaha – surely a sensible action as the rebellion threatened to spread.[25] "It was undesirable that they should be at large, and the cause of peace was certainly advanced by their capture." [26] There was a war of rebellion going on in which both soldiers and civilians were being killed.

Had Te Rauparaha been put on trial, it would have created more trouble and he would have had worse conditions if he was held in a common gaol. Instead, "Te Rauparaha was well treated; he was more a guest than a prisoner." [27] Te Rauparaha understood this, and had no complaint with his captivity. As Bishop Octavius Hadfield, who was generally sympathetic to Maori interests, noted: "Some years later Sir George Grey who had ascertained that his sympathy with his nephew,Te Rangihaeata, who was in open rebellion, had become dangerous, apprehended and detained him on board a man-of-war. He did not resent this, as he knew it had saved him and his people from trouble." [28]

Te Rauparaha and Te Rangihaeata had continued their aggressive actions after 1840, following Maori traditional ways, in contravention of the Treaty. At Wairau in 1843 they had burned down a hut belonging to a member of the surveying team and then resisted a police contingent – the lawful authorities under the terms of the Treaty. As Sir Apirana Ngata stated so clearly, "The main purport was the transferring of the authority of the Maori chiefs for making laws",[29] and the task of those police was to uphold those national laws. Just who fired the first shot in the resultant struggle is unclear. There is no doubt however that Maori executed eleven helpless captives, as a customary act of revenge (utu) for those Maori earlier killed.[30] The dead included a Nelson police magistrate, the Nelson chief constable, two constables and seven special constables. It is offensive that Government should compensate Ngai Toa for the treatment of Te Rauparaha and Te Rangihaeata in the 19th century - murderers of policemen - by giving their descendants the right to buy land now occupied by the Police College, Wellington central police station, and police stations at Upper Hutt, Lower Hutt and Porirua.[31] Such legal chicanery is only possible in a travesty of justice carried out behind closed doors.

The only people with any opportunity to raise questions have been the other powerful Wellington iwi, Te Atiawa and related tribes. A group of ten individuals led by Professor Sir Ralph Heberley Ngatata Love (the Port Nicholson Block Claims Team) filed a claim to the Waitangi Tribunal "on behalf of Taranaki *whanui* regarding the proposed comprehensive settlement of the Ngati Toa Rangatira historical claims with the Wellington region." [32] This grouping was identified as "Te Atiawa, Taranaki, Ngati Ruanui Ngati Tama and other iwi from the Taranaki region, for example Ngati Mutunga", who "had combined collectively to negotiate their claims under the general banner of Taranaki Whanui ki Te Upoko o Te Ika (Taranaki *whanui*)."

This group raised many issues with the proposed settlement, including a desire to protect their own special position.

"17.4 The grant of such properties and rights denigrates and reduces the *mana* of the Taranaki Whanui in Whanganui a Tara and erodes its already reduced position in the City of Wellington, the City of Lower Hutt and the City of Upper Hutt by giving Ngati Toa a standing beyond that recognised by the Waitangi Tribunal in the Report."

Unlike a non-Maori such as myself, they were able to raise the question of the island, Taputeranga, in Island Bay.

"22. Tapu Te Ranga island is part of the historic Taranaki Whanui traditional lands. The Crown is offering this Taranaki Whanui island as a gift to Ngati Toa, subject to the approval of Wellington City Council. Such an offering is a breach of the Treaty of Waitangi because the Island is not for the Crown (or Wellington City Council at the behest of the Crown) to gift to any *iwi* without *ahi ka* standing in the Port Nicholson Block and within the Island precincts in particular."

These Taranaki *iwi* laid claim to priority within Wellington in the section concerning "Occupation, rights and use of the land and resources".

"The traditional Maori occupation and use of the region was extensive. Archaeological evidence of this is still being discovered.

Occupation patterns changed over time with the earliest people choosing strategic locations for fortified *pa* not too distant from the key food resources of both the ocean and the forests with fish and birds a key source of protein supplemented by marine mammals such as seals and whales.

Those who were in occupation of the Port Nicholson Block when the Treaty of Waitangi was signed and whose rights had been confirmed in *tikanga* Maori through *raupatu* or conquest and *ahi roa* were Te Atiawa, Taranaki, Ngati Ruanui and Ngati Tama.

Based on the foregoing and by virtue of our association with the Port Nicholson Block since well before 1840, Taranaki Whanui ki Te Upoko o Te Ika assert *mana whenua* over the Port Nicholson Block."

There is sleight of hand here, a blurring of history. The extensive traditional occupation was by Ngati Ira and Ngati Tara, who were driven out in the bloody attacks of the 1820s. Ngati Toa, led by Te Rauparaha, had fought and conquered much of the land around Wellington, and raided across Cook Strait. Remarkably, the protection of other Maori and European settlers by the colonial government (as called for by the Treaty) by putting an end to that power to wage war is to be compensated by a $10 million payment to Ngati Toa for "loss of marine empire", which is simply a code for the right to take a fleet of canoes across Cook Strait in order to kill and eat the South Island Maori, as well as to prey on European shipping.

"Innumerable accounts have been related to me of Te Rauparaha's treachery ... in his intercourse with white whalers and traders and the shipping in the strait, he had universally distinguished himself by the same qualities." wrote Travers in *The Stiring Times of Te Rauparaha.*[33]

Te Atiawa were allies who were left in occupation of the Wellington city area. These two arguing *iwi*, and former allies, were latecomers to the Wellington region, and it is stretching things a bit to refer to 1830 as "well before 1840" when their occupation was for only around ten years before land sales began. The former inhabitants are forgotten, and the current inhabitants – of all ethnicities – are ignored.

Who are these people, these two privileged peoples? Despite their many claims on properties in Wellington, few Ngati Toa live there. Those 844 who identified as Ngati Toa in the 2006 census make up 1.53% of Wellington Maori, only 0.12% of the Wellington population.

The *manua whenua iwi*, who are recognised by the Wellington City Council, and given an important role in governing the Town Belt, are Te

182

Atiawa, Taranaki, Ngati Ruanui and Ngati Tama. These *iwi* together make up 8.1% of Maori, just 0.63% of the city's population. This is a minority of a minority. These 543 Te Atiawa, 144 Taranaki, 267 Ngati Ruanui and 30 Ngati Tama will not in reality choose the representatives to co-govern the Town Belt. That decision will be made by the controlling elites, many of whom live outside the city.[34]

Add the two groups together and these privileged few in these two *iwi* groups are 0.75% of the Wellington population – just one in 133. Meanwhile other Maori, including descendants of the defeated pre-1820 *iwi* and those who have moved to Wellington in the past 172 years from other parts of New Zealand, are grouped together with those of all other ethnicities as second-class citizens.

Settlement money is not equally divided amongst *iwi* members. The provision of considerable sums in settlement payments has resulted in the growth of "neotribal capitalism" and the dominance of a tribal elite, similar to the chiefs of traditional Maori culture.[35] As has become evident here in Wellington, benefits are not always for the ordinary members. The *Dominion Post* has reported a series of problems with various transactions.

•   The Serious Fraud Office is investigating the Wellington Tenths Trust over possible unlawful payments and transactions. This includes a $1.02 million payment into a joint account of Ngatata (Ralph) Love and his partner Lorraine Skiffington. On the same day that a ground lease of Pipitea House was signed, Skiffington's company, Pipitea House Developments, had signed an agreement to receive $3 million for consultancy services that Judge Kos described as "opaque", and that what she did for the money was "vague". The Tenths Trust business manager Keith Hindle and other senior members of the Tenth Trust community knew nothing about the deal between Pipitea Street Ltd and Skiffington. Love then stood down from all his positions representing Maori.[36]

•   The Serious Fraud Office had also received a complaint concerning the use of some of the $24.7 million Port Nicholson Block Treaty settlement for construction of Wellington's waterfront *wharewaka* building, claiming that due process was not followed and that the *wharewaka* "is a commercially run conference centre, café, and corporate catering kitchen.....in which Taranaki Whanui have no property or other financial interest." A Waiwhetu-based Atiawa faction had warned that the settlement trust was losing money and the proceeds could be squandered in ten years at the current rate.[37]

• Sir Peter Jackson's plans to build a world-class film museum in Shelly Bay, on land that has recently been given to the Tenths Trust, were scuppered when Skiffington sought $750,000 in consultancy fees to help secure the land. Jackson and partner Fran Walsh chose not to sign when presented with the proposed consultancy deal.[38]

• Sir Ngatata Love offered to sell Wellington railway station to a would-be casino developer as his partner Lorraine Skiffington sought a $35 million consultancy deal on the same development. Ms Skiffington proposed that, for her role in the development of a "major landmark hotel, convention and entertainment centre" at the railway station, she be paid: a $4 million signing fee, $7 million to secure ownership of the railway station, social hall and adjoining land on Waterloo Quay, a two-year "operational budget" of $9 million including $1.125 million on signing, $7 million to be paid directly to her for the "transfer of intellectual property", $8 million for securing air rights above the station, including $2 million up front. The Port Nicholson Block Settlement Trust had acquired the right to buy the railway station in 2009, as part of a Treaty of Waitangi settlement with the Crown.[39]

These examples demonstrate that, when some person or group has a controlling stake in properties or goods, agreement for action by their "partners" may come at a price. Soon Ngati Toa will have more of that power. One can but wonder at the demands to be met when Ngati Toa's maritime empire is recognised, with Ngati Toa – as *kaitiaki* (guardians) of Cook Strait and the coastal marine area in Port Underwood and Pelorus Sound (including Kenepuru Sound, Mahau Sound, and Tennyson Inlet) – developing a statutory plan "articulating Ngati Toa's values in relation to these areas". While those "values" remain undefined, it is well to recall the prominence of the murderous warrior chief Te Rauparaha in the history and the claims of this tribe. What will be the demands when a strategic advisory committee enhances Ngati Toa's involvement in the management of Kapiti Island? When the Crown grants overlay classifications over the Brothers Islands and Wairau Lagoon to acknowledge Ngati Toa "values" in relation to that area. When Mana Island, Taputeranga, Whitireia Park (Onehunga Bay), Akatarawa Road Conservation Area, Wainui Urupa, Queen Elizabeth Park, Onepoto Bay, Okatiki (Ohingaroa Scenic Reserve), Rarangi, Robin Hood Bay (Waikutakuta), Waihinau Bay, Elaine Bay, Pelorus

Bridge, Pakawau Inlet, and Queen Charlotte Forest (Crown forest licensed land) are vested in Ngati Toa in fee simple? When a Memorandum of Understanding is signed with Wellington City Council, Porirua City Council, Upper Hutt City Council, Lower Hutt City Council, Horizons Regional Council, Kapiti Coast District Council, the Greater Wellington Regional Council, the Nelson City Council, Tasman District Council, Marlborough District Council and Buller District Council?

While the people sleep, foxes are in the henhouse, having a mighty good feed.

STEALING THE BEACHES

Hugh Barr

This chapter considers one of the most astounding pieces of judicial activism ever seen in New Zealand – the Court of Appeal's 2003 decision to assist iwi privatisation of New Zealand's foreshore and seabed. This is a massive area of in excess of 100,000 sq km, amounting to the equivalent of 40% of our dry-land area. Since 1840 it had been considered as a public common, as is the custom in many countries, owned in common by all New Zealand citizens and equally their responsibility to manage sustainably and for the benefit of all. The ramifications of this decision have been splitting our society ever since.

Crown acquisition of land in New Zealand for settlement:
The Crown interpreted Article 2 of the Treaty of Waitangi to mean that all land had to be purchased from some tribe, and that there was no *terra nullius* (land owned by no-one). This was in spite of much of New Zealand, especially in the interior, mountain lands for instance, not being occupied at all by Maori, or rarely visited. This is currently reflected in the Maori Land Act by Section 129 (1) which states - For the purposes of this Act, all land in New Zealand shall have one of the following (six) statuses:
(a) Maori customary land
(b) Maori freehold land
(c) General land owned by Maori
(d) General land
(e) Crown land
(f) Crown land reserved for Maori

Maori customary land is that which is held communally by Maori, according to Maori custom. Originally, in 1840, most land in New Zealand was in this category. There was no provision for *terra nullius*. General land is freehold land, and has individual saleable title. It is now the largest category of land. However, where the land purchased was not occupied by the tribe, the implication was that the price paid for it was less, because of this non-occupancy.

In contrast, in Australia, where there was no Treaty with the aborigines, all land was considered as belonging to the colony initially, i.e. *terra nullius*. This meant that any aboriginal customary title to their lands was not recognised by the Australian colonial governments.

The British *terra nullius* doctrine applied only to "dry" land and did not extend to the foreshore or seabed. Crown purchases were only of "dry" land and there were no clauses saying that the foreshore and seabed were included. This was in line with British law that the foreshore and seabed are Crown owned. Hence this is the case in the Maori Land Act. It is not stated specifically because British (and therefore New Zealand) law assumed it. So the concept of the foreshore and seabed being "land" could never arise.

Maori were indeed fortunate that the British adopted the "no *terra nullius*" rule. There was, in fact, a large amount of land that was not occupied by any tribe. But the British were still prepared to purchase it from the nearest, or appropriate, tribal group, albeit at a discount. It was not always clear who the appropriate owner was and on occasions the Government paid more than one chief who claimed to be the owner.

One hundred and sixty-three years on, in 2003, the Court of Appeal, in the notorious *Ngati Apa* case, turned this settled law on its head.

Court of Appeal double-crosses the Crown

This privatisation of New Zealand's foreshore and seabed, initiated by the Court of Appeal in this case is probably the most audacious and irresponsible example of judicial activism ever seen in New Zealand. This has already been explained previously in Chapter Four.

This story began in the mid 1990s, when applications for mussel farms (now called aquaculture) in the sheltered Marlborough Sounds rose to gold-rush levels because of the high profitability of mussel farming at that time. The Marlborough District Council, the authority that then allocated the mussel farm permits under the Resource Management Act, had largely refused to grant permits to Maori groups, including any of the seven iwi whose tribal areas covered the Marlborough Sounds.

As a consequence, the seven iwi made a joint case to the Maori Land Court seeking a declaration as to whether the foreshore and seabed of the whole of the Marlborough Sounds was Maori customary land, or a variant of it. If this were the case, then the iwi between them would own the land under all the other permit areas, and could have then disrupted their activities.

The Maori Land Court is considered a minor court, dealing as it does with a small component of New Zealand society, Maori with disputes primarily over inheritance rights.

The case went to the Maori Appeal Court, and then to the High Court, before reaching the Court of Appeal. The Court of Appeal ruled that the case should go back to the Maori Land Court to decide, using Section 129 above.

However, the Court found as well that, firstly the foreshore and seabed should be considered as just like dry land, thereby expanding the area to which section 129 applied, namely the whole of New Zealand's territorial sea, which now covers the equivalent of 40% (100,000 square km) of New Zealand's (dry) land area (See Map 1 below).

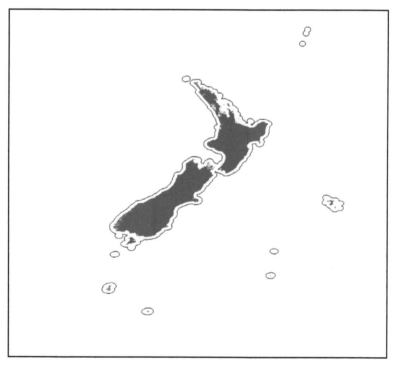

Map 1: New Zealand's Territorial Sea (Foreshore & Seabed) amounts to the equivalent of 40% of our dry-land area

To compound its mischief-making, the Court also declared that the foreshore and seabed could not be Crown land. This would allow any

188

Maori customary land on the foreshore/seabed to be recognised by S 129 as Maori customary land.

Consequently, by the simplistic rules of s. 129, the whole of the Marlborough Sounds could be Maori customary land since none of the other allowed land types of s. 129 were applicable.

The Crown could be forgiven if it felt that it had been ambushed by the five judges – Sian Elias and Judges Gault, Tipping, Anderson and Keith. This hefty spanner that the "foolish five" threw into the middle of New Zealand's race relations is still splitting our society nine years later and is likely to continue to do so.

The Court of Appeal had turned the honourable intentions of the British to observe no *terra nullius* when settling New Zealand into a weakness, whereby Maori coastal tribal groups could be awarded customary ownership of potentially ALL of New Zealand's 100,000 sq km of Territorial Sea, 163 years after the Treaty! This was achieved simply by five unelected judges saying that the foreshore and seabed was just like dry land and that, as the Crown had never legally annexed it, the Crown no longer owned it.

All five judges were more or less of one mind, based on Chief Justice, Sian Elias's leading decision. No judge dissented, which is surprising in itself on such a controversial decision. This looks to be a case of judicial groupthink - to make a political, not a legal decision.

"Groupthink", a term coined by the social psychologist, Irving Janis, occurs when a group makes faulty decisions because group pressures lead to a deterioration of "mental efficiency, reality testing, and moral judgment" Groups affected by groupthink ignore alternatives and tend to take irrational actions that dehumanize other groups.[1]

Barristers can argue cases from any viewpoint to achieve the outcome that they desire. Those who can argue successfully that "black is white", or even that "sea is land", are highly sought after. But judges are, by their oath of office, expected to be arbiters, and not protagonists. Reading the judges' decision, one is left with the uneasy feeling that this whole case was an ambush of the Crown (that is the people of New Zealand) by the plaintiffs and the judges.

This decision gives a disproportionate, unearned and undeserved advantage to coastal iwi. It is a racist violation of democracy, and discriminates against non-coastal-iwi New Zealanders. One has to wonder if these precious judges have any understanding of the treaty, of democracy or even of the law.

What is our territorial sea and why do we have it?

We hear a lot about the "foreshore and seabed" but what exactly does the term mean? As one walks down the beach, the foreshore starts at mean high water springs (spring high tide MHWS), followed by mean high water mark (MHWM), and then mean sea level (MSL), followed by mean low water mark (MLWM), and then finally mean low water springs (MLWS). This is followed by the seabed, which stretches from MLWS out to the limit of the territorial sea (12 nautical miles from land). All the foreshore and seabed is called New Zealand's territorial sea.

From March, 2011, when the Marine and Coastal Area Act was passed, the foreshore and seabed has also been called the Marine and Coastal Area – part of the National Government's attempt to confuse the public with new and misleading terms.

From the eighteenth century until the mid-twentieth century, the territorial waters of the British Empire, the United States, France, and many other nations were three nautical miles (5.6 km) wide. Originally, this was the length that a cannon could fire a shot, hence the portion of an ocean that a sovereign state could defend from shore at that time. However, in 1977 the area of territorial sea was extended from three nautical miles offshore to twelve. The state has sovereignty over the water, soil and air column through and above its territorial sea.

A nautical mile is 1,852 metres. It is also 2,025 yards long, that is 15% longer than a mile. Twelve nautical miles equal 22.22 km. New Zealand's foreshore and seabed (territorial sea) is shown in Map 1 above.

A 2003 LINZ (Land Information New Zealand) Report set out coastal ownership data – parcels of land adjoining the foreshore. This showed that the coastline was 19,883 km long. The Crown owned just over a third (37.6%, 7,455 km), mainly national parks and conservation land, and marginal strips. Local bodies owned almost one third (31.4%) being esplanade reserves, public recreation reserves including regional parks, etc, and road parcels. Privately owned land made up the remaining 30.4%, with 0.6% unresolved. General land adjoining the foreshore covers 3,979 km (20% of the total), and Maori land covers 2,053 km (10.4%).

Very little of the actual foreshore and seabed is privately owned – LINZ put this at 46.8 square km, compared with the total foreshore and seabed of over 100,000 sq km.

190

The UN Convention on the Law of the Sea (UNCLOS)

As already stated, for the 137 years from 1840 until 1977 the extent of New Zealand's territorial sea was only three nautical miles. In 1977, after nearly 20 years of negotiation at the UN Convention on the Law of the Sea (UNCLOS), the progress made allowed us to pass the New Zealand Territorial Sea, Contiguous Zone, and Exclusive Economic Zone Act, extending our territorial sea to twelve nautical miles from shore, thus more than quadrupling its size, as well as taking up an exclusive economic zone (EEZ) stretching 200 nautical miles (370 km) from the shore.

This major change was because of the ongoing UN Conferences on the Law of the Sea that started in 1958. New Zealand, as an independent state and founding member of the United Nations, had full national participation rights at these conferences.

The conferences had a number of goals, including giving maritime nations responsibility for far more of the oceans around their coastline, so that they would have the right to stop pirate plundering of adjacent fisheries and other resources, and to allow exploitation of, and responsibility for, their EEZ (Exclusive Economic Zone). Otherwise international fishing fleets would simply have plundered the nations' fisheries with no thought of sustainable practices, or ecosystem and biodiversity protection that the Convention provides for. This was what was happening in the North Sea, eastern North American fisheries, and other over-fished ocean areas at the time.

Under the UNCLOS Convention the owning state has sole control of exploitation rights, including commercial fishing, minerals, oil, etc. Each signatory state also has environmental responsibilities to protect the diversity of its ocean areas, and the sea species that live there. The Convention also guaranteed that ships of all states would enjoy the right of innocent passage through territorial seas. Generally international shipping sails round our coasts outside the territorial sea. Cook Strait, like the Straits of Malacca, the Strait of Gibraltar and other straits, is an international waterway, open to international shipping, in spite of being within New Zealand's territorial sea.

These privileges, benefits and responsibilities are the result of New Zealand's participation, as an independent sovereign nation, a member of the United Nations and a signatory to UNCLOS. It has nothing whatsoever to do with the Treaty of Waitangi or the British Crown.

The UNCLOS Convention Preamble talks about a "spirit of mutual understanding and co-operation" between states and says that the Convention "makes an important contribution to the maintenance of peace, justice and progress for all peoples of the world." The racist and confiscatory decision of the Court of Appeal, in the 2003 *Ngati Apa* case is an affront to this worthy international treaty that New Zealand has signed.

Public commons – the common property of humankind
There are certain resources essential to all human life which, because of their importance, most societies see as commonly owned by all humankind, and for which consequently, all humans have a responsibility to protect. In western society this principle was first written down, as far as records exist, by the Roman Emperor Justinian the Great, about 530 AD. He is famous for compiling and rewriting Roman law, which is still the basis of civil law in many modern states. His law of public commons states (in English) "By natural law itself these things are the common property of all: air, running water, the sea, and with it the shores of the sea."[2]

Environmental commons are usually considered to include forests, the atmosphere, rivers, water, fisheries, the oceans, land and water ecosystems, grazing land – things that can be shared, used and enjoyed by all. That the oceans and the foreshore and seabed are public commons is a fundamental consideration in the UNCLOS. States with EEZs have significant obligations to maintain these common areas and their ecosystems for future generations and to balance their short term exploitation rights with longer term conservation responsibilities.

An important aspect of commons is that they cannot be commodified, viz. bought and sold. If this happens, they cease to be commons since private ownership destroys the common rights of the community. A second aspect is that, unlike private property, commons are inclusive rather than exclusive. Their aim is to share ownership, and consequently responsibility, widely, rather than as narrowly as possible, as is the case with private ownership.

We receive them as shared gifts and have a duty to pass them on to future generations in at least the same condition as we received them. To achieve this, rules of use, etc. are usually required. In a predominantly capitalist world - or feudal society - any public commons are likely to be subject to privatisation threats so that those who become private owners can charge the community at large a rent to use what was previously theirs by right. This makes the "owners" (usually stealers) more wealthy, and the former commoners poorer.

In England this privatisation of the grazing commons happened during what was called the "enclosures" of the common land, where the villagers previously grazed their animals and grew their crops. This happened in the late eighteenth and early nineteenth centuries.

The first thing that the new, usually wealthy, landowners did was to fence off (enclose) their new estates so as to keep out the commoners who had traditionally used them. Thus the commoners, now unable to grow their own food, were of necessity driven out - either to the new, filthy industrial towns where they were forced to work for low wages, or to emigrate overseas to the "new lands".

It was the enclosures in England that were a major spur to Edward Gibbon Wakefield to form the New Zealand Company so as to enable the sturdy but dispossessed English country folk to emigrate to New Zealand in the 1840s and 1850s, thus providing his capitalist settlements with a source of reliable labour.

Environmental commons, like Justinian's natural law, are things that Elias, Anderson, Gault, Tipping and Keith in their *Ngati Apa* decision, had either forgotten or were ignorant of or chose to ignore. Instead, in defiance of the law of precedent (the *Ninety Mile Beach* case) they took it upon themselves to open the way to commodifying the public commons of the foreshore and seabed by turning the law on its head for no other easily apparent reason than to indulge their own prejudices. With judges like these, who needs courts?

Maori villages are not on the coast because of tsunamis

Maori had good reason not to live on the coast. James Goff and Bruce McFadgen have documented tsunamis around Cook Strait from the 13th century settlement of the area until the 1850s.[3]

The authors carried out field observations, assessing coastal gravels, etc. that had been washed inland by tsunamis. "We suggest that the abandonment of coastal settlements, the movement of people from the coast to inland areas, and a shift in settlement location from sheltered coastal bays to exposed headlands, was due to seismic activity, including tsunamis. We expect similar patterns to have occurred in other parts of New Zealand, and other coastal areas of the world with longer occupation histories."

193

Furthermore the Maoris were a warrior race where truth was not a major force since the best fighter usually decided what the truth would be with his *patu* (club) or *tao* (spear). After the introduction of muskets in the early 19th century, the intertribal warfare became so ferocious that fortified pas were built on hilltops and high points to make them easier to defend. Seaside villages were too easily overrun by fast approaching flotillas of war-canoes. Hence again, most settlement was away from the coast and beaches. The spread of agriculture too, with potato, wheat and the growing of other garden crops, after traders arrived, also encouraged tribes to move back from the coast to more fertile and less windy sites.

Before 1840 there was no Maori "nation", as most tribes were in a constant state of actual or potential war with each other, with no power or laws to create peace. One of the issues that tribes hoped would be resolved by British sovereignty was the introduction of law and order, and the outlawing of tribal warfare, cannibalism and slavery.

Labour's Response to the Court of Appeal – the Foreshore and Seabed Act 2004

Not surprisingly the 2003 Court of Appeal decision led immediately to a deluge of claims to the foreshore and seabed from opportunistic coastal tribes. Iwi understand the Maori Land Act very well, and must have laughed to themselves when they read that the Court had said that title to the foreshore and seabed "would be difficult to prove."

The Court of Appeal's *Ngati Apa* decision made it clear that additional amendments to the Maori Land Act, or a new Act, would be required to address possible foreshore and seabed customary rights.

There is still the contradiction that the Maori custom for dry land is to keep the fires of occupation, *ahi kaa*, burning, something not possible on the foreshore and seabed. This difficulty alone meant that any tribal customary claim to the foreshore and seabed, if valid at all, would be much weaker than customary title on dry land. The Court of Appeal decision acknowledged this.

Hence the Labour-led Government under Helen Clark had to address how best to amend the legislation to take account of the lesser rights of foreshore and seabed claims. Not doing so would create unacceptable precedents if the Maori Land Act was to be applied as it stood.

Without new legislation the Maori Land Court could automatically award applicant *iwi* all their sectors of the territorial sea, creating *iwi* property rights that the Crown would then have had to acknowledge and be potentially constrained by. New Zealanders who were not members of the privileged tribal groups being given ownership could have been locked out.

Our foreshore and seabed is, has been, and should be generally, the common property of all New Zealanders under Crown ownership. The arrogance of the Court of Appeal in undermining these common rights and paving the way for them to be given only to coastal iwi is an affront to non-Maori New Zealanders and is an important reason why Sian Elias's Court of Appeal was held in such low esteem.

The easiest response of the Government would have been to re-assert the long-standing Crown ownership of the foreshore and seabed since 1840. This was in line with Roman, European, British and other law, that the foreshore and seabed, along with the air we breathe, fresh water, sunlight, etc. is a public common, which, after all, is what it became upon the imposition of British law in 1840.

Alternatively, Government could have appealed the case to the Judicial Committee of the Privy Council. However, Labour had agreed that a New Zealand Supreme Court be established, and an Act setting it up was passed by Parliament on 14 October, 2003, less than four months after the Court of Appeal's *Ngati Apa* decision. The case could still have gone to London. But solving this issue quickly with amending legislation was preferable.

Getting a majority for the legislation was not easy. Winston Peters, the New Zealand First Party leader, supported Helen Clark, giving her a majority for the new legislation. Opposition came especially from National, who falsely accused Labour of selling out to Maori, even though that was not the case.[4]

Later, in 2010, National were to sing exactly the opposite tune when, with their new Coalition partner, the Maori Party, they were happy to take the whole of the coastline and seabed out of Crown ownership, to make it easier for iwi to claim.

The Labour Government released its framework in January, 2004. The Waitangi Tribunal held an urgent inquiry on it. This was, as one would expect, highly critical of the Crown's actions, on the grounds that, in Maori traditional stone-age beliefs, everything is connected to everything else, and so land, foreshore and seabed were as one. This mythical and religious approach is a very effective way of deflecting informed debate with semi-religious mumbo-jumbo.

The Maori gods of the land are different from those of the sea, e.g. Tane – god of the forest, and Tangaroa – god of the sea. So Maori gods can perceive a difference between the two, even if the Tribunal can't. By taking the approach that it did, the Tribunal isolated its position in an unassailable vacuum, where dialogue is impossible. It is still there, talking to itself.

The Tribunal's Report made no acknowledgement of New Zealand law, or of what New Zealand had gained for its citizens through the UNCLOS. The Tribunal's position appeared to be aimed at creating the arguments for supporting future iwi claims out to the edge of the EEZ, as well as to all other things that most of us consider public commons.

The Waitangi Tribunal has had a lot of experience in fooling pakeha, and there are any number of white politicians, journalists and judges who are only too happy to aid and abet its deceptions.

The Tribunal usually only hears and gives credence to Maori submissions and has become a cheerleader for Maori supremacist recommendations with the result that its interpretation of the treaty has now left the field of fact and entered that of propagandist agitation. It is not a court at all, in the sense of seeking alternative evidence and weighing the pros and cons. But this Maori supremacy advocacy racket is still funded by the long-suffering taxpayer.

The Deputy Prime Mminister, Michael Cullen, in a media release of 12th February, 2004, ("The rocky foreshore"), put Labour's case for a middle ground approach. He pointed out the obvious, that customary rights, if they still existed on the foreshore and seabed after 164 years of New Zealand nationhood, were and never had been, anywhere near as strong as private ownership rights on dry land.

There was conflict between the concept of "public domain", and the status quo of Crown ownership. In April, 2004, New Zealand First supported the Government on the condition that they chose the previous status quo of Crown ownership. This was a sensible move as Crown ownership is one of the six categories in s. 129 of the Maori Land Act, while the newly proposed "public domain" is not mentioned in any legislation. So it had no specific rights or case-law. The land status under the Maori Land Act would be important. "Public domain" is meaningless, and would not even return the law to the previous, well-understood status quo of Crown ownership.

196

With New Zealand First support Labour had enough votes to override desertions by its Maori M.P.s. Tariana Turia, a junior minister in the Labour government, voted against the Bill and was dismissed from Cabinet. In a huff, she resigned from Parliament and stood in a by-election for the newly formed Maori Party, which she helped establish. Labour M.P. Nania Mahuta also voted against the legislation but stayed with Labour.

A *hikoi* (long march) from Northland arrived in Wellington in early May, 2004, and an estimated 15,000 people turned up at Parliament to oppose the Government's plans. The size of a *hikoi* has no bearing on the legitimacy of its demands. *Hikois* are a show of force, designed to bully and scare the public and politicians.

It was essential for new legislation to provide for public access, and to ensure continuance of freedom of movement of vessels under the UNCLOS agreement. Michael Cullen also wanted the ability to recognise tribal historic association (*mana*) including *wahi tapu* (forbidden, usually burial, places where public access would be prohibited), but not any customary ownership titles. Winston Peters consulted with coastal iwi leaders as to whether this was acceptable, and broadly gained their approval.

Michael Cullen hosted numerous stakeholder meetings. New Zealand-wide recreational associations such as the Council of Outdoor Recreation Associations and angling and fishing groups strongly supported a return to the status quo, of Crown ownership (a public commons), with conservation management continuing, as before, under the Department of Conservation.

The Foreshore and Seabed Act 2004 was passed on 18 November, with 65 in favour and 55 against. For - Labour 50 M.P.s, NZ First 13, and Jim Anderton's Progressives (2); Against - National (27), Greens (9), ACT (9), United Future (8) and Turia (L) and Mahuta (L) (55 votes).

Labour, New Zealand First and the Progressive Party had protected New Zealand's sovereignty over the foreshore and seabed in spite of opposition from all other parties.

National voted against the Act, primarily because they said it gave too many rights to iwi. The Green Party - really a Brown-Green party, judging from their position - voted against it for the opposite reason, because they said that it did not recognise full iwi property rights. United Future voted against because the Act restored Crown ownership, and did not introduce Peter Dunne's foolish concept of "public domain". (To clarify: "public commons" protect public rights whereas "public domain" does not)

Although Labour had re-affirmed Crown ownership of the foreshore and seabed, it wasted no time in addressing the Marlborough Sounds iwi's grievances about not gaining a fair share of aquaculture sites in the Sounds. This problem was created by the Marlborough District Council, not by the Labour Government.

Iwi nationwide had received 20 percent of the total commercial fishery quota in the 1992 Sealords deal under the Bolger National Government. Labour confirmed this for aquaculture in the 2004 Maori Commercial Aquaculture Claims Settlement Act. Its purpose is to "provide a full and final settlement of Maori claims to commercial aquaculture", and "provide for the allocation and management of aquaculture settlement assets."

Foreshore stability: 2005 - 2008

After Labour was returned to power in the 2005 Election twelve tribes lodged claims under the Foreshore and Seabed Act over the next three years. Ngati Porou (Ruatoria) and Te Whanau a Apanui (eastern Bay of Plenty) negotiated with Michael Cullen. Ngati Porou claimed to have reached agreement in 2008.

National anticipated that it would be in coalition with the Maori Party, an expectation that List M.P. Christopher Finlayson appears to have sold to Prime Minister John Key in 2007. National talks with the Maori Party on replacing the 2004 Foreshore & Seabed Act seem to have started at least as early as January, 2008, as outlined by political columnist Chris Trotter, in the *Dominion-Post* of 8th February, 2008.

Trotter also wrote scathingly of John Key rubbing noses with the notorious Maori separatist, Tama Iti, at Waitangi. He asked "Is the National Party's determination to forge a coalition with the Maori Party now so great that it is prepared to clasp hands and rub noses with individuals whose long-term goal is to dissolve the New Zealand State into a patchwork of independent tribal cantons?

Are we to take from Mr. Key's gesture of friendship towards two of the staunchest proponents of Maori nationalism that the rumour going round about the Foreshore and Seabed Act is true?

That rumour had Mr. Christopher Finlayson, the man tipped to be New Zealand's next attorney-general, hard at work drafting legislation that will restore to our beaches the indeterminate legal status they enjoyed immediately after the Court of Appeal's bombshell judgement of 2003 and before the passage of the Foreshore and Seabed Act 2004."

If Mr Trotter, a man as far apart from the National Party as it is possible to imagine, had all this at his fingertips nine months before the election, why didn't Mr. Key come clean about it to the voters?

"If this is indeed National's intention," continued Mr. Trotter "Mr. Key's new found allies from the Maori nationalist movement have pulled off an extraordinary political coup. By convincing the National Party leader that the foreshore and seabed issue is nothing more than a dispute over property law, they have opened the way to a much more radical application of indigenous rights. ...And if they (Maoris) have a customary right to New Zealand's beaches, then why not its rivers, estuaries, swamps, lakes, forests and everything else?"

Mr Key's nose-rubbing mate, Tama Iti was later convicted of firearms offences in connection with the Urewera "terrorist" raids and was imprisoned.

National's 2008 secret and opportunist U-turn

Mr. Key studiously refrained from disclosing to voters that he would enter a coalition with the greedy and racially divisive Maori Party (which incidentally obtained a mere 2.39% of the total vote in the election). Nevertheless this is what he did, clinching a secret and unnatural deal with this Party, led by radical Maori activists, who are the exact antithesis of almost every person who voted National.

This deal, made within only days of the election, resulted in the repeal of the Foreshore and Seabed Act. It was a betrayal of the long held and valuable rights of all New Zealanders to enjoy the resources of our coast. It is also a violation of Article Three of the Treaty of Waitangi, which guaranteed legal equality between Maori and other New Zealanders.

Had Mr. Key told the voters *before* the election that he was going to repeal the 2004 Foreshore and Seabed Act so as to grant customary rights to a racial minority, then National would never have been elected. Those who still believe that Mr. Key is an honest politician should open their eyes. In opposition the National Party campaigned against special racial privilege for Maoris but, once elected, they did an immediate U-turn.

Writing in Wellington's *Dominion* on 14 December, 2004, National's then deputy-leader, Gerry Brownlee, promised: "National will ensure the beaches and lakes remain in Crown ownership for all New Zealanders, without the strings attached by Labour and New Zealand First." National's then leader, Bill English, and Murray McCully made similar statements.[5] But all three of these hypocrites later voted to steal the beaches off the public by the Marine and Coastal Area Act so as to make them available to tribes to claim.

National easily won the 2008 Election, increasing its party vote by 6% to 45% (58 seats) in a 122 seat Parliament. Labour dropped 7% to 34% (43 seats). The Maori Party won 5 electorate seats. NZ First did not get over the 5% threshold, so was eliminated from Parliament. But not for reasons relating to the 2004 Foreshore and Seabed Act.

National needed only five extra coalition seats to govern. The Maori Party could supply all of these. So could ACT (5 seats). Peter Dunne (1 seat) also supported National. So National was not forced to bow to the Maori Party's demands as a coalition partner.

National signed its coalition agreement with the Maori Party a week after the election. There was not much to discuss as presumably Finlayson, who seems more partial to the racist separatism of the Maori Party than to the principles of the National Party, had it all arranged before the Election. The main issue was to "revisit' (code for repealing) the 2004 Foreshore and Seabed legislation.

Finlayson's biased Review Panel

Having gained power by deceiving the voters, it didn't take National long to give effect to their pre-election plan. In early March, 2009, Finlayson announced an "independent" panel to review the 2004 Foreshore and Seabed Act as part of National's dirty deal with the Maori Party. Ministers have done this sort of thing in the past and they have usually tried to make such a panel as broadly based as possible so as to give it greater credibility. But not Mr. Finlayson. He went the other way and made it as narrow as possible – presumably because he had already decided that the Act was to be repealed and that customary rights over the foreshore and seabed would be granted to his *iwi* friends.

Any change in the Act would be likely to adversely affect fishermen, the aquaculture industry, beachgoers, business interests, local government, the mining industry, etc. One would have thought that representatives of these organisations would have something to offer and so could realistically sit on the panel. No way!

There was nothing independent about the panel of three - Eddie Durie, Richard Boast and Hana O'Regan. They had been chosen because of their record of political activism and supporting Maori treaty ambitions.

Eddie Durie was chief judge of the Maori Land Court from 1980 to 1998, and Chair of the Waitangi Tribunal from 1980 to 2004. During his judicial career he was criticised on a number of occasions for failing to declare possible conflicts of interest in relation to his lawyer wife, the Maori activist, Donna Hall. In a 1994 High Court case against the Maori Land Court and West Coast dissidents, the defendant, Rudolph Cecil Lousich, was represented by Durie's wife, Donna Hall.

In that case Justice Tipping found it proper that the case be heard in the High Court rather than in front of Durie, the Chief Maori Court judge at the time. Durie took great offence to this reference to his connection to Donna Hall and tried unsuccessfully to get the Solicitor-General's office to remove it. Durie is known for his strongly pro-Maori treaty rights views.

At the time of writing (November, 2012) Durie's wife, Donna Hall, is facing allegations before the Conveyancers' Disciplinary Tribunal, for which she could be struck off the roll of lawyers as being unfit to practice law.

In choosing Durie to be the chairman of this patsy panel Finlayson was creating a conflict of interest since it was Durie who first proposed that Maori should own the foreshore and seabed way back in 1985. In other words, put the guy in charge who first thought up the scam.

Hana O'Regan. is the daughter of Ngai Tahu and Maori advocate, Stephen O'Regan. She is Dean of Te Puna Wanaka at the Faculty of Maori Studies at Christchurch Polytechnic Institute of Technology and has been a member of the Maori Language Commission since 2003. She was brought up in the house of a very pale but leading Maori activist and has spent virtually her entire working life in Maori language studies.

Hana O'Regan should not be surprised that it might be widely thought that she was not the best person to advise the government on the repeal of a law that would have the potential to enrich her tribe, Ngai Tahu. It has 40% of the New Zealand coast in its tribal area - the biggest coastline of any tribe. Finlayson was the lawyer for Ngai Tahu in its greedy and dodgy treaty settlement.

Treaty lawyer Richard Boast is an associate professor of law at Victoria University, specialising in the roles of indigenous peoples and Treaty of Waitangi issues, including assisting the Waitangi Tribunal. He has been engaged by a Hawkes Bay *iwi* to do research work, and so his objectivity could be questioned.

With Finlayson's panel having a majority consisting of Durie and O'Regan and excluding anyone who was not steeped in Maori studies, this sounds very like letting the fox loose in the chicken coop.

When the panel was announced in the first week of March, 2009, Wellington's *Dominion-Post* reported, "All three [panel members] are considered likely to be sympathetic to changing or repealing the Act." When the Maori Party co-leader, Pita Sharples, was asked what would happen if the panel did not recommend change, he replied with all the arrogance and confidence of a man who was in control of the whole thing, "I would probably sack them and put another group in." [6]

This was not a joke and, so concerned was the Beehive that the cat was being let out of the bag, that a press secretary was sent to explain to journalists that Sharples was commenting as Maori Party co-leader and not as Maori Affairs Minister. If anyone believes that this unbalanced panel was appointed for any reason other than to dance to the Maori Party's tune by recommending the Act's repeal, then they must also believe in the tooth fairy.

New Zealand must be the only "democracy" that is controlled by a Party which won only 55,980 votes at the 2008 General Election – less than the population of Napier. It polled even less, (31,928 votes) in 2011. Yet it still retains its stranglehold on the National Party, through Key and Finlayson. Because of John Key's spinelessness the Maori Party is calling the shots on whatever issues it chooses to concentrate on, of which the foreshore and seabed has been the most notable.

The terrible truth is that the Maori Party, iwi, Finlayson, Key and the National Party constitute a very dangerous combination – a cabal working against the public at large.

I attended the Wellington hearing of the Panel and spoke on behalf of the Council of Outdoor Recreation Associations (CORANZ), a national council of seven major outdoor recreational associations and representing over 20,000 outdoor recreational users. CORANZ argued the very high importance of the foreshore and seabed for outdoor recreation and that free and unhindered public access for people and boats was essential. We urged that the area be managed as a public common, and that the 2004 Act be retained and its public commons focus be strengthened. Other large national associations made similar presentations.

At the hearing I was struck by the negative demeanour of the Chair, Judge Durie. He did not smile and he acted in an unfriendly manner, as if to say "Why have I come to hear these awful white people. They are beneath contempt". I was not surprised that the Panel came out so strongly for the Maori Party position.

Predictably, after consultation, most of it at marae meetings to which the public would not have been inclined to attend, the Panel made its Report, published by the Justice Department under the name of "Pakia ti uta, pakia te kai". An ever so politically correct phrase but deliberately confusing for the public. But, as we shall see, this whole process of stealing the beaches off the public was for the benefit of the tribal elite, and the public were to have virtually no say in the taking away of their rights.

It claimed that most of those giving oral or written submissions supported repeal of the 2004 Act. But submission opportunities for non-Maori were hardly publicised. One wonders why. Did the Government not want non-Maori to engage on this matter?

The 2004 Act worried iwi because they knew that it made it difficult to get customary title. They also knew they had never occupied the foreshore and seabed. Even under a more favourable regime, it would still be difficult to prove. What iwi wanted was certainty that they would have the right to claim customary title over potentially all the foreshore and seabed. Unsurprisingly this is what the Panel delivered. Discussion about whether iwi really owned the foreshore and seabed was absent. The Report was all about Maori thinking that they should own it. So, as in any warrior society, no proof was required.

The Panel proposed two options. First, a national Treaty of Waitangi framework, and nine principles with a "bicultural" body similar to the Waitangi Tribunal, that would:

- develop proposals for a national settlement
- develop proposals on the rights for *iwi* and *hapu* in the foreshore and seabed and how such rights could be implemented, recognised and enforced

203

- develop proposals for local co-management

The second option was for regional and national negotiations directly between the Crown and *hapu/iwi*.

The Panel's Report was a recipe for an *iwi/hapu* takeover of ownership of the foreshore and seabed, bypassing any involvement or role for non-iwi New Zealanders. The Panel further proposed an Act to repeal the 2004 Act, and assert *iwi/hapu* control of the foreshore and seabed.

This was a massive and unjustified Maori "land" and resources grab. Of course Maori would say "I want it", if they were asked. They realise that gaining ownership of this vast area would allow rentals to be charged from those who occupy foreshore and seabed space now and in the future. It is a major step in implemeting a Maori Apartheid society, with everyone else as second class citizens.

Customary title to the foreshore and seabed is generally considered extinguished if the Crown or another purchaser has legally purchased coastal land from Maori to the seaward boundary. This has clearly happened on large spans of New Zealand's coast, as shown in survey title records. The Land Information NZ (LINZ) report of December, 2003, states that only 10% (20,000 km) of the coast is now in Maori ownership, and that some of that may have been re-purchased back after a Crown purchase. Hence the Panel's proposal that the whole of the foreshore and seabed should be legislated to be Maori customary title was a massive, unjustified "land" grab.

When the Durie Review of the 2004 Foreshore Act appeared in early July, 2009, I commented as secretary of the Council of Outdoor Recreation Associations, on Radio New Zealand's Morning Report on 2 July, about the biased nature of the Panel and of the whole consultation process.

As a consequence I was invited by Maori TV to appear on their Current Affairs programme, Native Affairs, on 13 July, 2009, as their token white male, and opposed privatisation of the foreshore and seabed to *iwi*, because it was a public common for all New Zealanders.

New Zealand First leader, Winston Peters, temporarily out of office, broke a six-month silence by launching a blistering attack on the Durie Review on TVNZ's Q+A Current Affairs programme on 5 July, 2009. "You've heard about the separate court system, the separate prisons system, the separate education system. And now you've got a separate ownership system," Peters told ONE News political editor,

Guyon Espiner. "They are arguing about title. Make no mistake about it they are arguing something separatist. And, if that's the way that New Zealand is to go, then our future direction towards the Third World is certain. How do you construct a different world view when the mass majority of Maori activists I know have less than a quarter Maori in them and when I know so many Europeans who value the beach for its shellfish, for its contact with nature and for their love of New Zealand being the way it is?"

I also wrote an opinion piece of CORANZ's concerns for the *Dominion Post* and *New Zealand Herald*, 14 This article pointed out that National was putting public access to New Zealand's foreshore and seabed at risk by repealing Labour's 2004 Act. Getting rid of the 2004 Act would open a Pandora's box of very high risks for the rest of us. In contrast Labour's 2004 Act confirmed the foreshore and seabed as a public common for all New Zealanders, the way it had been treated in law since 1840 and before.

Treaty Negotiations Minister, Christopher Finlayson, responded to my article with a letter to the *New Zealand Herald*, saying that I was "misrepresenting" the issue of access to our beaches and pointed out that 85% of submitters favoured repealing the Act, most of whom appeared to be Maoris with a vested interest in the outcome since they would be the recipients of his Government's largesse through the transfer of publicly owned resources. Finlayson failed to mention the massive proposed privatisation, presumably because it was National's intention to fudge this central issue. Interestingly Finlayson signed his letter as Attorney-General, not as Treaty Minister. It is a travesty itself that the Prime Minister allows him to hold both these highly conflicting positions at the same time.

On Waitangi Day, 2010, *New Zealand Herald* columnist, Fran O'Sullivan, wrote a piece entitled "Foreshore Debate all about Big Bucks", in which she said, "Park the charming stories about the customary connections that Maori enjoy with the foreshore and seabed. What's really at stake are the big bucks that can be earned from commercial activities such as marine farming, mining iron-sands or even clipping the ticket on revenue from offshore gas and petroleum deposits.

That has always been the *iwi* bottom line. It's the real reason why Labour legislated to assert Crown ownership of the foreshore and seabed in the first place. Not to preserve the rights of all Kiwis to access the beaches to fry sausages at their summer barbies. If that was the only matter at stake, Maori would have been content with the then existing 2004 legislation, which enshrined their ability to apply for customary rights orders so they could undertake their traditional activities. But neither Labour nor now National is prepared to debate the real issues behind this lengthy controversy."

Finlayson's self-serving consultation process

Having got the findings that he wanted from the Panel, Christopher Finlayson produced a Consultation Document, that promoted his views on how to "balance" the interests between *iwi* and other New Zealanders – views that seem to have been influenced by his earlier deep professional advocacy links to the Ngai Tahu tribe, which potentially stood to gain more foreshore and seabed than any other tribe. This conflict of interest casts serious doubt on Finlayson's objectivity. As Ngai Tahu's former counsel, he was the last person who should have been entrusted with this issue.

The questions in the Consultation Document were phrased to favour a positive "yes" response. The document itself is extremely confusing, with many undefined and un-definable Maori phrases – presumably to confuse the public on this massive swindle of their rights. Then, after Finlayson's propaganda, there were 27 questions that submitters were asked to answer, of which the first two were the most important – Q.1: "Should the 2004 Foreshore & Seabed Act be repealed?" and Q.2, which really was "Should *hapu* and *iwi* be allowed to own and control New Zealand's foreshore & seabed?"

This "consultation" was announced on 31 March, 2010, as it happened, just before Easter (2-5 April) and was to close on 30 April, after only 20 working days. This is an extremely short period for such an important consultation, which entailed whether or not the National Government would privatise the 100,000 sq km of New Zealand's public foreshore and seabed to coastal *iwi* and *hapu*. No wonder this likely "theft of the century" from the public to *iwi* was phrased in such waffly words. If the public had been told the truth, they would have been up in arms – and rightly so. The document waffled on about the foreshore and seabed being "owned by no-one" to camouflage the fact that it would really be owned by *iwi*.

Even the National Government's controversial consultation on mining in national parks, miniscule in comparison to this issue, had 48 working days, including a time extension.

At the launch of the Foreshore and Seabed consultation, Prime Minister John Key gave his word that "if there was not wide support, then the current law could remain in place." [7]

Of this self-serving document, presented by a group of Treatyists who had been hand-picked by a biased Minister, the columnist Michael Coote wrote in the *National Business Review*, "the stench of a jack-up emanates from its every page, calculated to manipulate the alleged 'consultation' to the Government's own expedient ends...to create de facto Maori sovereignty for coastal tribes" [8] The National Party did not campaign on anything so radical or dilutive of Western civilisation and the rule of law in the 2008 general election.

On 28 April, 2010, a petition of 5,000 people asked the Government for an extension of submission time for another three months. Government refused immediately. A letter asking for an extension, sent by the Council of Outdoor Recreation Associations, was similarly refused by Finlayson.

Obviously National's political agenda was to get the Foreshore and Seabed issue out of the way as soon as possible. Public consultation was necessary for the sake of appearances but was really irrelevant, in the Minister's view.

Finlayson's rigged and undemocratic "Consultation" meetings

The National-Maori Government held eleven marae and eight public consultation meetings crammed into the two weeks after Easter. Please note – eleven meetings for Maori and only eight for other New Zealanders.

The process was driven by the eleven *iwi* marae meetings, which were usually scheduled for two and a half hours and often preceded by an iwi *hui*. The public meetings were usually in the evening, scheduled for only an hour, and poorly advertised. Iwi groups also attended the public meetings as a bullying tactic, specifically to crowd out what non-iwi may have wanted to say.

Coverage of the whole country's coastal areas was poor. In the South Island, only four meetings, two marae meetings at Picton and Akaroa, and public meetings in Christchurch and Blenheim, were held.

207

Thus all of Southland, Otago, the West Coast, South and Mid-Canterbury and Nelson were ignored.

North Island marae meetings were held at Kawerau, Kaukapakapa (Kaipara), Gisborne, Napier, Porirua, Otaki, Omapere, Hawera and Paeroa. Public meetings were held at Butterfly Creek, (wherever that is) in Manukau City, Gisborne, Napier, Wellington, Otaki, Kaitaia and New Plymouth.

Auckland, with a third of New Zealand's population, was badly served, with only one public meeting, the first, at a new, unknown tourism park, plagued by heavy traffic, near the Airport. There were no public meetings in the Wairarapa, Manawatu, Hamilton, Tauranga, North Shore City, Auckland City, Waitakere City or Whangarei - all major population areas. In terms of meeting non-Maori, it was a consultation evasion exercise.

I attended the Wellington public meeting. It was also attended by *iwi* representatives and others. There was a Maori facilitator as Chairwoman. Minister Finlayson arrived half an hour late, having been delayed at the marae meetings he said, and highlighting that he had little real interest in non-Maori views. He asked whether Labour M.P., Shane Jones, was present. On confirmation that he was not, Finlayson abused him in his absence for what the Minister claimed was his extreme lack of knowledge on the issue.

Finlayson said that the whole reason for National's change was to allow Maori "their day in Court". Finlayson's demeanour was very welcoming of Maori comments and offhand with non-Maori ones.

I supported the sea as a public common and asked if, in the event of the foreshore and seabed not being owned by the Crown, how was the new idea of "public domain" going to be managed? What agency would be responsible for it? I got no answer from Finlayson.

Morrie Love, a part-Maori Ati Awa spokesman, spoke aggressively and excitedly about how his Maori DNA was different from his European DNA. His Maori DNA could never agree to the foreshore and seabed being a public common, he said. This was an idiotic comment since most of his DNA is European. A young Ngati Kahungunu man said he "knew" the foreshore and seabed was Maori land. No need for any proof! Self-interest was obviously more important than needing proof. A reminder too, that "proof" is not a concept needed in stone-age warrior societies.

208

Historian, Graham Butterworth, said that non-Maori had been living on the coasts of New Zealand since at least 1800, and around Wellington since before 1840. Why couldn't they, because of their long association, claim private title to their foreshore and seabed just as *iwi* were, to be "allowed their day in court"?

At the end of the meeting the Minister said that he would be pleased to talk to me, and to others, about our concerns. I duly rang his office several times. But I was unable to get through to him. On 19 April I e-mailed him, saying that I would appreciate a meeting.

Prior to the Government's announcement of its policy, I was rung twice by the Minister's office to set a time to meet him and discuss the matter. On neither occasion could his secretary find a suitable time. This showed me that the Minister wasn't keen to meet me. He has criticised me publicly on a number of occasions, when I was not present to defend myself, saying that I should have responded to his invitation. There is no lie like the big lie – claim that your opponent is doing what you are doing yourself. However, in fairness it should be pointed out that Mr Finlayson is so busy running around maraes, talking to *iwi*, and encouraging their ever-increasing demands, that the time he could spend listening to non-iwi like me, representing 20,000 members of CORANZ, would be extremely limited indeed.

Public advocacy and fightback

There was much public concern leading up to the 30 April public consultation deadline. David Round wrote a piece in the Christchurch *Press* on 23 April 2010 – "Time to draw a line in the sand".

This former National Party candidate - and a co-author of this book - wrote that the 2004 Labour Government's decision to place the foreshore and seabed in Crown ownership was a sensible and courageous move to maintain it as a public common for all New Zealanders. He argued that the proposals of the Attorney-General and former Ngai Tahu Treaty negotiator, Chris Finlayson, to "settle" the matter was a betrayal of all non-Maori New Zealanders. "It deserves to be rejected with the same contempt which that gentleman (Finlayson) obviously has for us," he wrote.

I had opinion pieces in both the *Dominion-Post* (28 April) and the *New Zealand Herald* (29 April) "When the tide goes out, it will all belong to Maori". I said that National wanted a race-based privatisation of the community's foreshore and seabed to Maori, and that the concerned public should oppose repealing the 2004 Foreshore and Seabed Act. It is great that these two papers published these critiques in the interests of fair debate.

Another notable contribution was from Michael Coote, financial writer in the *National Business Review*. In his piece, "Business beware: Maori sovereignty is landing on a beach near you", he wrote that National's "final solution" to the foreshore and seabed was being deliberately trivialised by John Key.

> "For Maori the foreshore and seabed brouhaha is about racially privileged gold digging at the expense of the rest of New Zealand society. Yet opening up that vast natural domain – remembering that New Zealand has an enormous coast line – to Maori tribal claims of rights and titles is what the National Government's game is all about. The end result of the government achieving this goal will be exponential growth in the legalised corruption officially sanctioned for Maori tribes. Opportunities for legalised extortion, dane-gelding, and bribe taking will abound – note that these activities will all be perfectly legal – raising the cost of capital and passing that cost on to New Zealand's consumers as an effective 'Maori tax'."

He quoted the example of Meridian Energy buying off *iwi* concerns regarding their proposed Mokihinui hydro-electric dam near Westport.

> "The Maori tax will thus be levied on Meridian's customers. No country that has increased corruption – whether legalised or not – has ever prospered as a consequence, and so we can forget about all the government's half-hearted propaganda campaign over closing the living standard gaps with Australia in the event of these creeping 'Maori taxes'. That is why National should think twice before setting the Parliamentary seal of approval on Maori tribal ticket clipping all the way from the beach front to the limit of the territorial sea.
> Legalised corruption for Maori tribes is a zero sum game for our economy since a dollar paid to them is a dollar filched from someone else, meaning that there is no net productivity gain and so the gap with Australia will only widen. Instead of converging with Australia we will head in the direction of corruption crippled Third World countries."

Mr Coote also questioned National's "public domain" concept.

"If coastal iwi will be able to go to the High Court or some combination of that court with the Maori Land Court to seek their customary title, who would be the defendant since no one would own the foreshore and seabed? No entity would be able to mount a counterclaim against Maori claimants.

This means of the Crown divesting itself of responsibility to defend its title, which at present it holds on behalf of all New Zealanders, is being concealed from the public. For Maori a claim to the foreshore and seabed in the High Court becomes a mere box-ticking exercise. If they can correctly tick the boxes for the judge, then – hey presto – they will succeed in their claim and so the legalised corruption that will be part and parcel of customary title will get under way.

However, at least court proceedings are open to public scrutiny whereas the proffered alternative of negotiating directly with the government does not have even that protection since it is secretive and subject to arbitrary actions, non-judicial proceedings and undemocratic political influences. Nor is it open to appeal through the courts. We should not lose sight of the fact that in all of this, Maori tribal interests are always and everywhere private interests and in no way represent the public interest."

Opposing Finlayson's coastal give-away - formation of the Coastal Coalition

Former ACT Party M.P., Dr Muriel Newman and her husband Frank, run the centre-right blog website the New Zealand Centre for Political Research (www.nzcpr.co.nz). By the end of April, 2010, she had collected over 5,000 signatures for her petition opposing Finlayson's proposed tribal foreshore and seabed privatisation. It was obvious that this would be a continuing struggle, as certainly Ngai Tahu's past advocate, Finlayson, and also Prime Minister John Key seemed determined in pursuing their race-based privatisations, expecting to ride roughshod over public opinion by fair means or, in fact, foul.

In early May, 2010, we called our new activist group to fight these proposals the Coastal Coalition. Our policy was one of keeping the 2004 Foreshore and Seabed Act, namely almost the status quo of Crown ownership that had been the case from 1840 until those five wretched Court of Appeal judges muddied the waters in 2003 with their shameful *Ngati Apa* decision.

It is a David and Goliath battle. But it is a battle that has to be fought and won if New Zealand is to have a future as an advanced,

211

democratic nation rather than slip back to tribalism and graft as, for example, is the case in Tonga. That is why so many people across the political spectrum supported – and still support - our goal of Crown ownership of the foreshore and seabed.

The Coastal Coalition's worked to build our supporter numbers and encouraging them to oppose this theft of such a priceless resource. We wrote articles, held meetings, raised significant funds, and ran several advertisements in national and regional papers (see Appendix 4), distributed billboards (see the photo pages), lobbied other interested parties, etc. The Coalition was broad-based, with supporters across the political spectrum.

The Iwi Leaders Group's extreme views

The Iwi Leaders Group, the powerful umbrella group for major *iwi*, circulated a commentary to tribal groups in March, 2010, to "provoke discussion and debate among *iwi* and *hapu*" This was widely circulated and commented on in the media. The Iwi Leaders said that the Government's March, 2010, proposals "may not satisfy the rights, expectations and values of *iwi* and *hapū*."

They say that the new relationship with the Crown should be built on –

• *Mana* (power authority, control) – that *iwi* and *hapu* have inherited *mana* and the obligation to act as *kaitiaki* (guardians) of their tribal marine area

• *Tikanga* (customs and obligations) – the authorities and obligations that go with *mana* should be understood and defined only according to *tikanga* (not introduced English common law) and that *tikanga* should be given effect as law

• Treaty "partnership" – this partnership (Iwi superiority) should be provided for in a meaningful way which provides for the respective authorities and responsibilities of each partner

The Iwi Leaders' Group said they were concerned that the Government proposals did not –

• Address the cause of the issue – *iwi* and *hapu* claim of customary authority and control over the foreshore and seabed adjacent to their tribal area

• Redress the 1840 Treaty relationship – restore the relationship between the Crown and *iwi/hapu*. The Iwi Leaders group view this relationship as being able to behave as they like ("tino rangitiratanga") while the Government pays for everything ("kawanatanga") with everyone else being second-class citizens in a Maori Apartheid society.

• *Mana* – Iwi "know" that the foreshore and seabed is theirs. (stone-age religious view, and a view expressed only after the *Ngati Apa* decision as apparently they hadn't thought of it before then). The Crown must agree with this and not require *iwi/hapu* to prove it

• *Tikanga* - Maori *mana* must be recognised according to Maori customs, and not according to New Zealand law. There will be two laws – with *iwi* law prevailing on the foreshore and seabed

It is difficult to understand how any sane government could adopt what the Iwi Leaders Group proposed. It takes all influence away from the rest of the community, including the Government itself. That, no doubt, is what the Iwi Leaders Group would like to do. They are largely contemptuous of New Zealanders who are not of Maori descent. But since the Key Government treats them as its de facto "Treaty partner", with Key himself talking with them regularly, they are a very dangerous and extremist influence.

What the Iwi Leaders Group wants is the basis of a Maori supremacist state within New Zealand. It is a plan for domination of the foreshore and seabed by coastal *iwi/hapu*, to the detriment of all other New Zealanders, and the removal of New Zealand sovereignty and laws from it. This itself highlights that New Zealand is near to constitutional breakdown.

If this was not enough, the Iwi Leaders Group wanted further concessions from the Crown, namely:

• Public Domain – remove it, as it will greatly impede *iwi* title and control

• Resourcing the ownership transfer process – - legal aid to be available to claimants

• Universal recognition of *mana* without having to go to court or negotiate

• Strengthen *iwi/hapu* property rights – and widen the range of awards available, particularly those providing management powers

• Create a specialist court/tribunal (This was also a proposal of the Durie Review Panel)

• Ensure greater flexibility for *iwi/hapu* to design their own solutions i.e. lock the public and Government out of any role

213

Many of the Iwi Leaders Group demands are so outlandish that they do not deserve to be taken seriously. They are extreme, mirroring those of the Durie Panel. What is disturbing is that National has already surrendered to many of their demands and seems to have no strategy in place other than to appease them on issue after issue. One thing is certain, as former British Prime Minister, Neville Chamberlain proved when negotiating with Hitler, in the late 1930s - appeasement doesn't work. It just shows weakness and inspires new demands.

Iwi cheer-leader, Christopher Finlayson, the conflicted Attorney- General and Treaty Minister

Christopher Finlayson holds two key portfolios in John Key's Government – Treaty Settlements and Attorney-General. He is also the lead minister for the foreshore and seabed issue. It seems that Mr. Finlayson has a clear idea of his apparent goal – the alienation of as much of the coast and seabed (and other public resources) to his iwi friends and ex-clients as possible. This is typical of the ill thought out mess that the repeal of the Act became on his watch. To give but one example of his twisted thinking, he wrote in Wellington's *Dominion-Post* on 28th April, 2010, "By restoring the right of Maori to seek customary title in the court, the Government is ensuring there is one law for all."

The whole essence of Finlayson's repeal of the 2004 Act was to give customary title to Maori only. So it is Maori Apartheid (the beaches for *iwi*) and not "one law for all", just as South African apartheid was not "one law for all". He seems to have as little understanding of this law as he did of the law relating to the disclosure of M.P.s' pecuniary interests, which he breached on more than one occasion.

For example, on 22 April, 2010, Finlayson was caught out for not declaring that he was a director and shareholder of Te Puhi Trust Ltd, a failure which prompted Parliament's Registrar of Pecuniary interests, Dame Margaret Bazley, to declare that he was in breach of Parliament's rules. When Labour's Trevor Mallard brought this to the attention of the House, Finlayson, in yet another of his hysterical personal attacks, screamed that Mallard was "psychotic"

Not having learned his lesson, Finlayson was caught out again a week later for not declaring that he was a director of another trust company, Diana Bremner Trust Nominees Ltd. If Finlayson cannot even understand the simple rules relating to disclosure of Members' pecuniary interests, how on earth can he be trusted with the job of Attorney-General, the top law officer of the land? The answer is he shouldn't be holding it.

Finlayson's attitude to conflicts of interest is every bit as casual – or self-interested – as his defiance of the laws of Parliament. The fact that he was Ngai Tahu's Treaty lawyer, who enjoyed suing the Crown (i. e. the taxpayer) on behalf of *iwi,* and is now Treaty Minister, doling out public resources to tribes, is bad enough. But even worse is the fact that this biased Minister holds the dual and conflicting offices of Attorney-General and Minister of Treaty Settlements.

The Attorney-General is meant to protect the interests of the Crown, i.e. the public. Yet Finlayson spends much of his time undermining the Crown's interests, so as to give major resources and special legal privileges to *iwi,* to whom he seems to be in thrall, for reasons of political expedience or self-interest. Lawyers should be up in arms that the Attorney-General, the head of the legal profession, appears to be so deeply compromised but unfortunately many of the law societies have become politically correct, Treatyist outfits with so many of their members doing very nicely out of the Treaty industry.

As noted in Chapter Seven, when the Emissions Trading Scheme was introduced Ngai Tahu bleated that it would reduce the value of the forests that they got under their Treaty settlement and they threatened legal action against the Crown. Despite Crown legal advice that this claim could be resisted in the courts the government caved in and gave Ngai Tahu and four other tribes the rights to carbon credits for forestry on more than 35,000 hectares of Crown conservation land for 70 years.

It is unusual to reject Crown legal advice and it is likely that Finlayson, in his capacity of Attorney-General, had a big say, if not all the say, in granting this further benefit to his ex-client. Negotiator Willie Te Aho said the deal would be worth $2 billion over the years, but Climate Change Minister, Nick Smith, said that the total would be less than $70 million to $120 million.[9] The value of carbon credits in Ngai Tahu's 2010 report was $16.1 million

Of his one-sided Consultation Document, which was part of Finlayson's seriously flawed "process" to take the foreshore and seabed out of Crown ownership, so that *iwi* can claim it, Michael Coote wrote in the National Business Review, on 9 April, 2010: "Finlayson signed

215

off (the Consultation document) as Attorney-General, a role that should encompass diligently, dutifully and scrupulously impartial stewardship of the legal rights of all New Zealanders, without exception under the implied rule of law established by absolute parliamentary sovereignty"

What chance is there of Finlayson being "diligent" and "scrupulous" when this arrogant crusader for special Maori privileges spots an opportunity to advance the power and wealth of his ex-client, Ngai Tahu, or his other favoured tribes?

"Finlayson has a palpable conflict of interest in also being the Minister of Treaty of Waitangi Negotiations, the Government's head deal-maker, trouble-shooter and pay-off artist for Maori tribal compensation demands," wrote Mr Coote.

The Attorney-General would "report back to Parliament on how his own (Consultative Document) handiwork affects and interacts with the rest of our laws. Moreover, Mr Finlayson brags that he personally appointed the patsy panel that did what was expected of it, and declared the Foreshore and Seabed Act a 'failure'. The conflicted Minister then waited nine months to ambush business and the general public by releasing his Consultation Document on the brink of Easter, with a submission deadline of 30 April, (twenty working days later) for submitters to respond meaningfully and substantively to a set of complex far-reaching proposals." [10]

Finlayson's behaviour over this Consultation Document shows just how far this flawed and deeply compromised Minister is prepared to go to give potential riches to iwi, and especially his ex-client Ngai Tahu, who can claim a coastline that is 40% of New Zealand's total foreshore and seabed. As Treaty Minister, and Attorney-General, Finlayson does not appear to be acting for the general public of New Zealand but for Ngai Tahu and all other coastal iwi.

"The Minister who cannot guarantee anything to non-Maori"

David Garrett, when an ACT M.P., said that Finlayson makes up policy as he goes along and that he cannot guarantee anything. "Surely the Attorney-General of all people is in a position to know what will be permitted or prohibited under customary [marine] title. The most frightening thing is that he doesn't know." [11] Maybe he does but is not saying. He doesn't seem to be open about anything, which is necessary, of course, if you are stealing people's rights off them and don't want them to know too much about it. In the words of Mr. Ken Sims, the Co-

216

Chairman of the Council of Outdoor Recreation Associations, "He seems to specialise in making decisions behind closed doors." [12]

For example, on TV3's *The Nation* programme on 10th April, 2010, Finlayson invited Maoris to negotiate the proposed new customary title with him personally rather than openly through the courts. That way he would be in a position to dish out favours to Ngai Tahu and his other iwi friends in secret.

In the words of Labour M.P. Shane Jones, "It's preposterous that the Minister of Treaty Settlements can choose a few favoured Maori and then, in association with them, dream up ways that they can start to plan Club Med resorts dotted all around the coast line." [13]

On the same *Nation* programme Mr. Finlayson called customary title "a very vague concept" and "a constrained form of property right". He said, "If someone has customary title, certain rights will flow from that, just as happens with ordinary property owners, and I can't see that's necessarily a bad thing." [14]

That is how he presents it to the public – "vague" as part of his disinformation campaign but it seems that he has expressed himself a lot more clearly to his Maori Party friends. In the words of Tariana Turia, "We have been given an assurance that [customary title and customary rights] will be as sacrosanct as any other rights and title" [15] while Pita Sharples said that "significant property rights would flow from findings of customary title" [16] Sharples described customary title as "full blooded title similar to fee simple or freehold title".[17] This is the opposite of what the Court of Appeal said in *Ngati Apa*.

Remember how Sharples jumped up and down with joy in front of the cameras when the repeal of the Act was announced – reminiscent of Hitler dancing a jig when he heard that Paris had fallen to the Nazis. I think that tells us a lot more than Mr. Finlayson's evasive answers. By apparently telling one thing to the Maori Party and another to the largely non-Maori electorate, Finlayson demonstrates his great ability to talk out of both sides of his mouth at once.

National's "double-speak" confusion

National's orchestrated confusion about the issue continued with Key saying that "very little" will go to *iwi* by way of customary title while Finlayson said that "10%" might be lost in that way, based on present Maori ownership of the foreshore. This is what they tell the largely non-Maori electorate but it seems that they tell the Maori Party something quite different. In view of the Maori Party's insatiable greed it is unlikely that Sharples would have jumped up and down in the air for a mere 10%. After all, if you hand the keys of a house to someone, you can hardly expect them to stop at the front porch. And the pushy Maori activists and "corporate iwi" who were driving the campaign for customary marine title are hardly the types to stop at the front porch.

Mr Finlayson's long and deep links to Ngai Tahu should mean that he cannot be in a position as Treaty Minister to pass laws that steal assets like the beaches off the public so that his ex-client can benefirt from the theft. However no matter how biased and incompetent he is, he is unlikely to be moved, as it is believed that part of the secret coalition deal between National and the Maori Party was the Maori Party's insistence that Finlayson be in charge of Treaty Settlements and the foreshore and seabed. It is virtually tantamount to having someone from their own racist party in these two jobs.

For National to sign a coalition agreement with the Maori Party (2.39% of the total vote) was one thing. But to deliver the government and country heart and soul into the hands of these racist bullies in return for their five grotty Parliamentary votes was quite another. It shows Mr. Key's cowardice, opportunism and lack of both backbone and patriotism. By allowing *iwi* to claim customary rights (i.e. control) over the coast and seabed of New Zealand, Mr. Key is not only betraying the rights of the majority of New Zealanders but he is also turning the National Party into a traitor to its own founding principle of representing all New Zealanders without favouring any one group.

However, in fairness it should be pointed out that Mr. Key is a man whose roots in New Zealand do not run very deep. It is doubtful if he has ever read a book on New Zealand's history and constitution. With his currency-trader mentality he views everything in the short term and for cheap, opportunistic gain. If those Maori Party votes can keep him in power, then the permanent and wholesale alienation of the coast and seabed of New Zealand is, for his own purposes, a small price to pay. In other words, because of Mr. Key's temporary political needs, New Zealanders have compromised permanently our long held and unqualified rights to enjoy our coastal resources.

Mr. Key tries to mask his betrayal of his own voters by making endless and meaningless sound bites. Why doesn't he just say, "Listen, I'm a man of straw and I'll do whatever Finlayson and those two big bullies in the Maori Party tell me to do and, if that breaks any election promises, then more stupid the fools who voted for me."

No less alarming than this massive swindle of the public has been the failure of the mainstream media to question him on anything other than a superficial basis or take him to task for such an outrageous racist attack on our rights. It seems that, because he will always pose in a funny hat for photo-journalists and give them a slick sound-bite whenever they stuff a camera in his face, he can do no wrong. I was struck by the media's silence and lack of criticism at many times during our campaign. They rarely criticised Key or Finlayson.

Apart from a few principled and far-sighted commentators the silence of the media has been deafening, suggesting that it is not just currency traders whose world view extends no further than the hysteria of the moment – be it the latest murder, helicopter crash, cop killing, whale sighting, celebrity arrival or whatever.

Finlayson sneers at democracy

Since John Key is so busy rushing from one photo opportunity to the next, he has left the whole foreshore and seabed issue to Finlayson. Therefore it is necessary to look at the background, character and motivation of this thrice defeated candidate.

Mr. Finlayson seems to have a sneering contempt for democracy in general and for the ordinary voter in particular – probably because voters have refused to elect him on the three occasions on which he stood for Parliament in his home town of Wellington.

If Mr. Finlayson had any respect for democracy, he would have accepted the verdict of the voters and gone back to his law practice. Instead he hitched his horse to National's Party List and rode into Parliament and Cabinet that way. It was very foolish of the National Party to place him on their List as Mr. Finlayson does not appear to believe in National's founding principle that it is a Party to represent all New Zealanders and not any particular class or racial group. That was why it was formed in the first place – as an alternative to the then class-based Labour Party.

By pushing to give the Maori minority race customary rights to the foreshore and seabed Mr. Finlayson has rejected the core National Party philosophy of representing all groups rather than just one section of the community. So why does this man, out of accord with his Party's stated philosophy, stay in Parliament? There has to be a reason and for that we must go back and have a look at how he made his money during his legal career.

As a lawyer Mr. Finlayson fed himself lavishly off the "Treaty industry". He appears to be on a personal crusade to strip non-Maori of precious and long held rights and resources for no higher reason than to enrich his ex-Maori clients and other *iwi* friends. Whatever Mr. Finlayson's colours are, they certainly do not seem to be the blue of the National Party.

Mr. Finlayson's big client before he came to Parliament on the National list was the Ngai Tahu tribe. It seems that he might still be acting for them – this time in his ministerial capacity since, under his Marine and Coastal Area Act, Ngai Tahu stand to get customary title to much of the South Island foreshore and seabed. Why shouldn't he answer to Ngai Tahu? After all, as a thrice defeated candidate he is not answerable to any voters.

To give some idea of where Mr. Finlayson's true sympathies lie, we need go no further than his maiden speech to Parliament as a List M.P. on 16th November, 2005, "The proudest moment of my professional career," he crowed, "was being at Kaikoura on 21st November, 1997, when former Prime Minister, Jim Bolger, and Sir Tipene O'Regan for Ngai Tahu signed the deed of settlement." This was the dodgiest of all treaty settlements and should never have been made.

An even more revealing comment was that in the *Sunday Star Times* of 30th May, 2010, which has already been mentioned in an earlier chapter, when he bragged of his time acting for Ngai Tahu, "I used to love going to the office in the morning when we were suing the Crown . . . Ngai Tahu mastered the art of aggressive litigation....It was 'take no prisoners'." How can a man with such a one-tracked mind against the Government, but in favour of *iwi*, be trusted as Treaty Negotiations Minister? How can he be trusted to negotiate customary title with tribes who want all or most of the New Zealand foreshore and seabed? He appears to think even now that his only loyalty is to *iwi*.

Even that arch-Treatyist, Douglas Graham, found the approach by Ngai Tahu and its lawyer intimidating. As Graham wrote in his short book, *Trick or Treaty*, "There was an aggressive approach from Ngai Tahu that I found unhelpful at times.....their approach was quite hard-nosed." [18] Don't forget, Ngai Tahu were being *given* taxpayers' money for an undeserved settlement since they had had four previous

220

settlements, the last one being "full and final". And this was the attitude of Finlayson and O'Regan!

Finlayson's hysterical personal attacks

Further evidence of Mr. Finlayson's apparent dislike of democracy and its concomitant, robust public debate, is his preference for personal attacks on those with a different viewpoint rather than a genuine discussion of the issues. Since I am part of the following incident I shall put my pen down and let it be told in the words of the respected commentator, Chris Trotter, who wrote as follows about an interview that Finlayson gave to Mr. Geoff Robinson on *Morning Report* on Tuesday, 15th June, 2010.

In Mr. Trotter's words,

"Am I the only New Zealander feeling less than a respected citizen to-day? Or that the full and equal protection of the laws no longer applies to me? Am I alone in suspecting that, constitutionally speaking, something important is about to take place – without the nation's consent?

What set me to pondering these questions was an extraordinary interview broadcast by Radio New Zealand on Tuesday morning. Morning Report's Geoff Robinson was talking to Treaty Negotiations Minister, Chris Finlayson, about the agreement secured between National and the Maori Party over the repeal of the Foreshore and Seabed Act.

Preceding the interview listeners had heard reactions to that agreement from Dr. Grant Morris, a law lecturer at Victoria University, Michael Barnett, C.E.O. of the Auckland Chamber of Commerce, and Hugh Barr, spokesperson for the Coastal Coalition – a group devoted to preserving public access to New Zealand's beaches. All of these men had expressed critical views of the National-Maori Party deal and Finlayson had been asked to respond to their remarks. What followed was extraordinary. Rather than address the trio's arguments, the Treaty Negotiations Minister immediately launched into a series of aggressive put-downs of his critics.

'I didn't know that Grant Morris knew anything about this subject,' sneered the Minister. 'I thought his specialty was legal systems or feminist legal studies.' Michael Barnett, according to Finlayson, was 'just sounding off because it's Tuesday morning'. Hugh Barr received a ministerial tongue-lashing for 'writing some crummy article in the *Dominion Post* which contradicted everything I had told him.' Huffed Finlayson, 'I can't be bothered wasting my time with him.'

But, oh, what a difference a change of ethnicity produced in the Minister. When *Morning Report* asked for his reaction to the Maori M.P.,

Hone Harawira's, charge that the whole consultation exercise surrounding the Foreshore and Seabed issue had been 'bullshit', the Minister couldn't have been sweeter.

I'm a bit disappointed in Hone,' crooned Finlayson, 'because in my opinion he's a first class chap, and he's a fantastic M.P. for the Far North. But one of the things I picked up from his *rohe* (tribal territory) actually was the idea that folk didn't want to have to go to court or negotiate to prove their *mana*. And I thought that was a fair enough point. So we've added in the universal recognition order as a result of that. So, I think Hone's a little unfair, with the greatest of respect to him, because I was listening and I was the one who was up on the road hearing what people were saying.'

The contrast in the Minister's tone, in his careful choice of words, and most particularly in the extreme care he took not to give offence was, to say the least, instructive.

The Minister's Pakeha critics, the C.E.O. of the Auckland Chamber of Commerce (an institution not noted for its hostility to National governments), a university lecturer whose comments were measured and utterly lacking in any kind of personal animus, and a champion of New Zealanders' right to recreate themselves amidst this country's spectacular natural beauty, were all the recipients of Finlayson's disdain, and he expended no serious effort responding to their arguments or questions.

How different it was for the Te Tai Tokerau M.P. – the man who infamously referred to his fellow New Zealanders as 'white mother****ers' – who was responded to with the 'greatest of respect' because, in the assessment of the Treaty Negotiations Minister, he is a 'first class chap' and 'a fantastic M.P. for the Far North'.

The Minister's Pakeha critics had dared to suggest that the interests of thousands of New Zealanders had been sidelined in the Government's rush to reach an agreement with the Maori Party. As Mr. Barnett observed, 'We still don't know what contact has been made with the recreational and conservation interests, the business interests, the local interests. But we do know that Government has been dealing with Maori and that it doesn't seem to be the so-called 'balanced' conversation that they suggested that they were going to have'." [19]

And all this from a Minister who has been rejected by the voters on all three occasions that he has stood for Parliament! Still, he can't help his prejudices but a man so obviously racially bigoted in favour of one race (Maoris) is quite unfit to hold public office in a multi-racial nation such as New Zealand. His appointment to Cabinet is yet another example of John Key's poor judgement.

Like Uriah Heep in *David Copperfield*, Finlayson is obsequious to those above him but rude to and dismissive of those below him – usually a sign of poor breeding. He almost invariably abuses opponents when he is discussing his pet Maori giveaways with non-Maori. The saying in the legal profession is "No defence – then abuse" so, rather than show the lack of substance in his arguments, abusing his opponents is the easy way out. Finlayson did it with M.P. Shane Jones at the public meeting in Wellington. He did it to me in a TVNZ *Breakfast* interview in November, 2010. He did it again when he called the Coastal Coalition people "clowns". And he has done it regularly on Radio NZ interviews and elsewhere. It is a distraction to sideline real debate, as well as highlighting his angry and unstable personality.

Secrecy and Racism

On 14th June, 2010, Finlayson and Prime Minister John Key announced repeal of the 2004 Act, and the introduction of Finlayson's new Bill to allow *iwi* to gain ownership and development rights to the foreshore and seabed.[18] He also called it a "non-ownership" model in what appears to be yet another of his efforts to deceive the public.

However Michael Coote was closer to the truth when he wrote in the *National Business Review* that the Act would give coastal Maori "enduring, inalienable, quasi-sovereign, unaccountable, non-recource powers that would trump democratically elected central and local government authorities for commercial ends." [20]

Finlayson announced that it would include secret negotiations between *iwi* and the Government, "to save money". It was also to include a new right, "universal recognition" or *mana tuku iho* to the whole of the territorial sea. It shows clearly too that Prime Minister John Key was putty in Finlayson's hands, with little understanding of the issue. Key also said "the National government, the Maori Party, and iwi leaders, have agreed a common position on the foreshore and seabed issue." A most revealing comment. But what about the rest of New Zealand?

Secret negotiations aren't "to save money". They are to avoid democratic process and to lock out non-iwi stakeholders so that Finlayson can be unrestrained in his giveaways of public resources.

The Coastal Coalition (CC) continued our campaign to highlight the massive transfer of public resources to coastal *iwi*. We were fortunate in gaining the support of advertising guru, John Ansell. John was the brains behind the National Party's 2005 election Iwi-Kiwi billboards. He was furious at Prime Minister John Key's astounding U-turn to back Maori ownership of the foreshore and seabed for no more apparent reason than to please Finlayson and buy the parliamenmtary votes of the Maori Party.

Mr Ansell produced new Iwi-Kiwi type billboards for Coastal Coalition, showing John Key waving the Maori separatist flag and wearing a Maori cloak and Hone Harawira's tie. It was Key who allowed the Maori separatist flag to be flown on the Auckland Harbour Bridge, alongside the New Zealand flag, to highlight that New Zealand is really two nations; one, iwi, whose self-assumed claimed legal rights far exceed those of the other, non-iwi.. Any Prime Minister who won't even defend the Nation's flag is useless, if not treacherous.

The Coastal Coalition gained access to a number of commercial billboards around New Zealand, thanks to the generosity and support of their owners.

The first "Beaches" billboard showed Iwi in National blue, with John Key giving them ownership rights, development rights, mining rights, veto rights, etc. Kiwi were in the black half, having only questionable visiting rights. We tested it at two sites in Wellington and two in Auckland, and they went well. This was especially the case with a Wellington site at the Basin Reserve, with a very high daily vehicle count and where ministers flying in for Cabinet meetings would see it. Many of the billboards were distributed around the country – in Auckland, Tauranga, New Plymouth, Hawera, Napier, Sanson, Golden Bay, etc. and some were on trailers.

A second billboard "Visit your beach before I give it to iwi" was also used in February, 2011, on Wellington's busy Jervois Quay and elsewhere, while the Bill was proceeding through Parliament.

April 2010 Foreshore and Seabed Consultation: Finlayson suppresses submission summary

Obtaining the summary of the results of Finlayson's April, 2010, public "consultation", which he had promised during the Consultation, was difficult. There was no sign of it before 14 June, when Key and Finlayson announced that a new Act would replace the 2004 Act.

Finally, in early September, Finlayson's bill was tabled in Parliament. Coastal Coalition's request to Finlayson for the summary

The Iwi/Kiwi ads that advertising guru, John Ansell, created for Coastal Coalition.

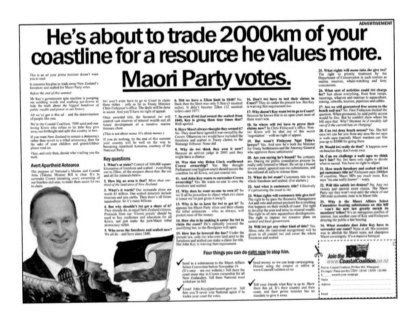

The Ansell created ad that Coastal Coalition inserted in the newspapers to inform the public of what was being taken off them by the National Government. To read this in bigger script see Appendix 4.

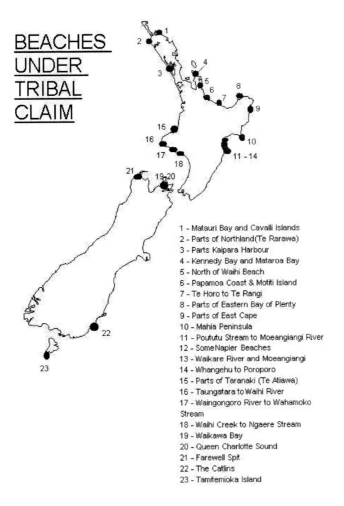

BEACHES UNDER TRIBAL CLAIM

1 – Matauri Bay and Cavalli Islands
2 – Parts of Northland (Te Rarawa)
3 – Parts Kaipara Harbour
4 – Kennedy Bay and Mataroa Bay
5 – North of Waihi Beach
6 – Papamoa Coast & Motiti Island
7 – Te Horo to Te Rangi
8 – Parts of Eastern Bay of Plenty
9 – Parts of East Cape
10 – Mahia Peninsula
11 – Poututu Stream to Moeangiangi River
12 – Some Napier Beaches
13 – Waikare River and Moeangiangi
14 – Whangehu to Poroporo
15 – Parts of Taranaki (Te Atiawa)
16 – Taungatara to Waihi River
17 – Waingongoro River to Wahamoko Stream
18 – Waihi Creek to Ngaere Stream
19 – Waikawa Bay
20 – Queen Charlotte Sound
21 – Farewell Spit
22 – The Catlins
23 – Tamitemioka Island

A map showing the areas that are likely to be the first to be lost to Maori "customary marine title" - effectively full ownership of our coasts.

The hillock off Cape Reinga, the uttermost point of New Zealand. It is from here that, according to Maori lore and the plaque (below), the spirits of dead Maoris leave on their journey to their homeland of Hawaiki, thus showing that even the Maoris don't believe that they are indigenous.

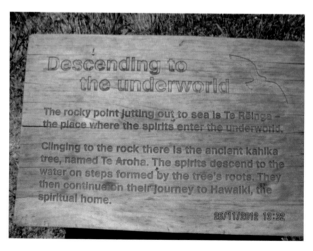

through Labour's David Parker, through a question in Parliament was refused. Typically, Labour just accepted this. But we did not.

Muriel Newman then requested the Report from the Justice Department under the Official Information Act. We only received a copy on 28 October, 2010, with the all-too-usual Departmental maximum delay of 20 working days. The Summary is now on the Ministry of Justice website

No wonder Finlayson refused to release it before his Bill was tabled in Parliament. The Summary showed that, despite all his bluster, rather than a majority wanting repeal of the 2004 Act, only 21% of those who answered the question, supported repeal. Instead the vast majority, 77% (over three out of four), supported keeping the 2004 Act.

The second question, "Do you support the Government's approach?" (privatising the foreshore and seabed to coastal tribal groups), was even more decisively rejected by submitters who answered the question. Ninety-one percent, more than nine out of ten, rejected it. Only 7% supported Finlayson's approach.

It was not even a close vote on either question. The public who had gone to the trouble to make submissions were overwhelmingly against Finlayson's new Bill. The whole submission process was a charade. Finlayson was hell-bent on pushing on regardless. To hell with open and accountable democracy. Just suppress the results!

These tactics, like his appointment of the Durie Panel, his shonky Consultation Document, and then handing the Bill to the self-interested Maori Affairs Committee rather than a less self-interested select committee, show Finlayson in his true colours – deceitful, secretive, biased and unscrupulous. In the words of Richard Long, a former Chief-of-Staff to former National Party leader, Don Brash, Finlayson is "as slippery as a barrel of eels from Maori lakes".[21]

Michael Coote has written, "Perhaps Mr Finlayson is a fool, but if he comprehends something like the true extent of the (foreshore and seabed) claims he has been seeking to minimise for public consumption, he is perhaps more a knave for talking them down in order to trick the vast majority of New Zealanders.".[22]

Yet this deeply flawed character – almost certainly the most distrusted and despised M.P. in living memory – is the man who is charged by John Key to "negotiate" the handover of large stretches of the coast, and public assets to his mates and ex-clients. In view of his temperamental and twisted nature, together with his dismissal of those who opposed the taking of our beautiful coasts out of public ownership, as "clowns", one has to wonder whether, in his vindictiveness towards his opponents, he will not throw a few more miles of valuable coastline into a tribal claim just to spite the Coastal Coalition "clowns". After all, a man who was prepared to chuck one of our precious national parks – the Urewera – into a Treaty Settlement, is capable of almost anything.

To have such a biased and manipulative person as Finlayson as Treaty Minister is deeply disturbing. Yet the apparent aim of this overly ambitious man to be the next Chief Justice in 2016, when the present incumbent retires, is so preposterous and so potentially harmful to the nation, that it must not be allowed to happen. How could such a biased person ever be a judge? How could one so unscrupulous in his methods ever be trusted on the Bench?

Given the huge public opposition that the Summary showed, Finlayson and Key displayed their usual arrogance. The Parliamentary media, primarily cheerleaders for the National Government, made hardly any use of the Coastal Coalition's media release on the actual consultation result.

On 15 November, 2010, I appeared on TVNZ's Breakfast programme, with Finlayson. However the interview soon descended into Finlayson's abuse, probably because he did not like hearing the truth.

Public submissions to the Maori Affairs Select Committee of Parliament on the Marine & Coastal Area Bill closed on 19 November, 2010. By directing these submissions to the Maori Affairs Select Committee Finlayson showed yet again his casual attitude to conflicts of interest since that committee consisted entirely of descendants of Maori who stood to gain from the Bill, whereas the issue was one that affected ALL New Zealanders. Interestingly, Helen Clark, faced with the same issue in 2004, recognised this conflict of interest, and required that submissions be heard by a special select committee, that was broadly based, and not by the self-interested Maori Affairs Committee.

Conflicts of Interest and why they need to be avoided
Conflicts of interest occur when a public decision is – or is seen to be – influenced by the decisionmaker's personal interests – either actual or potential. It is essential to guard against such bias and identify when it might occur, based on past experience and objective evidence. Conflicts of interest are a major cause of poor decision-making world-wide. Hence they are expected to be declared, and those with them are

expected to refrain from debate and voting on the particular issue. However, especially in feudal and stone-age societies, they are often condoned, e.g. in the dictatorships of Africa.

Many of Finlayson's actions seem aimed at creating conflicts of interest, so that the decision he seeks becomes the expected outcome, because the people making that decision will almost always decide according to their self-interests. Usually they do not suffer any penalty for doing so, and stand to reap large rewards.

The Cabinet Manual sets out the conduct of ministers:

A Minister of the Crown, while holding a ministerial warrant, acts in a number of different capacities

a) in a ministerial capacity, making decisions, and determining and promoting policy within particular portfolios;

b) in a political capacity as an M.P., representing a constituency or particular community of interest;

c) in a personal capacity.

"In all these roles and at all times, Ministers are expected to act lawfully and to behave in a way that upholds, and is seen to uphold, the highest ethical standards. Ultimately, Ministers are accountable to the Prime Minister for their behaviour", states the Manual.

In view of all the little tricks that he played on New Zealanders during the repeal of the Foreshore and Seabed Act it is hard to see how Finlayson complied with these high standards set out in the Cabinet Manual.

Similarly unjustifiable decisions are likely to arise with "by agreement" claims under the Marine and Coastal Area Act, where Finlayson will make these decisions in secret, with no other stakeholders represented. There isn't any need for proof in such one-sided, secret rip-offs of the taxpayer and community.

Prime Minister, John Key, set up a major conflict of interest when he appointed Finlayson as Treaty Claims Minister and Attorney-General. Why did he appoint Finlayson to these positions, given Finlayson's well understood prejudices favouring *iwi*?

Finlayson's and Sharples' appointment of the three 2009 Foreshore and Seabed Review Panel members, Eddie Durie, Hana O'Regan, and Richard Boast, was an example of creating a conflict of interest for the panellists so as to ensure the outcome that Finlayson and Sharples wanted. All three panellists are deeply into the Treaty industry and it could reasonably be predicted that they would make recommendations that all the foreshore and seabed be open to iwi ownership. As they did. Surely New Zealand deserves something better than this sort of behaviour.

Finlayson perfects Maori Apartheid Consultations

Finlayson has also perfected a Maori Apartheid consultation process in spite of New Zealand still being nominally a democracy. Minority groups that want to take over countries that are democracies must first subvert the democratic process.

New Zealand is fast becoming a Maori Apartheid country, where *iwi* have greater rights than other New Zealanders. Consequently, as with South African apartheid, consultations must bypass non-iwi with the result that their majority view is ignored. With South Africa, one had to be a white citizen. In New Zealand, one has to be descended from a Maori. Same race-based apartheid privileges.

Finlayson's "consultation" on repealing the 2004 Act and proceeding with what became the 2011 Act highlights his methods of operating. He spent most of the 20 working days consulting with and encouraging *iwi*. The public meetings weren't well advertised, and *iwi* also attended, giving their own rants about why they should have ownership, thus elbowing out non-iwi views. At the meeting I attended there was also a Maori moderator from the Justice Department.

As already stated, because the results did not suit Finlayson, he suppressed them until after he had convinced John Key and the National Cabinet to proceed with repealing the 2004 Act and introducing his new Marine and Coastal Area Bill. Non-Maori views just don't seem to count with Finlayson. Is this the "highest ethical standards" as required by the Cabinet Manual?

John Key just as responsible as Finlayson over their seabed give-away

There is no doubt that John Key, a man of weak character, dances to the tune that Finlayson and the Maori Party sing. In the words of Michael Coote, Key has "been relentlessly whiteanted by Treaty minister Finlayson, who has made his own substantial fortune by delivering imaginatively to acquisitive Maori tribal complainants as much juicily lucrative appeasement as they can swallow, whether as a top billing Treaty lawyer or a high paid minister of the Crown." [23] But that doesn't excuse Key's deceit over the foreshore and seabed issue. This deceit began even before Key became Prime Minister.

As we have seen, during the 2008 Election campaign, Key studiously refrained from telling the voters that, if National won, he would enter into a deal with the small racist Maori Party that would result in the public losing ownership of our beautiful beaches and valuable seabed.

When opposition began to mount against taking the beaches out of public ownership, Key said that "if there was not wide support, then the current law could remain in place." [24] There was indeed widespread opposition – over 90% of submissions – but Key still went ahead with the Bill. He deceived us by giving the impression that public support was a condition of the repeal of the Foreshore and Seabed Act when it quite plainly wasn't.

Then in February 2011, in "Key Notes" on www.johnkey.co.nz Mr Key wrote, "Our new approach (the Marine and Coastal Area Act) recognises the rights and interests of all New Zealanders, and is designed to put the issue to rest once and for all." This appears to be two lies in one sentence as, by taking the coast and seabed out of public ownership so that only *iwi* can claim it, National was not recognising "the rights and interests of all New Zealanders", but privatising public rights to *iwi*.

And how could the issue be put to rest once and for all when there was (and still is) such vehement public opposition to it. Over 90% of the 5,794 written submissions to the Select Committee were strongly opposed to the Bill. And so were an astounding 97% of the oral submissions. And let us not forget that all other parties in Parliament voted against it except for National, the Maori Party and National's little puppet, Peter Dunne?

In the words of Michael Coote, "The Government itself - principally in the persons of John Key and Chris Finlayson – have made repeated statements that have the appearance of being calculatedly false, misleading and deceptive about how minimal the changes that will flow through from the Marine and Coastal Area Act will be. The public should not be reassured by the Government's soothing words". [25]

It is bad enough to steal off the people, but to exacerbate it by what appears to be a litany of deceit, is about as low as one can go. That is what Key and Finlayson stand charged with over their Marine and

Coastal Area Act – the greatest and most disruptive swindle in New Zealand history, and one that will have to be overturned if New Zealand is to have any future as a modern democracy with "one law for all".

Finlayson creates conflict of interest in the Ngati Whatua Orakei Treaty Claim

Another marine related issue reflecting Christopher Finlayson's tendency to create conflicts of interest within our communities through the Treaty Claims process he controls, has occurred in the Ngati Whatua Orakei Claims Settlement Act.

Finlayson included a 3.2 hectare block of land worth $30 million, at Narrow Neck, on Auckland's North Shore, as part of this Treaty Claim Settlement. It is now used by the Royal New Zealand Navy. The deal is conditional on the Navy being offered a continuation of their lease, for a minimum of 15 and maximum of 150 years.

The land was subject to the Hauraki Gulf Maritime Park Act, under which it would become a reserve, should the Navy decide to end its lease after the minimum period. The $30 million cost of this block is a significant part of Ngati Whatua's "commercial redress".[26]

The land is being removed from the Marine Park Act, so that the tribe would be entitled to use it for commercial purposes, with no guarantee of public access. North Shore interests fought a charged legal battle 15 years ago to stop an 11.2-hectare site at Narrow Neck being sold for commercial development and succeeded in having its reserve status retained. So Finlayson's Treaty Claim settlement seems intended to set Ngati Whatua against the North Shore community. He was accused in Auckland's *North Shore Times* as being "plainly guilty in claiming to have consulted on this whereas he obviously tried to sneak this through under the radar".

As well the Settlement includes $95.63 million of Navy blocks and a five year lease-back and $10 million of nearby Navy land, as well as a 170 year right of first refusal over surplus Crown land[27] This raises conflict of interest issues, with strategic New Zealand military land being privatised to a local *iwi*.

After hearings before, guess who, the Maori Affairs Select Committee, the Committee ignored the North Shore community's pleas, and said that their opposition was based on "mistrust and misunderstanding". The Committee recommended passing the Bill with only minor changes.[28] Residents and Auckland councillors felt that the settlement was marred by secrecy and underhand tactics.

This deal creates a major conflict of interest for both Ngati Whatua and the Navy. Having private ownership of strategic Defence Force land or resources raises the issue of undermining their effectiveness to do their job. To compromise the Navy by having such an important base privately owned raises the issue of what happens in future if Ngati Whatua see their own interests as better served by taking control of this highly valued and potentially commercial land, and developing it for commercial purposes themselves.

The Navy deserves better than this. National has already delivered it a hammer-blow with Defence cuts of $355 million by 2015 – and this out of a lemon that had all but been squeezed dry by earlier governments. And now, by Finlayson's Ngati Whatua deal, the Navy is being forced to have this key base not on public land – as is the case with all other navies – but as a mere tenant of a private and race-based landlord, that could kick them off the base if a higher rent could be obtained by commercial means.

As Michael Coote has so astutely observed, "all Maori politics are essentially tribal, having nothing to do with New Zealand's national interests".[29] Examples of this are:

• The refusal of Ngai Tahu, after swiping $170 million dollars from the taxpayer, to let some of the rubble from the Christchurch earthquake be reclaimed into the sea, to provide some much needed land "because there might be some bones of our ancestors there".

• The refusal of the Tuwharetoa tribe to allow a mini-submarine, brought out from Germany at great expense, to enter Lake Taupo (under which is an active volcano) to carry out seismic research in the interests of public safety

• Another iwi's refusal to allow a small trench to be dug on Mount Ruapehu to prevent a life-threatening lahar

By putting the Navy in this undesirable position Finlayson stands charged with potentially undermining the defences of the nation, and one has to call into question the patriotism of this crusader for *iwi* rights. No part of our defence forces should be beholden to a private landowner, as that is a potential derogation of both sovereignty and naval power.

What was Finlayson thinking when he set up this conflict by including Defence Force land in the Treaty Settlement? Was it a view he has that the future of New Zealand will be a Maori feudal State, where the tribes will control most of what goes on and the rest of the community will be disenfranchised? Is that what he is working for?

I am reminded of Shakespeare's play *The Merchant of Venice*, where Shylock the Jew catches the Merchant in a vulnerable moment, and agrees that, if he cannot repay a friend's debt, then Shylock will get a pound of his flesh nearest the heart.

Privatising land to *iwi* in Treaty Settlements such as this, is potentially setting up a "pound of flesh next to the heart" for the Defence Force, and other agencies such as Crown Research Institutes (AgResearch), and Universities (Waikato), where privatisation to *iwi* of their land and buildings was part of Treaty Settlements.

Universities have traditionally been places of free speech. But at Waikato University, there is a reluctance to criticise Tainui – even in New Zealand history classes – for fear of upsetting the tribe that is the University's landlord.

The Marine & Coastal Area Act.

Finlayson shepherded the Marine and Coastal Area Bill through Parliament, with minimal changes to its structure. The Maori Affairs Select Committee heard submissions. Submitters were 95% opposed to the Bill, the majority because it took away the foreshore and seabed from ALL New Zealanders and privatised it to coastal iwi. Many Maori groups were opposed because it did not automatically give the foreshore and seabed to them, without them having to prove their claim.

After hearing submissions, the Maori Affairs Select Committee decided, based on its majority of National Party voting members, after only two hours' deliberation, to return the Bill to Parliament unchanged, presumably on Finlayson's orders. This caused uproar from the non-National M.P.s on the Committee. Consequently the only amendments made were by Finlayson's Supplementary Order Papers in Parliament. Perhaps even he did not trust the conflict of interest that the Maori Affairs Select Committee had. Then again, he himself is such a control freak that he trusts very few.

Concerns about the Marine and Coastal Area Act are that it sets up a Maori Apartheid system – only Maori tribal groups can apply - for

232

ownership and rights over the public common that is the foreshore and seabed. In summary-

1) The Act allows a massive transfer of the foreshore and seabed resources from the Crown (i.e. the New Zealand public) to coastal *iwi*, e.g. iron-sands, titanium, sand, gravel, etc. Customary marine title under the new Act gives tribal groups the ability to charge rents on all facilities in their tribal customary marine title area, e.g. boatsheds over the water, marinas, buoys, launching ramps, etc. in spite of coastal *iwi* never having occupied these areas. Finlayson tried unsuccessfully to speak with a forked tongue by telling non-iwi that "no-one owned it" while out of the other side of his mouth he told *iwi* about the great wealth that would accrue to them from these ownership rights.

2) It creates three increasingly valuable iwi-only property rights, in terms of being able to interfere with and control other people's, and the public's, property rights, structures and public access. These three rights are:

a) *Mana tuku iho* (ancestor recognition) – a right given to all tribal groups, who claimed *rohe* (tribal areas) with coastlines in 1840, if they apply for it. (And they would be mad not to) Rights include notification by the Department of Conservation (DOC) for concession applications, marine reserves, marine mammal sanctuaries, concessions, etc. [See Ss 47-50 of the Act.] This "right" gives coastal *iwi* a "holding right" out to 22.2 km (12 nautical miles) from shore, rather than the 5.5 km (3 nautical miles) that existed in and prior to 1840, had they actually occupied the foreshore and seabed - which they obviously didn't do, as they lived on the land.

b) Protected customary right – exercised since 1840, according to *tikanga* (custom), e. g. collecting *hangi* stones but excluding fishing, aquaculture, matters relating to wildlife or marine mammals, or spiritual or cultural associations [s. 51-57]

c) Customary marine title – [Ss. 58-93] This is the big one - a very strong property right (s. 60, 62), similar to private property ownership. To qualify, a tribal group must prove occupation of the adjacent coast since 1840, without substantial interruption, until the present day or have exercised customary fishing rights in the area from 1840 [s. 59] Tribal groups can create their own Resource Management Act plans for their area, independent of the rest of the community or the regional council, who must recognise their plans – foreign nation status, almost. The tribe becomes the authorising authority of any activity or consent by others, including aquaculture, mining, buildings or facilities. So they will be able to charge an *iwi* tax for approval to use these facilities and resources – since the owners have to get *iwi* sign-off. They can also create their own *wahi tapu* areas - where access is forbidden to the public. They have exclusive ownership rights to any minerals other than the Crown-owned minerals of petroleum, gold, silver, uranium. So they get iron-sands, titanium, gravel, sand, etc. which are of major value.

3) *Wahi tapu* [s. 78-81]: Any tribal group with customary marine title can seek to have *wahi tapu* areas declared in its customary marine title area. This can be done by "agreement" with the Minister in secret, but without any public input. Then it is bulldozed through a compliant Parliament and the public lose the right to walk on an area that has hitherto been open to them. The Act allows these *wahi tapu* areas to be across important fishing areas, so as to lock out non-tribal fishers [See S 28]. Wardens appointed by the group, and Ministry of Primary Industry fisheries officers, will police the exclusion area. Fines up to $5,000 can be imposed on other New Zealanders who enter these previously public zones.

So, the Government's claim that there is free public access over the foreshore and seabed, under their new regime is untrue. Should a tribal group gain Customary Marine Title, then its ability to determine *wahi tapu* in this tribal area would introduce additional Maori Apartheid to our coasts. The very concept of *wahi tapu* moves New Zealand back to stone-age thinking. In reality it is a way of creating 21st Century private property trespass offences, and will be misused in this way. There are no public rights of appeal - another feature of an apartheid system.

4) Secret process for determining protected customary rights or customary marine title: the tribes have always known that proving occupancy rights to foreshore and seabed is impossible. They didn't live on the beach, let alone on the seabed. So, to get over this legal impossibility, Finlayson agreed that they could negotiate with him in

234

secret, with no other interested parties present, and this will be the primary method of tribal groups gaining Title.

Finlayson said it was to "save iwi time and money going to court" Really! It is to allow secret deals that Finlayson alone controls.

Unlike Treaty claims, another parallel Maori Apartheid process, where no-one but the claimant *iwi* is part of the negotiation to be given public property, there is not even a memorandum of understanding (MOU) setting out what the Crown is giving away. At least the Treaty Claim MOU alerts other stakeholders, even though there is little they can do about it. This is an atrocious position to put other parties in.

Once a decision amenable to Finlayson and the tribal group is agreed, then it is railroaded through Parliament. There is no requirement for truth, or independent overview, or appeal.

The alternate process of going to the High Court is also difficult for non-iwi stakeholders to join. They have only a finite time to find out about the case and register [s 103 and 104] before the cut-off date. As there is no national register, including application dates, where there easily could be, it is clear that Finlayson has done his utmost to shut out other stakeholders, even from the High Court process. So much for non-Maori "having their day in court".

5) Removal of Crown and local body ownership of the Common Marine & Coastal Area [S 11]: This section removes Crown or local body ownership, now and in the future. But it still allows Crown or Local Body control where customary marine title does not exist. It weakens Government control of our territorial sea and opens the way in future for Maori Apartheid ownership of New Zealand's territorial sea - as if coastal tribal groups were mini-nation states. However, new areas designated as conservation area, national park, or reserve can still vest in the Crown.

Political party positions – years of Pakeha grievance ahead

Party votes cast as follows in the final parliamentary vote on the Marine and Coastal Area Act in March, 2011 were:

In favour of this swindle of the beaches from public ownership: National (58), Maori Party (4) and Peter Dunne (1) Total: 63 votes.

Against: Labour (39 – with 3 abstentions), Greens (9), ACT (5), Progressives (1), Chris Carter, Hone Harawira. Total: 56 votes, in the 122 seat Parliament. For a full list of those M.P.s who voted for this –

probably the greatest ever swindle in New Zealand history – see Appendix 5.

New Zealand First, which strongly supported Labour in passing the 2004 Act, was not in Parliament in 2011. It still strongly supports Crown ownership.

Though Labour opposed the 2011 Act, it does not now seek a return to Crown ownership. The Green Party supports even greater *iwi* ownership. Hence there is no likelihood of the 2011 Act being replaced by an Act restoring Crown ownership for some time. Not unless there is a major change in people's voting habits. And that is up to every New Zealander opening their eyes to what is really happening.

The Coastal Coalition campaigned strongly against the 2011 Act and stopped the likelihood of it being rammed through Parliament under urgency. The Coalition continued to run ads in the main Sunday papers and major dailies pointing out the downsides of the Bill. But no National M.P. broke ranks to vote against it. This in itself is a damning reflection of the puppet-like nature of this particular species.

Known Claims lodged under the Marine and Coastal Area Act

The 2011 Act process allows all "by agreement" claims to be dealt with in secret, until "final agreement". Hence the actual number of claims is not publicly available.

However, there were twelve claims registered under the 2004 Act process, which have been forwarded to the Wellington High Court, under s. 125 of the 2011 Act. These are known. As well, at the time of writing, there are believed to be around 15 separate claims for full blooded Customary Marine Title (CMT). However, any claim for a protected customary right can become a claim for CMT. So there is no certainty on CMT claims.

The Office of Treaty Settlements has a website listing some claims, on the Justice Department website.[29] This website has only eleven of the known 27 claims at present.

Three News documented claims in a news item it ran on 8 May, 2012, showing 21 separate claim areas, two areas being under multiple claims. Three additional claims in the Upper South Island have since been announced. The largest areas of coast at risk are:

a) the coastal area of the Te Rarawa tribe – from halfway up Ninety Mile Beach down the coast to the upper half of the Hokianga Harbour, including Herekino and Whangapae harbours.

236

b) the Ngati Porou claim on the East Coast

c) the the Marlborough Sounds, covering all of Queen Charlotte Sound, Gore Bay, Tory Channel, and the western side of Cook Strait.

d) Cape Farewell to Kahurangi Point, including Whanganui Inlet

But in many cases it is unclear just how much area of foreshore and seabed is being claimed.

The known 27 claims as at December, 2012, are shown in the map in the photo pages. It shows that tribes from all over New Zealand are seeking to take advantage of the new bonanza of Maori Apartheid rights and riches that National have dropped into their laps at the expense of your rights, resources and expectations, and mine.

Conclusion

Tribal claims to the coast will multiply over time as, possibly on Finlayson's secret advice, the tribes will not want to go too far too fast, for fear of creating a public backlash against this giveaway of our precious coast that has been so cleverly and deceitfully masterminded by Ngai Tahu's ex-lawyer.

But bit by bit and despite Finlayson's soothing words to the contrary, beaches and fishing grounds will be lost to public access through the creeping virus of *wahi tapu* and, although not at the 2011 Election, but certainly in the future, the names of Key and Finlayson will be damned as the two manipulative characters who stole the beaches off New Zealanders by such deceitful means.

THE EXTORTIONATE TREATY CLAIM TO NATIVE PLANTS, ANIMALS AND MAORI "KNOWLEDGE"

Hugh Barr

This Claim is about ownership of New Zealand's native flora and fauna (plants and animals), which the claimants argue they should own and control. They also claim that Maori should have much more control over the way that Maori art, culture and knowledge (*mātauranga Māori*) is used, and also want a return to Maori traditional healing.

Their summary statement of claim relates to "the protection, control, conservation, management, treatment, propagation, sale, dispersal, utilisation, and restriction on the use of and transmission of the knowledge of New Zealand indigenous flora and fauna and the genetic resources contained therein." It is a claim that *iwi* be given ownership and control over all New Zealand native plants and animals – a privatisation to *iwi* of what is a public common, owned and guarded by all New Zealanders, and managed by the New Zealand Government for us all.

The Claim is both absurd and racist. By taking it seriously and yielding to most of its greedy demands, the Waitangi Tribunal has proved yet again that it is a self-interested, racist racket. It is driving a sword through our society by its advocacy of racial separatism and privilege, and its denial of what the Treaty really said. This Report (WAI 262) highlights the tribunal's increasingly vengeful and provocative attacks on our democracy, sovereignty and way of life.

The claimants argue that *iwi* have "*tino rangitiratanga*" (chiefly control), as against the Crown's "*kawanatanga*" (governorship) in the Treaty. This is nonsense. Article 2 of the Treaty guaranteed to Maori their "lands, estates, property" until such time as they sold them. Nowhere in the Treaty is there any mention – implied or otherwise - of fauna and flora.

Species specifically mentioned for *iwi* privatisation and control include kumara, pohutukawa, koromiko, clematis, export timbers, tuatara, and kereru (wood pigeon). The original claim of 29 pages has been re-interpreted to 82 pages by the Tribunal's presiding Judge, Joe Williams.

This claim is a full frontal attack on government sovereignty and its control for all New Zealanders of our fauna and flora.

Privatisation to *iwi* would remove influence and control of native species by non-Maori New Zealanders - the very people who single-handedly have ensured that these species are protected. It is another proposed privatisation of a public "common" by the Waitangi Tribunal, similar to their proposals for radio waves, the foreshore and seabed, fisheries, fresh water, geothermal resources and anything else they can think of.

The claim was lodged with the Waitangi Tribunal in 1991 by representatives of six tribes. It gained three more tribes but was speeded up by Tribunal Chair, Judge Joe Williams, who took over in 2006. The Tribunal issued its findings on the claim in July, 2011. Action on the Claim now rests with Treaty Claims Minister, Christopher Finlayson.

The Waitangi Tribunal Report and its non-binding recommendations

The Tribunal Report is in three massive volumes, a condensed report (268 pages) and two supporting volumes (787 pages). Recommendations are at the end of each chapter. They involve Maori co-management committees throughout twenty Government departments and agencies. The Report is the Tribunal's king-hit for a whole-of-government take-over by what is euphemistically called "*iwi* co-management", but what is really *iwi* control.

Genetic and biological resources of native species: The Tribunal proposes Maori committees to advise on the Hazardous Substances and New Organisms (HSNO) Act, administered by the Environmental Protection Authority (EPA), and Patents Office decisions relating to these species. These committees would appear to have veto rights over departmental actions and policies.

The environment: The Tribunal said that the Environment was not a *taonga*, since it was ruled by Maori gods (*atua*). However, it decided that the relationship between *kaitiaki* (Maori food-gatherers) and the environment was crucial to Maori culture and identity, and therefore the Crown should actively protect this imagined *kaitiaki* relationship.

The Resource Management Act (RMA) in Section 6, (Matters of national importance), already acknowledges the relationship of Maori and their culture and traditions with their ancestral lands, water, sites, *wahi tapu*, and other *taonga*.

In Section 7 of the RMA *kaitiakitanga* (Maori "guardianship") is listed, along with the ethic of stewardship and nine other matters. As well, Section 8 states that those administrating the RMA "shall take into account the principles of the Treaty."

The Tribunal recommends Maori control of environmental management of *taonga*, partnership models, and veto rights in favour of *kaitiaki* interests. It recommends enhanced *iwi* management plans, improved mechanisms for *iwi* control, the Crown building *iwi* "capacity", and National Policy Statements giving *iwi* control, using current powers in the RMA. This will cut right across the rights of the rest of the community in Sections 6 and 7. It is a recommendation for special privileges based on a Maori ancestor and is contrary to both Article 3 of the Treaty and the UN Declaration against Racism.

Taonga (property) and the Conservation Estate The Tribunal backed the claimants' power-grab to exercise *kaitiakitanga* (guardianship/control) over *taonga* (property) within their tribal area, and over geographic features including forests, lakes, rivers, mountains and offshore islands. Its Report said the Crown should protect *kaitiaki* stone-age relationships, and ensure *iwi* control, guaranteed by tino *rangitiratanga*. All this after 170 years of developing the country along Western lines for the benefit of all. It is hard to take such rubbish seriously but that is exactly what Finlayson is doing instead of rejecting it out of hand as being unacceptable in a 21st century democracy.

DOC manages one third of New Zealand's total land area. The claimants want to control and own that too. They also want control in the concessions granted by DOC, which would allow them to levy *iwi* taxes on applicants. The "back to the Stone Age" Tribunal supported putting *iwi* members on the DOC payroll as DOC "iwi-liaison" staff as a great innovation for *iwi* – just like the "political commissars" in each element of the Soviet Army, who had the power to over-rule the colonel of the regiment.

This will simply provide more unnecessary taxpayer-funded jobs for the little coterie of tribal elite and give them scope to make more difficulties for the economy and more mischief for our society. It also raises major conflict-of-interest issues about whether they serve DOC or their greedy tribes.

The claimants want all public conservation land returned to them. There is no mention in the report of the rights of non-Maori New Zealanders. Or that the land was legitimately purchased in most instances. The Tribunal presumably ignores non-Maori as having no rights.

The Tribunal's wish-list of bullying legislative, policy and structural reform of DOC is that -
• There is a statutory partnership between DOC and *iwi* – with DOC's mission being achieved by respecting the *tino rangitiratanga* of *iwi*. This is bound to make *iwi* needs DOC's greatest priority
• All current and future Treaty principles, articulated by the Courts, should apply to DOC
• Full statutory co-management of customary use (taking plants and animals), and the making of joint decisions (DOC and Iwi)
• The Wildlife Act to be amended so that no-one owns protected wildlife, (c.f. Foreshore & Seabed, where nobody owns it so as to facilitate *iwi* claims) and that management is statutorily by the fraudulent "Partnership" Principle which, as seen in other areas where it has been tried, leads to.non-iwi having little or no say.
• Commercial concessions – *iwi* interests in *taonga* are to have preference when DOC makes decisions about commercial concessions on conservation land, e.g. skifields on Mount Ruapehu. This would allow *iwi* to blackmail developers over *iwi* culture, which is already happening with the Auckland Super Council's unelected Maori members, e. g. the cafeteria at the Aotea Centre being forced to have a Maori décor, at the request of these unelected members.

There are also Tribunal chapters on the Maori Language, and Crown control of Maori knowledge, namely Te Papa, the National Library, Archives, education agencies, Te Puni Kokiri. There are also recommendations on Maori traditional healing. The Tribunal recommends "Maori partnership" models for all.

Maori traditional healing is not science-based. It looks to the past, using *tohunga* (priest) traditions passed down usually by word of mouth with all its unreliability. Modern healthcare is based on testing and analysis, development of drugs and treatment, and a massive body of medical, psychological, chemical, physical and other scientific knowledge, that has been, and is still being, gathered through time, from all around the world. The Tribunal obviously has no understanding of the capability and effectiveness of modern, science-based health systems. Instead it proposes that the Crown give greater support to Maori "traditional medicine" which, before the introduction of Western medicine, led to Maoris having an average life-span of fewer than 30 years.[1]. How cruel to try to go back to those methods.

241

Maori *tohunga* "health" knowledge prior to European settlement was highly likely to kill the patient. It often consisted of putting sick people outside in the cold and rain and leaving them there. This approach was so bad that the young, educated twentieth century Maoris such as Sir Apirana Ngata, Sir Maui Pomare (a medical doctor) and Sir James Carroll actively supported the Tohunga Suppression Act, 1907,[2] because of the damage that many *tohunga* teachings were doing to Maoris.

These educated Maori men worked to establish modern medical practice and hygiene for Maori. Now the Waitangi Tribunal is recommending that Maori medicine go back to the Stone Age of damaging *tohunga* folk-lore remedies again. An astounding, incomprehensible and incompetent blunder, which confirms that the Tribunal knows nothing about medicine or science. This decision would certainly create a Treaty breach by any Government stupid enough to implement it, and massive damage to any tribe who followed it. It is a classic example of the Tribunal putting its racism ahead of humanity and compassion towards the Maori people.

Traditional "knowledge" impossible to verify

The difficulty in defining "traditional" knowledge is seen from the much-talked about "healing" properties of Manuka honey. Neither beehives nor the domestic bees that collect the honey are Maori inventions; they were brought here by early European settlers. Hence the ability to use Manuka honey was not available to *iwi* prior to European settlement.

There is no satisfactory way of identifying how, by whom or when the healing properties were identified. It is only since 2000 that production of Manuka honey for healing purposes has blossomed, 160 years after New Zealand became a British Colony.

Reaching this stage with the honey has required much scientific research to confirm and make the product acceptable in the medical industry. Dressings are now sold to hospitals, etc. But constant research continues to be needed to develop the product further. Modern science requires this additional research, simply to maintain present markets, something that neither the Claimants nor the Tribunal appear to understand. Knowledge today does not stand still or look to the past, as in a stone-age society. However, one of the significant producers of the honey is an East Coast company operated by Maori. They have got off

242

their butts and worked hard to create this industry. Good on them. They have succeeded in the open market and don't need any form of racist protection from people like Judge Joe Williams. And they are contributing far more to the economy and society than Williams is.

The areas hit hardest by the Tribunal's pompous, overblown, racist and one-sided Report are the environment, fauna and flora, public conservation lands, and Maori "knowledge". For these massive interests it advocates co-management with *iwi* within twenty major government agencies.

The Tribunal's recommendations are clearly separatist - one co-management law for *iwi*, and no comparable rights for anyone else. It is a "whole-of-government", Maori supremacist policy, based on stone-age practices, masquerading as a "partnership" by a Tribunal, presided over by a Maori Judge (Joe Williams) who seems to have a very limited understanding of how New Zealand has developed.

From these rantings of the Tribunal in this unprecedented power grab for tribal purposes Joe Williams should not be surprised if people suspect him of putting the interests of his race and his tribe ahead of the general good of having a fair society with democratic accountability.

Joe Williams' letter to the National Cabinet

The Chairman of the Waitangi Tribunal, "Judge" Joe William,s circulated the Report to the whole of the National Party Cabinet, with a vague and threatening covering letter saying that New Zealand was at a cross-roads and that, in his opinion, there should be much more control for "Maori", who apparently will know how to solve New Zealand's problems their way.

He claims that New Zealand must recognise "Maori" culture as well as non-Maori (New Zealand or European-based society and culture). But he makes no reference to Pacific or Asian culture. He says that there is a tidal population wave of more "Maori" but produces no evidence for this. There isn't any. How much is a 1/32nd or 1/64th Maori, really "Maori"? His recipe for Maori success is to have Maori controlling twenty Government agencies and departments, instead of the democracy that we have always known. His solution is a Maori Apartheid system, though he does not call it that. It will be up to Treaty Minister, Christopher Finlayson, to decide whether or not to implement the Tribunal's Report. New Zealand democracy is in for a rough time if these two Maori Apartheid proponents get their way.

243

Redefining key words to twist the Treaty

Since 1975 the meaning of the Treaty of Waitangi has been hijacked by special interest groups and has changed significantly. Much of this re-interpretation has been by redefining the words – *taonga*, "partnership", "principles", and *kaitiaki*, to create the legality of New Zealand as a Maori Apartheid state.

In 1840 *taonga*, the first syllable of which - *tao* means spear – was "property procured by the spear". Even more concerning is the appearance of the Principles of the Treaty. Neither the Maori version of the Treaty, which almost all chiefs signed, nor the English version, referred to principles or partnership.

Any government that is in "partnership" with a minority group of its citizens soon becomes a dictatorship run by that minority group. The minority, unelected group effectively ends up running the government, (in partnership of course) The South African government was in partnership with the white minority and embarked on a white apartheid regime, Governments in communist (single party) states are in partnership with the Communist Party, Hitler's government was in partnership with the Nazi Party, Mussolini with Italy's Fascist party, etc.

This is already happening now with Maori becoming increasingly in "partnership" with the New Zealand Government, resulting in a tribal dominated state. And the progressive privatisation of the beaches and seabed by means of "customary marine title" will only expedite this sinister process.

These three changes in meaning - *taonga*, "partnership" and *kaitiaki* (kai food, tiaki – look after) are being used cunningly, if not dishonestly, by the Tribunal to create a Maori supremacist state. *Taonga* has now been greatly broadened to mean anything *iwi* desire out of non-iwi e.g. radio spectrum, Maori language, rights to all native plants and animals, key species like tuatara, pohutukawa, and wood pigeon, fresh water and geothermal resources.

Having a "partnership" between Government and *iwi*, is now interpreted by the Tribunal to allow *iwi* to run the country, as the Wai 262 Report vividly demonstrates. *Kaitiaki* (guardians) was a very limited concept, usually relating to food gathering, and *rahui* (food gathering prohibited) only in rare instances like when there had been a drowning.

Underlying the Tribunal's recommendation that Maori should have equal rights with local authorities, DOC and the Environmental

244

Protection Authority, etc. is the lie that Maori are better guardians of nature than the rest of us. This view was given oxygen when former Treaty Claims Minister, Douglas Graham, stated "To most of us a river is something to use. We fish in it, swim in it, launch our boats into it and may enjoy just looking at it flow by. But we don't revere it as Maori do." [3]

Now let us look at the record of Mr Graham's fellow Maoris in looking after the environment. According to Australian palaeontologist Tim Flannery, author of *The Future Eaters*, what Maori found when they first landed in New Zealand was "the most extraordinary, indeed unbelievable, assemblage of birds. Nothing like it was found anywhere else on earth." [4]

In the ensuing years, under Maori "guardianship", approximately thirty species became extinct, and around one third of New Zealand's forest cover was destroyed. In the words of Bill Benfield, in his book *The Third Wave: Poisoning the land*, "At times the killing of the moa assumed an almost industrial scale.....It was a blitzkrieg of butchery. If it was there, Maori killed it. It wasn't only moa. It was also the easily harvested bird-life – the kakapo, the adze-bill, the flightless geese and ducks, even the flighted black swan." [5]

Maori had little understanding of over-gathering finite food resources. In the constant state of tribal warfare that plagued Maori society from the 17th century, tribes were not worrying about finite food resources. Their main concern was not to be someone else's dinner. *Kaitiaki* was a word more likely invented to camouflage Maoridon's awful record of driving species, and other tribes, to extinction, This compares with the much better record of European New Zealanders, who realised the risks of extinction. Conserving species, was recognised in the late 1890s, with the setting aside of sanctuaries on Little Barrier Island (1894), Kapiti Island (1897) Stephens Island (1896).

Why "truth" doesn't exist in a stone-age warrior society

Maori societies had no written language until after 1820, when the missionaries provided one. Prior to that time stories were handed down by storytellers, and word of mouth, from generation to generation. These tend to glorify and flatter the tribe and its chiefs, if only for the narrator's self-preservation. The story-tellers who were best at glorifying the tribe and chiefs would prevail. Often the most repeated story, or the best story, becomes the "true" one. There is no understanding of truth, which is a scientific idea that includes collecting information, and verification.

In science, questioning assumptions and conclusions is a central part of the process. It is a major difference between the forward-looking western system and the backward-looking Maori world-view. There is no ready way of verifying the truth of what *iwi* say especially about things long ago. When Maori words are used in Acts, what they mean is controlled by the users of the language today, as with *taonga* and *kaitiaki*. As is clear with these two words, meanings can change rapidly where self-interest is involved.

The Tribunal's Report starts by comparing "Kupe's people" – Maori, with "Cook's people" - descendants of Europeans. This seems to be the Tribunal's race-based way of claiming that Polynesian voyaging customs and processes were somehow as good as, or better than, European navigation technology. It appears to be a lead-in to arguing that Maori medical and health knowledge prior to 1840 was on a par with modern New Zealand health services, which themselves by the process of discovery and invention in medicine and science, have been revolutionised since 1840.

Errors in and counter-arguments to the Tribunal's Report

Much could be said here. Only a few important points are made:

a) The Public Conservation Estate and the Department of Conservation (DOC) were created almost solely by non-iwi New Zealanders, who wanted to see New Zealand's scenic diversity protected, the wildlands used for outdoor recreation, and native plants and animals protected in sanctuaries and thriving in the wild. The main contribution from Maoris was in setting in process the formation of Tongariro National Park in 1887, when Paramount Chief Tukino Te Heu Heu gifted the tops of the peaks of Tongariro, Ngauruhoe and half of the summit of Ruapehu to the people of New Zealand. This later became the core of Tongariro National Park after major additional government land purchases.

Like the original gift of Tongariro National Park, most of the 9 million hectares in the public conservation estate (33% of New Zealand's land area) is almost worthless for agricultural production, being of low fertility, steep, with heavy frosts, often with winter snow, glaciers and wind. But it is valuable for stopping downstream flooding, and reducing erosion, and for recreation and tourism. Green fertile looking native forests belie the rocks under only five centimetres of topsoil. Campaigns to form national and forest parks, and protect kauri forests, and tussock grasslands have come from pakeha, not Maori.

No proof of Maori "knowledge"

With patents, proof of who was the first to develop and register the idea, process or product, and how the product works, is required. Contrast this with the Maori claimants' sense of entitlement and unproved ownership. Why should Maori be given exclusive ownership of natural herbs and plants, based on unsubstantiated mythology - often deliberately twisted to suit the claimants' needs?

Patents, on the other hand, last only a limited time, after which anyone can use the patent for free, and the community benefits from lower costs for the use of the product. Examples are generic drugs including penicillin, etc.

There is no registration possible with Maori "knowledge", and it will usually not be clear what the key component of any Maori natural remedy is. Leaves of some plants are sometimes very effective. But usually pharmaceuticals are manufactured to treat the same symptoms, probably more effectively.

Massive benefits to Maori from Western inventions and technology

Tribal Maori have benefitted enormously from the patents of modern technology, ranging from penicillin to electricity, telephones, motor vehicles, ships, aircraft, televisions, cameras, sewing machines, radios, etc – almost every aspect of modern life. There is very little that they can point to in return as having contributed the other way. Yet reciprocity is said to be a fundamental concept of Maoridom. If what the Wai 262 claimants want is a payment every time their "knowledge" is used then, by reciprocity, they would agree that Maori should be charged a fee every time they use one of these non-Maori inventions.

That is why WAI 262 can better be described as the Jealousy Claim, or the Revenge Claim. It has very little merit and, if the Waitangi Tribunal was not a race-based advocacy group, it would have thrown out the claim long ago.

The non-Maori community, and no doubt much of the Maori community too, believe that these benefits, the work of human ingenuity, should be shared for the benefit of all mankind when a patent expires. They have compassion, the basis of Christianity, and something taught by the missionaries. It is probably something that every major civilisation needs in order to survive.

However it is something that the WAI 262 claimants obviously don't have. Compassion is a trait that would not survive in a warrior society, where the rule is "kill or be killed". Compassion would be seen as weakness and would be ruthlessly eliminated. That is what things would be like if this selfish, callous and backward looking claim should be implemented – even in part.

Political comment

After the Tribunal's report, Treaty Claims Minister Christopher Finlayson said that he would "carefully consider" it. As Finlayson is the man who stole the beaches off the public with his thieving and racist Marine and Coastal Area Act 2011, his "carefully considering" yet another *iwi* attempt to grab resources that belong to all New Zealanders, regardless of racial ancestry, is very alarming.

Don Brash, a former National Party leader and past Governor of the Reserve Bank, said the Tribunal's WAI 262 recommendations that resource management decisions should be made between government and *iwi*, was inappropriate, and "a recipe for long-term stagnation of the New Zealand economy".

Most people, once they understand the implications of the recommendations, would go far further and say it was the finalisation of New Zealand as a Maori Apartheid, stone-age state, in which non-iwi would have no say in the way the country would be run.

FISH

Hugh Barr

As we have seen in Chapter Two the word "fisheries" was not mentioned in Te Tiriti (the real Treaty of Waitangi) that was signed by almost all the chiefs. This being so, all demands for Maori quotas for fish, etc. based on the 1840 situation are entirely spurious and irrelevant.

The modern preferential fishing treatment given to Maoris – or, to be more exact, part-Maoris – does not derive from the 1840 Treaty of Waitangi but from the mischievously reinvented treaty that was dreamt up 150 years later by politicians, bureaucrats and tribal leaders for spurious purposes. Under this "Palmer-Cooke" treaty part of the national quota of deep sea fishing has been granted to part-Maoris on the basis of race alone. From that point everything went awry.

The recent advantages give to Maoris in the fishing industry goes to the root of the matter since Maori were not deep sea fishermen. Unlike the inhabitants of some of the small but heavily populated islands of Polynesia, the Maoris never needed to go out beyond the local bay to catch fish since New Zealand has a long coast and the Maori population was small relative to the large land mass of our two main islands.

Basing his findings on fish remains found on archaeological sites rather than the notoriously unreliable and sometimes deliberately false stories of "Maori lore" Doctor Foss Leach in his authoritative book, *Fishing in pre-European New Zealand,*[1] concluded that the pre-1840 Maoris were not deep sea fishermen. He referred to "the complete absence of any indicators of fishing for species which inhabit the clear oceanic waters near the edge of the continental shelf and beyond".[2] He also wrote that "there are no signs in New Zealand of the development of an aquaculture industry such as took place in Hawaii during the pre-historic period".[3] By the eighteenth and nineteenth centuries Maori had lost the ability to build and sail ocean going craft and could only do so after Europeans arrived and built European style boats for them.

Unhappy with the quotas that were allocated by the Ministry of Fisheries, when the government privatised the commercial fishery, some Far North tribes made a claim to the Waitangi Tribunal in 1985 under the joint name of the Muriwhenua Claim, alleging that the commercial quota system breached their rights under Article 2 of the Treaty even though there is no mention of fisheries in Te Tiriti, that the chiefs

249

signed. The Tribunal chairman, Eddie Durie, made the absurd ruling that the sea was owned in the same way as land – a mistake that the Court of Appeal also made in their notorious *Ngati Apa* case. Durie also said that, if the government wished to develop the sea commercially by way of quota, it must acquire the right to do so from the "traditional users" who were, of course, Durie's fellow part-Maoris.

In the High Court Justice Greig agreed that the quota management system contravened the rights of the Far North people and made the equally absurd finding that there was a case for a highly developed and controlled Maori fishery over the whole coast of New Zealand before 1840. He thereby proved that historical confusion, if not ignorance, is no bar to judicial promotion in our new dumbed down society.

The Government then bought back 10% of the commercial quota that it had given out and in 1985 transferred it (60,000 tonnes) to the Maori controlled Waitangi Fisheries Commission as well as shareholdings in fishing companies and $50 million of taxpayers' money. But that little bonanza was only the first part of the deal. In 1992 a second dollop of largesse was given out to the privileged tribal elite by National's Treaty Minister, Douglas Graham, via the Treaty of Waitangi (Fisheries Claims) Settlement Act 1992. This included 50% of Sealord Fisheries (New Zealand's largest fish company) as well as 20% of all new species brought under the quota system in the future.

The Act also required the Crown (i.e. the taxpayer) to pay $150 million, as specified in the Deed of Settlement, to the Treaty of Waitangi Fisheries Commission, for the implied commercial quota purchase of the 60% share of Sealords. This Act makes it clear that the National government of the time saw the whole fisheries as a breach of the treaty in spite of it not being so. Maoris also argued that their fishing rights were *customary* ones because they knew that the Maori version of the treaty did not mention fisheries.

Sealord had 24% of the national fishing quota and so, with their half share in this company plus their existing 10%, Maori now had 22% of the quota. However, by 1997 they had managed to increase this to a whopping 50% of New Zealand's fish resources – not bad considering that fisheries were not even mentioned in Te Tiriti.

This extension of racism into the fishing industry where it does not and should not belong was "sold" to the New Zealand public as providing opportunities for young Maori men to find jobs in the fishing industry. The only problem was that, once the tribal leaders scored their

El Dorado of fishing quota, many of them, instead of providing jobs for their needy and jobless tribesmen found it more profitable to sub-lease their valuable quotas to Asian crews on overcrowded vessels, which are not much more than floating sweatshops.

In the words of prominent Hawkes Bay businessman and former Napier city councillor, John Harrison, commenting on a Bloomberg Businessweek report revealing the slavery and debt bondage on these foreign fishing vessels operating in our waters, "Two hundred years ago Maori enslaved other Maori....Now they're actively partaking in modern-day slavery of Indonesians and others while their jobless numbers climb still higher. Perhaps in the name of humanity, less Maori unemployment, endless hui and taxpayer funded talk-fests, Maori should man the boats themselves to tackle their self-imposed position at the top of our unemployment statistics. It would be a win-win for all concerned."[4] Yes, but that will never happen so long as the tribal leaders can get more money from employing the slave labour of foreign vessels. For them it is not about helping their fellow tribesmen but about enriching the fat cats at the top.

The most vehement supporter of this modern Maori slave-use is the Maori Party whose overwhelming concern, as seen throughout this book, is the enrichment of the tribal elite. They don't care how many people are exploited or impoverished in the process.

Whenever there is a prospect of the government making moves to bring an end to this national embarrassment of Maori chartered "slave" vessels, the Maori Party screams, "Hands off our little racket!" In the words of Maori Party co-leader, Tariana Turia, "We're standing by Maori people involved in the fishing industry who have expressed huge concern that unwarranted government interference [code for ending this form of slavery] in arrangements with foreign chartered fishing vessels will render many *iwi* businesses marginal or uneconomic.....The significant increase of up to $2 extra an hour over and above the minimum wage [payable to the Asian fishermen] will hurt Maori more than any other as the vast majority of *iwi* are principally dependent on foreign charter vessels to catch quota." [5]

Her support for these appalling conditions is a throwback to the Maori slave owning days before the Treaty. This is the woman who, in her capacity as *Associate* Housing Minister, swanned off to Vancouver with her private secretary to attend a conference on "indigenous housing". They stayed seven nights at Vancouver's luxurious Hyatt

Hotel on the taxpayers' tab and the bill for the two of them came to $26,000[6] This seems to have been an entirely unnecessary trip as firstly these conferences can now be done by video link without leaving one's office and secondly it was of no relevance to New Zealand since the Maoris are not indigenous. Yet she screams against a pay rise of a $2 above the minimum wage for men who are effective slaves on Maori controlled vessels. Her little jaunt to Vancouver Hyatt Hotel cost more than what these poor seamen are paid in a year.

Turia's co-leader of the Maori Party, Peter Sharples, spoke in April, 2011, of the tribal exploitation of this form of slavery, declaring that it "would not be appropriate for the government to interfere in their decision making." [7]

"The Maori Party was profoundly compromised by advocating the pro-slavery clause in opposition to the Labour Government's earlier reforms to foreign charter vessel regulations in October, 2006," [8] wrote Michael Coote in the *National Business Review*.

After being shamed into requiring these foreign charter vessels to bring themselves under the New Zealand flag by 2016 with improved conditions, the government is now poised to pay its friends in the tribal elite $300 million as "compensation" for ending the slavery!

In the words of Michael Coote, "New Zealand has descended into the hell of becoming a Treaty of Waitangi-driven madhouse of incontinent cargo cult compensation.....Until the reflagging is done New Zealanders should take care to boycott any seafood products, related businesses and Maori tribes associated with fishing slavery.....Just like the Southern slavers after the American Civil War, modern day Maori tribalists should not be paid one cent in compensation for abolition of the fishing slavery they profited from." [9]

In 2012 there were twenty-seven foreign charter vessels, which were catching about $650 million of fish a year, the majority of it for Maori *iwi* quota, in an export industry valued at an annual $1.5 billion.[10]

So, the taxpayer has been seriously short changed by

a) First, having the quota given out racially rather than commercially. Commercial operators must have a catch history with boats, etc. to get their quota but Maori get their quota free – paid for by the taxpayer. They don't need boats and other expenses to achieve it.

b) Then not getting the young Maoris off the dole and into the fishing industry as intended

c) Then not getting any tax from these foreign vessels while corporate *iwi* are laughing all the way to the bank, having scored a valuable quota non-commercially and then benefitting from it by onselling it at a profit without having to do any work to develop it

d) And now facing a demand for $300 million as "compensation" for ending a system of slavery that should never have arisen in the first place if Maori had manned the boats themselves as was intended. But Sharples said that young Maori men don't like to be too far away from their "whanau". We are talking about fishing in a zone no more than 370 kilometres from New Zealand's shore with frequent trips back to port.

With high unemployment – especially in respect of young Maori men – we have the non-employment of tax paying New Zealand crews for a large part of our national fishing quota and the non-employment of an onshore work force to process the catch since foreign crews on foreign vessels take it back to their own countries to process.

Contemporaneous with this transfer of so much fish, jobs and boats to cheap labour Asian countries has been the collapse of several small-time New Zealand European owned fishing enterprises in the last five to ten years. So, the actions of the tribal elite in grabbing an undeserved quota in the first place and then hiving the benefits offshore while pocketing the profits themselves is not only greedy but also unpatriotic, leading to both the loss of jobs and tax revenue for New Zealand.

Since so many *iwi* have not performed their part of the deal, that part of the quota should be taken away from them. But it appears that n government would be prepared to take a stand as principled as that.

Unfortunately, the preferential treatment given to Maoris goes much further than the generous and undeserved quota that was bestowed on them solely because of their tribal ancestors. They also have special rights at a lower level, which works to the disadvantage of the recreational fishermen of New Zealand. I am talking about *taiapure* and *mataitais*, two categories of Maori customary fishing reserves.

Taiapure come under Part 9 of the Fisheries Act 1996 while *mataitai* are covered by regulations – Fisheries (Kaimoana Customary Fishing) Regulations 1998 and the Fisheries (South Island Customary Fishing) Regulations 1999. Both these types of Maori controlled fishing reserves were created a sa consequence of the Treaty of Waitangi (Fisheries Claims) Settlement Act 1992, via the 1996 Fisheries Act.

Taiapure were proposed to give better provision for *rangatiratanga*, and ownership rights under s. 2. They can occur in

253

coastal or estuary areas which are of special customary fishing significance to the tribes. They require a Maori management committee and there may be representatives from other fisher stakeholders. There are high upkeep costs as the Ministry has to pay the Maori community involved yet another taxpayer subsidy to support this racist system. Although popular initially, only eight of them have so far been set up – Palliser Bay, Wellington (3 sq. km), Maketu, Bay of Plenty (55 sq. km), Porangahau, south of Cape Kidnappers (67 sq km), Waikare Inlet, Bay of Islands (18 sq km), Kawhia-Aotea (137 sq km), East Otago (23 sq km), Delaware Bay, east of Nelson (25 sq km) and Banks Peninsula (45 sq km), making a total of 373 sq km so far.

Under *mataitai* regulations special Maori customary fishing reserves in "traditional fishing areas" can be set up. These regulations require tribal groups to appoint their own "kaitiaki". In Maori this word means literally "those who look after (tiaki) food (kai)."

Mataitais are a privatisation of the control of non-commercial fishing to the tribal group setting it up. Commercial fishing is usually excluded – in contrast to *Taiapure,* where commercial fishing is allowed. The public have the right to fish recreationally in a mataitai, subject to its rules. The public are also able to make submissions on any proposal. Nevertheless, it is a race based reserve since only tribal groups have the right to set up these reserves and patrol them.

Parliament initially said that *mataitais* would be "small, discreet areas of special importance to Maori such as reefs and shell beds".[12]

In 1998 Rapaki in Lyttelton harbour became the first *mataitai*, (covering about 25 hectares and 2.5 km of coastline). "But sloppy administration of *mataitai* regulations encourages *mataitai* to grow – both in area and scope. Customary Maori seized the chance to take control of coastal fisheries," wrote Roger Beattie in his article, Maori Fishery Reserves – Bureaucratic Racism" for the New Zealand Centre for Political Research.

"Late 2004 saw an 8,000 hectare *mataitai* declared over Paterson Inlet on Stewart Island. Other large *mataitais* followed: in 2005 Moremore off Napier (9,000 hectares and about 20 km of coast line), Raukokere in 2005 at East Cape (2,600 hectares and about 13 km of coast line), and Aotea harbour in 2008 (4,000 hectares and about 45 km of shore line). Applications are also in process or planned for Tory Channel (2,500 hectares and 80 km of shore line), Otago harbour (5,000 hectares and 45 km plus of shore line), and Lyttelton harbour (4,000 hectares and 30 km plus of shore line),......

Recreational fishing loses out badly with the rush to large *mataitai*. Recreational fishing operates by way of a common law tradition handed down since time immemorial. Common law gives the public right of access to sea fisheries."[13]

Despite the smooth talk of the Ministry of Fisheries the fact is that mataitais deprive recreational fishermen of their ancient and precious common law rights. In Mr. Beattie's words, "All recreational fishing in a *mataitai* is by way of privilege granted by the Maori owners. The very nature of privileges means that they can be revoked at will.

The Tangata Tiaka/Katikati [now called "guardians" rather than "gatherers"] can make bylaws that determine the what, how, when and where of fishing. Recreational fishing can be excluded either by species or through a general closure. *Iwi, hapu* and *whanau* are exempt: *mataitai* bylaws don't apply to fishing under customary rules.

It's one thing for recreational fishers to give up common law rights over particular shell beds and reefs. However, it's a very different story when it comes to giving up common law rights over thousands of hectares of prime recreational fishing area and tens of kilometres of coast line......[as is now happening]

Privileges are no substitute for rights. Only a fool would trade away common law rights to fish recreationally over huge areas of coastal water in return for being granted a privilege based on someone else's preferences. .....Politicians of the day like Sir Douglas Graham, gave assurances that *mataitai* would be small and discreet areas. Now they don't want to know and don't care."[14]

By 2012 the Ministry of Primary Industry (formerly the Ministry of Fisheries) had set up seven maitaitais in the North Island and nineteen in the South Island and Stewart Island, twenty-six in all, covering hundreds of square kilometres and significant areas of coast.

Mataitais are a threat to New Zealand recreational fishers and to all who love the outdoors. No democratic government should be allowed to tolerate them. If that means a massive shift in the political landscape, that could hardly be worse than the present. National and Labour have led us into this hell-hole of having important rights determined by race and they are not the ones to lead us out of it. These unnecessary, historically dubious and ever expanding Maori private fishing rights are incompatible with a fair, decent and non-racist society.

WATER

Hugh Barr

"By the law of nature these things are common to mankind – the air, running water, the sea, and consequently the shores of the sea."
The Institutes of Justinian, 529 A.D.

Encouraged by the racist extremism of the Waitangi Tribunal and by the endless concessions that have been made by appeasing and cowardly governments, the tribal elite has claimed the foreshore and seabed, the fish of the ocean, water (both fresh and salt) and even wind. Their ultimate aim is to get us all to pay for these things which in other countries are not handed out on a racist basis to those who scream the loudest. By claiming the wind they are laying the ground for charging us even for the air that we breathe in our own country.

It seems bizarre that in this so-called "advanced" 21st century we have to waste time telling a small, racist corporate elite why they do not and can not own the water that God gave to mankind for the use and pleasure of all of us and which, as shown by the quote from the Institutes of Justinian at the head of this Section, has been recognised in the law of civilised societies as being common to mankind for at least 1,600 years. But the greed of Maoridom's tribal elite has forced us to go back to basics.

Water is a natural and – so far – constantly renewing resource. Common sense dictates that no one can actually own any specific drops of water. If water "belongs" to anyone, it belongs to the entire nation. Therefore, although its actual ownership is incapable in law – be it the Institutes of Justinian or even the Treaty of Waitangi - its use and accessibility can be regulated (e.g. to discourage wastage) but only by the State on behalf of us all.

No citizen, company or tribe should be granted rights over water in public places which would allow it to be sold or access to it to be withheld. In other words, water should be free for recreational and reasonable domestic use as it has been ever since 1840, while commercial use of it may be taxed with the tax going to the government on behalf of the nation and not into the pockets of any particular tribe. And let it not be forgotten that it was Western invention and technology that developed the use of water in New Zealand – taps, dams, flushing toilets, baths, etc. – from which we all benefit but which those of European descent are not using as an excuse to extort money out of Maoris for this efficient provision of water to their homes. For Maoris the Western ways are so much superior to their bucket system of pre-1840.

Nowhere in any of the Treaty of Waitangi's several versions is there any mention of water, and the modern claim is made under the all encompassing word "Taonga" which, as we have seen, was wrongly translated by Professor Hugh Kawharu in 1987 since its real meaning at the time of the treaty was "goods" or, more specifically, "goods acquired at the point of a spear", which was the usual way of acquiring anything in pre-1840 New Zealand be it a pa, village, goods and chattels, or even females.

It is Kawharu's mistranslation of this word that has opened virtually the whole universe to Maori claims on the grounds that they are "treasures". The British, at the height of their Industrial Revolution where water powered all the steam engines that made the British Empire the mighty force that it was, would never have signed the treaty if "taonga" was to embrace all natural resources, some invisible and not even discovered such as radio frequencies, instead of its real meaning at the time, viz. "goods".

In the interests of both historical accuracy and national integrity Kawharu's deeply flawed translation of this word should be confined to the waste paper basket as it has – very likely by deliberate intent – caused a mistranslation of the treaty which has driven a sword through the nation, endangering both our race relations and the economy in general since almost everything is now claimed under this wrong translation of "taonga".

For tribes to seek "recognition" of some special relationship with all water is preposterous since all New Zealanders have a similar relationship to this natural element. For Christians it has an even more meaningful and spiritual relationship since it is the essence of baptism yet we don't see the churches claiming that they own all the water of the land.

For those who came from Europe in the 19th century to settle the country and make it what it is to-day water had been the staff of life for millennia – for boiling food, for washing body and clothes, for fishing and sailing, for making ale and whisky and, as already mentioned, for powering the new steam engines. But the descendants of these people are not claiming that they own the nation's water. Only the greedy and not very well educated tribal leaders are spouting that nonsense, with the prize for the silliest comment going to Maori Council co-chairman, Maanu Paul, who was quoted in the *Otago Daily Times* as saying, "As far as my people are concerned we are the water and the water is us." [1] Yes, well no doubt a lot of white surfers feel the same way but they don't claim ownership of it.

Into this cesspool of racism and opportunism stepped a Waikato chief called Tuheitia who is wrongly called "the Maori king". Like all other New Zealanders he is a subject of Queen Elizabeth II and no monarch can be the subject of another. It is legally impossible. Tuheitia, described by *New Zealand Herald* commentator, Bob Jones, as "the comical Ngaruawahia ex-truck driver who can't speak Maori and struggles with English but calls himself king of Maoridom despite his realm ending at his letter-box" [2] is encouraged in his pretensions by gullible journalists in our dumbed down society – people like the *Dominion Post's* political reporter, Tracy Watkins, who displayed her constitutional ignorance when she wrote, "For King Tuheitia, whose reign has so far been underwhelming, the *hui* was a giant step toward making the kingship relevant".[3] Three bits of nonsense in one sentence as he is not a king, does not reign and there is no kingship.

Tuheitia's cheap and opportunistic claim that "we have always owned the water" is every bit as nonsensical as Tracy Watkins' reporting. In fact, almost every time that this foul mouthed fraud opens his mouth and claims to speak for "Maoridom" he creates more embarrassment for Maoris – especially the growing number of Maori achievers who have higher aspirations than forever bludging off their fellow countrymen on the grounds of spurious race claims.

The only honest and reasonable conclusion and one that is in harmony with the treaty signed at Waitangi – but not with the reinvented treaty of the Treaty of Waitangi Act 1975 – is that *iwi* should have the same – and no greater – rights to use water as everyone else in New Zealand.

John Key, in one of his several prevarications on this issue, has said that "no one owns the water" but, like his government's equally nonsensical Marine and Coastal Area Act (which says that no one owns the foreshore and seabed, thereby taking it out of Crown , i.e. public, ownership), this "no one owns" concept opens up a can of worms. Water should be regarded unequivocally as a natural resource, which in effect "belongs" to the nation and all its citizens. Any other interpretation, such as allowing a tribe to own it racially, opens the way to holding the public to ransom over this resource which is so vital for human life – all the more so since some Maori leaders have said that they are Maoris first and New Zealanders second. .

For examples of holding the public to ransom over water we only need to look at the case of the hydro dam that Meridian Energy wanted to build on the Mokihinui River on the West Coast to provide electricity to consumers. Initially the local *iwi*, a sub-tribe of Ngai Tahu, opposed the dam. But this position was changed by the majority of the group when Meridian offered them a substantial payment – the "Maori tax" that seems to attach to these sorts of things and which we all have to pay for in higher prices.

Another instance of tribal defiance of the general good occurred on the Kapiti coast, north of Wellington, which has a perennial shortage of water. To supplement the meagre supplies the local council looked at drawing some water from the nearby Otaki River. But the local *iwi*, the Ngati Raukawa *runanga*, refused, its chairman, Waari Carkeek, screaming, "I want to remind council that taking water from the Otaki River is non-negotiable." [4] To which Kapiti's mayor, the craven and ever so politically correct Jenny Rowan, replied ever so meekly, "We will not go there if you say no." [5]. These and other examples show the utter folly of putting the future of our water supplies in the hands of greedy and not very patriotic tribes.

And, of course, if they don't get their own way legally, they can always resort to thuggery as happened at Lake Horowhenua in September, 2012. In the words of Wellington's *Dominion Post*, "Young rowers face a bleak season after arriving at one of the country's poorest clubs to find all but two of their boats smashed and strewn around the clubhouse. The attack has come in the midst of what Horowhenua Rowing Club members describe as mounting abuse and threats from Maori activists over ownership of Lake Horowhenua....Twenty-five boats were pulled off the racks and had holes stabbed through the bottoms of them." [6] Police counted seventy-five holes in total and the damaged boats had to be taken all the way to Lake Karapiro to be repaired at an estimated cost that was in six figures, meaning that the boats would be out of action for much of the coming regatta season.

As already stated water should be free for recreational and reasonable domestic use. Hence rainwater collected in roof tanks, artesian wells on private property, and rain which falls on private land and stays in the soil, is a simple, free and natural benefit of living in a well-watered country like New Zealand.

However, as soon as a farmer or a local industry puts a pipe into a river and pumps out water for crop spraying, dairying, irrigation, etc., they are using the state's (i.e. everyone's) water for their own commercial advantage. It is only fair and logical that they should pay a tax to the state as the "owner" of the water and that is where Mr. Key's argument that "no one owns the water" falls down. How can the state (or local authority) make a charge on water used for commercial purposes if they don't "own" the water?

We, the people of New Zealand, have already lost the foreshore and seabed through Mr. Key's taking it out of Crown ownership so that "no one owns it", thereby making it easier for tribes to grab under National's new ownership concept of "customary marine title", and, if this constitutional ignoramus is not more careful, we, the people of New Zealand, will lose our fresh water as well. In fact, in his usual wishy-washy way of trying to please everybody Key has already conceded the point. In a letter to *iwi* leaders in May, 2009, Mr. Key acknowledged that *iwi* have "specific interests and rights in fresh water" [7] The problem is that Key is just a glib day trader without an understanding of the past and without a care for the future.

Key's statement is false. If the Treaty gave Maori rights over water, then from 1840 the authorities would have been paying the ever-grasping tribes for the use of such. But that is not the case.

Where water is collected by local bodies, purified and reticulated for domestic use, the costs of doing this can be – and sometimes are – recovered by means of a water rate but the charge is for the "value added" to the water (e.g. guaranteeing its purity) and not for the water itself. The idea of acknowledging that the ever extorting tribes own such a natural resource as water or indeed have any rights in it greater than those of other citizens is so bizarre, legally flawed and morally unacceptable that it is doubtful it would have got as far as it has but for the National government earlier caving in to the equally preposterous claim that the Crown no longer owns the foreshore and seabed on behalf of the people of New Zealand. Both these outrageous claims are alien to our nation, extremely dubious in law, and subversive of both our democracy and our ancient rights which were brought from Britain, the home of the common law, by our ancestors more than 170 years ago.

However, encouraged by their success at getting the opportunity to grab long stretches of our rich and beautiful coast line by National's Marine and Coastal Area Act, is it any wonder that the tribal leaders should stretch their luck and try for a second bite of the cherry by going for our water as well?

As with the Emissions Trading Scheme, by which National handed corporate iwi "up to $2 billion" [8] on a golden plate so as to buy the support of the Maori Party in Parliament, it could well just be posturing so that, when these energy companies are eventually put up for sale, corporate *iwi* will get preferential treatment in any rush for shares. Indeed, the Minister of Finance, Bill English, has already intimated something along these lines when he said that the problems could be sorted out by effectively giving "koha" to certain tribes that prove obstructive. "Koha" is the gift that one is expected to leave on the marae after one has visited it – a complete reversal of the usual rules of hospitality that are followed in other cultures, viz. of giving hospitality to a guest without expecting – or demanding – something in return. Mr. English's words were, "As you get down the track there will be some kind of settlement which generally involves some cash, or involves the transfer of some Crown assets to them".[9] This is the same Mr. English, offering to use taxpayers' money for what is effectively political bribery with a racist tinge, who as Leader of the Opposition campaigned for "one law for all". Ah yes, there is nothing like a politician of conviction!

"Koha" should be left on the marae and should have no presence where public funds are involved. In fact, where a government buys off tribes by giving them "koha" out of taxpayers' funds, we are talking about bribery and corruption. That the Deputy Prime Minister should be airing this possibility shows just how rotten and corrupt is this Key government and how different it is from previous National administrations.

This stench of corruption seems to go to the very heart of National's proposed sale of these particular assets at this particular time as only a fool or a traitor would sell vital state assets in the depths of a recession when prices are at their lowest – and made even lower by the government's indecision over water rights. Just like when Gordon Brown, as Chancellor of the Exchequer, sold the Bank of England's gold reserves when prices were particularly low but which shot up rapidly not long afterwards. No wonder this bungler left the British economy in such a mess.

261

In the words of Michael Coote in the *National Business Review*, "Maori water rights claims have gone viral and the beginning of an era looms of a pervasive 'Maori tax' inflicted upon the economy via blanket rent-seeking activities imposed on natural resources.

All-tactics-and-no-strategy Mr. Key faces further corrosion of his tarnished political credibility as New Zealanders find they have increasingly little reason to trust in his hubristic and vainglorious underestimation of limitless and litigious Maori demands for racial superiority".[10]

Finance Minister Bill English claims that it is necessary to sell these strategic state assets to reduce the national debt which, on his watch, ballooned into the record books, touching a Budget deficit of just on $10 billion for the eight months to the end of February, 2012.

However, according to former Labour leader, Phil Goff, using figures prepared by his office, the government – or, if you like, the taxpayer – would be throwing away $900 million in annual payments from these forfeited state enterprises.[11]. That is what the four targeted state owned enterprises paid to the government in the year to 30th June, 2011 (Air New Zealand $55 million, Meridian Energy $684 million, Mighty River Power $110 million, Solid Energy $50 million)[12]

It seems that the main beneficiary of this reckless throwaway will be Mr. Key's colleagues in the finance industry – the "service providers" (Computershare Investor Services, and Clemenger) which, it is believed, will pocket between them $140 million.[13] Seen from their point of view – and only from their point of view - the sale of state assets in the depths of a recession does make sense.

Another of Mr. English's tricks was to fly to Singapore and Hong Kong within hours of announcing in the 2011 Budget that the government was going to sell parts of various state assets. The purpose of his trip was to interest Asian investors in this massive privatisation. "Asian investor" is code for China's sovereign companies and those controlled by Li Ka-shing, Hong Kong's richest man, which kowtow to China's brutal communist dictatorship. Mr. English went so far as to say that he met the "top brass" of the Chinese Investment Corporation (C.I.C.) in Peking in April, 2011 – a company that is reported to have set aside $6 billion to "invest" in little old New Zealand [14]

China is in the business of trying to control the world by means of owning vital assets like the strategically important, formerly U.S. owned Panama Canal and, on a more local level, Wellington's electricity network – both owned by companies controlled by that lackey of China's government, Li Ka-shing, through his Hutchison Corporation. The reason why China chose New Zealand as the first Western country with which to make a "free trade" deal was because New Zealand was regarded as more gullible than other countries and therefore less averse to putting itself in the jaws of the dragon.

The postponement of this landmark privatisation in the face of spurious Maori claims to ownership of the nation's water suggests that appeasement is something that Mr. Key can never shake off but, even if he were to find a piece of bone in his back that could be recognised as a spine and face down this latest and most absurd challenge of corporate *iwi*, that would not entitle him to the gratitude of the voters. He would have to restore the foreshore and seabed to Crown ownership before he could deserve that.

It should not be forgotten that control of water and water rights on a planet with increasing population and growing aridity will be a leading issue through the 21st century. At this point in our history, to place our water supply at the mercy of the extortionists of corporate *iwi* would be the final death knell of Hobson's noble aspiration of "We are now one people". It would endanger the welfare and economy of the country to the detriment of everyone – Maori and non-Maori – who are not part of the corporate *iwi* elite.

We owe it to ourselves and our descendants to keep this priceless natural resource in the hands of the State for the benefit of all and not to trade away any rights in it for the political convenience of the present government. Water is too valuable, powerful and important to our daily lives for it to be "racialised" in any shape, manner or form. When a state loses control of its water it also loses much of its sovereignty and freedom to operate.

SEPARATE AND PRIVILEGED

Mike Butler

D. McMaster of Auckland filed a claim with the Waitangi Tribuna, in February 1985, stating that a number of special privileges were accorded to Maori people by virtue of their race but these privileges were at variance with the Treaty of Waitangi. He asked the tribunal to end such special privilege. Mr McMaster was asked whether he was a Maori. He replied that he was not, and so he was required to withdraw his claim because Section 6 of the Treaty of Waitangi Act 1975 says *only* Maori people can bring a claim.[1] The word "privilege", according to the Concise Oxford Dictionary, means the "right, advantage, or immunity belonging to person, class, or office . . . a special advantage or benefit".

The New Zealand government has fostered a myriad of privileges for those who claim Maori ancestry. Such race-based privilege is not restricted to claims under the Treaty of Waitangi Act, as this chapter will show. It extends to special funding for those claiming Maori ancestry and huge tax advantages for tribal trusts. Administration of this government largesse is so loose that a criminal gang was able to access funding from a race-backed programme to finance a drugs operation. Anyone who dares criticise this privilege is called racist and reminded of all the poverty, bad housing, educational disadvantage, and general under-performance that are attributed to Maori.

How much does separate treatment cost?

Separate treatment along racial lines is costly as a result of barmy initiatives, non-essential bureaucratic structures, and duplicated services. Race-based funding in 2011 cost $1.324 billion. This comprises $280 million a year to settle historical grievances since $1.4 billion has been set aside over five years from 2011 for this purpose. Budget 2011 showed that $79 million was set aside for treaty negotiations, and $10.519 million kept the Waitangi Tribunal running. Co-governance of the Waikato River costs $16 million a year. The budget for Te Puni Kokiri (formerly the Ministry of Maori Affairs) was

$208.54 million which included $4 -million for Whanau Ora. Devolved social services may cost $730.8 million a year. Those who do not like to hear about the high annual cost of race-based funding point to the $1.7 billion taxpayer bailout of South Canterbury Finance in 2010. But here's the thing. Race-based funding costs almost that amount *every year*, and this is all for the benefit of one racial group or, to be more truthful, the tribal elite of one particular racial group.

Whanau Ora creates new funding trough

The Whanau Ora scheme, a Maori Party initiative, was set up as an interagency approach to provide health and social services focussing on Maori families, known as *"whanau"*, as a whole. The scheme was allocated $134.3 million in funding over four years from 2010 when it was launched.[2] The taskforce report was 70 pages of platitudes. Critics said the scheme was poorly defined, and predicted numerous back-office jobs and private ticket clipping for no actual change. But none of its numerous critics expected the type of rorting that appeared when the scheme got under way in 2010.

For instance, who would imagine that thousands could access up to $20,000 of Whanau Ora cash for family get-togethers, as New Zealand First leader Winston Peters told parliament on February 7, 2012? One Wellington family, supported by three successful businesses, had collected funding for a family reunion, he said. Whanau Ora Minister Tariana Turia confirmed that more than $6 million had been paid to over 2,000 applicants to the scheme labelled "Whanau Integration, Innovation, and Engagement". Application documents for the funding say that "any New Zealand *whanau*" can apply for between $5,000 and $20,000 in assistance that must be paid to a legal entity "or family or *whanau* trust". Activities that may be funded include "facilitation and reasonable costs of *whanau hui* or *wananga* to develop *whanau* plans" as well as "support for *whanau*-based activities".[3]

A Northland television station and an arts career planning service were among 150 organisations to have banked funds for the Whanau Ora scheme, the Stuff news website reported on February 9, 2012. Peters suggested that private individuals who allocated Whanau Ora funding were working for the recipients, which was an arrangement ripe for conflicts of interest. About 25 "provider collectives" involving more than 150 health and social service providers had been signed up to Whanau Ora by that date, many of which were Maori trust boards, working on social services. The Te Tai Tokerau collective included the Northland TV Charitable Trust, which runs a community television station in Whangarei, while the Kaipara collective included Kumarani Productions - which runs performing arts programmes for special needs adults and children.[4]

Otaki's Rahui Rugby and Sports Club received $60,000 in 2011 to "undertake *whanau* development research" on resilience, "*whanau* connectedness" and community leadership in a scheme that Peters said was proof that the Whanau Ora scheme was a "bro-ocracy".[5] The *Dominion Post* obtained under the Official Information Act details of 25 successful applicants to the *whanau* innovation fund. One $5,000 contract between Te Puni Kokiri and an unnamed Hawke's Bay *whanau* of 20 members said that a *hui* to finalise "spiritual balance" and "family development" would pay $500 each for two facilitators, $400 for a venue, $1,000 for a hangi, $600 for a chef, a $500 administration fee, $300 for travel, and $1,200 for resources. The agreement was signed on January 12, 2012, with $4,000 paid up front on the understanding that the report would be filed with Te Puni Kokiri by the end of April. The final $1,000 would be paid when the *whanau* plans were completed at the end of June.[6]

It got worse as the criminal underbelly got involved. Four members of the We Against Violence charitable trust, that Dunedin police said were known members of the Mongrel Mob, were charged in May, 2012, after nearly $100,000 worth of cannabis was seized, and alleged misuse of government funding was uncovered. Ten were arrested. In November one of those arrested was jailed for four years for dishonestly converting $20,000 of trust money, conspiring to sell cannabis and possessing cannabis for supply. At the time of the offending he was on bail for violence charges. In calls intercepted by police, this person told other gang members that the Dunedin Notorious Mongrel Mob was a model for how other gangs could access Whanau Ora funding.[7]

At the time of the arrests Maori Party co-leader Tariana Turia said there was no evidence that Mongrel Mob members misused $20,000 of Whanau Ora funds, arguing that "there is quite a stringent process to go through and my understanding is that this particular funding was managed by another organisation on their behalf".[8] After the conviction, John Key defended the scheme by saying that Whanau Ora was in its infancy and working with high-risk families. He did not see a need for an investigation because there had not been any "proven substantial issues". After all, Whanau Ora is a Maori Party initiative and Mr. Key is always very careful not to offend the Maori Party.[9]

Wealthy tribes pay little tax

Tribalists assert that tribal businesses contribute significantly to the economy but they don't say that little returns to the public purse as tax. Accountants and tax lawyers who do work for Maori authorities will be all too familiar with this section. When the Crown settles with a tribe, they demand that the settlement is with a "post settlement governance entity", which cannot be tax-exempt. So the settlement usually goes to a Maori authority, which pays tax at 17.5 percent. A Maori authority may give or settle money to a charity (usually a charity of the same tribe), and the Income Tax Act was amended so as to include *iwi* since, under common law, marae activities were not charitable since there is no proof of the members being poor or in need; they might all be very rich. The amendment added "bloodline for Maori" in order to give them the charitable status that, for very good reasons, the common law denied them. Under common law, if the beneficiaries were, for example, restricted to workers from a particular factory rather than the general public, then it would not qualify them as a charity. If the charity was for the benefit of an *iwi*, as it now can be, then that charity can get a distribution from the Maori authority.

The tax paid by the Maori authority comes down as an imputation credit. Companies that pay tax at 28 percent also have an imputation credit, but there is a difference. If a Maori authority pays 17.5 percent tax on $100, it is left with $82.50. It can then distribute the $82.50 to the *iwi* charity that may claim a refund of the $17.50 already paid in tax. In this way a tax credit is available for the tribe but not for an ordinary company, which pays $28 tax on $100 profit, and is left with $72 and no ability to claim a refund on the $28 paid. The Maori authority distributes $82.50 and the tribe gets a refund of $17.50 so that the government gets nothing.

A charity may run a business and not pay any tax on it so long as the purpose of the business is charitable, such as running maraes, promoting welfare, education, etc for *iwi* only. The 17-5 percent that Maori authorities pay in tax is the second-lowest tax rate. A Maori authority may make a non-taxable distribution as it is considered a capital gain, and capital gains are not taxed. A company can also do this if it winds up. There is no obligation to distribute. Charities must pay

GST on commercial activities. These commercial entities can build up a capital empire and employ *iwi* members at an arm's length rate. This is a way of distributing to members. Most tribes have a tax-paying entity as well as a charity.

The newly created Charities Commission was absorbed into a government department in 2012 to cut costs. The commission was policing charities and was getting results from prosecutions. Now there is no strong control of charities, and so no restraint on marae activities. Numerous marae expenses are listed as "koha", mostly without a description of what the "koha" entailed. If funds go missing, they can be written up as "koha". The lack of detail means "koha" entries cannot be audited. Non-Maori companies may not use the term "koha" as a book entry.

The Inland Revenue page on Maori organisations says that from April 1, 2003, any organisation that administers a marae situated on a Maori reservation has been able to qualify for an income tax exemption as a charity as long as it uses its funds to administer and maintain the marae's physical structure and land, or for charitable purposes. As of July 1, 2008, the marae needed to be registered by the Charities Commission to qualify for an exemption from income tax.[10] The exemption is for the organisation that is responsible for the marae, not for the marae itself. The tax exemption is further detailed in Part 1, Section 5 of the Charities Act 2005. Maori authorities have had a special tax status for a long time. The rate was 19.5 percent, reduced to 17.5 percent from the 2012 income year. This was at a time of record deficits when no tax advantages were offered to anyone else.

To show the scale of tax that the government is missing out on, here are returns reported by the two wealthiest tribes. Ngai Tahu is registered as the Ngai Tahu Charitable Trust, a tax-exempt body. For the June, 2012, year, Ngai Tahu reported a profit of $95.66 million, helped by a revaluation of three new dairy farms and the sale of Ryman healthcare shares for $27 million. The trust distributed $26.26 million to the tribe, including $240,000 to each of the tribe's 18 runanga in the South Island.[11] Ngai Tahu makes money from commercial property, vineyards, fisheries, seafood distribution, safaris, Shotover Jet, Huka Falls Jet, finance, forestry, dairy farming, among other ventures. Ngai Tahu's commercial operations claim and pay GST like non-tribal businesses, but the Ngai Tahu bottom line is tax-exempt.

268

Tainui Group Holdings, whose core business is property investment, listed 15 subsidiaries in its 2010 report comprising three seafood companies, two hotels, The Base retail complex at Te Rapa, forestry, and boating. Eight of these had charitable status and seven did not. On its annual report web page it says it "reports its annual results in a slightly different way from most companies because its commercial activities are undertaken ultimately for charitable purposes ... (so) it does not pay tax."[12] For the June 2010 year, Tainui Group Holdings posted a net profit of $39.9 million and distributed an $11 million dividend to its sole shareholder, Waikato-Tainui Te Kauhanganui Incorporated.

In their 2010-11 report, Tainui Group Holdings and Waikato Tainui Fisheries announced, as they were poised to open six new cinemas at The Base, which followed the opening of the $65 million Novotel Auckland Airport hotel that was 70 percent owned by the tribe, that they wanted $1 billion of high quality assets by 2021.[13] Responding in 2011 to a *Waikato Times* report headlined "Super-rich tribes pay no tax", a Tainui Group Holdings spokesman said they did pay GST, and argued that its tax-exempt status also meant that the tribe could not claim depreciation or the interest costs of its borrowing. That spokesman would know but did not say that, with no tax required, there would be no need to minimise profit by claiming all possible deductions.

Tribal entities have been given a competitive advantage over non-tribal businesses by claiming charitable status. The amount not paid in tax is reinvested, thus making them stronger vis-a-vis their competitors in the industries in which they operate and bringing their monopolistic goals closer. Former National Party leader and Reserve Bank Governor, Don Brash, vehemently opposed treating tribes as charities. He suggested one way to make the tax treatment of tribal businesses more equitable would be "to make the payment to the shareholding charity a deductible payment and then have them pay tax, at the same tax rate as any other company would, on what is left," This proposal is similar to charitable tax law reforms planned in Australia.[14] But it remains – and will remain – only a proposal.

BERL finds Maori asset base $36.9b

After decades of statistics that claimed to show that Maori were poor because they were Maori, Business and Economic Research Ltd

269

chief economist Dr Ganesh Nana came up with the somewhat surprising finding that the asset base of enterprises in the 2010 Maori economy totalled at least $36.9 billion. Presenting to the 2011 Maori Economic Summit a summary of findings of projects undertaken for the Maori Economic Taskforce and Te Puni Kokiri, he said that figure was an increase of $20.4 billion from the 2006 estimate of $16.5 billion.

In gross domestic product terms, the operating surplus income of Maori enterprises totalled $3.3 billion, while capital spending totalled $1.4 billion. The employment and capital income of Maori households totalled $10 billion, and spending amounted to $16.6 billion. The Maori enterprise sector recorded gross output of $22.2 billion, resulting in net savings of $0.2 billion. National net savings of the enterprise sector totalled $10.3 billion. The Maori household sector recorded total income of $14.8 billion and total outlays of $20.3 billion, resulting in net savings of (-)$5.5 billion. National net savings of the household sector totalled (-)$7.8 billion.[15] New Zealand's total annual GDP is around $200 billion.

Maori draw disproportionately more welfare

Nevertheless, Maori continue to draw disproportionately more welfare. Te Puni Kokiri advised the incoming Minister of Maori Affairs, in December, 2011, that welfare payments to Maori exceeded tax paid by Maori,[16] an assertion made without evidence. When ACT Party members made this claim with supporting evidence around 2003, they were howled down. At that time, the Institute of Economic Research showed that Maori were paying slightly more in tax than they received in transfers - they paid $2.404 in tax and received $2.312 in social benefits.[17] Has the situation worsened since 2003? Why did Te Puni Kokiri make this claim in 2011? Either the claim is factual, or it is made to perpetuate the tale of Maori deprivation to keep the funds flowing.

Ministry of Social Development fact sheets for June, 2012, revealed that, of the 50,000 working-age people receiving an unemployment benefit, 36.5 percent or 18,250 were Maori and 9.3 percent were Pacific Islanders. Of the 59,000 working-age people receiving a sickness benefit, 28 percent, or 16,520, were Maori, and 7 percent were Islanders. Of the 84,000 working-age people receiving an invalid's benefit, 22.4 percent, or 18,816, were Maori and 5.1 percent were Islanders. And of the 112,000 working-age people receiving a domestic purposes benefit, 42.7 percent, or 47,824, were Maori, and

10.2 percent were Islanders.[18] A total of 673,000 Maori made up 15 percent of the population in 2006. In 2012, 101,410, or 27 percent, of an estimated 380,000 working-age Maori (18–64 years) were receiving a benefit. More positively, 73 percent of working-age Maori were not receiving a benefit.

Former Prime Minister Helen Clark summed up the grim nature of intergenerational welfare in 2004 when she said: "In some parts of our country, whether it's the Far North or East Coast, you've got kids who have never seen Mum or Dad, or even Granddad or Grandma, go to work and you get long term demoralisation set in in those communities and that's where crime's rife, the drug take is rife, alcoholism's rife, the ill health-overweight's rife and you have trouble just getting people off their backsides and into a job because of the problems." [19] Of course this grim situation is a socio-economic problem, not a racial problem, and is not limited to Maori.

Should blood quantum be a part of definition of Maori?

New Zealand First leader Winston Peters pushed an argument over Maori identity into the headlines in September, 2012, when he said "if cynical backroom deals between the National and Maori parties lead to preferential treatment for Maori over water rights, then all New Zealanders should claim to be Maori". He said "such a move would force the Government to declare exactly who it considers to be Maori enough to get special deals on assets already owned by all New Zealanders".[20] Peters argued his point in a two-on-one debate on TV One's *Close-Up* on September 13, 2012.

The debate raised the concept of blood quantum, which refers to describing the degree of ancestry for an individual of a specific ethnic group. For instance, 1/4 Omaha tribe, was widely applied in the United States after the Indian Reorganization Act of 1934. The government used it to establish which individuals could be recognised as Native American and be eligible for financial and other benefits. On the *Close-Up* debate, Waikato University sociologist, Tahu Kukutai, asserted: "Blood quantum is a colonial fantasy. There is no scientific basis for racial purity. Blood quantum is tied to the nasty history of racial exclusion".

Statistics New Zealand in 2005 defined ethnicity as the ethnic group or groups that people identify with or feel they belong to, and noted that people can belong to more than one ethnic group. But to be on the Maori electoral roll and gain access to education scholarships, evidence of Maori descent is required. If Statistics New Zealand adopted the electoral roll or Maori scholarship criteria for "Maoriness", the Maori population would immediately shrink and the woeful welfare, education, and crime rates would merge with the socio-economic data of the rest of the population.

Why should the government continue with a separate Maori department?

Separate treatment along racial lines is deeply rooted. The government has had a Minister of Maori Affairs and a Maori Affairs department since responsible government began in 1853. The Minister of Maori Affairs supervised the Maori Affairs Department, while having input into other portfolios to the extent that they affect Maori. In 1989, the Department of Maori Affairs was broken up. Its policy function was vested in Manata Maori (the Ministry of Maori Affairs), and its operational and service functions in Te Tira Ahu Ihu (the Iwi Transition Agency), which was to manage their transfer to mainstream agencies or devolution to tribe-based assemblies over a period of five years. A change of government late in 1990 meant that the enabling Runanga a Iwi Act, enacted in mid-1990, was repealed in mid-1991 and the Iwi Transition Agency was abolished, Manatu Maori was beefed up into Te Puni Kokiri (the Ministry of Maori Development), and most service functions were mainstreamed or contracted out.[21]

Section 5 of the Ministry of Maori Development Act 1991 outlines the statutory responsibilities of the ministry, which include increasing achievement by Maori in education, training and employment, health, and economic resource development.[22] Separate Maori affairs administration has created a source of power and money that is not available to non-Maori, and persists unquestioned, apart from the occasional misuse of a work credit card by staff for private spending.

The scale of funding for Te Puni Kokiri is shown in the 2011 Budget that allocated a total of $208.54 million. An amount of $27 million was allocated for policy advice, $9 million for the Land Management Unit, $7 million for community level social assistance to Maori *whanau* including Maori wardens, $7 million for "strengthening relationships" with Maori, $75 million for the promotion of Maori language and culture through Te Mangai Paho, Maori Television

272

Services and Te Putahi Paoho, and the Maori Language Commission, $10 million for the Maori Trustee, $3 million for Maori economic development initiatives across tourism and the productive sectors, $21 million for Maori Potential through community investment programmes and "rangatiratanga" grants, $4 million for Iwi Housing Support, Maori Registration Service, Maori Wardens, NZ Maori Council and Maori Women's Development Fund, $500,000 for addressing treaty and contemporary claims, $43,000 for various legislative payments administered by Te Puni Kokiri, $2 million for capital investment in the Maori Trustee and departmental capital expenditure, and $43 million for Whanau Ora..[23]

Te Puni Kokiri has a policy section, known as "policy wahanga", which aims to lead and influence public policy, particularly that which "impacts on Crown-Maori relationships, the protection and promotion of Maori rights, interests and development opportunities in cultural, natural and other resources; the promotion of economic opportunities for Maori; and the systems of government".

It would appear that political appointees and employees working in Te Puni Kokiri are controlling the above-stated policy areas for the government, which is possibly the single biggest reason that the government-driven Maori privilege behemoth continues irrespective of any political administration and would seem unstoppable. Moreover, research detailed in this chapter that, as well as failure in Whanau Ora, poor uptake in the use of the Maori language, increasing unpopularity of Maori immersion schools, and increasing numbers of Maori on welfare, would indicate that the $200 million plus a year spent on Te Puni Kokiri is an epic waste of money. This raises the question of why, after 173 years of shared history, should a separate Maori department still exist?

Should the question of separate Maori seats be left to Maori to decide?

Separate political representation has existed since 1867, when the Maori Representation Act provided for the election of four Maori MPs by Maori males (including half-castes) aged 21 and over. The Act was deemed necessary in the mid-19th century when the right to vote was based on individual ownership of a freehold estate to the value of £25. Disputed ownership of customary Maori land that had no title meant many Maori who wanted to vote could not provide the proof to meet the electoral requirement. Some Maori could supply this proof and

273

some did vote. It is worthwhile to note that the 1867 Act gave Maori men a non-property right to vote 12 years before European males, which occurred in 1879 through the Qualification of Electors Act.[24]

The 1867 Act established four Maori electorates as an interim measure for five years. Parliament had the view that the Maori Land Court, established in 1865, would resolve title issues for Maori within that time. The 1867 Act was extended a further five years in 1872, and extended again in 1876, this time indefinitely. Maori males who met the property qualification were entitled to vote in either Maori or European constituencies. When, in 1893, universal suffrage extended voting rights to all New Zealanders, subject only to an age qualification, any practical reason for separate Maori seats had disappeared.[25]

Nevertheless, separate seats continued, and this separate representation took on a life of its own as political parties courted Maori support. For instance, in the 1946 general election, the National and Labour parties were tied for general seats, and it was only Labour's hold on the four Maori seats which enabled it to stay in power. The National Party feared that cutting the Maori seats would bring thousands of Labour-voting Maori on to the general roll in its marginal rural electorates. When Parliament reviewed the Maori seats in 1953 while re-aligning Maori electoral boundaries, the vested interests of both Labour and National meant that Maori seats remained.

More than 173 years of intermarriage meant that those of Maori ancestry often had more blood of the colonisers. By 1975, the Maori Electoral Option allowed for electors of Maori descent to choose whether to be enrolled on the general or Maori roll. This option occurs after every census and is the only time Maori voters can switch between the general and the Maori rolls. Those wishing to register on the Maori roll must answer a Maori-descent question, and may have only a minute trace of Maori blood. During the 1980s the Maori seats became linked with the Maori separatist movement. The Report of the Royal Commission into the Electoral System in 1986 noted that separate representation disadvantaged Maori in a number of ways. In recommending a change from the old first-past-the-post voting system to MMP, which eventuated, this commission predicted that MMP would bring more Maori MPs to Parliament, which has also eventuated. This commission recommended the abolition of the Maori seats if MMP was introduced.

MMP was introduced in the 1996 election and the Maori seats stayed. Not only did they remain but pressure exerted by Maori nationalist groups meant that the number of Maori seats became tied to the number of New Zealanders electing to register on the Maori roll, creating an incentive to promote registration on the Maori roll. Several well-publicised, taxpayer-funded enrolment drives increased the number of Maori seats from four to seven. In the 2011 general election only 53 percent of the 233,568 registered on the Maori roll bothered to vote.

The National Party quietly morphed from having a policy of phasing out the separate Maori parliamentary seats to leaving it up to Maori to decide. This change appeared in a leaders' debate in the 2011 election when it seemed that National Party leader, John Key, was making up policy on the hoof. The Maori Party wants the Maori parliamentary seats to be entrenched in law and, like the Afrikaner Nationalists in apartheid South Africa, wants every New Zealander classified by ethnicity, with all 18-year-olds of even remotely Maori descent placed automatically on to the Maori electoral roll so as to increase it.

Should this occur, the number of Maori seats would need to be expanded every election to keep pace with an ever-growing "Maori" population of one-eighths, one-sixteenths, etc. The "overhang" that occurs when a party wins more electorate seats than their party vote entitles them to, means that the number of confidence votes needed to form a government increases from 61 to 62. This would give the Maori Party disproportionate leverage in coalition talks, should the highest polling party find itself unable to form a government in its own right or with other coalition partners. Entrenching separate Maori political representation would embed a self-anointed racial aristocracy, a situation that numerous non-Maori New Zealanders would have a strong opinion on. Therefore, the question of whether or not to retain the Maori seats should be made only by the New Zealand public by way of binding referendum.

The Maori Council – created by, but enemy of, the government
The government created a further separate political hierarchy under the New Zealand Maori Council in 1962. This replaced tribal committees, recognised through the Maori Social and Economic Advancement Act 1945 after being praised for their contribution to the war effort from 1939 to 1945.[26] The Maori Welfare Act 1962 was a

275

response to more Maori moving to the cities after that war. That Act brought into being the Maori Council that was the top of a four-tier bureaucracy, with neighbourhood committees on the bottom tier. Executives supervised the bottom tier committees, and district councils, based on Maori Land Court boundaries, supervised the executives. Elections at three levels were held every three years. Each district council sent three delegates to the national council that elected a president. The government disbursed subsidies through this structure. Since a number of its presidents were National Party stalwarts, the Maori Council became identified with the National Party.

The Maori Council's Legislative Review Committee began to advocate biculturalism, called for law changes to allow Maori self-determination, asserted the principle that in Maori society the group is more important than the individual, and demanded a new law to support retention, use, and management of Maori land by the tribe. It also asserted that the constitutional right of government to rule, that emanated from the Treaty of Waitangi, was balanced by a fiduciary responsibility that the government had toward Maori.[27]

Is Maori immersion schooling saving the Maori language?

Over a billion dollars has been directed over the last twenty years[28] toward funding *kohanga reo*, which are early childhood education centres for children from birth to five years old and their families that involve total immersion in the Maori language, according to Education Minister Hekia Parata. The Waitangi Tribunal's 2012 report, *Matua Rautia: The Report on the Kohanga Reo Claim*, predictably upheld the claimants' view that a decline in the number of *kohanga reo* and the number of children enrolled in *kohanga reo* could be blamed on Crown actions and omissions. Always blame the Crown! Close to 9,000 children and members of their wider family attended the 471 *kohanga reo* across the country in 2012, whereas in 1990, there were 616 *kohanga reo* with 10,108 children.

Concern at the decline of the language, especially after a 1971 report,[29] led to a push to save it by establishing pre-schools and schools in which Maori would be the language of instruction. The first *kohanga reo* opened at Pukeatua Marae in Wainuiomata in April, 1982, and by 1985 the number was approaching 400, taking in more than 6,000 children.

The 20 hours per week early childhood education subsidy comprised 20.9 per cent of total Government funding for *kohanga reo* in 2010–11. Licensed *kohanga reo* are eligible for "standard" early childhood education funding rates of $7.70 per funded child hour up to 20 hours a week. *Kohanga reo* could also access equity funding, which was targeted at reducing educational disparities, as well as the childcare subsidy, which contributed a higher share of Government funding than for the rest of the early childhood education sector.[30] The Maori Party secured $19 million in Budget 2012 for Maori medium early childhood education providers. The umbrella Kohanga Reo National Trust receives $2.643 million a year for "administration".

"Kura kaupapa Maori" are state schools established under section 155 of the Education Act 1989 for pupils six and over in which Maori is the principal language of instruction. Kaupapa Maori education aims to educate children and young people into tribal society and into Maori knowledge using the Maori language. Kura kaupapa schools adhere to "Te Aho Matua", which is a set of principles underpinned by Maori values, beliefs and customs. The board of Te Kura Kaupapa Maori ensures that the principles are met along with the national curriculum framework. All *kura kaupapa* schools are co-educational and are part of the compulsory schooling sector of New Zealand state schools, while early childhood centres, *kohanga reo*, universities, technical institutes or "*whare wananga*" are not part of the compulsory sector.

How many parents opt for Maori-language immersion schooling? Auckland University Associate Professor of Education, Elizabeth Rata, said that about 14 percent of the school age population are identified as Maori. Of these, about 84 percent are in mainstream schools while about 16 percent are in Maori-medium education, where the Maori language makes up 12 percent or more of the instruction. Nearly 4 percent are in the separate *kaupapa* Maori education system where 80-100 percent of the instruction is in the Maori language. This includes institutions for early childhood, primary, secondary, tertiary sectors, and the production of Maori indigenous knowledge.[31]

Are these Maori language schools successful? The Ministry of Education continues to support *kura kaupapa* schools and a UNESCO report found that Year 11 candidates at Maori-medium schools were more likely to meet both the NCEA literacy and numeracy requirements than the other Maori candidates. However, pupils from Maori

277

immersion schools did not do well in science, and there is a warning on the accuracy of the statistics because there are vastly more students in mainstream schools than in Maori-medium schools.[32]

Despite the claims of the Waitangi Tribunal report, the decline in *kohanga reo* numbers and pupils in *kura kaupapa* primary schools probably indicates that Maori parents are voting with their feet. The *kohanga reo* share of total Maori enrolment in early childhood education dropped from 33 percent in 2002 to 26 per cent in 2007 and 22 per cent in 2011. In contrast, the share of Maori children enrolled in non Maori-language education and day care centres open rose from 32 per cent to 47 per cent over the decade.

In *kura kaupapa* Maori primary schools, where instruction is 80-100 percent in the Maori language, the School Roll Summary Report of 2009 showed that the number of Maori learners dropped from 1,092 in year eight to 545 in year nine.[33] Are parents acting in their children's best interests by sending them to schools where instruction is solely in a barely used language? Put it this way, migrant families insist on their children learning English so that they can have the best opportunity at school to do well in their working life. While Maori-language schools are taking their Maori pupils back to a Stone Age culture, migrant families who arrive from places like Vietnam and China without a word of English send their children to mainstream schools and provide a good learning environment in the home with the result that these students shine, especially in science and maths, and often go on to take university honours. How many parents find that, after putting their children through a Maori-language primary school, they have to send them to Kip McGrath for extra tuition to bring them up to speed for secondary school exams?

Have the Maori language schools increased the number of Maori speakers? The uptake of the Maori language remains limited because it has limited use. It is spoken only in New Zealand, and by very few. A national census undertaken in 2006 suggests there were approximately 157,000 speakers of Maori (around 4 percent of all those living in New Zealand). The Survey on the Health of the Maori Language 2001 suggests there were approximately 29,000 (9 percent) of Maori adults who were fluent speakers of Maori. Many fluent speakers of Maori were likely to be over 50 years old.[34] And among the young there is a decline in Maori language use. A total of 35,148 people (16.7 percent) aged 15 years and under could hold a conversation in Maori in

2006 compared with 19.7 percent in 2001. However, these figures are a dramatic improvement on 1975, when fewer than 5 percent of children could speak Maori, according to the Waitangi Tribunal's Te Reo report.[35]

A gap in educational achievement between Maori and non-Maori continues. Statistics on the National Certificate of Educational Achievement for 2009 show that 48 percent of year 11 Maori students gained an NCEA qualification at typical level or above which compares with 69 percent of non-Maori. Some 53 percent of Maori and 70 percent of non-Maori in year 12 achieved NCEA level 2, while 35 percent of year 13 Maori gained a level 3 qualification or above which compares with 57 percent of non-Maori. A Ministry of Education report written in 1997 said: "The main reason for this is mainly because Maori parents have less money and less education than non-Maori parents".[37] This is nonsense, as the key to a child's educational success is a stable and congenial home environment for learning and not the amount of the family income.

Privatising state wealth into new tribal elites

The process of treaty settlements since 1989 has fostered the emergence of new tribal elites, which claim an ancestral connection to groups that existed in 1840 but in fact are new creations. For this reason they are "new tribal elites"[38]. The process assumes that the claimant group is alienated from the Crown and so seeks to restore a relationship between the two groups, with a goal contributing to a claimants' economic development through financial and commercial redress from the general taxpayer.[39]

The claimant group must provide a deed of mandate stating who has the authority to represent the claimants in negotiations with the Crown, describing how this mandate was obtained and how the negotiators are to be held accountable, and defining the claimant group, the claim area, and the claims that are to be settled.[40] The Office of Treaty Settlements uses taxpayer money to contribute towards costs of the settlement negotiation process, although the Crown Forestry Rental Trust may also contribute. Up to $50,000 may be provided for any one group towards pre-mandate phase activities including treaty settlement education and awareness, claimant communications, facilitation, legal or specialist advice and project management, and up to $150,000 may be available for legal or specialist assistance.[41]

279

The Crown and mandated representatives negotiate: the historical basis of the claims, the Crown's alleged "breaches", the wording of the Crown's apology; what commercial settlement assets might be transferred, and on what terms; and the various items of cultural redress that are offered. Once agreed, details are set out in a draft Deed of Settlement for approval by Cabinet. This is initialled by both the Crown and the mandated representatives, and is ratified by the claimant group.[42] Claimants must set up a governance entity to hold and manage settlement assets and exercise cultural redress provided for in the settlement. Because the Crown is obliged to ensure the settlement assets are managed by and for those who will rightfully benefit from the settlement, the Crown will assess representation, transparency, dispute resolution procedures, accountability, and ratification of the proposed governance entity.[43]

Legislation implements a settlement. This removes the ability of the courts and the Waitangi Tribunal to re-open the historical claims or the Deed of Settlement. A select committee may investigate any aspect of the settlement but, apart from purely technical changes, it must approve the legislation as a whole, or not at all. The Bill is then passed and signed by the Governor-General, allowing settlement assets to be transferred to the lucky tribe.[44]

Therefore a claimant group, which may comprise a handful of people, provides a deed of mandate, accesses the $50,000 for pre-mandate costs, $150,000 for legal aid, negotiates cultural and financial redress, agrees on a re-written history, sest up a governance entity, and receives a settlement worth from $43,000 to $170-million. While that claimant group is responsible for managing the - let's say - $20 million asset on behalf of everyone in their kinship unit, they control the money. A new tribal elite is created.

Members of each one of these groups have established personal relationships with people in the Waitangi Tribunal, the Office of Treaty Settlements, as well as with an array of government ministers and politicians. In some cases, claimant groups include government employees. The nature of that relationship was described in Te Puni Kokiri's briefing to the Minister of Maori Affairs in December, 2011:

> Settlement negotiations create intensive relationships between iwi and the Crown, and a pathway through which wide-ranging dialogue occurs. Although framed in a settlement context, much of this

dialogue tends to be forward looking and is laying the foundations for a changing relationship with particularly iwi interests in the post-settlement environment. Key dimensions of that dialogue which are influencing the nature of Crown-iwi relationships include: iwi rights and interests in, and shared governance and management arrangements over, natural resources; expectations regarding the accessibility, quality and effectiveness of services provided by the social sector; and future investment and growth opportunities.[45]

These sound like audacious proposals from a government department. The government appears to be fostering the emergence of semi-autonomous tribal states, apparently united as long as the government remains the great cash cow that it has been over the past 30 years. Many of the 77 such governance entities and claimant groups, listed on the Office of Treaty Settlements website in 2012, have coalesced into the Iwi Leadership Group which expect ongoing special deals from the government, as became apparent in their demands for rights over the foreshore and seabed, water, and air.

How the Maori Council squeezes assets out of the government
The 1980s Labour government brought unexpected benefits for tribalists. As already stated, in 1985, Attorney-General Geoffrey Palmer enabled the Waitangi Tribunal to investigate claims all the way back to 1840, which set the stage for more than 20 years of lucrative treaty settlements. Another windfall came from a decision to change most government trading departments into corporations run for profit. Much Crown property and extensive tracts of Crown land were to be transferred to these corporations. When the legislation to do this, known as the State-Owned Enterprises Act, came into effect in December, 1986, the Maori Council became worried about the implications for treaty claims if the State-owned corporations sold land. The purchasers would get fee simple title, putting that land out of reach of claimants. The Maori Council sought a High Court injunction to stop the transfer of Crown land into the State-owned corporations until legislation was changed to enable land to be recovered should the Waitangi Tribunal rule in favour of a claimant.[46]

The Maori Council injunction rested on section 9 of the State-Owned Enterprises Act, which, as we have seen, says: "Nothing in the Act shall permit the Crown to act in a manner that is inconsistent with

281

the principles of the Treaty of Waitangi". The Crown was directed to make available to the Maori Council schedules of land to be transferred to State-owned enterprises, which revealed assets worth $11.8-billion. In the verdict on June 29, 1987, five judges ruled that Section 9 of the Act enabled the Treaty of Waitangi to prevent the transfer of assets without protecting Maori claims. The only claims cited at that time were: the Otago block in the South Island, where insufficient reserves were alleged; the Woodhill State Forest, where land taken near Muriwai in 1934 under the Public Works Act for sand dune reclamation had been planted in forest; and a 1,600 hectare Ngai Tama block in Taranaki confiscated although that tribe did not fight in the 1860 war.[47]

Through the State-Owned Enterprises battle, the Maori Council discovered a basic strategy to squeeze assets from the government. That strategy was used in September, 1987, to extract the commercial fisheries settlement from the government. The strategy was in use during 2012 in an injunction seeking to stop the Key-led government from partly privatising state-owned electricity generators. The process shows government dysfunction at its worst. The Maori Council, as a government-created and funded body, seeks a sympathetic ruling from the Waitangi Tribunal, another government body, to seek a ruling from the High Court, consisting of the same types of people, to get a result from the government. All these arms of officialdom at war with each other and the taxpayer paying for all of them!

How Maori groups came to control welfare funding

Privatisation of government social services by the 1980s Labour government, with Roger Douglas controlling the finance portfolio, meant the government began to devolve services to tribal authorities. This created a stepping-stone towards the splintering of welfare administration. A number of multi-tribal organisations existed in the 1980s, including Te Whanau o Waipareira Trust (West Auckland), founded in 1984, the Manukau Urban Maori Authority (South Auckland), Te Runanga o Kirikiriroa Trust (Hamilton), Te Runanganui o te Upoko o Te Ika (Wellington), and Te Runanga o Nga Maata Waka (Christchurch). These organisations forged links with central government and local bodies and became active in education, commercial ventures in health, pre-employment, and other social services, while tribal organisations in rural areas increasingly did the same.

The short-lived Runanga-a-Iwi Act 1990 empowered tribal authorities to deliver government programmes until it was repealed by the incoming National government. In 1994, the Waipareira Trust made a claim to the Waitangi Tribunal for recognition as a representative of urban Maori. Subsequent law changes allowed the trust to assume welfare responsibilities from government agencies, heralding a change in the way the government viewed urban Maori authorities.[48]

There are numerous such agencies throughout New Zealand. For instance, 57 Maori social service providers from five regions participated in research conducted in 2002.[49] That report said: "The successful delivery of services and programmes by Maori and *iwi* providers is key to building Maori community capacity and therefore in addressing Maori/non-Maori disparities". The amount of funding consumed by these agencies may be seen in the Hastings-based Te Taiwhenua o Heretaunga 2009 annual report that showed operating revenue of $8.4 million and total assets of $10.2 million. It offered general practitioner, dentist and mental health services; family start, youth transition, and teen parent social services; as well as early childhood education and other education and training.[50] If 57 agencies operated on the scale of the Taiwhenua in Hastings, the total funding bill would be nearly half a billion a year, all paid for by the taxpayer but benefiting a limited number of New Zealanders based on race.

A former Race Relations Conciliator, Dr Rajen Prasad, who became a Labour Member of Parliament, pointed out that delivering social services through tribal groups and other Maori structures would result in discrimination against non-Maori.[51]

Race-based affirmative action called "social apartheid"

"Closing the Gaps" was the name given to a race-based policy of the Helen Clark Labour-led government and involved assisting disadvantaged ethnic groups, particularly Maori and Pacific Islanders, through targeted programmes. The phrase came to prominence as a slogan of the Labour Party in the 1999 election, although race-based affirmative action had already appeared in policies of the 1980s Labour government. In June, 2000, New Zealand First party leader Winston Peters described Closing the Gaps as "social apartheid",[52] alluding to the racial segregation policies of pre-black rule South Africa. The *Dominion* newspaper criticised the policy, saying that sprinkling legislation with race-based clauses is out of place in a multi-racial society" and "it is no wonder that this is creating a backlash".[53]

Reacting to concern that a lot of money was being spent on Maori with little accountability, the government introduced checks on spending that included: public service chiefs having to demonstrate how they were acting to improve outcomes for Maori, stipulations in employment contracts that bonuses would not be paid if these bosses do not achieve Maori improvement targets, all departments being required to provide Te Puni Kokiri with details of planned Maori spending, effectiveness audits by Te Puni Kokiri, a section in annual reports on the effectiveness of Maori programmes, and an annual aggregated report on Maori. Prime Minister Helen Clark used this refinement to argue that that the government would need to increase funding for Maori development.[54]

The New Zealand Public Health and Disability Act 2000 has clauses that give Maori priority for health treatment. Section 3 of Part 1 of the Act says the purpose is "to reduce health disparities by improving the health outcomes of Maori and other population groups", and section 4 says "in order to recognise and respect the principles of the Treaty of Waitangi, and with a view to improving health outcomes for Maori, Part 3 provides for mechanisms to enable Maori to contribute to decision-making on, and to participate in the delivery of, health and disability services". Clause 23 lists the 15 functions of district health boards, three of which refer specifically to Maori. Besides the elected members of district health boards (who can be Maori and who are elected by all electors including Maori) there must be four appointed members, of whom at least two must be Maori, while the Maori membership of the board is proportional to the number of Maori in the DHB's resident population.[55]

Canterbury University law lecturer David Round, a co-author of this book, has noted that, since the Act requires boards to establish special partnership relationships with *"mana whenua"* Maori, or those of the 1840 tribe of the area, the Act creates divisions between different tribes by preferring some over others. Moreover, the basic premise of a "special relationship between Maori and the Crown" implies a special claim by Maori on publicly funded resources, Round wrote.[56]

Disadvantage not to do with race

Disadvantage in New Zealand is more closely tied to age, marital status, education, skills, and geographic location, than it is to ethnicity, according to Simon Chapple, a senior analyst in the Department of Labour. In 2000, Chapple wrote *Maori Socio-Economic Disparity* Although his paper did not issue clear recommendations for policy, Chapple's conclusions pointed toward a gap-closing policy that would target pockets of disadvantage defined geographically and perhaps by sub-cultural features, rather than by targeting services to Maori as Maori.[57]

'Closing the gaps' vanishes but race-based affirmative action continues

Leaders of the ACT party used the Chapple paper to fuel a backlash against "closing the gaps" policy in early 2000. The attacks by MPs Muriel Newman and Richard Prebble were reinforced by favourable commentary on Chapple's analysis from National Party MP Simon Upton's web-based opinion column. Ultimately, the momentum of the Chapple-induced debates contributed to the Government's decision to remove the phrase "closing the gaps" from its vocabulary, to re-label its policy "social equity," and to commit to fighting economic disadvantage rather than ethnic disparities.[58] Opposition politicians observed that the Labour-led government still had a "closing the gaps" policy objective, but no longer referred to the policy by that name.

Attempts to re-brand "closing the gaps" were undermined by a clause in the Apprenticeship Training Act 2001 which required apprenticeship co-ordinators to "have particular regard to the needs of Maori [and] Pacific Island peoples of New Zealand" as well as "disabled people and women".

The complexity of administering such legislation, together with its inconsistencies, was illustrated when New Zealand First M.P, Brian Donnelly, said he had two adopted children of Pacific Island descent, who would qualify for help under the bill because of their ethnicity. But his eldest daughter would qualify for the same attention because she was a woman, although if she had been a boy she would have missed out. He said he couldn't comprehend the different treatment despite the fact that his children came "from the same family background, they come from the same household. The two parents who brought them up are exactly the same and yet two of them are privileged and one of them is not". NZ

First MP, Ron Mark, said the Bill demeaned Maori people because it told them that they were not capable of achieving without special recognition and attention.[59] National MP, Nick Smith, said that the race clause could open the doors to legal grievances lodged by unsuccessful Maori and Pacific Island applicants, "who naturally expect to get in because of their skin colour".[60]

Over the term of the 1999-2008 Labour government, social statistics for Maori and Pacific Islanders did generally improve. However, the statistics for white New Zealanders showed a greater improvement, resulting in "gaps" actually increasing. The Ministry of Health and Otago University's series of Decades of Disparities reports observed such changes.[61]

The Maori Party – how a tiny tail wags the body politic

The Maori Party, which attracted only 2.39 percent of the party vote in 2008, has furthered the separatist agenda by being in coalition with the governing National Party. The Maori Party got into Parliament by dominating the vote on a number of the Maori seats. This party has never competed in a general electorate.

In the 2005 election, the party won four out of seven Maori seats and 2.12 percent of the party vote, which entitled them to three List seats. They stayed in Opposition, snubbing the Helen Clark led-Labour Party that Tariana Turia had left. They were also unwilling to co-operate with the "one law for all" Don Brash-led National Party – hardly surprising for a party based on advancing the interests of one race at the expense of others..

In the 2008 general election the Maori Party retained the four seats it won in 2005, plus Te Tai Tonga that Rahui Katene won from Labour. Their 2.39 percent share of the party vote entitled them to three List MPs. The party entered into a confidence-and supply agreement with the new National government. Sharples became Minister of Maori Affairs, Associate Minister of Corrections, and Associate Minister of Education. Turia became Minister for the Community and Voluntary Sector, Associate Minister of Health, and Associate Minister for Social Development and Employment. Maori Party president Whatarangi Winiata said with prescience that "there won't be a piece of legislation that can be passed without a Maori signatory to the treaty agreeing to it".[62]

As part of the government, Sharples and Turia made an impact. The agreement with National resulted in the red, black and white "*tino rangatiratanga*" flag appearing on the Auckland harbour bridge and other official buildings on Waitangi Day, 2010, sending a message to New Zealand that Prime Minister John Key had agreed to an important goal of the Maori Party and the Maori sovereignty movement. Turia launched Whanau Ora to provide health and social services focussing on Maori families on April 8 that year. Two weeks later, Sharples quietly slipped out of the country and signed New Zealand up to the UN Declaration on the Rights of Indigenous Peoples on April 20, even though Maori people migrated to New Zealand just like everyone else and so are not indigenous. Sharples and Turia set in motion a process that led to the Marine and Coastal Area Act 2011 replacing the Foreshore and Seabed Act 2004, thus enabling tribal groups to claim customary title to the coastal area. Sharples in conjunction with Finance Minister Bill English set up an ideologically and racially biased Constitutional Advisory Panel to push for a written constitution based on the Treaty of Waitangi.

At the 2011 election, the Maori Party slipped back, taking 1.4 percent of the vote, and only three of the Maori seats, largely because of Hone Harawira's exit to form his own Mana Party. The Maori Party continued with the confidence-and-supply agreement with National. It appears that somewhere along the line the Maori Party convinced soft-touch Key to move from National's position of abolishing the Maori seats to leaving the decision to abolish them up to Maori.

Commissioner's double standard on race relations

Joris de Bres, as Human Rights Commissioner, stirred up hostility by a number of other initiatives. He was in the hot seat when Maori Party MP Hone Harawira's "white motherf***er" reference in an email was publicised by the recipient. This prompted 814 complaints, which was a record considering that the total number of race-related complaints received by the commission for the whole of the previous year in 2008 was only 407. What did de Bres do about the Harawira complaints? He publicly asked himself what to do when a public figure makes a racially offensive statement. He said that "it is incumbent on the Maori Party to address the issue to uphold its standards and values and to provide assurance to the public." He published the Human Rights Commission's section on freedom of expression. That was it! .

In 2012, de Bres accused non-Maori of not being generous enough and called for more race-based programmes for disadvantaged Maori. This provoked a welter of letters to the *Dominion Post* and other newspapers. Wellington historian John McLean wrote that "Pakeha don't mind helping the needy, but object doing so on a racist basis". Vipi Gregory-Meredith of Otaki said that de Bres "would do well to accept that his role is to represent all races in New Zealand", Jenny Miller of Belmont said that she saw "a lack of generosity being shown by (de Bres) toward those Pakeha who have a different viewpoint from that which he holds".[63]

Wish-lists and the Auckland Maori Statutory Board

Maori representation on the new Auckland super city became controversial with the undemocratic establishment of a Maori statutory board of unelected Maori members but paid for by Auckland ratepayers.

The Local Government (Auckland Law Reform) Act 2009 set up the nine-member statutory board that must appoint a maximum of two persons to sit on each of the Auckland Council's committees that deal with the management and stewardship of natural and physical resources.[64] Board members were there to promote cultural, economic, environmental, and social issues of significance for *mana whenua* and Maori of Tamaki Makaurau to assist the Auckland Council in making decisions, performing functions, and exercising powers. According to the Maori dictionary the term *"mana whenua"* means "territorial rights and power......associated with possession and occupation of tribal land".[65] There is tribal land dotted around Auckland but not a huge amount. Therefore the *"mana whenua"* rights would appear to be restricted to that limited possession and occupation. Not so.

These unelected Maori members of an otherwise democratically elected council had a $3.4 million budget of ratepayers' money for their "board" and then submitted a $295-million wish list for the draft 10-year plan on December 1, 2011. That list, published in the *New Zealand Herald* on December 1, 2011, included $72.37 million for guardianship of the sky, sea, and land, $11.84 million for sacred sites, $31.75 million for the life force of ancestral lands and waters, $116.14 million for chiefly authority over resources and affairs, $7.78 million for treaty rights and obligations, $9.25 million for the right to participate within the community, $42.8 million for the "mana of Tamaki Makaurau *iwi* and *hapu* co-governance arrangements", and $3.29 million for Maori "knowledge".

The board was asked by a nervous council to reconsider. They did and returned on September 2, 2012, to release 49 cultural, social, economic and environmental goals that included the compulsory teaching of Maori in all Auckland schools, a naming protocol in Maori, financial literacy programmes to promote Maori engagement in trade delegations, foreign direct investment, innovation and export. The Auckland Council was asked to facilitate a relationship between 19 *mana whenua* tribes, the council's Auckland Property Ltd (APL) and Auckland Council Investments Ltd (ACIL) concerning "management, acquisition and divesting of land and other strategic assets." [66] The total cost over 10 years would be the same - $295 million.

How many would this benefit? A total 157,500 Maori lived in Tamaki Makaurau in 2012, mostly in Manurewa-Papakura, and 85.5 percent belong to non-Tamaki Makaurau *iwi*. The total population of Auckland was one million.[67]

Commissioner's drive for separate Maori representation in local government

Maori involvement in decision-making on the new Auckland Council created an opportunity for Human Rights Commissioner, Joris De Bres, to push local government towards setting up special Maori seats in other parts of the country. In 2011 he wrote to all councils asking them to consider the question of Maori seats in their three-yearly representation review. He provided a copy of a 2010 Human Rights Commission report titled "Maori Representation in Local Government – The Continuing Challenge",[68] which identified Maori local government representation and Maori involvement in the decisions of the new Auckland Council as being among the top ten race relations priorities for 2010. In response, of the 78 councils nationwide, 49 told De Bres that they had already considered the Maori seats option but had not taken it any further, and three councils – the Nelson City Council, the Wairoa District Council, and the Waikato District Council – agreed to start the process of establishing Maori seats.[69]

Affected electors were entitled to demand a poll. When a poll was demanded in Nelson, a 43.4 percent return in May, 2012, showed 79.4 percent against the proposal and 20.2 percent for it. Results of the official poll in Wairoa showed that only 47.3 percent of electors opted to exercise their right to vote, with 51.9 percent against and 47.9 percent for. And Wairoa is a very Maori area. A similar poll held by the Waikato District Council in April, 2012, also rejected separate Maori representation. Of the 12,762 (30.2 percent) of electors who voted, 10,111 were against the idea, while 2,517 favoured it. It is quite clear that ratepayers do not want separate Maori representation on their councils – a wish that should be respected in any country that calls itself a "democracy". But the ratepayers of Auckland were never given the choice, instead incurring expensive and unnecessary Maori influence in their council thanks to the Key government.

In March, 2012, Consumerlink, a private research department of Colmar Brunton, carried out a poll which questioned 1,031 people throughout New Zealand. The responses showed that 70.5 percent (73.2 percent non-Maori) of those who responded yes or no believe that separate Maori representation on local bodies (where it already exists in the Bay of Plenty) should be abolished. That poll also found that 69.4 percent (72.4 percent non-Maori) thought that Maori seats and the Maori electoral roll should be abolished, and 67.8 percent (70.1 percent non-Maori) were in favour of abolishing the Waitangi Tribunal.[70] Maori Party policy in 2011 was to establish "*mana whenua*" statutory boards at local government level, thus spreading the type of costly wish lists as seen in Auckland all around New Zealand.

Power and money through co-governance

Co-governance deals have evolved from a simple agreement to co-manage a mountain into multi-year, multi-million co-governances arrangements that create cash flow for years to come plus an extra portion of political power for tribes. Co-management first appeared in the multi-tribal Poukani settlement of $2.65 million in 2000, which related to the 49,514 hectare Pouakani block situated between Lake Taupo and Mangakino, and including co-management of Tiraupenga Mountain.

Co-governance agreements are very expensive for the taxpayer since members of the tribal elite are paid huge amounts for attending meetings and consulting among themselves. These agreements took off with the Waikato River settlements of 2010 that included five tribes. The Waikato Raupatu River Trust was established. Waikato-Tainui received a $20 million publicly funded Sir Robert Mahuta endowment, a $10 million river initiatives fund, a $40 million river initiatives fund, $3 million co-management funding, $1 million co-management funding a year for 27 years, and a $2.8 million ex-gratia payment. Te Arawa received a $3 million initial payment, $7 million after three months, and $1 million co-management funding a year for 19 years.

Raukawa received a $21 million initial payment, $7 million a year for 27 years, $3 million to the Raukawa Settlement Trust followed by $7 million three months later, and $1 million a year for 20 years. The government pledged to contribute towards costs incurred by Tuwharetoa Maori Trust Board. Maniapoto received an initial $3 million co-management payment, $7 million three months later, and $1 million co-management funding a year for 19 years. The total amount over 27 years is $400.8 million, and there was no indication whether this funding had anything to do with improving the quality of Waikato River water. This took place with the Key-led National Party government with Treaty Negotiations Minister, Christopher Finlayson, at the helm. All this is in addition to Tainui's huge Treaty settlement.

Efforts to co-govern on the Hauraki Gulf Forum became difficult, prompting veteran Auckland politician, Christine Fletcher, to quit in disgust from two positions in gulf leadership.[71]The Hauraki Gulf Forum is a statutory body administered by Auckland Council to manage the Hauraki Gulf under the Hauraki Gulf Marine Park Act 2000. Its 21 members include five Auckland councillors, two Auckland council local board members, three ministry representatives (Conservation, Fisheries, Maori Affairs), five other local body representatives (Hauraki, Thames-Coromandel, Matamata-Piako, Waikato district, Waikato regional), and six "*tangata whenua*" members.[72]

Dissatisfied with having only five out of 21 votes, the "*mana whenua*" group started pushing for equal voting powers. On 2nd October, 2012, the council debated a proposal for a steering group of 26 Maori representatives and 26 councis and government agency representatives. The steering or leadership group of 52 would be in addition to a stakeholder forum (of 200 representatives), an expert advisory group and a project team.[73] It appears that co-governance bodies will become a battleground for control of power and assets – as is already happening.

The model for racially separate states within a state
Some tribal authorities view themselves as states within a state. Ngai Tuhoe of the Urewera region describe themselves as the Tuhoe nation, and Ngati Kahungunu listed the top three points in their 25-year vision

to 2026 as: "Economic strength, to participate as a contributing nation in the world, and *tino rangatiratanga*: independence and self-determination".[74] Maori studies professor, Margaret Mutu, in 2012 advocated the constitution of Bolivia, formally known as the Plurinational State of Bolivia, as the model for New Zealand. This model involves nations within a nation.[75] Many would be surprised to find out that the "one people" view of New Zealand society that is taken for granted by many is, in the eyes of Maori nationalists, nothing more than a coloniser myth.

Maori self-determination specialist, Whatarangi Winiata, a retired professor who became president of the Maori Party, designed a racially separate administrative set-up for the Anglican Church in New Zealand, which has three churches in one – Pacifika, Maori and Pakeha – so designed ostensibly to free Maori from a dominant, assimilative culture. According to the revised Anglican constitution of 1992, each Anglican "*tikanga*" as the sub-groups are so confusingly called, has its own language, church buildings, clergy and customs. This has led to triplication, e.g. three archbishops, and insufficient resources to cater for all three. Communication and understanding between the sub-groups has become more difficult. In this set-up, the 1840 Treaty of Waitangi overshadows the Bible and Anglican theology. Bicultural partnership has become the Anglicans' supreme value, and a necessary skill for a bishop is knowledge, understanding, and commitment to things Maori.[76] So the once great Anglican Church has been reduced, in New Zealand, to a three-ghetto organisation based on politics rather than Christianity.

Winiata asked the Anglican Church general synod in 2012 for half the $315 million worth of assets in a church trust, claiming that the Anglican hierarchy didn't do enough to save or support dying Maori boarding schools. He asked that 50 per cent of the St John's College Trust Board's assets be put under the control of Te Pihopatanga o Aotearoa - the Maori partner and one of the three arms of the church.[77]

The synod unanimously passed Winiata's motion which sought a six-person working party to advise on how this should be done. This "three *tikanga*" working party was to report back to the next general synod in 2014 at Paihia, near Waitangi.[78]

The splintering of New Zealand into an array of tribal "nations" that depend on contributions from the surrounding "coloniser" culture not only threatens the administrative integrity of the nation but also puts its viability at risk. Let's remember that the Communist International fostered the nationalistic aspirations of ethnic groups to weaken existing nations and eventually take them over. Forget the warm fuzzies about the great "earth mother" and Stone Age tribal spirituality – any reader should be aware that, if you choose to go down the "nations within a nation" path, you are signing away your rights as well as your security.

Conclusion

The high use of welfare by those claiming Maori ancestry enables politicians to argue for increasing race-based affirmative action. This has the unintended consequence of de-emphasising, for Maori, the value of rising by merit, as everyone else does. It also enables the new tribal capitalists to argue that the apparent poverty of "their people" is grounds for their businesses to be treated as charities. Race-based funding costs more than $1.3 billion every year. Whanau Ora rorting shows the ease with which the government may be fleeced. A separate Maori department is an anachronism, as are separate Maori seats, and separate local government representation. Maori immersion schooling has had little impact on the Maori language. There was a time when radicals were fringe activists who excitedly daubed "honour the treaty" on factory walls in the dead of night. Those radicals have now become very influential in government but their spots have not changed.

The willingness of successive governments to cave in to outrageous tribalist demands gives the appearance that the radicals have taken control. We can see the strategy that the Maori Council uses to squeeze assets out of the government. The Maori Council was created by and funded by the government but is perhaps the government's worst enemy. It certainly is one of the taxpayer's worst enemies. State wealth is being privatised into new tribal elites while opponents of privatisation stay silent, frightened of being called racist.

THE BROWNWASHING OF NEW ZEALAND – TREATY INDOCTRINATION

"Not to know what happened before we were born is to remain perpetually a child."
Cicero, c. 60 B.C.

The unprecedented, unjustified and economically harmful transfer of massive public resources and rights to a greedy and unworthy elite of part-Maoris solely on the basis of accidental birth could never have succeeded in a twenty-first century democracy without a massive propaganda campaign. This has been going on for twenty to thirty years and, through lies both blatant and subtle, organised deception, the rewriting of history, selective reporting by the media, and the intimidation and bullying of virtually all public officials, it has succeeded in brainwashing large numbers of people – especially the young.

This chapter will expose some of these methods of indoctrination and explain the harm that they are doing to freedom of thought and speech, standards of education, national pride, and the unity and sovereignty of the nation.

Like the best of the propagandists, the Treatyists start their distortion of history in the schools, where they are aided by a bullying education bureaucracy in Wellington, currently presided over by National's disastrous Education Minister, Hekia Parata – an arch-Treatyist. The state education system is being used to establish a form of separatism that is said to be "Treaty based" but which, in fact, is in violation of the Treaty and of all the worthy principles on which New Zealand was founded.

The new and false version of the treaty – the "Cooke-Palmer treaty" – with its carefully crafted "principles" which are unrelated to the real treaty but serve the needs of the devious and manipulative political elite, is being instilled into young minds at an early age at the behest of the Ministry of Education.

The government is using education for social and political or, if you like, indoctrination purposes and this is at the expense of teaching children what they need to know to get through life successfully in the Western world – not only mathematics and science but also a thorough understanding of our beautiful English language. In many cases kids know how to scream a *haka* (a violent and unfriendly manifestation of a Stone Age culture to which the vast majority of New Zealanders have no cultural connections) before they learn to read properly, to speak correctly, to write clearly and legibly, to spell, punctuate, parse, divide, multiply, add and subtract.

They are taught endless Maori myths and songs, with an ever so correct pronunciation of course, but many of them finish up not being able to utter an English sentence in a clear and grammatically correct way or to put a punctuation mark in its right place.

Yes, in the twenty-first century there is a time and a place for learning traditional Maori songs and dances but that is on the *marae* in out-of-school hours and should not be forcibly rammed down the throats of young, impressionable students of all races by a mischievous and manipulative bureaucracy with an agenda that is far removed from teaching the young what they need to know for the challenges of a fast changing world.

James Cowan, the foremost historian of the period of the Maori wars of the nineteenth century, wrote, "The young generation would be better for a more systematic schooling in the facts of national pioneer life and achievements, which are a necessary foundation for the larger patriotism." [1] That is a worthy sentiment but it is not being honoured to-day when New Zealand history, and the Treaty of Waitangi and the Maori Wars in particular, are being taught in such a manner as to separate the races in every possible way so as to fuel the grievance industry.

The situation is made worse by the new breed of "revisionist" historians, whose modus operandi seems to be to take a position on something without knowing much about it and then scouring the sources not to find out what really happened but to bolster the prejudices of the position that was taken in the first place. This selective use of sources is not history but indoctrination.

This cosy little coterie of revisionists all pat each other on the back, favourably review each other's books, and gang up on anyone who dares to think for himself or herself by going "off message".

The widely acclaimed Queen Bee of revisionist historians is Claudia Orange. Although her understanding of the treaty and the events at Waitangi around 1840 is somewhat flawed that doesn't matter a bit as she has interpreted these in line with current official policy and has been richly rewarded in well-paid (quasi) government jobs/contracts and even a title – Dame Claudia Orange!

In her book *The Treaty of Waitangi* she criticises Sir Apirana Ngata, the greatest mind that Maoridom has ever produced, with the words, "Ngata's explanation of the treaty is not a reliable, authoritative statement of the Maori understanding (of the treaty) in 1840." [2] What patronising nonsense!

She then compounds her misunderstanding by adding "(Ngata's) pamphlet perpetuates other erroneous notions that there had been no law and order in New Zealand before 1840." [3] This is contrary to the evidence of both Maori and Europeans of the time and denies the reason why the chiefs ceded their authority to Britain, viz. to provide the law and order that was so patently lacking. Either Orange's research is shoddy or her understanding of "law and order" is seriously deficient. "Europeans crowded to buy land for themselves...." wrote Ngata. "Many claims were made by various Europeans for the one piece of land sold to each of them by various Maori chiefs. Where was the law in those times to decide what was right?.....The Maori did not have any government when the European first came to these islands. There was no unified chiefly authority over man or land....How could such an organisation as a Government be established under Maori custom?" [4]

Can there really be law and order where the law of the gun prevails, resulting in the deaths of an estimated 43,000 Maoris (one third of their population)? Come on, Claudia, we're not that stupid.

On Page 7 of her book she states that Maori had lived in New Zealand for more than 1,000 years before 1840. At the time she wrote this statement the most widely agreed date of the first Maori settlement in New Zealand was around 1250 A.D., a mere 600 years before 1840. This was reinforced by peer reviewed and published findings of a research group led by Atholl Anderson from the Australian National University in Canberra and Janet Wilmshurst from New Zealand's Landcare Research, that was published in *The Proceedings of the National Academy of Sciences in the United States*. Analysing 1,400 radiocarbon dates from 47 Pacific Islands, they showed that Polynesian migration to New Zealand took place around 1250 A.D.

But it reinforces the spurious claim of Maori to be "indigenous" if the date can be stretched back earlier. So, does Claudia Orange know something that the rest of us don't or did she just extend the date backwards so as to fool the reader into thinking that the Maoris have a greater claim to being "indigenous" and using such to extract more out of the taxpayer in claims? Or perhaps she just can't count.

On Page 92 of her book Orange claims, "The Waitangi Treaty gave Britain only a partial entitlement to the country." If she had read and understood Article One of the treaty, she would know that the chiefs ceded sovereignty of the country to Queen Victoria. If it were qualified in any way, the chiefs would have kept their slaves and retained their cannibalism, both of which meant a lot to certain chiefs. To make the ridiculous claim – 150 years later! – that only partial sovereignty was ceded does boost the credentials of the grievance industry and it is hard to resist the conclusion that this was Orange's main purpose in creating such a strange reinvention of New Zealand's hitherto clearly understood history.

On Page 117 of her increasingly bizarre book she called the Wairau massacre a "confrontation....Twenty-two settlers were killed." What she doesn't mention – perhaps deliberately – is that eleven of these settlers were murdered by the Maoris after they had surrendered. Either shoddy research or a selective presentation of the facts.

The rebellion of the Kingites in the Waikato was an act of treason against the Crown but anyone who says that is labelled by Orange as an "extremist" – "To extremists the King movement was treasonable", she wrote on Page 117.

So, she doesn't understand that a direct and violent challenge to the legal sovereignty of the Queen, which developed into armed rebellion, is treasonable? Instead she labels those who call it so as "extremists". Well, as they say, it takes one to know one. The treaty imposed duties as well as rights and one of the duties of a British subject is not to rebel against the Crown.

She seems to be equally confused over the confiscations of land after the wars. On Page 196 she wrote of, "confiscations which contravened the land guarantee of the treaty". All she needed to do here was to apply some logic and common sense which, it should be noted, do not seem to be in large supply in academia.

If certain tribes rebelled against the Crown in violation of the first Article of the treaty (which ceded sovereignty to Queen Victoria), then they lost the protection of the second Article in relation to their lands. Even Claudia Orange should be able to work out that, if you rebel against one article of a treaty, then you can not rely on a guarantee or protection from another article of the same treaty.

If these rebellious tribes claimed that they were not bound by the treaty, then the law of nations allowed land seizure from belligerents after a war which was lost. In either event they had put themselves outside the protection of the treaty. Sir Apirana Ngata declared in his excellent pamphlet aforementioned that the land confiscations were not in contravention of the treaty. In the words of Ngata writing in 1922, "Some have said these confiscations were wrong and that they contravened the Treaty of Waitangi but the chiefs placed in the hands of the Queen of England the sovereignty and authority to make laws. Some sections of the Maori people violated that authority. War arose from this and blood was spilled. The law came into operation and land was taken in payment. This itself is a Maori custom – revenge, plunder to avenge a wrong. It was their own chiefs who ceded that right to the Queen. The confiscations can not therefore be objected to in the light of the treaty." [5]

The fact is that Ngata understood what the Treaty of Waitangi meant for him and his fellow Maoris better than this "johnny come lately" revisionist historian whom the Treatyists – and the government – so questionably hold up as a "modern authority" on the treaty of 1840.

When a historian makes as many mistakes as Orange has made in her book it is stretching credulity to regard her as an "authority" on the events of 1840. But she is a cheerleader of the Treaty industry and it seems that that is all that matters.

Perhaps the key to the flawed, if not biased, history that she writes can be found in the title of the last chapter of her book- "A Residue of Guilt" Guilt for what? For saving the Maoris from racial extinction, which would probably have occurred if they had continued killing each other on the industrial scale that was assumed in the 1820s and 1830s? For ending cannibalism, slavery and infanticide by a treaty that was designed by worthy humanitarians at the Colonial Office in London? For introducing law and order to a land that had never known it? For bringing settlers who paid for their land and who, using British construction and engineering skills, transformed the country for the better by building wharves, steamships, roads, bridges, railways, dams and large and beautiful buildings? For giving their lives for putting down the tribal rebellion of the 1860s so that New Zealand could develop as a peaceful and prosperous society? Guilt indeed!

Claudia Orange can have her own guilt trip but, when she tries to inflict it on the public by means of her history books, she should be seen for what she really is – an historian with an agenda. That her deeply flawed, if not ridiculous, book has been taken seriously instead of being laughed out of the library is an indication of the vice-like grip that the Treatyists have established over the media and minds of New Zealand. Whatever honours might have been showered on Orange by grateful governments one could do a lot better than accept her revisionist version of the Treaty of Waitangi and the events of 1840.

One of Orange's little tricks, for which she was well paid out of a $6.5 million "propaganda fund" that the government allocated in 2006, was to help set up the "Treaty 2U" caravan (or, if you like, circus) that spent four months travelling round the country brainwashing schoolchildren in the interests of the grievance industry.

In the words of Ross Baker, the head of the One New Zealand Foundation, who trailed the caravan for a while in order to expose the distortions that it was peddling to all the groups of schoolchildren who were dragged along by their teachers to see it, "In truth the exhibition had little or nothing to do with the Treaty of Waitangi *per se* or anything much that actually occurred on the ground in New Zealand history. The so-called 'treaty' subject matter merely provided an excuse for the well-funded Maori grievance industry to propagandise New Zealanders and, more importantly, impressionable schoolchildren, who were forcibly bussed in to the exhibit as captive audiences." [6]

Using their $6.5 million budget, they handed out free books, videos, and pamphlets to youngsters who were forced into their claws. The reason for this ham-fisted indoctrination exercise was that the Littlewood treaty (See: Chapter 2) had recently been discovered and which, if accepted as the final English draft from which Te Tiriti was created (as it should have been), would have blown the grievance industry to smithereens and so it was necessary to suppress its emergence with this hurriedly put together road show. It would be really terrible if the public were ever given the true facts about the treaty as that would enable them to make up their own minds instead of being directed how to think by the likes of Claudia Orange.

Another field where Orange has stuck her oar in is the so-called series of "Treaty of Waitangi debates" that have been held at the National Museum in Wellington (Te Papa). These have been presided over by Orange. In the words of Malcolm Geard, a good burger of the suburb of Hataitai in Wellington, who attended one of these, "The only problem with these debates is that nobody is debating anything. Instead, we have an assortment of Maori elite, academics and lawyers, all of whom have powerful vested interests, engaging in endless lectures to persuade us that reparations for wrongs to Maori will be eternal." [7]

In the words of *Dominion* commentator, Karl du Fresne, writing in his column of 8 February, 2013, "Only one view – the pro-Treaty one – was represented in the 'debate' I attended, and the few dissenters were silenced by moderator, Kim Hill, with the vocal support of the audience."

John Ansell expressed similar sentiments. "For the last several years that bastion of bias, Te Papa, and its in-house history twister, Dame Claudia Orange, have been staging what they laughingly call 'debates' about the Treaty. I am not sure what dictionary Dame Claudia uses but her debates feature several members of the affirmative, no members of the negative and no audience please!"

John Ansell should know as on the evening of 24th January, 2013, he and some others who are committed to an open debate on the Treaty attended one of Claudia Orange's Te Papa debates. Knowing how one-sided it was all going to be, he and some others started handing out a brochure entitled "Nine Things You Won't Hear at Te Papa".

Immediately they were pounced on by the Te Papaganda Cultural Safety Police who told them that they couldn't distribute pamphlets inside the building even though a few yards away was a table loaded with the Treatyists' pamphlets.

So they went outside the building, followed by Te Papa's uniformed goons, and attempted to hand out the brochures to people arriving for the "debate".

"No, you can't stand there", screamed the goons and so they had to retreat behind an imaginary "Orange line" on the plaza, which apparently delineated where Te Papa's property ended and the Free World begins.

So, from here – a good fifteen yards away from the Te Papa building – they handed the pamphlets to those who were arriving for this Orange show. The pamphlets were accepted by Maori radical, Moana Jackson, and by Human Rights Commissioner, Joris de Bres, but not by Stephen O'Regan or Geoffrey Palmer who obviously did not want any contrary – and, for them, uncomfortable – arguments to intrude into their smug and smarmy world - a world where both of them have spent much of the past two decades living off the taxpayer in a very big way.

While this Stasi-type stand-off was going on outside Te Papa, inside Orange and her little coterie of supporters were "debating" the place in modern New Zealand of a treaty that by the end of 1840 was regarded as redundant, having performed the task for which it was created, viz. to bring New Zealand under British sovereignty.

The four "debaters" were Moana Jackson, Claudia Orange, her fellow Treatyist, the part-Maori Carwyn Jones, and Matthew Palmer. The last mentioned is the son of Geoffrey Palmer and that probably tells us all that we need to know. More about this bogus debate can be found on John Ansell's website www.johnansell.wordpress.com

So, that is how Te Papa, a body funded by the taxpayer to the tune of $32.5 million a year and by Wellington ratepayers ($2.5 million a year), treats freedom of speech – something that our servicemen died for in the two world wars. It's time that this "bastion of bias" was cleaned out, purged of its ridiculous, overbearing and censorious political correctness, and turned into a proper museum. There is a place for open debate but not for the exclusive propaganda of a deeply flawed view, supported by only a very small minority of the population, of such an important aspect of our history, which has a bearing on the rights that we are losing to-day as a result of distorted history and Treatyist indoctrination.

So closed is Te Papa's "mind" that, to get a job there, one must accept Te Papa's flawed view of the Treaty of Waitangi. A very good venue for Claudia Orange to spout her stuff.

History is further distorted by the so-called "historical accounts" that support claims to the Waitangi Tribunal. As such, they are carefully crafted to create a compensatable "grievance" in defiance of historical truth. So bad is this racket that some historians have been forced to change their honest findings in order to get paid their fee by the claimant tribe. And then it becomes an "historical account of the Waitangi Tribunal"!

Te Papa is not the only publicly run museum that seeks to twist our history. One of the worst offenders in this area is Puke Ariki, the New Plymouth District Council owned museum in the centre of that city.

There has already been mention in Chapter Seven of the exhibition that was put on by this museum in 2012 entitled "The Taranaki War, 1860-2012; Our Legacy, Our Challenge" and of the bare-faced lie that it seeks to perpetrate by stating that there was no cannibalism of the captured crew members of the unfortunate *Harriet*. Of course, cannibalism denial is on the rise. The stronger the evidence becomes of cannibalism among pre-treaty Maoris, the more strongly the propagandists, who are rewriting our history into a distorted, politically-correct form, choose to proclaim the contrary.

Unfortunately that was not the only lie or distortion that the exhibition spun to the public. It said that there were seven Maori language copies of the treaty whereas there were only five. It said that Te Tiriti, which the chiefs signed, did not cede sovereignty but that is exactly what it did – completely and forever - as a result of which the Crown has exercised sovereignty ever since. All the chiefs at Waitangi understood this and said so in their speeches in the marquee at Waitangi.

This seriously flawed exhibition also claims that "taonga" at the time meant "all Maori treasures, material and non-material" whereas, as we have seen, it meant only "goods acquired at the point of a spear".

It also claims that there was "government burning, killing and looting" (rare occurrences indeed) but there is no mention of the 177 farms of Taranaki settlers that were destroyed or the several farming families who were killed by the rebels. And no compensation out of the obscene "Treaty settlements" to rebellious Taranaki tribes for the descendants of these Europeans who were victims of the farm burnings and other atrocities.

Another distortion of this little propaganda exercise is that "dodgy" land deals by the government caused the rebellion. The authorities did their best in very difficult circumstances and in some cases the same piece of land was paid for three and four times over. The deals were complicated due to the unsatisfactory nature of so-called Maori land ownership but good faith was the Crown's guiding principle. And was there "good faith" on the Maori side? The multiple – and often fraudulent - claims to the same piece of land would suggest not.

It also declares that in 1868-9 Maori "clawed back some of the land seized" whereas the truth was that some land, confiscated legitimately, was generously and voluntarily returned to the tribes after peace was restored.

It is not surprising that this scandal of an "exhibition" should be so seriously flawed since its organiser/creator, Kelvin Day, has written "The content (of the exhibition) attempts to recognise that there is no such thing as one true history".[8] So, Mr. Day, there is no true history? Then who won the Battle of Waterloo? The French? Mr. Day's statement seems to be part of the new mantra that history is all a matter of perception and the facts don't matter.

What is surprising is that a man who openly (and apparently without embarrassment) declares that there is no true history should be paid ratepayers' money by the New Plymouth District Council to work as their "historian" for an exhibition or, if you like, an exercise in propaganda. Perhaps the answer to this riddle is that, in Mr. Day's own words, "I would highly recommend the Waitangi Tribunal's report The Taranaki Report Kaupapa Tuatahi (1996). We drew heavily on this report...during our research and it offers some good insights into the Taranaki context". [9]

Since this is the report that propagated the lie that the colonisation of Taranaki was a "holocaust" it is surprising that any reputable historian would rely on it for anything. That he did so seems to be an indication of Mr. Day's poor judgment and his historical confusion. The poor man doesn't even know the name of the country he lives in, wrongly writing of it as "Aotearoa New Zealand", which is nothing more than a figment of his imagination – just like so much of his exhibition seems to be. Because of all its many mistakes this whole exhibition was a waste of money for the New Plymouth ratepayers. One can't help feeling that this was just an expensive exercise for Mr. Day to indulge his own prejudices.

When these errors were pointed out to Mr. Day he refused to correct anything, thereby suggesting that he is impervious to reason and unable to comprehend that he might be wrong – the arrogance of the politically correct. He admitted that the exhibition's video account of the *Harriet* episode was "different from accounts people have encountered in the past". [10] Of course it's different as no other historian has ever had the nerve or the lack of professional standards to propagate such a lie.

There seems to be an appalling lack of knowledge of their own history among the people of Taranaki, and the New Plymouth District Council and its museum, Puke Ariki, are very much to blame for that. A useful first step would be the replacement of Mr. Day by a more objective historian with better judgement, e.g. one who relies on contemporary records of the time like Jacky Guard's diary and the reports of the Royal Navy officers on *HMS Alligator* who took part in the rescue of the *Harriet* people rather than the one-sided distortions that are put out in the Waitangi Tribunal's biased and historically wrong reports, of which its Taranaki Report, the one relied on by Mr. Day, is by far the worst.

Politicians are also pretty good at twisting history for their own purposes. Take Finlayson for example. In the *New Zealand Herald* of 10th January, 2013, he claimed that Sir George Grey was a racist (against Maoris). To get some idea of the truth or falsity of this allegation let us look at what Professor Keith Sinlclair wrote of Grey in his authoritative and classic *A History of New Zealand.*

"Grey did everything he could to encourage Maori agriculture. He made them private and public loans (which they almost invariably repaid) for the purchase of ploughs, mills or small vessels. And throughout his governorship he laboured to establish other measures calculated to improve the condition of the Maori people and to 'elevate' them in the scale of civilisation....

Grey subsidised mission schools, and encouraged the missionaries to start new ones. Several co-educational Industrial Boarding Schools were established, in which the pupils received training in carpentry and agriculture, or sewing, as well as in arithmetic, English and Maori....In four of the North Island towns he built hospitals where Maoris received free treatment." [11] Do these words of Sinclair, a man who spent a lifetime researching early New Zealand history, suggest that Grey was "racist"?

And then there is the media which so often report Treaty matters from a tribal perspective and from no other, thus giving a false picture. "Objective reporting" is now a dirty phrase and New Zealand's schools of journalism now discredit it to their students. Yet, in the words of that experienced newspaperman, Karl du Fresne, the long-established rule that journalists should try to remain impartial and present facts and opinions in a balanced manner "has underpinned good journalism in Western democracies for decades" [12] This is good advice for all those fans of special tribal rights in the media – especially the young ones whose minds have been indoctrinated right through their education and whose knowledge of our early history leaves a lot to be desired.

However, all is not lost for those who seek the truth of how our country was founded and how it developed. There are so many good books, often written in the 1800s by well-educated, literary men who were close to the events they describe and, in many cases, saw with their own eyes the making of the nation. These can be found in libraries and second hand bookshops and, together with a few modern books written by open-minded historians, are a wonderful counter-balance to the mischievous nonsense that is being written by some of the new breed of "revisionist" historians. The difference between a master historian like James Cowan, who reports historical events in the way that they happened, and a revisionist historian like Claudia Orange, who "interprets" them – apparently to suit her own Treatyist agenda, is like the difference between champagne and beer.

Michael King, another historian engaged in the business of rewriting New Zealand's history to suit the grievance industry ("noble Maoris, wicked pioneer settlers"), has been strongly criticised by Ian Wishart in his well-researched book, *The Great Divide*, such criticism being well-founded, while James Belich, another of this ilk, has had his book on the Maori Wars heavily criticised by historians like Matthew Wright and John Robinson. Where there is Cowan, who needs Belich?

We owe it to ourselves to seek nothing less than the truth about what really happened – especially when these events are being called upon to justify massive compensation claims from the taxpayers of the twenty-first century. A true scholar will always rigorously test what he or she finds out. In the words of Lord Bledisloe, the Governor-General who donated the Treaty House and grounds at Waitangi to the nation, in his farewell address to New Zealand, "In the Kingdom of the Blind the one-eyed man is King, and he that does not know his own history is at the mercy of every lying windbag."

THE CONSTITUTIONAL ADVISORY PANEL – A VERY NASTY SMELL

David Round

(This chapter, a commentary on "New Zealand's Constitution; The Conversation So Far", published by the government's Constitutional Advisory Panel in September 2012, first appeared in the electronic newsletter of the New Zealand Centre for Political Research on the 4th of November 2012. Minor amendments have been made.)

A "conversation". The very word fills us with foreboding. "Conversations" are creatures of the caring classes; the schoolteachers and academics, the higher-paid end of the public service and all the professional carers in charities, lobby groups, trusts and the social sciences; all comfortably off, and all dedicated to their own deadly vision of a truly caring and happy world where they and people just like them intend to be in charge. The very word has echoes of nanny telling us that we must be civilised and behave like grownups, and that our silly childish prejudices do not justify us depriving other people, the poor, for example, or even Maori, say, of their rights under the Treaty.....That is the sort of context in which we hear the word, anyway. "Conversations", although allegedly two way, inevitably end up with us having to listen to a small group of the shrill self-interested and self-righteous lecturing us on why we need to change.

There are other words that could have been used to describe this process of constitutional review. Why not "review"? Or we could try inquiry, or consultation, or discussion? What is wrong with "discussion"? That is friendly and relaxed enough. Or stock-take, or study, or examination? Some of those words - although not all of them - might be said to smack too much of officialdom and bossy people being in charge; but that would, after all, be no more than the honest truth. Besides, we surely want a word with some overtones of officialdom, because this is, after all, a proper, sober, official inquiry. Isn't it? We would not want to mislead New Zealanders into thinking that this was just some casual random chat that they might like to get involved in or might not, depending on how they felt on the day. Isn't this something important, which ought to be named with an appropriate important word? New Zealanders, surely, are not so feeble that they will be intimidated by a word like "review". The very word "conversation" is patronising. It implies that we are so timid or pathetic that we need special reassurance and moral assistance before we dare poke our shy little noses out of our hidey-holes.

And by the same token, why an "advisory panel"? Why not a "commission"? "Advisory Panel" is hardly an appropriate name. New Zealanders are being asked for their opinions on immensely important matters. This inquiry is far more important for the country's future well-being than one, if I may be forgiven for taking the longer view, into the causes of a mine explosion or even the collapse of buildings in an earthquake. Those inquiries were important, and deserved commissions of inquiry. But the future constitutional shape of our country, something that will affect us and our descendants, our prosperity and our very identity; this is shoved away in a corner to be considered by a mere "advisory panel"?

Something funny is going on here. This behaviour is not honest. It is stealthy. Someone is about to be ambushed. It might, perhaps, be radical Maori and the Maori Party, misled by National into believing that they might really be able to acquire serious legal privilege for ever. (Even if they do not succeed in doing that, of course, harm will have been done, because their expectations will have been raised, and they will feel aggrieved that they have once again (so they will say) been swindled out of their rights.) They will only have been defeated, of course, because a thoroughly alarmed population will finally have been aroused out of its longstanding apathy. But it might be that the majority of our population is not alarmed, but continues in its inert torpor, and so it – we - are the ones who are ambushed. I am inclined to think this will not be the case; there seem to be stirrings, and I certainly hope they are more than just that; but I have been hopeful before. If we are not alarmed and angry, then bad things will happen.

I read the Panel's recently published "The Conversation So Far", of course, with suspicion, and you might argue that such an attitude naturally leads one into paranoia, and to see plotting and treachery - or, to use gentler terms, self-interest and personal agendas - where none exist. But of course there are personal and political agendas. This whole inquiry is a concession to the Maori Party. It is not a disinterested review where no-one involved has any axe to grind. Why would we not think that there are private agendas? This is radical Maori's big chance. If they pull this one off, they will have won. They will be on top forever, the rest of us - those who have not decided to flee to Australia - helots in our own land. So why, even before we look at them and see who they are - would we not think that many members of the Panel and their friends and allies might have some axes to grind?

We might not expect anything particularly blatant in an introductory document such as this, but without being blatantly biased - without saying anything that is not perfectly reasonable and accurate - one can nevertheless contrive to give a certain tone, a certain slant, a certain colour and direction to a perfectly neutral document. Just ask Sir Humphrey Appleby of *Yes, Minister*. This is done here. I shall give some examples below. But, as we shall see, there is more than mere delicate slanting in the Panel's chapter on "Crown-Maori Relationship Matters". In that chapter there are many statements which are actively misleading. Their presence does not do the Panel any credit. Nor does it give us any faith in their fairness and openmindedness.

After a ten page description of our present constitutional arrangements, the document has two big chapters – "Electoral Matters" and "Crown-Maori Relationship Matters". Crown-Maori matters, note. The fiction is maintained that the Crown - our government, the government of the people by the people - is somehow quite a separate thing from the people, with the implication that the settling of claims and the "honouring" of "Treaty principles" is a matter in which we, the people, are not entitled to interfere. To speak of "Crown-Maori Relationship Matters", rather than presenting the matter as one of universal and legitimate public interest, also tends to imply, quite incorrectly, that the Treaty established a "partnership" between Maori and the Crown. It did no such thing, of course; it was an agreement that Maori were to be the Queen's subjects like anyone else. In Captain Hobson's words, "Now we are one people". But the very existence and agenda of this review begins from the opposite assumption.

The first chapter, "Electoral Matters", covers several issues. There is the size of Parliament - should it stay the same, or be reduced to perhaps 100? Then there is the question of the term of Parliament - three or four years? Should the date of elections be fixed well in advance, or should an early election date be left, as it is now, to the Prime Minister? Then there is mention of the number and size of electorates, and finally the possibility of "electoral integrity legislation", such as was enacted in 2001 (but expired in 2005) to deal with the "waka-jumping" of Alamein Kopu and others, who were elected as list M.P.s for one party but then decided to leave it and support another.

Yes, these are not unimportant issues, but they are entirely a smokescreen. There is no need to include these in the review at all. They must be included, it must be explained, because the Panel's terms of reference require them to be; but this is not the Panel's purpose. The Minister of Maori Affairs, Dr Peter Sharples, for example, who, with the Deputy Prime Minister Mr Bill English set the terms of reference, has said that the purpose of the review is that "Maori want to talk about the place of the Treaty in our constitution", and "how our legal and political systems can reflect *tikanga* Maori". We all know this. Their hope is, I imagine, that the raising of these electoral issues will divert some public attention away from the Panel's real purpose, and perhaps lend an air of spurious legitimacy to that actual purpose.

Bear in mind that nearly all of these electoral issues have either been recently settled or are just non-starters in the first place. The size of Parliament? A select committee considered this in 2001. Submissions to the committee were 99 for the present size and 55 for smaller. In 2006 the Justice and Electoral Select Committee also recommended that a member's bill to reduce the number of seats not be passed, for eminently reasonable and practical reasons. But the point is that the issue has often been canvassed recently. Are M.P.s of any party seriously willing to consider reducing the number of seats? I think not. So why is it being raised again?

The second issue, the term of parliament (three or four years?) is one where there can be not the slightest doubt of public feeling. In referenda in both 1967 and 1990 just under 70% of the population voted firmly for three years. The proportion of those favouring three years was actually up slightly (69.3%) in 1990. So why is this mentioned again?

Then, third, there is the matter of the number and size of electorates. The reason for the presence of this issue is a little more perplexing. Surely, we might think to ourselves, the number of electorates depends on our answer to the first question, the size of parliament. Parliament of course has both constituency and list M.P.s, but nevertheless we thought we could assume a general rule that any reduction or increase in electorates will just be the other side of the coin of changing the size of parliament and number of MPs. How can it be a separate issue? This question seems unnecessary. But here is concealed something that could be very unpleasant. The document's discussion raises several possibilities: that the South Island quota of constituencies might be abolished, that the present rule that the population of different electorates must not vary by more than 5% be relaxed to allow a 10% variation, and that certain physically large electorates (Maori electorates are specifically mentioned) might also be able to be reduced in population size because of the inconvenience to the M.P. of properly servicing the larger electorate. We can easily see the foundations being laid here for a Maori gerrymander. Abolish the minimum number of seats for the South Island - even though it has big electorates they are all white people down there - and give the extra representation to an increasing number of Maori seats with the smallest legally possible populations. Watch out for trickery here.

Finally, there is the proposal to create new laws against 'waka-jumping'. I was not aware that this was a burning issue. After an initial period of instability after MMP's appearance, political parties are settling down. ACT will be gone at the next election, if not before, and United Future and New Zealand First are unlikely to outlive their present leaders. The Mana Party will last only as long as Hone Harawira does - which may be some time, admittedly - and the Maori Party's future seems to be quite uncertain. So again, electoral integrity legislation seems to be nothing but a smokescreen.

And so, behind the smoke, we come to "Crown~Maori Relationship Matters", the real interest and purpose of the advisory panel. This chapter is divided into three headings; Maori representation in Parliament, Maori representation in local government, and the "role" of the Treaty of Waitangi. Again, these headings and their sub-headings are prescribed in the Terms of Reference. The observant reader notices at once that this chapter of the Panel's is much more detailed than the previous one. There are numerous references to various Acts of Parliament; so many, indeed, as to cause a little disquiet, as we realise what inroads Maori have already made into our supposed democracy of equals. This may well be part of the purpose of the description - to suggest to the reader that these things are already established and accepted, and so we might as well put provisions of a similar nature in a written constitution. Our reaction might well be the opposite, however - horror at the discovery of how far down the slippery slope we already are, and determination to arrest and reverse the slide.

The Waitangi Tribunal is also often quoted, but always with the greatest deference. This is a real cause of dismay, and good evidence of the Advisory Panel's bias. Yes, we know that the Waitangi Tribunal is established by law (the Treaty of Waitangi Act 1975) and we know that it is empowered to make recommendations based on its views of what "Treaty principles" require. The Advisory Panel would doubtless argue that that fully justifies the frequent quoting of Tribunal "findings". But it does not - because, as we are all well aware, the Tribunal is not even an impartial finder of historical fact, and its view of what Treaty "principles" are and require is always strongly politicised and slanted to the benefit of claimants. This is beyond dispute. Even admirers of the Tribunal say as much. Reading the "Conversation" one would get the impression that the Tribunal is an absolutely authoritative and unquestioned authority, but in fact its findings are often factually and logically shaky, and with motivations which have no place in a proper judicial tribunal. To quote it as an authority, then, and say absolutely nothing to indicate the tendentious and disputed nature of its "findings", is no less than misrepresentation; it is to be guilty of a confidence trick against the public.

Let us go into more detail over the Panel's report on the "conversation so far".

1. Maori Representation in Parliament

Page 41: "Over the years, the Maori seats have provided a voice for Maori perspectives and interest in parliament. Commentators say the Maori seats serve as a reminder to successive governments of the promises made through the Treaty."

Some commentators may say that. Other commentators point out that the seats have nothing to do with the Treaty, that they were introduced almost thirty years later and that they were intended to be a merely temporary measure. For much of their more recent history they have, in effect, been captured by the Labour Party, and their usefulness in providing a voice for Maori perspectives in Parliament has been entirely questionable.

Page 43: The Waitangi Tribunal is quoted as finding that the Crown is obliged under the Treaty "actively to protect Maori citizenship rights and in particular existing …rights to political representation…" That is to say, the Tribunal "finds" that the Treaty requires the Maori seats to remain. No comment on this finding is given; the impression is that the matter is settled, instead of being just one political opinion and hardly justified by the historical facts.

Earlier on that page we are told that the 1987 select committee considering the future of the Maori seats "was not convinced by the Royal Commission's position [the 1986 report of the Royal Commission on the Electoral System] that the introduction of MMP would enhance Maori representation in parliament". 1987 was twenty-five years ago; the issue of whether the Royal Commission was correct or not is completely ignored. It would be very simple to provide an answer. The Panel simply fails to answer this obvious question one way or the other. Why? We are forced to speculate, and I am afraid my speculation suggests that the Panel knows but simply does not like the answer.

To be fair, page 44 tells us of the view of the (un-named) ACT Party member of a 2001 Review Committee that the Maori electoral option was undesirable in that it promoted racial distinction and tensions. But even then, it does not tell us of ACT opposition to the seats themselves. It does tell us that Professor Joseph, my learned colleague at the University of Canterbury Law School, "did not see separate Maori representation as being critical to the integrity of the electoral system and therefore did not see it as legitimate subject-matter of constitutional entrenchment". We note with interest that both the Greens and Labour supported entrenchment of the Maori seats; although given the things which National is doing now and Helen Clark never did ~ establishing this review, for a start, signing up to the United Nations Declaration on the Rights of Indigenous Peoples, and passing the new, dangerous and racist foreshore and seabed legislation - I do not think we should necessarily be unkind to Labour. Credit where credit is due.

And then, after considering the questions of maintaining Maori seats, their entrenchment, and the Maori electoral option, the Panel helpfully raises the subjects of waiving the 5% requirement before a list party can get its candidates into parliament (an idea unanimously rejected by the 2001 committee) and mentions a Ngati Porou proposal to establish a completely new Maori Representation Commission "to return to first principles and new forms of Maori representation in a three year consultation process". At this point I think we have reached the stage where the Panel is putting ideas into people's heads. Why raise again something that has been unanimously rejected by a select committee? The answer, I suggest, is this - that these ideas are the logical next steps which Maori will want to take in their slow, stealthy power grab. They have the Maori seats - perhaps they even have the Maori seats entrenched. So what next? How can the radical racist Maori

312

agenda go forward from here? Let us think..... But what is this? Good heavens! Right here, as it happens, a suggestion - from the traditional leaders of one tribe, no-one else - that Maori representation cease to be a matter for Parliament, but should be handed over to a permanent Maori committee. Well, that would be handy! The Maori seats, then, would no longer be a matter for the wider public, but just for Maori - some Maori, just a small elite - themselves. This Maori committee will inform us from time to time about their latest demand - I am sorry, they will tell us what they have discovered the latest of our ever-evolving duties under the Treaty to be-~ and we will then have no choice but to do as we are told. (The Treaty is, the late unlamented Sir Robin Cooke told us, "an embryo, not a fully-developed set of ideas". In other words, it is a blank cheque, so of course there will be all sorts of surprises in future as we continue to keep what is evidently our side of the bargain. Bargain?! As currently interpreted, it is a very expensive 'bargain'. And so now the Panel mentions this interesting idea in passing and, if anyone wants to follow it up, well…This is what is known in the law as leading the witness, and, except in cross-examination, is generally considered improper.

2. Maori Representation in Local Government In this section we are told on page 47 that "'as *tangata whenua,* Maori have a close and direct concern with the management of natural resources. Maori therefore have a close interest in effective representation in local government to ensure their views and perspectives are represented". Now what is that but a blatant statement that Maori deserve something more than just one normal vote each just like everyone else? "'As *tangata whenua*"? As inhabitants of New Zealand we all have a very great interest in the management of natural resources right now, but that seems not to concern the Panel. Some of the ancestors of present-day "Maori", usually a small minority of their ancestors, were of the Maori race, yes. How does that give them a special right in the management of natural resources?

The Panel then tells us as a fact that "historically Maori exercised *kaitiakitanga,* managing all of New Zealand's natural resources. Maori and the Crown agreed, through the Treaty, that Maori would maintain authority and control over their *taonga,* including natural resources. Now, much of the management and regulation of these resources is the responsibility of local government".

313

Put it like that, and the only conclusion is that local government (all of us) should hand over to Maori (just some of us) more control over the natural resources on which this country's economy and life are based. If Maori were promised the right to manage everything, even after they'd sold it (a point the Panel does not touch on) - and if they don't have that right now - well, clearly (in the eyes of the Panel) we've taken it away from them, and we have to give it back. That is the only conclusion that paragraph can lead you to.

Yet there is not a single fact in that paragraph. For a start, pre-European Maori were not "managers" - in their own way, they over-exploited resources and lived beyond their environmental means as much as anyone else. The record of Maori environmental destruction is clear - perhaps thirty or more bird species rendered extinct, between a third and a half of our pre-human forests burnt, and other resources used unsustainably. Dr Tim Flannery, the respected author of *The Future Eaters*, suggests that by the late eighteenth century a Maori "resource crisis" was in full swing and, had it not been for the white man's pork and potatoes, that would soon have led to a catastrophic collapse in the Maori population. And then *"kaitiakitanga"* - the word, for a start, is a missionary word, coined by Henry Williams for insertion into the Treaty. How could Maori have exercised something they did not even have a word for? I notice that the panel's definition of *kaitiakitanga*, in a footnote, defines it "in a modern resource management context". Very wisely, there is no attempt to define it as it was understood environmentally in 1840. It would have been nonsensical to try, because no-one in 1840 was thinking about "natural resources", and the understanding would certainly have been that, if lands and rivers, say, were sold to the Crown, then Maori rights over them would cease. There is nothing in the words or even in the "principles" of the Treaty which says that, even after Maori have sold land, they are still entitled to all sorts of rights over it to "manage" its natural resources, which they have just sold. But the panel presents this as a statement of fact which, it also makes clear, obliges us to "return" to Maori the rights of governance that local government stole from them. This really is part of the next stage of the radical Maori agenda; it is time that Maori really got their hooks into local government as well as central government. This is one of the logical new fields of Maori takeover attempts. But we do not expect an allegedly impartial and open-minded review panel to instruct us that this is our duty.

This section then goes on to describe the opportunities already presented by the Local Electoral Act, the Local Government Act and the Resource Management Act for privileged Maori representation and participation in local government. This is followed by a section on "Questions and Perspectives". The first question is whether special Maori representation on councils should be "guaranteed" - that is, whether this racist affront to democracy should be made compulsory, rather than, as now, merely an option which local ratepayers may - and often do - vote against. If Maori had their own special representation on local councils it would usually mean that Maori were over-represented; that in one way or another their vote gave them more influence around the council table than the vote of a non-Maori. This offends against our most deeply-held egalitarian and democratic instincts. But the paper makes absolutely no remarks, here or anywhere else, about the virtues of equality of voting power and representation. There is not a single remark that "some commentators" might think that inequality of voting power is objectionable in principle. Clearly the Panel does not think it is.

The section then goes on to talk about "other ways" of achieving Maori representation, mentioning in particular some Treaty settlements, and the restructuring of the new Auckland City Council. But nowhere does it even consider the possibility that Maori should just be like everyone else and vote just like everyone else. The thought obviously never entered the Panel's head. Neutral? I think not.

3. The Role of the Treaty of Waitangi. Here things start to get really bad. This section, which claims to be a summary of the present situation so as "to inform a conversation about the future", is subtitled "The Treaty of Waitangi in Our Constitution". This of itself is misleading. The Treaty is not part of our constitution. The panel claims that the Treaty has an "accepted position as the founding document of New Zealand". At a legal level, this is simply untrue. The Treaty, as every judge still says, has no legal status. It is, of itself, not part of our law. Yes, we may say that at a political level the Treaty marks the beginning of the establishment of the state of New Zealand, but it has no legal status. It was a mere preliminary political proceeding to a land of warring tribes becoming a unitary colony under a British governor, then a self-governing dominion, and, finally, the fully independent democratic state which we are fortunate enough to inhabit today. Yet anyone reading this section would naturally assume from this description as our "founding document" that it was the legal foundation of our state. Not to spell this out carefully is, putting the best interpretation upon it, negligent - and since it is impossible to believe that this document was not extremely carefully written, we must suspect that it is deceitful.

The section then goes on to give examples of how "the Treaty influences the exercise of public power". The examples it gives are (first) references to the principles of the Treaty in some statutes, (second) the Maori seats, (third) the Waitangi Tribunal and, (fourth), the explaining and application of the principles by the courts and the Tribunal. The impression given is that the Treaty is already well-established in our constitution. Now all of this dishonest. For a start, the third and fourth items are nothing more than a part of the first. The courts and the Tribunal refer to the principles of the Treaty because they are referred to in statutes. So items one, three and four are exactly the same. Cross numbers three and four off the list, then. Second, as already explained, the Maori seats have nothing whatever to do with the Treaty. So cross number two off. Third, and most important, when the courts and the Tribunal do consider Treaty principles, they do so not because of any place the Treaty has in our constitution, but because a particular Act of Parliament has authorised such consideration. (After all, it is the "principles" of the Treaty, not the Treaty itself, that are being considered!) For an ordinary Act of Parliament to say that in certain cases decision makers must take the principles of the Treaty into account hardly makes the Treaty itself part of our constitution. An Act of Parliament might say that sustainable management of resources, say, is to be considered in decision making. Does that make sustainable management part of our constitution? I think not.

The next paragraph tells us that governments have "acknowledged that the Treaty's guarantees have not been consistently honoured, and have taken responsibility for redressing breaches through the settlement process. They have also accepted that the principles of the Treaty must be considered when making decisions, if future breaches are to be avoided."

There is no mention of previous full and final settlements. There is no acknowledgement that the current growing Maori grudge industry is the child just of the last two or three decades. There is no contemplation of any other possibility than that New Zealand's history has been nothing but one long heroic struggle of Maori to keep alive their *mana* while gallantly resisting the onslaught of the *pakeha* oppressor....The Panel does not even mention in passing the central fact of New Zealand history, the pioneers' labour to bring to a turbulent and wild country the gifts of civilisation, peace and law, and to build the still prosperous and smiling country which we know today. This silence of the Panel is disgusting.

It certainly is true that more recent feeble governments have allowed the grievance settlement process to be opened all over again, and that even the Crown seems reluctant to mention earlier full and final settlements; but nevertheless, those settlements, and our past peaceful race relations, have to be known. They make an enormous difference.

Moreover, governments have not officially accepted that Treaty principles must be considered in future decision-making. The Panel's statement suggests some sort of official declared policy, embedded now in law or at least government practice. But there is no law or generally-established principle to that effect, and, since the "principles of the Treaty" are so elastic, it would be disastrous if there were. The Panel, I notice, does not provide any footnote - very prudently!

International Context - Declaration on the Rights of Indigenous Peoples

To be fair, the Panel does note that this United Nations Declaration is "an aspirational document that does not bind the government". Most of this section repeats not the Declaration itself but the National and Maori Party government's statement of support for it, which "reaffirms the importance of the Treaty" and "recognises that Maori have an interest in all policy and legislative matters". Well they do have such an interest, of course; but so does everybody else.

'Treaty principles'. This begins with misrepresentations. It claims that there are "differences between the two texts of the Treaty". Now in fact there is really only one text of the Treaty, the Maori one, which is the one that nearly all chiefs signed. The English version most familiar to us is just a back-translation of that. But (apart from the obvious difference that they are in different languages!) there is no difference in substance between the English and Maori texts. Both recognise the sovereignty of the Crown, the status of Maori as British subjects - no less and no more - and continued Maori ownership of their property. The Panel claims that it was because of this invented "difference", and "the need to apply the Treaty to changing conditions" that "attempts have been made to distil a set of principles from the Treaty". The distillation of principles, however, occurred only because Parliament has referred to them in various statutes. Parliament was in no way prompted by alleged differences between the texts. Parliament acted for entirely political reasons, not out of any "need to apply the Treaty to changing conditions". Indeed, a very strong case can be made that Parliament considered the mention of principles in section 9 of the State-Owned Enterprises Act to be nothing but meaningless lip-service. The "need to apply the Treaty to changing conditions" could very fairly be described as an admission that the Treaty in its actual terms is now irrelevant, and has nothing further to say to a country where there is no doubt that the Queen is sovereign, and Maori are her subjects just like everyone else. Agitation for the "development" of Treaty "principles" (the "living document" fallacy) is an admission that the agitators are unhappy with that situation of equality before the law.

The Panel accepts that the list of Treaty principles "is not definitive". It "continues to evolve as the understanding of what it means to be a Treaty partner evolves". Yes indeed. Every day someone tells us of some new obligation we have. This lack of definition "provides flexibility for the Crown-Maori relationship to develop". You can say that again. But it can be "the cause of frustration for those who seek clarity and certainty of meaning". Well again, I must agree. And should we not have clarity and certainty of meaning in a constitution? But the Panel does not appear to be aware of this basic axiom of common sense. It prefers a situation where we are tied to a blank cheque - where our new constitutional arrangements will compel us to comply with "Treaty principles" without knowing what they entail. The principles "evolve" - at our cost, and to Maori benefit, for ever and ever.

Then there is a section on the principles in Acts of Parliament. Various statutes are mentioned but for some reason there is no mention of the number of statutes containing these references. The number is small, and would be easy to ascertain exactly. I am not 100% sure of the present figure myself, but it is a comparative handful, although including some quite important statutes.

'Who decides what the Treaty principles are?' This section says that the Waitangi Tribunal is "the body responsible for deciding what the Treaty means in a modern context". This is only half true. The Tribunal is not that mighty and authoritative. It is empowered to hear complaints of breach of Treaty principles, certainly, and make recommendations based on its "understanding" of the "principles", but it has no wider authority to deliberate on what those principles are. It may only say what they are in the claims before it; where, as we all know - see the recommendations on radio waves, and, much more recently, water, to take but two examples - its interpretations are often absurd. Moreover, the courts also make decisions about Treaty principles, when a statute refers to them. The Panel then talks about judicial decisions on the principles, but does not explain how the courts are able to adjudicate on those principles if the Tribunal (as they have just said) is "the body" responsible for defining the Treaty's "modern meaning". One might almost get the impression that the courts are bound by the mighty Tribunal - which is, thank heaven, still the opposite of the truth. For the time being, at least.

The final paragraph in this section mentions the Court of Appeal's 2003 decision in the *Ngati Apa* case, which began the whole foreshore and seabed controversy. That decision has been condemned by a significant body of opinion as disgraceful, and it was clearly improper according to the Court's own rules about abiding by earlier decisions, but there is no mention of that here. But on its face, anyway, the decision had nothing to do with "Treaty principles", being rather a matter of the interpretation of various statutory provisions. So why is it mentioned here at all? This is interesting. Is there a Freudian slip here? Is it possible that the prominent people on the Panel understand that the real secret reason why the Court of Appeal decided as it did was for the sake of enforcing its version of the "principles" of the Treaty.

Treaty settlements. It quite rightly admits that a claim before the Tribunal is only one way of making a claim and obtaining a settlement. It is also possible to enter into direct negotiations with the Crown. I comment that any future abolition of the Tribunal could, of course, do nothing to stop such claims. There will always be this option for the redress of genuine grievances, even after that biased Maori lobby-group, the Waitangi Tribunal, is deservedly consigned to the scrap-heap of history.

But, as we all know, we are nearing the end of the current round of "full and final settlements". The Panel itself does note, although only in a footnote, that all historical Treaty claims had to be filed with the Tribunal by 2008. So what happens then? Ah, yes indeed! It would be dreadful if the end of historical claims were to mean an end of the Treaty industry. And so, unsurprisingly, under "Questions and Perspectives", the next section, the question is asked - it has all been thought out, you see! - the question is asked, "What will happen once all historical Treaty grievances are settled?" Not all that long ago we were being told by important people like Sir Douglas Graham that, once historic claims were over, we would all be able to put the past behind us and move forward together happily into the future as one people. That assertion, however, was as accurate as the statements made to the Lombard investors for which the Honourable Sir Douglas was convicted in a criminal court. But the Panel clearly takes a different view from Sir Douglas. It instructs us that the Treaty "will continue to impact the Crown actions"

'The principles of the Treaty must be considered when making decisions if future breaches are to be avoided." "Must"? "Must"! Isn't the Panel supposed to be *asking* us, instead of telling us? But here it is once more lecturing us on what we "must" do. What the Treaty actually says is that Maori are to be the Queen's subjects - to put it into modern parlance, they are to be New Zealanders - like everyone else. Genuine historic wrongs against them may be righted - but after that, we are, in Captain Hobson's words, to be one people. Yet here is an allegedly impartial panel, set up to seek our opinion, telling us that the "principles" of the Treaty - by which they mean, a special place for Maori – "must" be considered - and, it is clearly implied, "must" be in our new constitutional arrangements.

This is a carefully coded but nevertheless openly racist political speech, clearly leading to a predetermined outcome. One would expect nothing more from some of the Panel's membership.

This section then quotes the recent report on the WAI 262 claim (for flora, fauna, culture, etc.) as being "future-focussed" and "setting out building blocks for a constructive and positive post-Treaty relationship between Crown and Maori based on mutual respect". Yeah, yeah. Clearly, again, the Panel thinks that this is the way to go. But you and I know perfectly well where we will end up.

Then finally in this section we have the question "Should the Treaty be entrenched?" The answer begins by describing an ill-conceived 1985 suggestion by the then Minister of Justice in a draft bill of rights, which would "recognise and affirm" the rights of "the Maori people" under the Treaty, and provide that the Treaty "shall be regarded as always speaking and shall be applied to circumstances as they arise so that effect may be given to its spirit and true intent". (Again the "living document" nonsense)   It was further proposed that the courts would be able to strike down any Acts of Parliament which they considered to be "inconsistent with the Treaty". Well, we were lucky not to get that, but here is the Panel raising the suggestion for us again. The Panel alleges, somewhat illogically, that the reason this suggestion never appeared in the Bill of Rights Act was that Maori objected that the Treaty would be demeaned unless it was entrenched as higher law. That was only one part of the reason. The other part was the fear of many of us that Treaty principles would be a blank cheque, and would authorise judges to embark on disastrous political adventures. But the Panel mentions only the one reason, objections by Maori themselves. That being so, it would   follow that, if Maori now had no objection to entrenching the Treaty as higher law, there would be no reason why it could not be done. Maori, are you listening?

'Other Constitutional Matters'.

This, the title of the final chapter, suggests that it is merely a ragbag of odds and ends. It mentions only two things. One is "Bill of Rights issues". As I am sure you recall, the New Zealand Bill of Rights Act 1990 sets out in extremely general terms various fundamental rights and freedoms which we usually ought to have. Time and space, mercifully, do not encourage me to go into the issues here, and the question is of course not one of the Panel's central preoccupations. But I note that the Panel lists the rights protected by the Bill of Rights Act, and includes in its list "democratic and civil rights such as electoral rights…". We might have thought that the Panel would dwell on those electoral rights a bit, given its keenness to give Maori special electoral privileges. How would those two things fit together, now? Would that not be a matter requiring a little careful consideration? But the introduction of racial inequality in voting is not pursued any further. Our country's intellectual and political elite have now moved to the stage where racial privilege, which we thought we never had, is now back as the only morally and intellectually accepted position. It requires no justification; it is self-evident. It is just that Maori - or, to be more correct, corporate *iwi*, assisted by their "useful idiots" -~will be holding the whip.

The other issue in this ragbag is 'Written Constitution'. Much of this section is pretty fair. But string these quotations together:

Page 70: A constitution's preamble "may talk about why the constitution has been developed, what kind of government it is establishing and the values it promotes. A preamble can be inspirational and aspirational. Preambles are not generally enforceable by courts, but can give a context for interpretation of other sections of the constitution."

Page 71: "Some countries have autonomous territories, generally where a minority ethnic group exercises some powers of self-governance independently from the national government." This is code for the break-up of our country into Bantustans.

Page 72: "Many constitutions also provide for group or community rights, particularly the rights of minority and indigenous groups. Mechanisms for implementing these rights may include:

- A requirement to consult these groups about decisions that affect them
- Providing for effective participation in decision-making and elected bodies through, for example, guaranteed representation in federal or central parliaments.'

"Decisions that affect them" in fact means *all* decisions.

On page 75, the "issues that might arise" (that word "might" is a charming touch) "in developing a written constitution" include, at the very top of the list – "How would a written constitution reflect the Treaty of Waitangi and the future position of Maori *iwi* and *hapu*?"

I am detecting a pattern here. It is a violation of every democratic and egalitarian principle our country possesses.

A lady recently sent me a news item reporting that Peter Sharples, the leader of the Maori Party and Minister of Maori Affairs, wanted to see more teaching of "Maori history" in schools. The lady commented "They never stop pushing, do they?" No, they never do stop pushing, and that is why they are succeeding. That is why we are on the back foot - because we sit quietly and comfortably at home while the rabble-rousers of Maoridom are imbuing their followers-~ both the no-hopers and the youug flash ones who are doing very well - with a sense of perpetual grievance. And now their respectable friends have engineered a committee which is no more than a group of like-minded radical

Maori and sickly white liberals to make recommendations about how "Maori" should be more in charge in future.

That is all this is. And it is so frighteningly easy to imagine the headlines just a year or two down the track after the Panel "reports" to Parliament. "A committee of prominent New Zealanders from all sides of the political spectrum has recommended that greater respect be paid to the principles of the Treaty in a new written constitution for Aotearoa/New Zealand." ("New Zealand", the land for which tens of thousands of soldiers, sailors and airmen, our ancestors and kinsmen, died in two world wars – "New Zealand" will ultimately be phased out, but that will take some time. The atlases....)

Then, an announcement after a close general election, when neither Labour nor National would be able to form a government by itself, and the Mana or Maori Parties hold the balance of power, that laws along these lines are being drafted for consideration the following year....A big *hikoi* of the disaffected and the weeping and wailing classes to Wellington when the select committee is sitting - a bit of muscle, perhaps, the odd threat of rebellious, impatient, young Maori anger, a bit of aggro, the fortuitous discovery of an arms cache in the bush somewhere.... - and politicians, practically all of them, end up as unscrupulous cowards - what would the politicians in our Chamber of Chamberlains do then? Three guesses. So statesmanlike! "Now is a time for healing." Then the *hongis*, the *karakias*, the little old ladies, the pompous orators with their big carved walking sticks, the windbaggery.

And then the deluge.

MEET THE MEMBERS OF THE CONSTITUTIONAL ADVISORY PANEL

In 2004 Parliament set up an all-party Constitutional Arrangements Committee to review New Zealand's existing constitutional arrangements. It conducted a "stocktaking exercise", at the end of which it concluded that "[no problems] are so apparent or urgent that they compel change now or attract the consensus required for significant reform".[1]

On 8th December, 2010, the National-Maori Party government announced a full blooded review of New Zealand's constitution and democratic processes, to be carried out by a carefully stacked "Constitutional Advisory Panel" with a predominance of Maori radicals and their sympathisers.

So, what changed between 2005 (Constitutional Arrangements Committee report) and 2010? Nothing – except John Key's perceived need to buy the three parliamentary votes of the small, unrepresentative and racist Maori Party.

Like the sham "Review Panel" that Finlayson set up to "review" the Foreshore and Seabed Act 2004, the Constitutional Advisory Panel appears to be a "done deal" masquerading as a "consultation". After all, if National could get away with a prejudiced panel on the foreshore and seabed, why shouldn't they try the same trick on the public again?

The Panel's task has already been covered in the previous chapter and here it is only necessary to quote what Peter Sharples, the co-leader of the Maori Party, said when he launched the Panel. "An important part of the review process will be consultation with Maori, particularly on the place of the Treaty of Waitangi in our constitution. The business over the Treaty has gone on for so long now and there's been year after year of demonstrations up at Waitangi because of the people feeling the treaty has not been acknowledged and implemented in this way. The members of the panel are well-placed [surely "well chosen"] to seek out and understand the perspective of Maori on these important issues." [2] In other words, the rest of us don't count.

In this chapter we are going to take a look at the members of the panel in order to judge the likelihood of it delivering an independent, honest and objective report free from racism, self-interest and Treatyism.

324

The co-chairman of the Panel is Professor John Burrows, a law professor at the University of Canterbury who has specialised in and taught the law of torts and contracts but strangely not constitutional law.

The other co-chairman is Stephen Gerard O'Regan, an Irish New Zealander who, to take advantage of his small smattering of Maori blood (he is believed to be only one-sixteenth Maori), changed his name to Tipene. This was at a time when it was becoming obvious that there were some big bucks to be made out of the soon-to-mushroom Treaty industry.

Both O'Regan and his daughter, Hana, (whom Finlayson appointed as one of the three members of his heavily stacked foreshore and seabed panel), have done very nicely out of the Maori gravy train with Stephen (or, if you are having a "Maori moment", "Tipene") reputed to be a multi-millionaire and one of Canterbury's richest citizens. Hardly surprising as he has extracted payment after payment from the public purse in various capacities – chief negotiator for Ngai Tahu in their dodgy Treaty claim, chairman of Ngai Tahu Maori Trust Board, the Mawhera Corporation and Sealord Ltd., a director of Television New Zealand, Deputy Chairman of Transit New Zealand, a member of the Geographical Board (where he stamped on his real heritage – Irish/British – to rename parts of the South Island with Maori names), and several other capacities. Money seems to be his real motivation – not Maoridom.

Stephen O'Regan and his daughter are more "make believe" Maoris than real Maoris. They can not even be described as "Irish Maoris" since that implies something like 50/50 whereas the Irish component of their genetic make-up is so much greater than their tiny smattering of Maori blood. (Hana O'Regan is believed to be one thirty-second Maori).

In claiming that such a tiny proportion of Maori blood makes them "Maori" the O'Regans are fooling not only themselves but others as well. If this absurdity – this distortion of biology – is allowed to continue, then no doubt in a hundred years time we will still have greedy O'Regans with 1/256th part of Maori blood still extracting everything they can out of the taxpayer on the grounds that they are "Maori".

By the natural and immutable laws of biology Stephen O'Regan's mother's family ceased being Maori and became European when Stephen's grandmother, Rena Harwood, was born a quarter caste Maori. Furthermore Stephen was brought up in a New Zealand European household with an adopted sister and an adopted brother – both totally white. The Maori persona – including the name change – came later and coincided with the financial bonanza of the Treaty industry. The O'Regans were an extremely well-off family and the idea that the taxpayers should have to "compensate" one of them for historical "grievances" of more than a century ago based on dodgy gtounds is so absurd that we really are in Alice in Wonderland territory. It is only fair to add that, unlike her son, Stephen's mother (one-eighth Maori) would have been the last person to ask for or expect anything from anybody.

The presence of Stephen O'Regan on the Constitutional Advisory Panel is an indication of how rotten is the present National-Maori Party government as this is a man who, as a director of the failed Hanover Finance racket, is currently facing a claim of $35 million that is being brought against him and his fellow directors by the government's Financial Markets Authority. So, while one branch of government is suing him, another branch is asking him to advise on the future constitutional rights of every New Zealander!

This type of thing is common in the tinpot dictatorships of Africa but it is a slur on the good name of New Zealand to have a man facing such legal action on such an important panel. Among O'Regan's co-defendants in this case are Mark Hotchin and Eric Watson. When Hanover collapsed in 2008 it owed $554 million to approximately 16,500 investors.

O'Regan, a former socialist turned greedy capitalist, has made his career out of grabbing money and resources off the taxpayer for himself and his tribe and, like his daughter on Finlayson's "review" panel for the foreshore and seabed, can hardly be regarded as an objective member when it comes to the panel's main task of entrenching the mischievously re-invented version of the Treaty of Waitangi, thus making it a straightjacket on our future rights, including the right to govern ourselves by the democratic principle. Unless O'Regan, facing this massive legal action brought by a public body, is sacked, the Constitutional Advisory Panel will have little or no credibility.

But he is not the only one. To back him up is that ardent and rather unbalanced crusader for Maori privilege, Ranginui Walker, a member of that notoriously racist, slanted and mischievous body, the Waitangi Tribunal. Walker was formerly a member of the Maori activist group, Nga Tamatoa (The Young Warriors) who, as pointed out in Chapter Seven, took inspiration from Marxist liberation and indigenous rights movements around the world, including the gun carrying Maoist Black Panthers in America. He wrote a book, *Struggle Without End,* and that probably tells us all we need to know about the "objectivity" of this particular member of the heavily slanted Constitutional Advisory Panel.

But it doesn't stop there. After all, it was the Maori Party, with only 2.39% of the vote at the 2008 election, which recommended the Panel and is calling the shots – even to the extent of apparently naming all the members of the Panel. Just like when the police investigate themselves.

Another member of the Panel is Leonie Pihama who, with very decided, if not extreme, views on "Maori rights", can hardly be expected to bring any objectivity to the Panel's task, thus further reinforcing the view that this is very definitely a Panel with a pre-conceived view of what it is going to report, in which case the so-called "conversation" that it is having with selected members of the public in an effort to give it some much needed credibility is just downright dishonest. How can you "consult" with someone when the reason for setting up the Panel – and its membership – is designed to reach a foregone conclusion?

So, who is Leonie Pihama? She has had extensive involvement in Maori education, Te Kohanga Reo, Maori language immersion units and Te Kura Kaupapa Maori. She did a Ph.D. on "Mana Wahine, A Maori Woman's theoretical framework based within Kaupapa Maori". She has done work for the Ministry of Maori Affairs. She was a director of the publicly funded Maori Television for four years and serves on the Maori Health Committee of the Health Research Council. She is also a research director of Maori and Indigenous Analysis Limited. Many, many organisations but not one of them dedicated to the general public – only to those of her own race. Can she really be expected to bring anything other than a narrow minded Maori opinion to these so-called deliberations? Oh, and she has two facial tattooes – one on the forehead and the other extending from her lip to the bottom of her chin.

As can be seen, she has done – and is doing – very nicely out of the publicly funded Maori gravy train and she shouldn't complain if people regard her as not typical of New Zealand women and with a vested interest in entrenching Maori privilege into a written constitution that would bind us forever to recognising that Maori have superior rights to the rest of us.

To give some idea of Leonie Pihama's "objectivity" it need only be recorded that she has declared that "holocaust is an appropriate and valid description of the impact of colonial genocide on Maori", which, of course, is complete nonsense since the "genocide" of the Maori people occurred during the musket wars of the 1820s and 1830s and was inflicted by fellow Maori. Since being appointed to the Constitutional Advisory Panel Pihama has publicly supported Keri Opae, a Maori teacher who in February, 2011, repeated the insulting and groundless allegation that the British settlers who came to New Zealand made a "holocaust" of the Maori.

To have on the Panel a person of such warped and racist views deciding the future rights of all New Zealanders is deeply concerning to those who care about the future of the country. No wonder the spokeswoman for the Maori Party, Rahui Katene M.P., exulted when the Panel membership was announced, "Our constitutional pathway is in good hands." Indeed it is – if you are trying to turn non-Maori New Zealanders into second class citizens after 172 years of hitherto equal citizenship rights.

To give further support to the radical Maori position the Panel also contains Linda Tuhiwai Smith who, like Leonie Pihama, has immersed herself in "Maori studies" which does not exactly give one a very broad view of the world.

Linda Tuhiwai Smith is "an internationally renowned researcher in Maori and indigenous education" and is Pro Vice-Chancellor (Maori) of that den of Maori radicalism, the University of Waikato. She has been joint director of Nga Pae o te Maramatanga, which translates as "Horizons of Insight", and of the National Institute of Research Excellence in Maori Development and Advancement as well as the Maori Tertiary Reference Group for the Ministry of Education.. She has been central to the development of a tribal university, Te Whare Wananga o Awanuiarangi, and to the nationwide movement for an alternative schooling system, Kura Kupapa Maori. With this narrow background, dedicated almost entirely to the advancement of interests that are exclusively Maori, how can she be regarded as "objective"? And isn't it remarkable how many of these organisations are set up at public expense to line the pockets of the corporate iwi/Maori academic elite?

In her book, *Decolonising Methodologies; Research and Indigenous People* (How's that for plain English?), Smith "presents a cogent critique not only of anthropology but of the cultural evolution of the entire Western concept of research. The author describes the devastating effects of such research on indigenous peoples and articulates a new Indigenous Research Agenda which aims to replace former Western academic methods." [3]

By calling in her book for the "decolonisation of research methods" this Maori activist is rejecting the time-tested, objective, logical and scientific methods of Western learning for the notoriously unreliable (and often deliberately slanted to fit compensation claims) Maori "lore" – e.g. that the North Island was formed by some guy called Maui pulling it up on his fish-hook! Smith's call for the "decolonisation of research methods" would be a step backwards for everybody, including Maori. The only ones who would be likely to benefit would be "Maori academics" like Linda Smith and her colleagues, who would no doubt grab a whole wad of further public funding to advance their "back to the Stone Age thinking". Like Leonie Pihama, Linda Smith seems to have done nothing else in life except take money from the public purse for advancing Maori rights and culture.

Yet another "Maori academic" on this twelve person Panel is Hinurewa Poutu, a teacher at Te Kura Kaupapa Maori o Mana Tamariki. She has an academic and work record in studying, researching and teaching the Maori language. She has also worked as a Maori language media consultant. In other words, another one steeped in the Maori culture and not much else.

So, that is five Maoris – all apparently professional Treatyists and doing very nicely out of the Maori gravy train. Since Maoris constitute 14% of the population and are outnumbered by Europeans by 5 or 6 to 1, we would expect that, to reflect the composition of the nation, there would be a proportional number of Europeans on this racially chosen panel. Not at all. This thing is the Maori Party's creation with John Key, the ever smiling poodle, trailing along.

There are a mere five Europeans on the Panel (to match the five Maoris) and even these are, to a large extent, supporters of the Treatyist agenda, starting with former Deputy Prime Minister, Michael Cullen, who in April, 2008, - a time when the writing was on the wall for electoral defeat for Labour in November - gave an exceedingly generous settlement of approximately $1 billion of Crown forests that had hitherto been owned by all New Zealanders to nine rather small central North Island tribes. These forests, that were added to the assets of the tribal elite that controls corporate iwi, were the Horohoro Forest, Whakarewarewa Forest adjoining Rotorua, the Crater Forest, the huge

Kaingaroa Forest, Waimihia Forest, Marotiri Forest, Pureora Forest, Waituhi Forest and Taurewa Forest.

The total area of these forests in this "Treelords" deal is 176,000 hectares and Cullen crowed that it was "the largest single treaty settlement package to be developed to date" [4] Together with benefits under the Emissions Trading Scheme, Cullen's gift of these forests is believed to be worth more than a billion dollars, thus enriching the nearly $40 billion corporate iwi assets even further.

One of the tribes benefiting from this settlement is Ngati Tuwharetoa. Then lo and behold, after leaving Parliament, Michael Cullen was appointed by Tuwharetoa as their "Principal Treaty Claims Negotiator" on, no doubt, a very handsome salary.

There appear to be two possible scenarios here. Either Michael Cullen is that rare species - a nice, honest politician who would never dream of using public money to give an advantage to an entity such as Tuwharetoa in return for a future favour. This would mean that it was nothing more than a mere coincidence that he would be engaged by Tuwharetoa so soon after leaving Parliament. There is, of course, another scenario and we leave it to the reader to decide which is the more likely.

In any event, the fact that he is apparently currently being paid by Tuwharetoa at the same time as pocketing his fees for being on the Constitutional Advisory Panel would seem to create a conflict of interests, thus bringing into question his objectivity and therefore his suitability as a Panel member. But this is not about objectivity but about appeasing the Maori Party and in the process normal considerations such as "not only must justice be done but it must be seen to be done" are thrown out the window.

A further mark against Cullen's objectivity is that he is on record as saying that the Treaty of Waitangi is a "living document". This suits the grievance industry very nicely as they can use it for whatever new opportunities crop up from time to time (e.g. claiming the spectrum – unknown in 1840) but it is factually wrong as the treaty was merely the mechanism to change the status of the country. After that was done there was no further use for the treaty which had performed the task for which it was created.

How can the Treaty of Waitangi be a "living document" in 2013 when its authors considered it a dead letter by the end of the year in which it was signed since it had achieved its purpose and, by later

Proclamations, New Zealand had been declared a British colony? With the British flag flying over New Zealand and the Maoris all full British subjects the treaty had fulfilled its purpose.

It is only a "living document" for Treatyists like Cullen to invoke for their own political, if not spurious, purposes. As an advocate for the Tuwharetoa tribe it is not surprising that Cullen has pushed the false "living document" line but it suggests that he has a preconceived position or, if you like, prejudice on the whole Treaty issue and there could hardly be a more unsuitable person to put on the Panel to represent, by the implied nature of the racial selection process, the interests of European New Zealanders. Cullen should not be surprised if European New Zealanders regard his appointment to this heavily stacked Panel with the gravest suspicion. But he probably doesn't care as, now that he is out of Parliament, he is no longer answerable to anyone – except, apparently, the tribe that is paying him. And, as the saying goes, he who pays the piper can call the tune. So, why not lump Cullen with the five radical Maori Treatyists? That would give these types six votes out of twelve on the Panel. But it gets worse.

We also have Deborah Coddington, a former A.C.T. Member of Parliament. But her views on Maori racial privileges are not those of most A.C.T. supporters. In an article that she wrote in the *New Zealand Herald* on 5th December, 2010, she claimed that Maori are not getting special treatment, which is contrary to the evidence.(See Chapter 13 of this book - "Special and Privileged").

Does Deborah Coddington turn a deliberate blind eye to what has been going on in New Zealand in recent years or is she so ignorant and/or gullible that she believes this unsubstantiated nonsense? With views like these she was a shoo-in for a place on the Constitutional Advisory Panel, whose prime aim seems to be to entrench Maori privilege over the rest of us. One wonders if she wrote the article in an effort to be nominated to this lucrative panel.

To reinforce her credentials as a Treatyist Coddington made the nasty and unsubstantiated allegation that Rev. Henry Williams deliberately mistranslated the treaty so as to protect his land holdings. This, like her belief that Maori to-day are not getting any special treatment, is contrary to the evidence but it does bolster the claims of the grievance industry. Oh, and let's not forget that Deborah Coddington is married to Colin Carruthers, who was the lead barrister for the Maori

Council in their greedy case against the government for rights over the nation's water.

Then there is John Luxton, a former National Minister of Maori Affairs (1993-6) who, if form is anything to go by in respect of National M.P.s and ex- M.P.s, can be expected to do whatever John Key wants him to do and what John Key wants above all else is to continue his appeasement of the Maori Party so as to keep his minority government in office.

Luxton was a director of Blue Chip which, like O'Regan's Hanover company, cheated many investors of their money. The liquidator said that the only reason that he was not suing Luxton and the other directors was that he lacked the funds to do so. It seems that an important qualification to be a member of the Constitutional Advisory Panel is to have been a director of a company that cheated its investors – just as the Panel is all but certain to cheat New Zealanders of our long-held rights.

As Minister of Maori Affairs Luxton wrote a paper *Te Oranga o te Iwi Maori: A Study of Maori Economic and Social Progress*. In this he wrote, "The Treaty of Waitangi has moved from being a way of protecting the rights of all when first signed in 1840.....to legislative recognition with a focus on protecting rights and allowing a Maori perspective to be considered where appropriate in government decision making" The true treaty never said that. So Luxton is accepting the new reinvention of the treaty which gives Maori an extra say in decision making over and above the rest of us, that Te Tiriti, signed by the chiefs, did not. With beliefs like that Luxton can not be considered to have an open mind or even an understanding of what the treaty was all about. But with such views he is eminently suited to be a member of this wretched panel.

So Luxton can probably be added to those others on the panel who want to entrench into a binding written constitution the reinvented treaty, containing new and false concepts such as special privileges for Maoris that were not part of the original treaty. That would give the Maori Party's lot on the Panel eight votes out of twelve – a majority.

Another member of the panel is Peter Tennent, a former mayor of New Plymouth, who is believed to be a strong National Party supporter which, of course, would explain why he was appointed since, with his career as a hotelier, his knowledge of constitutional matters could be reasonably expected to be somewhat limited unless, of course, he has spent the idle hours behind the bar reading Justinian and Taswell-Langmead and other tomes on constitutional law.

It is believed that Mr. Tennent has political ambitions on a wider canvas than the New Plymouth mayoralty and so how do we know whether or not National has promised him a reward – a position on the Party List for example – if he "does the right thing" for the National Party? However, to "do the right thing" for the new Key/Finlayson National Party would be to do the wrong thing for New Zealand as it would entrench in law a "Treaty based" written constitution that would relegate all non-Maori New Zealanders to a class of second rate citizenship.

If Mr. Tennent should "do the right thing" by John Key and support what will be the majority verdict of this slanted panel, then he will be betraying not only future generations of New Zealanders but also those many early settlers of New Plymouth who were literally murdered in their beds by rebel Maoris – people like William Brown, a merchant of New Plymouth who died on 22nd August, 1860, at Waitara from wounds received in an ambush by the rebels, Ephraim Coad, the 43 year old publican – like Mr. Tennent – of New Plymouth's Marsland Hotel, who was murdered at the mouth of New Plymouth's Henui River on 17th August, 1860, while taking some blankets to the soldiers who were guarding the wrecked sailing ship, the *George Henderson*, Lieutenant and Mrs. Gascoigne and their four young children and Messrs. Milne and Richards who were all massacred at the Pukearuha Redoubt on the outskirts of New Plymouth on 13th February, 1869, and sixteen year old Joseph Sarten of Henui, New Plymouth, who, on 4th December, 1860, was on his horse looking for a lost bullock when he was shot by a gang of Maoris hiding in the bushes, his body being mutilated by tomahawks.

And let's not forget all those brave men of the Taranaki Volunteer Rifle Corps and the Taranaki Military Settlers who gave their lives so that New Plymouth would be a safe and prosperous settlement for, in agreeing to a "Treaty based" constitution giving privileges to part-Maoris, Mr. Tennent would be helping to reverse the outcome of the Maori Wars in which Taranaki – and New Plymouth in particular – took the brunt of the casualties. Whether he has the spine and the patriotism to defy what will be the Panel's majority finding remains to be seen.

However, the signs don't appear very hopeful. During his time as New Plymouth's mayor Tennent did not bother to repair the city's fine monument on Marsland Hill to the British soldiers and sailors who defended and gave their lives so that New Plymouth could survive. This memorial, put up by the citizens of New Plymouth to commemorate their defenders, was smashed some years ago by Maori vandals and no mayor has been brave enough – or patriotic enough - to repair it. The smashed memorial, standing atop the hill from which the town was defended, is a continuing slur on New Plymouth's reputation and a sad reminder that political correctness, cowardice and appeasement seem to be the dominant forces on the New Plymouth District Council.

So there are the five Europeans who were chosen racially for this Panel – Burrows, Luxton, Cullen, Coddington and Tennent. By the nature of the racial selection process these five, equaling in number the five Maori Treatyists, should be expected to stand up for the rights of the 80% European component of the population. But don't count on it. If Sharples, who seems to have complete control of this process, thought that they were likely to oppose his cunning treaty entrenchment scheme, it is unlikely that they would have been appointed.

Since the Panel is selected on race alone rather than merit or constitutional knowledge it is only fair that there should be a Pacific Islander on board and that is Bernice Mene, the former netball champion, whose father was Samoan. No doubt Bernice is a very nice person and a good mother to her three children but what would she know about constitutional law? Still, it could be worse. If the criterion for selection to the Panel is as bizarre as a sports champion with the required amount of Polynesian blood, they could have appointed Sonny Bill Williams.

The last member of this twelve person panel is Peter Chin, the former mayor of Dunedin who is Chinese and it is hard to resist the conclusion that, if he wasn't of that ethnicity, he would not have been appointed.

The views of Chin and Bernice Mene are not really relevant since the Treatyists – both Maoris and some of their white lackeys – seem to have a majority on the Panel without the votes of Mene and Chin. However, in a replay of what Hugh Barr in his chapter on the foreshore and seabed calls "groupthink" among the Court of Appeal judges in the *Ngati Apa* case, we could be presented with a unanimous decision by this Panel to entrench the new version of the treaty in a written constitution. In fact, it is hard to believe that any of these carefully selected people would have been appointed unless they were "a safe pair of hands" for doing the Maori Party's dirty work of entrenching racial privilege, based on the false Cooke-Palmer treaty, into a permanent, written constitution. No wonder the Maori Party's M.P., Rahui Katene so smugly declared, "Our constitutional pathway is in good hands".

It is not beyond the realms of possibility that, in selecting the Panel, Sharples got guarantees from enough of them to ensure the desired outcome for the Maori Party. Of course, John Key would probably deny that this happened but, since Key deceived the public over the foreshore and seabed issue, why shouldn't he do so again?

To counteract this trick that is being played on the people of New Zealand by the Maori Party and their National lapdogs a group of well-qualified, knowledgeable and concerned people have got together to form a genuinely independent Constitutional Review Panel (as opposed to the Government's "Constitutional Advisory Panel"). Two of them are co-authors of this book – David Round and Mike Butler.

The others are the former ACT M.P. and its Deputy Leader, Dr.Muriel Newman, who has a B. Sc. Degree from Auckland University and is a Doctor of Education from Rutgers State University of New York, Emeritus Professor Martin Devlin O.N.Z., an ex-Army officer who taught education and business management at Massey University, Doctor Elizabeth Rata, Associate Professor of Sociology at Auckland University, and Professor James Allen, the Garrick Professor of Law at the University of Queensland and a former law teacher at Otago University and Cornell University in the United States.

Not only is this Panel truly independent – unlike the Constitutional Advisory Panel – but its members have far more legal expertise and knowledge of constitutional law than all the intellectual featherweights on Sharples' Panel. The report that will be made by this independent and unofficial panel will be free of the self-interest and racism that has infected the government's panel from the day it was announced.

It has been necessary to spell out the real backgrounds of the people on Sharples' race based Panel that appears to have been carefully stacked so as to achieve a particular outcome in spite of how unwelcome this outcome might be to the people whose rights it is determining. As such, this whole Panel is so flawed that anything it recommends will lack even an atom of credibility.

One example of the Panel's bias from the beginning is its referring to our country's name as "Aotearoa New Zealand". They don't seem to understand that their job is to ASK New Zealanders what changes, if any, they want, and not to dictate such important things as changing the name of the country from above.

The Constitutional Advisory Panel is the greatest threat to the rights of New Zealanders in living memory. It has been constructed for a purpose, viz. as Key's ongoing appeasement of the Maori Party. The Panel is not representative of New Zealanders at large but of a particular special interest group – the Maori grievance industry. It is deliberately, racially and mischievously slanted to advance by a huge leap the rights of those who happen to have been born part-Maori, thus relegating all others into a second class citizenship. All sorts of soothing words will be used to achieve this unfair, undemocratic and racist purpose – just as was the case over the foreshore and seabed - but they should not be believed.

The Constitutional Advisory Panel is due to make its recommendation in September, 2013, and that recommendation will be that, for the first time in 173 years, New Zealand must now have an unnecessary written constitution, entrenching newly invented "Treaty rights" for Maoris that were never part of the real treaty. This whole exercise is a Maori Party push to get control of New Zealand. Since it is almost certain that the Maori Party will be out of government after the 2014 election Sharples and his mob know that they will never have a better chance for this unprecedented power grab that under the present situation where Key has shown that he will never say "No" to the Maori Party on any substantive issue for fear of losing their parliamentary support. Therefore, we can expect the usual Maori Party/Treatyist tactics of intimidation, manipulatrion and control so that this grasping minority can yet again dominate the majority.

Should John Key continue his appeasement by accepting the Panel's recommendations, then every person who supports the National Party will be complicit in the crime of taking long held rights off New Zealanders for ever more and pushing our wonderful country down the slippery slope of apartheid where a greedy, selfish and unpatriotic tribal elite will call the shots with everyone else kowtowing to them. Try explaining that to your children and grandchildren.

As the Constitutional Arrangements Committee of Parliament reported in 2005 "there are no problems so apparent or urgent that they compel change now or attract the consensus required for significant reform". So, hands off!

EPILOGUE

This Land is your Land, This Land is my Land,
From Cape Reinga to Stewart Island
From the Kauri Forest to the Southern Waters
This Land was made for you and me.

As was noted in the first two chapters, in handing New Zealand over to Britain in the treaty of 1840 the Maoris were fortunate in their timing, since that was the high point of the humanitarian movement in Britain and of the influence of that benign force on the Colonial Office. The Maoris were doubly fortunate since the years following the treaty were also the golden age of British engineering and construction. Throughout the Victorian era, Britain was the pre-eminent engineering nation. As a brand new country that needed infrastructure, New Zealand was a beneficiary of this flowering of inventiveness and precision engineering, with many skilled engineers and contractors, who had gained their experience in Britain, coming here to build the country.

The Polynesians were experts at building canoes but that was about the limit of their shipbuilding skills. In 1792, when Captain George Vancouver sailed his ship, *HMS Discovery* (not Cook's vessel, but another of the same name) into Kealakekua Bay, Hawaii, he had to put his ship's carpenters to work to finish building a 36 foot schooner that the chief, Kamehameha, had started. However work had come to a grinding halt as the Hawaiians knew not how to proceed. Into the breach stepped the carpenters of the Royal Navy who finished the job to their own exacting standards, borne of years of experience and tradition, as well as providing the cordage and canvas to make the vessel seaworthy.

The Maoris too were canoe builders but not shipbuilders, commissioning Europeans to do such skilled and intricate work. For example, in 1876 Tenetahi Pohuehue, the chief at Pakiri, Northland, commissioned the Scottish Nova Scotian shipbuilder, Angus Matheson of nearby Matheson's Bay, to build him the *Rangitira*, "which was coppered and well fastened throughout," [1]. This was the fourth vessel that Angus Matheson had built for the Maoris, the others being two cutters of 27 feet each and another, described as "a rather smart looking craft." [2]

Angus Matheson and his shipbuilding brother, Duncan, had settled with their families at Matheson's Bay in 1859 – not long after their arrival from Nova Scotia as part of the migration of Highlanders from there to Waipu in North Auckland. The boat building yard that they established at Matheson's Bay was a continuation of the one that they had left behind on Cape Breton Island, Nova Scotia. They were a good example of hard working settlers who got on well with local Maori, and their bay came to be known as Matheson's Bay.

The Matheson family contributed enormously to the shipbuilding industry and the local economy. It was natural that their name should grace the bay in which they worked so hard. But 150 years later that crass and historically ignorant philistine, Christopher Finlayson in his capacity as Treaty Minister, denigrated the memory of the Mathesons by changing the name of this lovely bay to oblige his iwi friends. So, Finlayson has not only stolen the beaches off us, the public, by his thieving and racist Marine and Coastal Area Act but also, by his name changing, he is trying to strip us of our heritage as well.

Ship building was only one of several industries that got off the ground thanks to British engineering skills, coupled with the energy and enterprise of the pioneers. Wharves were built, harbours were surveyed and charted by the Royal Navy, and dredged when necessary, and lighthouses were erected on dangerous rocks and points.

Inland New Zealand, with its wide, fast flowing rivers and mountainous terrain, was a particularly difficult place in which to build infrastructure. Across the Tasman it was possible to lay a railway across flat, treeless land for a hundred miles or more at a trot, but in New Zealand the same railway would have required several bridges over raging rivers and tunnels through solid rock (or, worse, loose and ever falling shale)

As more settlers arrived more and better roads had to be built as well as railways, docks, drainage systems, reservoirs, bridges, tunnels and, later, tramways, cable cars, viaducts and telegraph lines. Some of today's best farmland in the Waikato is the result of the draining of the marshes near the Waikato River by pioneer entrepreneurs and engineers. Wiremu Tamihana (the Maori "kingmaker") sold "land that was swampy to the Scottish Morrin brothers [after whom Morrinsville was named] who hired Irish navvies to dig ditches and drain the land and turn it into some of the most fertile dairy land in New Zealand." [3]

The bulk of all this difficult and back breaking work was done by the skilled tradesmen and labourers among the pioneers although Maoris also increasingly worked as navvies (labourers) and bushfellers.

338

"Navvy", the nineteenth century word for a labourer, derives from "navigation worker" – those who dug the canals in England in the early stages of the Industrial Revolution.

The infrastructure so created was for the benefit of the whole country, and the Maoris, who had not even invented the wheel before Europeans arrived, were particularly keen for the 'iron horse' (railway) and other wonders of Western technology to be brought to their villages. As Sir John Logan Campbell wrote in his book, *Poenamo*, "The one desire of the Maori at that epoch (1840) was to get the Pakeha to come and live at their settlements".

That is how Auckland began and became the capital of New Zealand for a few years. In 1841 a delegation of chiefs went north and offered land in return for the Governor moving his establishment to what is now Auckland. Thus did the Auckland Maoris acquire both protection from their enemies and the thriving trade of a growing town.

In the words of the pioneer surveyor and author, S. Percy Smith, "It was not entirely an unselfish offer on their part, for the Tamaki Isthmus had been the constant highway of hostile war-parties both from north and south for ages past, and they thought that, if they could get the white man to settle there, these hostile incursions would cease, which in fact they did, for ever." [4]

It was the same elsewhere. For example, when John and Isaac McLeod, Scottish brothers who came to New Zealand with their families from New Brunswick in 1862, set up a timber mill at Helensville to cut the kauri of the Kaipara, their enterprise was welcomed by the local Maoris, not least because it provided them with employment in an economy where cash was becoming ever more important. The McLeods cut and milled timber, built a jetty and wooden huts for their expanding work-force, made bricks and founded the town of Helensville – named after John McLeod's hard working pioneer wife, Helen. In the words of Auckland's *Southern Cross*, "No more useful settler was in this community than Mr. McLeod." The young colony did well out of this "useful settler" who, besides establishing the timber industry of the Kaipara, also developed a coal mine at Kawakawa, lime kilns at Whangarei and Freeman's Bay, Auckland, and sat as M.P. for the Bay of Islands.

Even those Maori who resisted the British with armed force were happy to receive the benefits of the pioneers' engineering and construction efforts. After the Maori War in the Waikato, "Big John"

McLean, "a shrewd and dependable contractor whose word was his bond" [5], arrived in Pirongia, south-west of Hamilton, to build a 264 foot bridge over the Waipa River. Like Angus Matheson, this tall, bearded Highlander was also from Nova Scotia. He was told by the suspicious settlers of the district "that he would not be able to keep a tool or a piece of loose timber on the ground as it would be stolen by the natives" [6] who, a year after Tawhiao's surrender, were still obstructing surveyors and railway builders. "Big John" McLean went straight to Tawhiao and, after a long pow wow in the chief's meeting house, managed to convince him that the bridge would be of benefit to the Maoris of the area. Tawhiao's surliness ripened into enthusiasm – so much so that he instructed the Maniapoto chief, Wahanui, to put a *tapu* on the tools and materials, thereby forbidding any Maori from stealing them with the result that, at the end of the contract, "Big John" McLean said that he had never been so fairly dealt with than by Tawhiao and his people. And Tawhiao was very happy with the bridge, which was paid for by public funds.

While Maoris played a role in the development of New Zealand it was the pioneers (mostly from Britain) who, by their larger numbers and more advanced skills, made by far the greatest contribution to the physical building of the country that we know today.

They would venture into the bush and work long hours to bridge a river or dig a tunnel through a rocky hill before returning at dusk to their tents where the contractor's cook would have a hot meal waiting. Besides earning a living they were also building a country for themselves and their descendants.

Nobody has a greater claim to the rights and riches of New Zealand than the descendants of these doughty pioneers who applied their energy and skills to building New Zealand and, when called upon, their blood to defend it – in both the Maori Wars and the world wars. These are the real title deeds to a nation. Yet, by the Treaty industry as recently reinvented to strip non-Maoris of long held rights, it is the descendants of the people who built the land who are being made second class citizens in their own country.

The priceless egalitarian society that was created in New Zealand is far too precious to throw away. A self-serving Treaty industry, obsessed with racial privilege and the enrichment of corporate iwi, can only tear apart a beautiful country if it is allowed to continue.

A little bit of common sense, honesty and spine is all that is needed to lead New Zealand away from its present path of driving a sledgehammer through our sovereignty and breaking up the nation by "co-governance" agreements with chosen tribes.

Ordinary Maoris – often needy, particularly in the remoter rural areas – see little, if anything of the proceeds of Treaty settlements. Worse, they are used by the Maori Party and corporate iwi for selfish, if not corrupt, purposes, viz. furtherance of their monopolistic aims and the feathering of their nests. The last thing that the Maori Party would want to see would be the ending of Maori poverty as that would take away their main bargaining chip in extracting ever more public funds for corporate iwi.

Today, New Zealand has already gone too far down the path of separate racial development, with ever more legal rights for those who are part-Maori. The only solution is for the people to insist on the "colour blind state" where there must be no laws that give special rights, resources or privileges to anyone on the basis of race. There must be an end to all the race based funding that is crippling the economy and driving our "best and brightest" to Australia and other countries. Anything less will lead to an apartheid-like state – as is already happening.

Because of the corruption of New Zealand's political system, caused largely by the lack of a second chamber of Parliament as is enjoyed in Britain and the United States as well as in our sister realms of Australia and Canada – the people must take matters into their own hands and stop acting like fools by voting for the man with the most permanent smile.

The Treaty industry is a massive fraud that is based on a mischievous misinterpretation of the wrong Treaty – as we saw in Chapter Two. Sadly, at this point in our history, New Zealand is facing a "perfect storm" on three fronts – a) the most deceitful, unpatriotic and corrupt government in our history, that takes basic rights off the citizen to buy the support of the Maori Party, b) judges who can't be trusted because they are playing fast and loose with the law in order to indulge their own ideological political agendas, and c) a dumbed down, air-headed media so obsessed with "celebrities" and the trivia of the moment that they have lost touch with both reality and perspective and fail to ask the hard questions.

First the government. It is a terrible thing to call a New Zealand government "corrupt" but how else can one describe this government whose Deputy Prime Minister and Minister of Finance, Bill English, is on record as openly talking about paying – with taxpayers' money - what are effectively bribes to various *iwi* or other Maori groups that get in the way of National's asset sales programme? And, if Mr. English feels comfortable enough to talk like this, one has to wonder what other bribes this secretive government has paid to *iwi* and others that we don't know about.

Finlayson too adds to the impression of corruption, e.g. his spokesman admitted that tribes with customary marine title could refuse access to areas of seabed where Crown owned minerals such as petroleum or iron-sands are being mined or "come to an access agreement which could carry commercial benefits for the *iwi*" [7] – apparently code for paying a bribe.

Second, the judges. Of all the many benefits that the early settlers brought from Britain – Christianity, parliamentary democracy, engineering and agricultural knowledge, flocks of sheep and herds of cows, art, architecture, games like rugby, cricket and tennis, our beautiful English language with its rich and inspiring literature – there is none more precious than the common law which, with its precedents and centuries of wisdom, has traditionally protected our ancient rights, some of which stretch back as far as Magna Carta. That is why it is so disturbing that the two most senior legal offices in the land, those of Chief Justice and Attorney-General, should be held by manipulative Treatyists who seem to have scant respect for ancient rights or the preservation of a fair, non-racial society.

Sian Elias, Mrs. Hugh Fletcher, will have to retire as Chief Justice upon reaching the required age in 2016 but this woman, who seems to have such a cavalier attitude to the supremacy of Parliament and thereby to democracy itself, can do a lot more harm to the country between now and then.

And the media. Our once high quality newspapers are now like women's magazines that it takes intelligent people about four minutes to read while what is shown on the TV news is determined largely by corporate interests. That is why we never see footage of the atrocities being committed by the Chinese in Tibet as that would upset the corporate interests behind New Zealand's "Free Trade" Agreement with

China which is so harmful to our sovereignty and our manufacturing industry.

And as for Finlayson – the sooner he is got rid of from public life, the better. This aggressive, bullying and unscrupulous former counsel for Ngai Tahu appears to be so deeply compromised that he takes long held rights and resources off New Zealanders for the potential benefit of Ngai Tahu. From his own actions and methods – as exposed in this book – Finlayson gives the impression that his primary purpose in government is to advance the interests of Ngai Tahu and his other favoured tribes at the expense of the rights, resources and expectations of the rest of us.

To remove any doubts about Finlayson's fitness for public office we need only recall his reaction when asked what he thought of idea of a "colour blind state" with "one law for all" and no special privileges or funding for any particular race. "Nuts" was his reply – presumably because it would get in the way of Ngai Tahu's continuing race based privileges such as their undeserved monopoly over all greenstone in the South Island, the odious *nohoanga* (one hectare sites on *public* land from which non-Maoris are excluded for 210 days a year) and the advantages that they received under the Emissions Trading Scheme when the government, presumably at Finlayson's insistence, rejected the legal advice that the tribe's claim to carbon credits on Crown-owned forests should be refused.

From his actions, his words and his use – or, if you like, abuse – of office it seems clear that Finlayson wants a racially divided society with his friends among the tribal elite sitting on top of everyone else. This amounts to a return to the tribalism that the chiefs wanted to abandon when they signed the treaty. And the terrible thing is that the National Party, founded on the worthy principle of representing all New Zealanders equally, is tolerating it.

If this biased and deceitful minister is not got rid of, then he will continue to break up our wonderful country that thousands have died for on the battlefield as he sticks his knife further into our national sovereignty. He has started with his Tuhoe "co-governance" deal – no longer one sovereignty in New Zealand, as has been the case since 1840, but more than one, with the democratically elected government no longer being able to govern in certain areas without getting the consent of the small, private, greedy and backward Tuhoe tribe.

If Finlayson is not sacked, there will be more and more of his unnecessary, if not treacherous, "co-governance" deals stitched up behind closed doors with no public input for the benefit of his favoured tribes.

And why, after 170 years as a united, sovereign nation, do we suddenly need to dilute the country's sovereignty with "co-governance" agreements? For the same reason that we had the beaches stolen off us so that they can be claimed by tribes – Finlayson's pro-Maori bias and John Key's cowardly inability to stand up to him.

Surely every National Party member who feels unease – or revulsion – at Finlayson's antics has a patriotic duty to bring pressure on the Prime Minister to get rid of Finlayson in the interests of both the National Party and the country.

Of course, Key's answer to that would be that the Maori Party likes having Finlayson as Treaty Minister for obvious (and racist) reasons and that Key's supreme need is to oblige the Maori Party so as to continue to enjoy the support of their three wretched M.P.s, who keep Key in office and in a position to help Sky City and his other corporate friends.

If Key won't get rid of Finlayson, National will lose a growing number of its traditional, core and is likely to be "history" come the 2014 election. Especially if another party be formed – a type of traditional National Party where Nationalists would feel more comfortable – rather like the way that the U.K. Independence Party has destroyed the Conservatives' natural advantage. Margaret Thatcher had a 120 seat majority in a 630 seat parliament but, even after Gordon Brown's bungling, the Tories could not muster even a simple a majority because the UK Independence Party takes thousands of former Tory votes in every constituency.

No party can survive the loss of its traditional core and, because of the betrayal by Key and Finlayson of National's founding principle of representing all New Zealanders without favouring any particular group, there is no longer a reason for any traditional National Party supporter to continue to vote for what is effectively a new and different party. People who are more loyal to a political party than to their country are not much more than traitors. New Zealand deserves better than to be manipulated by these two ill-intentioned politicians who know how to con the public and do it very well.

For the sake of ourselves, our rights, our future and our country we must move away from entrenching the racial privileges of part-Maoris to a completely colour-blind state. That would be of benefit to everyone – especially the Maoris who would then have to stand on their own feet instead of being increasingly regarded as bludgers off the taxpayer. No doubt the Maoris would be surprised at what they could achieve without the ongoing benefit of special funding and legal racial privileges. Of course, any suggestion that Maori can be as good as their equals would upset the corporate iwi interests that the Maori Party represents. But this racist and tribalist party is such a feudal anomaly in the 21st century that it would have already died a natural death but for the helping and appeasing hand of John Key.

It is time that the tribal leaders started to behave like the citizens of a democracy rather than like the spoilt brats that the ever indulgent Treaty industry has turned them in to. And has there ever been a word of gratitude to the modern and hard pressed taxpayer for providing these endless funds to these fortunate tribes? Just more demands in the almost certain knowledge that appeasement pays. In fact, the irreconcilable ill will of Maori radicals has grown in proportion to the goodwill showered on them by taxpayer dollars.

What a terrible irony it would be if our wonderful country, built on the sweat of the pioneers (and the blood of their sons and grandsons in both the Maori Wars and the two world wars) was to destroy itself and all that has been accomplished through the corrupt interpretation of a simple document and the small-minded greed of an elite of tribal leaders and their political and judicial lackeys.

The treaty was a document for its time and for a specific purpose, viz. to bring New Zealand under British sovereignty and to make the Maoris British subjects. It is not a "living document" as claimed by the Treatyists so that they can put their own "spin" on it for their own greedy and ignoble purposes. It was simply the necessary piece of paper (well, dogskin) to change the staus of 1840 New Zealand so as to get the country up and running under the peace and good order of British rule and was never intended to put the nation in an apartheid like straightjacket 170 years down the line. We need to look forward and not backwards. "It is dangerous, it paralyses a people, to live in the past," wrote that astute observer of the twentieth century, Douglas Reed.[8] A major drawback about a policy based on past resentments is that you can not check it when the grievances have disappeared. The part-Maori winner of the Krypton Factor, Dr. Brian McDonnell, believes that a treaty based constitution would trap Maori in a "suffocating self-deception as in need of special pleading and a special status".[9] In other words, permanent and inter-generational dependence on the rest of us.

Speaking at the centennial celebrations at Waitangi in 1940, Sir Apirana Ngata said that the treaty was "a gentleman's agreement which on the whole has been not badly observed"[10] In the words of Sydney's *Daily Telegraph* in 1901, New Zealand's native policy was "a shining example of honourable intention and solicitous administration".[11]

How would history regard a democratic nation that allowed all its hard-won laws and privileges to be monopolised by a tiny, greedy minority? Laws and privileges based upon race can only lead to deep discontent, burning resentment, and a divided society. There are no shortages of examples throughout history, and there have never been happy endings to race-based laws.

To progress as one nation rather than the country breaking up into a patchwork of semi self-governing tribal Bantustans, it will be necessary to claw back some of the nation's resources and sovereignty that have been hived off to tribes for the political convenience of the mainstream parties – from Douglas Graham's racialisation of our fish and the dodgy Ngai Tahu settlement that he masterminded to Finlayson's theft of the foreshore and seabed and his dilution of the nation's sovereignty by "co-governance" agreements with chosen tribes.

That deceitful, racist and biased body, the Waitangi Tribunal, will have to go – preferably "by lunchtime". It is like a cancer on the body politic of the country, distorting history for the benefit of claimants, acting racistly and against the general good of a fair and united society and costing the taxpayer a sum of money that is now approaching $2 billion as it enriches a tribal elite at the expense of the rest of us. And the only way to get rid of a cancer is to cut it out completely.

Geoffrey Palmer must shoulder a very large part of the blame for the out-of-control Treaty industry that he did so much to create by his foolish decision to allow tribes to take their claims for "grievances" all the way back to 1840 – way beyond the experiences or knowledge of anybody living and so ripe for malicious fabrication by tribal leaders, revisionist historians and story-tellers. It is hard to believe that any average "man of the world" would have made such a disastrous decision and Palmer should apologise to the taxpayers of New Zealand for the billion dollars plus of largely unnecessary settlements that have flowed from his act of folly. He should also be stripped of all the perks that he currently receives from the taxpayer as an ex-Prime Minister. That is the least that he could do to reimburse the taxpayer a tiny fraction of what he has cost them.

Anything less than a colour-blind society would be a betrayal of the wonderful egalitarian society that was produced in New Zealand with equal rights and equal opportunities for all. Men have died for that noble cause and, if we let the country slide into an apartheid-like state by our laziness, apathy or ignorance, then we will be every bit as responsible for losing our country and our inheritance as the treacherous politicians and judges.

We have reached a critical point in our history where a devious, tribal elite of unlimited greed is making an unprecedented bid for control of vital resources and even part or all of the sovereignty of the nation so as to hold the rest of us to ransom.

In the interests of everyone outside this crooked elite (including ordinary Maoris who are being exploited and used by these master manipulators) these elitists and their intimidating "shock troops" of young Maori radicals and gang members must be faced down at whatever cost it takes to defeat their racist, economically crippling and nationally destructive grab for power, rights and resources.

New Zealanders have faced challenges before and on two occasions the threat to our continued existence has been dire. In the 1860s the worthy combination of the British Army, the Royal Navy, colonial militia and kupapa (friendly Maoris) faced down the threat to life, limb and property that was posed by the rebels of the Kingite and Hauhau movements. A lot of innocent blood was spilled but the expurgation of these unacceptable movements was worth it as thenceforth New Zealand developed as a single, peaceful and prosperous nation with fair and egalitarian values – at least until the Treatyist challenge of recent times.

Again in 1942 we stood naked and undefended against the Japanese menace until the U.S. Navy and Marines came mercifully to our aid.

Yes, we have got through troubles in the past and we must display similar common sense, discipline and courage in dealing with this latest threat to our rights, inheritance and expectations.

The challenge of radical Maori for New Zealand's resources and sovereignty, aided and abetted by the mischievous and racist Waitangi Tribunal, is now a serious threat to the nation, e.g. the amassing of guns at weapons camps by Tuhoe. These people are, in fact, enemies of a united and non-racial nation. And the only way to deal with an enemy is to defeat him – not appease him.

It has often been said that New Zealanders are easygoing, gullible and lazy people who are too busy watching TV and following the horses and the rugby to care about the wider issues of life. Some might be offended at this description but, if people don't start thinking about their ever increasing loss of rights and resources on a racist basis – stealing from the many for the benefit of the few – then this description will be proved not only true but also disastrous to each and every one of us.

If a majority of New Zealanders could get a grip on the facts and arguments related in this book, then rapid change could occur to end the racialisation of our once united country. The more people who find out what is really happening behind all the smoke and mirrors of the Treaty industry, the better.

On the site of the old Featherston Military Camp, several miles north of Wellington on State Highway 2, stands a monument containing the words: "This camp was the last New Zealand home for thousands of World War One soldiers. Let us keep New Zealand worthy of their dying." Yes, let's. They did not die to make non-Maori second class citizens in a racially divided society.

The Treaty of Waitangi ceded the sovereignty of New Zealand to Queen Victoria and was not a "partnership" between the Crown and Maori. Nor were there any "principles" of the treaty. The treaty gave Maoris no special rights that were not available to other New Zealanders. The Maoris are not indigenous to New Zealand; they are migrants like the rest of us albeit a little earlier than Tasman. They are New Zealand citizens of mixed race just like so many other non-European New Zealanders. They have no reason to think and act like a nation apart, which is a recipe for division, conflict and the break-up of the nation. We are not "guests" in New Zealand as some radical Maoris like Margaret Mutu have so erroneously claimed. All who came to New Zealand from Britain did so as of right since, by the Treaty of Waitangi, New Zealand became British territory and one had just as much right to sail from Liverpool to Wellington as to cross the Tamar River from Devon into Cornwall. Those who came later from other countries and who are now New Zealand citizens are also in this country AS OF RIGHT. The Maoris do not own New Zealand. It belongs to all of us.

APPENDIX 1

The final English draft of the Treaty of Waitangi, written by James Busby on 4th February 1840 and translated to Maori by H. & E.M. Williams on 4/5th February, 1840.

Her Majesty Victoria Queen of England in her gracious consideration for the chiefs and people of New Zealand, and her desire to preserve to them their land and to maintain peace and order amongst them, has been pleased to appoint an officer to treat with them for the cession of the Sovreignty of their country and of the Islands adjacent to the Queen. Seeing that many of Her Majesty's subjects have already settled in the country and are constantly arriving: And that it is desirable for their protection as well as the protection of the natives to establish a government amongst them.

Her Majesty has accordingly been pleased to appoint me William Hobson a captain in the Royal Navy to be Governor of such parts of New Zealand as may now or hereafter be ceided to her Majesty and proposes to the chiefs of the Confederation of the United Tribes of New Zealand and the other chiefs to agree to the following articles.–

Article first

The chiefs of the Confederation of the United Tribes of New Zealand and the other chiefs who have not joined the confederation, cede to the Queen of England for ever the entire Sovreignty of their country.

Article Second

The Queen of England confirms and guarantees to the chiefs and tribes and to all the people of New Zealand the possession of their lands, dwellings and all their property. But the chiefs of the Confederation and the other chiefs grant to the chiefs Queen the exclusive right of purchasing such land as the proprietors thereof may be disposed to sell at such prices as shall be agreed upon between them and the persons appointed by the Queen to purchase from them.

Article Third.

In return for the cession of the Sovreignty to the Queen, the people of New Zealand shall be protected by the Queen of England and the rights and privileges of British subjects shall be granted to them. –

Signed,

William Hobson,   Consul and Lieut. Governor

349

Now we the chiefs of the Confederation of the United tribes of New Zealand being assembled at Waitangi, and we the other chiefs of New Zealand having understood the meaning of these articles, accept of them and agree to them all

In witness whereof our names or marks are affixed. Done at Waitangi on the 4th Feb 1840. —

APPENDIX 2

Captain Gordon Brown's back-translation of the Treaty of Waitangi, March 1840

Victoria Queen of England, with her affectionate remembrance to the chiefs and tribes of New Zealand. Desires to point out to them their chieftainship in their lands, and that they may keep in peace and live in comfort thinks it right to send an English chief to advise with the natives of New Zealand, that they may accept the Government of the Queen over all their land and islands, Because there will be thousands of the Queens subjects to reside in the lands, and they are coming

The Queen is desirous of establishing a Government that all the ills now upon the natives from the English living in idleness and lawlessness may be removed.

Now the Queen is pleased to send me Wm Hobson, Captain Royal Navy, as Governor of all the island of New Zealand which will at another time be given to the Queen. The Queen says to the collection of the chiefs tribes of New Zealand and all other tribes of New Zealand, these are the laws that we have spoken of

First: That the chiefs at the assembly and those and those [sic] that are not at the assembly hereby give up entirely to the Queen forever the Govt of all their land.

Secondly. The Queen of England agrees and commits to secure to all the tribes, chiefs and all men in New Zealand, and the head chiefs to all their rights in their land, villages and other property. But the chiefs are to give to the Queen the right of purchasing all the lands that the owners are willing to sell, at the price they choose to put on it, and the Queen says she will pay for it herself.

Thirdly. This is the consent to the Govt of the Queen – The Queen will protect all the natives of New Zealand and secure to them all the rights and privileges of the people of England.

(Signed) . . Wm Hobson –
Consul and Lt Govnr

We the chiefs at the collection of the tribes of New Zealand, assembled at Waitangi, are the chiefs of New Zealand and also see the truth of these words and accept them, and therefore we put our names and marks hereto.

Done at Waitangi on the 6th day of Febr in the year of our Lord one thousand eight hundred and forty – .

APPENDIX 3

The false treaty, a composition by J.S. Freeman, Hobson's private secretary, 3rd class clerk. This is now legislated to be the official treaty.

Her Majesty Victoria Queen of the United Kingdom of Great Britain and Ireland regarding with Her Royal Favor the Native Chiefs and Tribes of New Zealand and anxious to protect their just Rights and Property and to secure to them the enjoyment of Peace and Good Order has deemed it necessary in consequence of the great number of Her Majesty's Subjects who have already settled in New Zealand and the rapid expansion of Emigration both from Europe and Australia which is still in progress to constitute and appoint a functionary properly authorized to treat with the Aborigines of New Zealand for the recognition of Her Majesty's sovereign authority over the whole or any part of those islands – Her Majesty therefore being desirous to establish a settled form of Civil Government with a view to avert the evil consequences which must result from the absence of the necessary Laws and Institutions alike to the native population and to Her subjects has been graciously pleased to empower and to authorize me William Hobson a Captain in Her Majesty's Royal Navy Consul and Lieutenant Governor of such parts of New Zealand as may be or hereafter shall be ceded to Her Majesty to invite the confederated and independent chiefs of New Zealand to concur to the following Articles and Conditions.

Article the First

The Chiefs of the Confederation of the United Tribes of New Zealand and the separate and independent Chiefs who have not become members of the Confederation cede to Her Majesty the Queen of England absolutely and without reservation all the rights and powers of

351

Sovereignty which the said Confederation or Individual Chiefs respectively exercise or possess or may be supposed to exercise or possess over their respective Territories as the sole sovereigns thereof.

Article the Second

Her Majesty the Queen of England confirms and guarantees to the Chiefs and Tribes of New Zealand and to the respective families and individuals thereof the full exclusive and undisturbed possession of their Lands and Estates Forests Fisheries and other properties which they may collectively or individually possess so long as it is their wish and desire to retain the same in their possession; but the Chiefs of the United Tribes and the individual Chiefs yield to Her Majesty the exclusive right of Preemption over such lands as the proprietors thereof may   be disposed to alienate as such prices as may be agreed upon between the respective Proprietors and persons appointed by Her Majesty to treat with them in that behalf.

Article the Third

In consideration thereof Her Majesty the Queen of England extends to the Natives of New Zealand Her royal protection and imparts to them all the Rights and Privileges of British Subjects.

[signed] W. Hobson Lieutenant Governor

Now therefore We the Chiefs of the Confederation of the United Tribes of New Zealand being assembled in Congress at Victoria in Waitangi and We the Separate and Independent Chiefs of New Zealand claiming authority over the Tribes and Territories which are specified after our respective names, having been made fully to understand the Provisions of the foregoing Treaty, accept and enter into the same in the spirit and meaning thereof in witness of which we have attached our signatures or marks at the places and the dates respectively specified. —

Done at Waitangi this Sixth day of February in the year of Our Lord one thousand eight hundred and forty. —

APPENDIX 4

Coastal Coalition Advertisement about the Foreshore and Seabed, which appeared in major daily newspapers in late 2010 and early 2011. The detailed text is as follows:

He's about to trade 2000 km of your coastline for a resource he values more. Maori Party votes.

This is an ad your prime minister doesn't want you to read. It concerns his plan to trade away New Zealand's foreshore and seabed for Maori Party votes.

Before the end of this summer:

Mr Key's government spin machine is pumping out soothing words and scathing put-downs to hide the truth about the biggest handover of public wealth and power in our history.

All we've got is this ad - and the determination of people like you.

We're the Coastal Coalition, 7,000 sand-and-sea loving Kiwis who refuse to let John Key give away our birthright and split this country in two. If you want New Zealand to remain a democracy rather than revert to a tribal aristocracy, then for the sake of your children and grandchildren please read on.

Then, and only then, decide who's telling you the truth.

Avert Apartheid Aotearoa

The purpose of National's Marine and Coastal Area (Takutai Moana) Bill is clear. It's to surrender Crown (meaning your) ownership of our beaches and seas, to make them easier for iwi. Iwi won't even have to go to Court to claim these riches - only as far as Treaty Minister Chris Finlayson's office. The deals will be done in secret. And you'll have no right of appeal.

Once awarded title, the favoured iwi will control vast reserves of mineral wealth and all future development of a massive marine treasure chest. (This is not about *mana*. It's about money.)

If you do nothing, by the end of this summer your country will be well on the way to becoming Apartheid Aotearoa, courtesy of the National Party.

353

Key questions and concerns

1. What's at stake? Control of 100,000 square kilometres of foreshore and seabed – everything out to 22km, all the airspace above that, the sea and all the minerals below.

2. How big an area is that? More than one third of the land area of New Zealand.

3. What's it worth? Our ironsands alone are worth $1 trillion. Our seabed minerals include titanium and rare earths. Then there's all future aquaculture. So it's many billions.

4. But why shouldn't iwi get a share of it?
They already do, as equal New Zealand citizens. Proceeds from our "Crown jewels" should be used to buy medicines and education for all Kiwis, not just make the part-Maori tribal aristocracy richer.

5. Who owns the foreshore and seabed now?
We all do - and have since 1840.

6. Did we have a 22 km limit in 1840? No. Back then the limit was only 5.5km (3 nautical miles). It didn't become 22krn (12 nautical miles) until 1977.

7. So, even if iwi had owned the seabed from 1840, Key is giving them four times that?
Well-spotted.

8. Have Maori always thought they owned it?
No. They must have agreed it was owned by the Crown. Otherwise iwi would have included the foreshore and seabed in Treaty claims to the Waitangi Tribunal. None did.

9. Why do iwi think they own it now?
Because a Bench of activist judges in 2003 said they might have a chance.

10. Was that why Helen Clark reaffirmed Crown ownership?

Yes. She thought Parliament (our highest court) should secure the coastline for all Kiwis, not just coastal iwi.

11. And John Key wants to surrender Crown ownership?
Yes. He wants no-one to own the foreshore and seabed.

12. Why does he want no-one to own it?
So we'll all be powerless to object when iwi claim it (since we've just given it away!).

13. Why is he so keen for iwi to get it?
To appease his Maori Party allies and their clients the tribal aristocrats - who, as always, will pocket most of the money.

14. How else is he making it easier for iwi to claim the coast?
He's radically lowered the qualifying bar, so the floodgates will open.

15. How has he lowered the bar? Under the present law, only iwi who own land next to the foreshore and seabed can make a claim for title. But John Key is waiving that requirement

16. Don't iwi have to test their claims in Court?
They do under the present law. But Key is waiving that requirement too.

17. Why doesn't Key want iwi to go to Court?
Because he knows that in an open court most of them won't win.

18. So where will iwi have to prove their claims now?
In Chris Finlayson's office. Non-iwi Kiwis will be shut out of this secret 'negotiation' - with no right of appeal.

19. But wasn't Finlayson Ngai Tahu's lawyer?
Yes. And now he's both the Minister for Treaty Settlements and the Attorney-General who approves those settlements!

20. Are you saying he's biased? We certainly are. During the public consultation process he really only listened to Maori. He set up a biased

review panel, ignored non-iwi submissions, and has refused all calls to release the summary of them.

21. What do iwi want? Customary title to the whole foreshore and seabed (for starters)

22. And what is customary title?
Effectively it's privatising the coast to iwi.

23. What rights will customary title give iwi?
The right to by-pass the Resource Management Act and veto and extract payment for everything that happens on their stretch of coast. The right to develop the area and mine its mineral wealth. The right to all new aquaculture developments. The right to impose iwi resource plans on central and local government.

24. Will iwi get any other kind of title?
Yes. *Mana tuku iho* (ancesatral recognition) will be given to all coastal iwi and cover the whole foreshore and seabed

25 What sort of activities could iwi charge for?
Just about everything, from boat ramps, moorings, wharves and marinas to aquaculture, mining, oilwells, tourism, pipelines and cables.

26 Are we still guaranteed free access to the beach and sea?
No. First Chris Finlayson ducked the question. Under pressure, he said public access would be free. But he couldn't show where his Bill says that. Why? Because he'd sneakily left out the current ban on charging!

27 Can iwi deny beach access?
Yes. The government says iwi can bar the public from any area the iwi decides is *wahi tapu* (sacred). Maori wardens can fine you up to $5,000 for going there.

28 Would iwi really do that?
It happens now on beaches they don't even own. Former Maori M.P. Dover Samuels said, "We'll eventually get the whole coast under *wahi tapu*, since every part of it contains the bones of our ancestors."

29. Can we challenge a *wahi tapu* we think isn't fair? No. Iwi have sole rights to decide what is sacred. You have no right to object.

30. How much foreshore and seabed will iwi get customary title to? Finlayson says 2,000km

31. Will this satisfy iwi desires?
No. Any iwi victory just spawns more claims. The Maori Party say they won't stop until the whole of our 200-nautical mile economic zone is in Maori title.

32. Why is the Maori Affairs Select Committee hearing submissions on this bill - won't the new law greatly enrich its members' tribes?
It's an outrageous conflict of interest. Just another case of Key and Finlayson denying the public a fair hearing.

33. What mandate does John Key have to surrender our coast?
None at all. His mandate was to abolish the Maori seats, not champion Maori sovereignty. It's a massive betrayal

Four things you can do right now to stop him.

1 Send in a submission to the Maori Affairs Select Committee before November 19. (It's easy - see our website.) Tell them the coast must stay in Crown ownership for all New Zealanders. Tell them National must withdraw its bill.

2 Email John.Key@parliament.govt.nz. Tell him you'll never vote National again if he trades your coast for votes.

3 Send money so we can keep campaigning. Donate using the coupon or online at www.CoastalCoalition.co.nz

4 Tell your friends what John Key is up to. Show them this ad. It's their country and their coast, and their Prime Minister has no mandate to give it away.

APPENDIX 5

Roll of Infamy – The M.P.s who stole the beaches off the people of New Zealand by voting for the Marine and Coastal Area Act at its final reading:

National Electorate MPs (41):

John Key, Helensville,
Bill English, Clutha-Southland,
Gerry Brownlee, Ilam,
Simon Power, Rangitikei,
Anne Tolley; East Coast,
Tony Ryall, Bay of Plenty,
Nick Smith, Nelson,
Judith Collins, Papakura
Paula Bennett, Waitakere
Wayne Mapp, North Shore
Nathan Guy, Otaki
Chris Tremain, Napier
Lockwood Smith, Rodney
Eric Roy, Invercargill
Murray McCully, East Coast Bays
Lindsay Tisch, Waikato
Phil Heatley, Whangarei
Jonothan Coleman, Northcote
John Carter, Northland
Maurice Williamson, Pakuranga
Shane Arden, Taranaki-King Country
Paul Hutchison, Hunua
Colin King, Kaikoura
Sandra Goudie, Coromandel
Chris Auchinvolke, West Coast
Jo Goodhew, Rangitata
Nicky Kaye, Auckland Central
Jacqui Dean, Waitaki
Lotuhiga Peseta Sam, Maungakiekie
Chester Borrows, Wanganui
David Bennett, Hamilton East

Tim Macindoe, Hamilton West
Amy Adams, Selwyn
Simon Bridges, Tauranga
Louise Upston, Taupo
Craig Foss, Tukituki
John Hayes, Wairarapa
Alan Peachey, Tamaki
Todd McLay, Rotorua
Jonathan Young, New Plymouth
Jamie Lee Ross, Botany

National List MPs (17):

Chris Finlayson; Georgina Te Heu Heu, Tim Groser, David Carter, Stephen Joyce, Kate Wilkinson, Tau Henare, Nicky Wagner, Jacky Blue, Katrina Shanks, Melissa Lee, Bakshi Kanwaljit Singh, Aaron Gilmore, Paul Quinn, Hekia Parata, Michael Woodhouse, Cam Calder

Maori Party MPs (4):

Pita Sharples (Tamaki Makaurau),
Tariana Turia (Te Tai Hauauru),
Te Ururoa Flavell (Waiariki),
Rahui Katene (Te Tai Tonga)

Peter Dunne (Ohariu)

Total: 63

Appendix 6

Treaty Settlements in detail

Treaty of Waitangi settlements detailed in the following pages come from the Office of Treaty Settlements website. The data is arranged into self-explanatory columns, and the table shows how settlements have evolved over the past 23 years. Total redress agreed to and mostly paid to January 9, 2013, is $1.98-billion, as shown. The financial redress total became sensitive as it approached the $1-billion figure (in 1994 dollars or $1.5-billion today), which is the figure that triggers relativity clauses (top-ups) in the Waikato-Tainui and Ngai Tahu settlements. Persistent questioning got the Office of Treaty Settlements and South Island-based tribe Ngai Tahu to confirm that the relativity clause was triggered for the year ended June 30, 2012. Those clauses would provide Waikato-Tainui with 17 percent of settlements over $1-billion and Ngai Tahu with 16.1 percent.

The Office of Treaty Settlements argues that Waikato River settlements are not historical redress despite the preamble of the river settlement deed saying that the "1995 Waikato Raupatu Claims Settlement Act expressly excluded certain claims from the settlement including the claims of Waikato-Tainui in relation to the Waikato River which arise as a result of the Raupatu [confiscations] of the 1860s and its consequences".

Anybody studying this information should be aware that the financial value of the settlement is always greater than the dollar amount shown because settlements include unspecified accumulated interest, leases for buildings, land, and forestland, and rights of first refusal (RFR) to buy surplus properties for up to 172 years. In addition, no dollar value has been given for the substantial number of cultural redress properties transferred. Forestry rentals are not included in the redress total even though forestry rentals were transferred to tribal ownership in 1989.

The National-led government had an election promise to settle all treaty claims by 2014, but has since said that it would not meet that deadline. With 37 settlements completed, 17 awaiting legislation, three awaiting tribal ratification, 15 at the detailed negotiations stage, and a number of others yet to be negotiated, there is a long way to go.

Prime Minister Jim Bolger at the Ngai Tahu settlement signing on November 21, 1997, said: "It will allow Ngai Tahu as a tribe to develop a workable economic base". Subsequently, some have assumed that treaty settlements would bring some kind of economic salvation to Maori. But this is not the case. If total settlements of $3.5-billion were divided among an estimated total Maori population of 673,000, each person would receive about $5,200, which is hardly life-changing. However, settlement cash is not shared among rank and file but is mostly kept by the tribal elite.

There is little sign of interest beyond the individuals directly involved in settlements or tribal business. Only around 50 percent of registered members of tribes are concerned enough to vote on whether to accept settlement deals. Non-Maori are by definition excluded from the whole process. The directors of today's tribal corporations have only slim ancestral links to the people who allegedly suffered up to 172 years ago, and have, in most cases, more blood of the coloniser.

The information here was first published at www.nzcpr.co.nz and may be found there under the "Treaty Transparency" panel on the New Zealand Centre for Political Research home page, where it is regularly updated. Otherwise, information may be found at the Office of Treaty Settlements website "Progress of Claims" page at http://nz01.terabyte.co.nz/ots/fb.asp?url=livearticle.asp?ArtID=-1243035403

Treaty of Waitangi settlements January 9, 2013.

Settlement	Year bill passed	Financial and commercial redress
## *Awaiting legislation*		
Te Atiawa o Te Waka-a-Maui		
Picton, Waikawa Bay		$11.76m plus interest purchase and leaseback of four properties 19 deferred-selection properties, right to buy 11,750ha of forest land and receive $7.75m in accumulated rentals 169-year RFR over listed properties including Nelson Marlborough Institute of Technology 100-year shared RFR
Ngāti Koata		
Northern South Island		$11.76m plus interest purchase and leaseback of four properties 16 deferred-selection properties right to buy 9000ha of forest land and receive $7.75m in accumulated rentals 169-year RFR over listed properties including Nelson Marlborough Institute of Technology 100-year shared RFR

Cultural redress	Co-management	Value $m
flora and fauna guardians in five areas 13 sites vested in the tribe, 7 with others two sites totalling 28,602ha jointly vested overlay classifications over Farewell Spit, Heaphy Track, Waikoropupu Springs Statutory Acknowledgements, Deeds of Recognition over 29 headlands, mountains, reserves, rivers, streams associated with the banded dotterel 53 names to change, 12 sites named	relationship accords with local councils Conservation, fisheries, taonga, minerals protocols Letters of introduction to museums River and freshwater advisory committee Conservation memorandum	11.76
co-operation payment of $500,000 right to erect a pouwhenua advice on Waikawa Bay marine environment mineral fossicking rights		0.5
six sites vested in the tribe, one with others four overlay classifications Statutory Acknowledgements, Deeds of Recognition over 12 areas Statutory Acknowledgement over the northern South Island coastal marine area tribal trustee to advise on conservation plan for customary use of fauna and flora association with Separation Point affirmed statement of maritime association 53 geographic names change, 12 new names mineral fossicking rights Moawhitu fishing reserve right of way	relationship accords with local councils Conservation, fisheries, taonga, minerals protocols Letters of introduction to museums River and freshwater advisory committee Conservation memorandum	11.76

Settlement	Year bill passed	Financial and commercial redress
Ngāti Koroki Kahukura		
3500 members Karapiro area		$3m plus interest Right to buy and lease back Pukeatua school 172-year RFR on surplus Crown properties $250,000 towards Manu Tioriori Visitor Centre
Ngāti Rangiwewehi		
1100 members Te Puke area		Financial redress $6m in cash, property Option to buy Crown property 171-year RFR over Kaharoa Primary School land (1.3364ha)
Tapuika		
420 members Te Puke area subgroup of Te Arawa		Financial redress $6m ($2.5m already received in 2008) includes 12 Te Puke commercial properties Kaharoa Forest, Te Matai North, Te Matai South, and Puwhenua Forest with with Ranginui and Rangiwehi.
Ngāti Toa		
4500 members Cook Strait area		$75.235m financial redress including $10m for loss of maritime empire Option to buy 19 properties Will buy 34,000ha of the Crown forest land in the northern South Island

Cultural redress	Co-management	Value $m
Maungatautari mountain reserve to hapu $3.73m cultural funding Statutory acknowledgements over Waikato River, lakes Arapuni and Karapiro and three other areas Deeds of recognition for rivers, lakes, streams	Letters of introduction Waikato River co-management	3 3.73
Hamurana Springs, Penny Road Scenic Reserve, and other sites vested in tribe.	Protocols with Conservation, Energy and Resources	6
Lower Kaituna Wildlife Management Reserve vested jointly in Tapuika and Ngati Whakaue,who will gift it to the Crown $500,000 for Te Puke cultural presence 12 sites totalling 209ha vested in Tapuika overlay classification over 65ha Opoutihi deeds of recognition over sites, waterways five geographic name changes	Protocols with Arts, Culture and Heritage, and Energy and Resources. Conservation Agreement Kaituna River co-governance	6
20 sites totalling 267ha vested in Ngati Toa 54ha in 3 sites vested with Ngati Toa, others Vested, gifting back, overlay classifications on parts of Kapiti Island Statutory acknowledgements over Cook	Te Tau Ihu River/Fresh water advisory Committee Regional councils recognise Ngati Toa Cook Strait guardian plan Letters of introduction	75.235

Settlement	Year bill passed	Financial and commercial redress
		RFR for surplus Crown properties -- of 169 years in North Island, 100 years in S.I.
Raukawa		
29,421 members Waikato		$21.143-million being the balance of $50-million, $28.857-million of which was paid in the CNI forestry settlement $530,000 on settlement day Right to buy deferred selection properties listed A right of first refusal for 172 years to surplus Crown property in the tribe's area $8-million for Mighty River Power deal
Ngai Ranginui		
7647 members Tauranga		$38.0276-million Right of first refusal for fish species introduced into the quota management system

Cultural redress	Co-management	Value $m
Strait, northern South Island coastal marine area, Porirua Harbour, Wellington Harbour, four other areas Statutory acknowledgements and deeds of recognition over 23 areas, rivers, scenic reserves, and coastal areas. Overlay classifications over Brother Islands and Wairau Lagoon $500,000 for Ngati Toa's southern claims Place-name changes for 12 North Island sites and 9 South Island sites Legislation to acknowledge Ka Mate haka	Joint board for Whitireia Park reserve Ngati Toa to manage the Queen Elizabeth Park campground site	
Wharepūhunga, Pureora o Kahu overlay classifications	Waikato River co-management Waipa River co-management in negotiation	21.143
Statutory acknowledgements over eight sites, three rivers, seven lakes, seven geothermal fields.		0.53
Deeds of recognition over four sites, three rivers, seven lakes.		
Eight cultural redress properties vested		8
Two new geographic names and one change		
$3-million for the cultural fund		3
$50,000 for pouwhenua marker poles		0.05
13 cultural redress sites vested in Ranginui Site on public conservation land at Oraeroa vested in Ranginui as sacred (wahi tapu),	Six names change and two sites named Management role in the Margaret Jackson Wildlife Management Reserve	38.028

Settlement	Year bill passed	Financial and commercial redress
		48 land bank properties for Ranginui to buy 3 LINZ sites for Ranginui to buy Puwhenua Forest Lands will transfer to an entity with Ngati Rangiwewehi and Tapuika.
Tamaki Collective		
Auckland		Financial redress addressed through specific tribal negotiations. 172-year RFR for surplus land deferred selection purchse rights
Te Rarawa		
9871 members Far North		$33.84-million plus interest 172 years RFR on surplus govt property May buy Te Karae and part of Sweetwater farms, six schools (leased back), 526.36ha Takahue Block forest, 6 LINZ properties, eight land bank properties, and two more jointly joint ownership of 21,283ha Aupori forest land $2.2m share of forestry accumulated rentals
NgaiTakoto		
489 members Far North		$21.04 million plus interest, discount on farm purchase price part of Sweetwater Crown-owned farm NgaiTakoto, Te Aupouri, Te Rarawa, and Ngati Kuri will jointly own the 21,283ha forest land on the Aupouri peninsula and will receive a share of accumulated rentals -- $2.2m

Cultural redress	Co-management	Value $m
subject to conservation covenant to protect biodiversity values, no public access. Te Hopuni site transferred Omokoroa School land transferred sale and leaseback to Education Ministry	Relationship protocols with Conservation, Primary Industries, Arts Culture and Heritage	
14 mountains vested in collective four islands vested in collective acknowledgement of importance of Waitemata, Manukau harbours 18 names to change, two new names	mountains except North Head and Mt Smart subject to co-governance creation of mountain authority conservation land co-governance conservation management plan	
17 cultural redress properties transferred	Warawara Forest Park co-governance	33.84
$137,500 in recognition of associations with Ninety Mile Beach	Protocols with Culture and Heritage, Primary Industries	0.138
$530,000 to preserve taonga and promote Rarawa history	joint conservation input	0.53
statutory acknowledgements over a harbour, two rivers, coastal marine area		
four names change		2.2
$2.4 million cultural redress fund , $812,500 social accord implementation	relationship protocols to be issued by the ministers for Culture and Heritage, Energy and Resources, Primary Industries.	21.04 2.4 0.813
$137,500 in recognition of associations with part of the $400,000 Ninety Mile Beach Board Ninety Mile Beach contribution		0.138

Settlement	Year bill passed	Financial and commercial redress
		NgāiTakoto will own an undivided 20 percent share of future rentals

Te Aupōuri

9300 members, one of five Te Hiku o Te Ika iwi Far North		$21.040m plus interest, to be used to buy: Te Aupouri's share of Aupouri Crown Forest Land, Te Raite and Cape View Farms, part of Te Kao School, residential property at Te Kao $2.2m share of accumulated forest rentals collective redress involves joint ownership of Aupouri forest 172-year RFR to surplus Crown properties

Waitaha

2000 members Tauranga		$7.5m plus interest Right to buy three landbank properties Right to buy and lease back five education properties in Te Puke Right to buy eight remaining land banked properties if not bought by others

Cultural redress	Co-management	Value $m
10 properties vested in NgāiTakoto six jointly vested with other Te Hiku iwi Six place names will be altered		 2.2
11 properties totalling 1300.1ha will be vested in Te Aupōuri 7 properties 245.5ha total incl 2 lake beds and 1 island vested jointly with other iwi cultural redress fund of $380,000 Statutory acknowledgements over 6 sites 19 name changes includes Te Oneroa-a-Tōhe /Ninety Mile Beach and Cape Reinga / Te Rerenga Wairua $812,500 towards social accord implementation part of the $400,000 Ninety Mile Beach Board contribution $137,500 to install signs, raise pouwhenua	relationship protocols with Culture and Heritage, Energy and Resources, and Primary Industries. joint committee to manage Ninety Mile Beach A new Te Hiku Conservation Board	21.04 0.38 2.2 0.813 0.4 0.138
Eight sites vested Deeds of Recognition on conservation areas Statutory acknowledgements over: Ōtanewainuku Peak, three creeks eight streams, one river and coastal area from Maketū to Mauao $3m for an education fund in the name of prophet Hakaraia $300,000 to document the story of Waitaha and of Hakaraia $500,000 to restore Hei Marae $500,000 to fund a needs assessment	Relationship protocols with Conservation,Culture and Heritage, and Energy and Resources	7.5 3 0.3 0.5 0.5

Settlement	Year bill passed	Financial and commercial redress
Ngati Whatua o Kaipara		
A subgroup of Ngati Whatua which has 14,724 members Kaipara		$22.1m plus interest Right to buy: Woodhill Forest and receive accumulated rentals, as well as the land under six schools, which will all be back to the Crown leased, plus properties at 8, 16 and 20 Old Woodcocks Rd, Kaipara Flats 169-year RFR over listed surplus properties 170-year RFR over Paremoremo Prison
Ngati Apa ki te Ra To		
700 members Northern South Island		$28.374m, including interest, $12.24m redress in lieu of licensed Crown Forest Land deferred selection purchase rights 169-year RFR over surplus Crown properties
Rangitane o Wairau		
1000 members Northern South Island		$25.374m including $12.24m in lieu of licensed Crown Forest Land, plus interest Deferred selection right to buy govt properties Right to buy, lease-back Crown properties 169-year RFR over surplus Crown properties

Cultural redress	Co-management	Value $m
Nine sites totalling 675ha vested in the tribe: Statutory acknowledgements over seven conservation areas and over coastal area. Six place names change, nine sites named.	Relationship protocols with Conservation, Culture and Heritage and Economic Development, and Agriculture and Forestry.	22.1
Overlay classifications over alpine tarns, and Heaphy Track jointly Alpine tarns and 28,500ha of North West Nelson Forest Park vested in Ngāti Apa jointly with other Te Tau Ihu iwi to be gifted back. Four sites totalling 29ha vested in Ngati Apa. A 0.2061ha Matangi Awhio site jointly vested Statutory acknowledgment over all the Te Tau Ihu coastal marine area, and over five rivers 12 further acknowledgements over six areas, and acknowledgements jointly with other iwi May apply to take Nelson Lakes park eels Right to take by hand any sand, shingle or natural material from a river bed 65 geographic name changes	involvement in advisory committee on local authority planning and decision making Relationship protocols with Conservation, Fisheries, Energy, and Arts, Culture and Heritage.	28.374
Overlay classifications over Lake Rotoiti and Lake Rotoroa (jointly with Ngāti Apa), and Wairau Lagoons and Boulder Bank.	involvement in advisory committee on local authority planning Relationship protocols with Conservation, Fisheries, Energy, and Arts, Culture and Heritage	$25.37

Settlement	Year bill passed	Financial and commercial redress
Ngati Kuia		
1600 members Northern South Island		$24.874m including $12.24m in lieu of licensed Crown Forest Land, plus interest Deferred selection right to buy govt properties Lease-back right to buy Crown properties 169-year RFR over surplus Crown properties
TOTAL		

Cultural redress	Co-management	Value $m
Vests nine sites totalling approximately 20ha in Rangitāne, A 0.2061ha Matangi Awhio site jointly vested Statutory acknowledgment over all the Te Tau Ihu coastal marine area and over four rivers Eight further acknowledgements relating to Wairau Lagoon, plus joint acknowledgements May remove argillite boulders by hand. May apply to hunt muttonbirds on Titi and Chetwode Island 65 geographic name changes		
Eight sites totalling 16ha transferred A 0.2061ha Matangi Awhio site jointly vested Overlay classifications over Titi, Chetwode and Maud islands, statutory acknowledgements over coastal area and five rivers 15 further acknowledgements and deeds Right to remove argillite boulders by hand. Right to take by hand any sand, shingle or natural material from a river bed 65 geographic name changes	Establishes a stand-alone iwi advisory committee for local councils Relationship protocols with Conservation, Fisheries, Energy, and Arts, Culture and Heritage	24.874
		389.525

Settlement	Year bill passed	Financial and commercial redress
Completed		
Ngati Manuhiri		
Subgroup of Ngati Wai which has 4869 members. East coast north of Auckland	2012	$9m plus interest Warkworth District Court land to be leased back to the Crown Pakiri School land leased back to Crown South Mangawhai Crown forest land and the accumulated rentals 169 years RFR over 82 Crown properties
Ngati Whatua o Orakei		
Part of Ngati Whatua which has 14724 members	2012	$18m plus interest $2m received in 1993 Railways Settlement 170 year RFR over surplus Crown properties
Rongawhakaata		
4700 members Gisborne	2012	$22.24m plus interest five properties transferred from landbank may buy two sale and leaseback properties 169-year RFR over five properties 100-years RFR over two conservation sites Right to buy four surplus Crown properties in six-month deferred selection

Cultural redress	Co-management	Value $m
Little Barrier Island nature reserve vested in Ngati Manuhiri then gifted to people of NZ Five other sites totalling 70ha vested in Ngati Manuhiri Two overlay classifications Statutory acknowledgements over Crown-owned portion of Mt Tamahunga, coast area, six rivers, Ngaroto lakes, Tohitohi o Reipae (The Dome); Pohuehue Scenic Reserve and Kawau Island.;	Relationship protocols with Conservation, Economic Development, Culture and Heritage.	9
Tamaki isthmus mountains, Hauraki Gulf islands redress Statutory acknowledgements over Kauri Point Purewa Creek renamed as Pourewa Creek	Relationship protocols with Conservation, Culture, Heritage, Economic Development Inclusion on fisheries advisory committee	18 2
original features of Te Hau ki Tūranga vested in Rongawhakaata. Eight sites transferred Cultural redress for Ngā Uri o Te Kooti Rikirangi includes: Vesting of Matawhero Government Purpose Reserve, Wharerata Rd. $500,000 to Te Whare Rakei o Te Kooti $200,000 for Ngā Uri o Te Kooti Rikirangi Te Kooti relationship with Conservation Statutory acknowledgements: Rongowhakaata coastal marine area, and seven rivers. $360,000 for Rongawhakaata culture revamp $100,000 to Te Rūnanga o Tūranganui a Kiwa for a memorial to those killed by the Crown	Relationship protocols with Conservation, Culture, Heritage, Economic Development, Energy Resources, Environment, Fisheries.	22.24 0.5 0.2 0.36 0.1

Settlement	Year bill passed	Financial and commercial redress
Ngai Tāmanuhiri		
1700 members Gisborne	2012	$11.07m plus interest 1858 Waingake Rd vested in Ngai Tāmanuhiri Wharerata Forest transfers to a company in which Ngai Tamanuhiri buys a 50% share. two year deferred selection purchase of land under Muriwai School and leaseback or 169-year RFR on land under Muriwai School, and Pakowhai Reserve.
Ngati Makino		
2000 members Bay of Plenty	2012	$9.8m plus interest $1.5m already paid for marae restoration RFR over five sites of public conservation land right to a sale and leaseback of the Otamarakau School land
Maraeroa A and B Blocks		
Lake Taupo area	2012	$1.578m $220,000 commercial redress property

Cultural redress	Co-management	Value $m
Young Nick's Head, Mangapoike transferred Statutory acknowledgements over Waipaoa River, Ngai Tamanuhiri coastal marine area. $180,000 for cultural revitalisation $100,000 for memorial to those killed by the Crown	Relationship protocols with Conservation, Economic Development, Fisheries, Culture and Heritage, and Environment.	11.07 0.18 0.1
8 sites totalling 720ha be vested in tribe Overlay classification over 256ha of Lake Rotoma Scenic Reserve. Deed of recognition and statutory acknowledgement over 256ha of Lake Rotoma Scenic Reserve. Statutory acknowledgement over 416.2ha of Lake Rotoiti Scenic Reserve.	Relationship protocols with Arts, Culture and Heritage and Energy and Resources	9.8 1.5
Overlay classification for Pureora o Kahu Statutory acknowledgement of ancestors' relationship with the site Five sites vested in governance entity $40,000 to buy culturally significant land $11,600 to buy land not available for transfer	Govt must consult with governance entity Partnership deal over 16 areas and streams	1.578 0.22 0.04 0.01

Settlement	Year bill passed	Financial and commercial redress
Ngati Porou		
72,000 members East Coast north of Gisborne	2012	$90m plus interest Six Crown properties will be vested in Ngāti Porou Ngāti Porou will buy Ruatoria and Tokomaru Licensed Crown Forest Land two year deferred selection purchase and leaseback of 21 Crown properties 170 year RFR to buy surplus Crown-owned and Housing New Zealand Corporation properties within the Ngāti Porou area The return of surplus Crown properties subject to Public Works Act offer-back requirements.
Ngāti Pahauwera		
6000 members East Coast south of Wairoa	2012	$20m plus interest, which includes the value of any Crown forest land purchased Thirteen Crown properties will be vested in Ngāti Pähauwera, including Mohaka Crown Forest Land, Rawhiti Station, five surplus Wairoa District Council properties. 100 year RFR on surplus Crown properties in the area
Ngati Manawa		
3500 members. Central North Island based in Murupara	2012	$12.2m of the CNI forest lands, plus interest $2.6m for special projects Right to buy four land bank properties Right to buy five deferred selected properties 50-year RFR for one surplus Crown property

Cultural redress	Co-management	Value $m
$20m plus interest Strategic conservation partnership Fifteen sites totalling 5898ha vested in Ngāti Porou. DOC to manage some sites. Statutory acknowledgements over the Waiapu and Uawa Rivers and their tributaries, the Tūranganui River and the Waimata River	Relationship protocols with Conservation, Economic Development, Culture, Heritage	110
Te Heru o Tūreia Conservation Area to be vested in Ngäti Pahauwera Iwi to retain 160ha at summit of Te Heru o Tūreia and 52.9ha by Mohaka River most of which is to be gifted to people of NZ 16 sites totalling 1087ha transferred to Ngäti Pahauwera Statutory Acknowledgement over part of the Earthquake Slip Conservation Area Ngäti Pähauwera to manage hangi stone removal	Conservation co-management charter rights to nominate members to discuss Mohaka River water Joint Regional Planning committee involvement Relationships introduction letters Fisheries sustainability input. Resource consent input Gravel extraction agreement	20
Five sites totalling 744ha transferred Nine wāhi tapu sites vested fee simple. Three schools transferred with lease-back 4 sites vested with Ngati Manawa and Ngati Whare. Statutory acknowledgements over five sites, four waterways. Overlay classifications and transfer and gift back of Tāwhiuau (a mountain). Deed of Recognition regarding Pukehinau and Te Kōhua. Two place names to change. RFR on five freshwater fish.	Appointment Conservation and Fisheries advisory committee, input into the management of freshwater fisheries, dams Relationship protocols with Conservation, Fisheries, Energy, and Arts, Culture and Heritage, letters of introduction	12.2 2.6

Settlement	Year bill passed	Financial and commercial redress
Ngati Whare		
3400 members Central North Island	2012	$15.7m comprising redress already provided in the 2008 CNI Settlement
Ngati Apa (North Island)		

Rangitikei-Manawatu area 3200 members	2010	$16m plus interest
		$6m forestry rentals .
		NZ Units (carbon credits) allocation
		Sale and leaseback of:
		  403ha of Wanganui forest
		  Marton Court House
		  Marton Police Station
		  Wanganui Prison

Cultural redress	Co-management	Value $m
Deeds of Recognition over four rivers. Framework for agreement on a management system for the Rangitaiki River Recognition of relationship with pou rāhui sites in Crown ownership		
$1.976m in cultural redress giftings Redress related to Tūwatawata (mountain), and Te Whāiti-Nui-a-Toi Canyon $1m for Project Whirinaki Regeneration Trust Transfer seven cultural sites totalling 36.2ha Return five wāhi tapu sites totalling 10.2952ha Joint vesting of four sites totalling 13ha Three place names to change Statutory Acknowledgements over two sites and Whirinaki River. Deed of Recognition over parts of Urewera National Park, Whirinaki River $200,000 to restore Te Whaiti Court House	Whirinaki Conservation Park co-governance Relationship protocols with Conservation, Fisheries, and Arts, Culture and Heritage Letters of engagement	15.7 1.976 1 0.2
12 sites totalling 214ha transferred to tribe Statutory acknowledgements for nine rivers, lakes, lagoons and coastal area Deeds of recognition for five sites Two name changes		$16.00

Settlement	Year bill passed	Financial and commercial redress
Waikato River		
Waikato-Tainui 33,429 members	2010	$20m Sir Robert Mahuta endowment $10m river initiatives fund $40m river initiatives fund $3m co-management funding $1m for co-management a year for 27 years $2.8m ex-gratia payment
Te Arawa 42,159 members		$3m initial payment $7m after three months $1m co-management funding a year for 19 years
Ngāti Raukawa	2010	$21m given after clean-up trust is set up. $7m a year for 27 years $3m to the Raukawa Settlement Trust Followed by $7m three months later And $1m a year for 20 years
Ngāti Tuwharetoa 34,674 members		Crown pledges to contribute towards costs incurred by Tuwharetoa Maori Trust Board
Maniapoto 33627 members	2012	$3m co-management funding for Maniopoto $7m three months later $1m for co-management a year for 19 years
Taranaki Whanui ki Te Upoko o Te Ika		
17,000 members	2009	$25.025m cash plus interest, 10-years right to buy and lease back land under Archives NZ, the National Library, the High Court, and Wellington Girls' College, 100-year RFR on certain Crown-owned land, entities, and State-owned enterprises, a two-year right to buy surplus govt properties a six-month right to buy Defence properties at Shelly Bay.

Cultural redress	Co-management	Value $m
34 sites of significance vest in Waikato Raupatu River Trust 120 managed properties vest in tribe to be transferred to Waikato Regional Council Statutory acknowledgement for Waikato River	Waikato Raupatu River Trust established Waikato River Authority set up Waikato River Clean-up Trust established The Crown and Waikato-Tainui begin co-management of Waikato River	$20.00 $10.00 $40.00 $3.00 $27.00 $2.80
	co-management of river begins	$3.00 $7.00 $19.00
Acknowledgement that Waikato River represents Raukawa	co-management of river begins	$21.00 $189.00 $3.00 $7.00 $20.00
		$3.00 $7.00 $19.00
33 sites including lakes,Ward Island, urupa,schools and other transferred Statutory acknowledgements include: Wellington Harbour bed, coastal area, Hutt River, Rimutuka Forest Park Deeds of recognition include Rimutaka Forest Park, Wainuiomata Scenic ReserveTurakirae Head Scientific Reserve Eight name changes		$25.03

Settlement	Year bill passed	Financial and commercial redress
Central North Island Forests Iwi Collective		
Ngäi Tühoe - 32670 Ngäti Tuwharetoa - 34674 members Ngäti Whakaue Ngäti Whare Ngäti Manawa Ngäti Rangitihi, who did not agree, Raukawa	2008	$223m rentals held in trust since 1989. $13m a year rentals for 35 years from 2008 an allocation of NZ Units (carbon credits) 176,000ha of the CNI licensed Crown forest land worth $149.564 m transferred to CNI Iwi Holdings Ltd. The Collective owns 86.7 percent, the Crown 13.3 percent.
Te Pumautanga o Te Arawa		
24,000 members	2008	Whakarewarewa Village $295,000 debt forgiven $38.6m to buy 18% of Rotoehu forest land share in CNI deal replaces $36m forest deal
Te Roroa		
3000 members	2008	$9.5m cash and land plus interest plus cost of transferring sites
Ngati Mutunga		
1300 members	2006	$14.9m Plus interest Plus right to buy surplus Crown property

Cultural redress	Co-management	Value $m
		$149.56
19 sites transferred including: Whakarewarewa Thermal Springs Reserve lake beds. Statutory acknowledgements over seven sites including Rotorua geothermal area Deeds of recognition over five sites including Mt Ngongotaha Scenic Reserve		$0.30 $38.60
24 sites totalling 2000ha transferred Including Waipoua Forest sites		$9.50
10 sites totalling 168ha.Statutory acknowledgements for 18 areas Including 4 rivers, 4 scenic reserves, a coastal area Deeds of recognition for 12 sites One name change, one new name		$14.90

Settlement	Year bill passed	Financial and commercial redress
Te Arawa Lakes		
42,159 members Located from Maketu to Tongariro	2006	$2.7m cash, $7.3m to capitalise annuity plus interest from the date of the signing plus the cost of the lakebeds returned plus $400,000 for 200 fish licences a year
Ngaa Rauru Kiitahi		
3000 members Taranaki	2005	$31m plus accrued interest plus RFR properties RFR to buy shellfish quota
Tuwharetoa (Bay of Plenty)		
3000 members	2005	$10.5m in cash and properties plus interest from the date of the signing Plus cost of transferring sites Plus the right to buy 844ha of forest land RFR to Crown geothermal assets for Tasman Pulp and Paper Mill. RFR to a Crown-owned geothermal bore and associated land
Ngati Awa		
13,000 members Eastern Bay of Plenty	2005	$42.39m of land and cash plus interest from the date of the signing $1m to restore Mataatua meeting house Ngati Awa Station Right to buy 5 percent of Owhiwa Harbour RFR to Crown-owned land

Cultural redress	Co-management	Value $m
13 lakebeds transferred to Arawa Spelling of some placenames amended		$10.40
7 cultural sites transferred Statutory acknowledgements for 3 areas topuni over Lake Beds Conservation Area Deeds of recognition for 4 sites One name change. Commercial taking of shellfish in area prohibited for 12 areas	Protocols with Conservation, Fisheries, Energy, Arts Culture and Heritage. Appointment of a governance entity	$31.00
5 sites transferred total 66ha, 1ha nohoanga camp area at Matatā Wildlife Refuge Reserve Access to traditional food restored Statutory acknowledgements for 3 areas And 1 river Deeds of recognition for 6 sites		$10.50
7 sites transferred Statutory acknowledgements over 9 areas four Deeds of Recognition 5 name changes Four camping licences (1ha nohoanga)		$43.39

Settlement	Year bill passed	Financial and commercial redress
Ngati Tama		
1000 members Taranaki	2003	$14.5m in cash plus interest from the date of the signing RFR to Crown-owned land. RFR to Crown surf clams and kina surplus quota Right to buy 10% of coast for aquaculture
Ngati Ruanui		
4000 members Taranaki	2003	$41m cash and land plus interest from the date of the signing
Te Uri o Hau		
6000 members Northern Kaipara	2002	$15.6m land and cash includes Crown Forests accumulated rentals held in trust since 1989 plus interest from the date of the signing RFR to surplus Crown-owned property RFR to quota for surf clams, tuatua, paddlecrab and toheroa
Pouakani		
Not a tribal settlement	2000	$2.65m plus the cost of the 1922ha Tahae Farm Plus interest from the date of the signing Plus the right to buy up to 1679 hectares of Pureora Central Forest

Cultural redress	Co-management	Value $m
5 sites totalling 1870ha transferred Statutory acknowledgements over 12 areas including two rivers, a swamp, the coastal marine area, three conservation areas and an historic reserve. Deeds of recognition over the same	Joint advisory committees on conservation, recreation, fisheries protocols on working with govt, local govt, fish and game	$14.50
6 cultural redress sites transferred 5 statutory acknowledgements, 4 deeds of recognition, 1 name change, 3 new names, 2 camping sites	fisheries advisory committee protocols on working with govt	$41.00
12 cultural sites totalling 30ha transferred 6 statutory acknowledgements 3 nohoanga camping sites 9 name changes, 7 new names	joint management of Haumoewaarangi's pa protocols on working with govt fisheries advisory committee	$15.60
	co-management of Titiraupenga Mountain	$2.65

Settlement	Year bill passed	Financial and commercial redress
Ngati Turangitukua		
Tuwharetoa hapu (Turangi town grievance)	1999	$5m ($304,299 cash, leaseback properties) Plus interest from the date of the signing Plus leaseback property interim payments
Ngai Tahu		
29,133 members South Island	1998	$170m total, comprising: 63 commercial properties 116 farms totalling 96,426ha 34 forests totalling 174,930ha Sale and leaseback of 7 commercial properties RFR to 4 major South Island airports, and Timberlands West Coast, Plus other properties
Te Maunga		
Re 6070m2 of land at Te Maunga	1996	$0.129m
Rotoma		
Concerns 5.2678 hectares of land	1995	$0.043m
Waimakuku		
	1995	$0.375m

Cultural redress	Co-management	Value $m
Kutai St Reserves transferred 1 name change Wahi tapu sites to be investigated		$5.00
Aoraki Mt Cook vested in tribe, gifted to Crown 17 cultural redress sites transferred runanga appointed to hold, administer 7 areas historic reserves created at 7 areas Statutory acknowledgements over 64 mountains, lakes, rivers, wetlands, lagoons 64 deeds of recognition over the same 14 topuni (overlay of Ngai Tahu values) created nohoanga camping areas created		$170.00
		$0.13
		$0.04
		$0.38

Settlement	Year bill passed	Financial and commercial redress
Waikato/Tainui raupatu		
33,429 members	1995	$170m total, comprising: about 200 unimproved properties plus 200 improved properties Leased for 31 years RFR over certain Crown-owned properties
Ngati Whakaue		
Re establishment of Rotorua	1994	$5.21m
Hauai		
Re 25.4932 hectares of land	1993	$0.716m
Ngati Rangiteaorere		
Re Te Ngae Mission Farm	1993	$0.76m
Commercial Fisheries		
	1992	$170m total An interim agreement in 1989 transferred to the Waitangi Fisheries Commission About 10 per cent of NZ's commercial quota or 60,000 tonnes Shareholdings in fishing companies $50m in cash The second part of the deal, the Sealord deal, in 1992, included: 50 per cent of Sealord Fisheries 20 per cent of new species in quota system $18m in cash
Waitomo		
	1989	The Crown transferred land at the Waitomo Caves to the claimant group, subject to a lease, and provided a loan $1m
Completed settlements total		
Grand TOTAL		

Cultural redress	Co-management	Value $m
no cultural redress included		$170.00
		$5.21
		$0.72
		$0.76
		$170.00
		$1,586.53

		$1,976.05

REFERENCES

Introduction
1. *History of the American People*, Paul Johnson, p. 434
2. *A Grammar and Vocabulary of the Language of New Zealand*, Thomas Kendall and Samuel Lee, 1820
3. *A Dictionary of the New Zealand Language*, William Williams
4. *Adventure in New Zealand from 1839 to 1844*, Edward Jerningham Wakefield, 1845, p. 409 and Old Tasman Bay, J.D. Peart, 1937, p. 68
5. *The Treaty of Waitangi*, Claudia Orange, p. 265
6. *Old New Zealand*, F.E. Maning, p. 6
7. *Maori Chiefs Asked for Queen Victoria's Laws*, Jean Jackson, Book 9, p. 161
8. The Asset Base, Income, Expenditure and GDP of the 2010 Maori Economy http://berl.co.nz/assets/Economic-Insights/Economic-Development/Maori-Economy/BERL-2011-The-Asset-Base-Income-Expenditure-and-GDP-of-the-2010-Maori-Economy.pdf

Why the Treaty?

1. *From Hongi Hika to Hone Heke,* O. Wilson, 1985, pp 17-19
2. *The Long White Cloud,* William Pember Reeves, p 111-113
3. Ibid
4. *Between Worlds; first meetings between Maori and Europeans, 1778-1815* Anne Salmond (1997), p 177
5. *Note on Maori casualties in their tribal wars 1801-1840*, James Rutherford papers. MSS and Archives A-42, Box 16, Folder 6, Special Collections, the University of Auckland Library
6. *When two Cultures Meet*, John Robinson, p 109-11
7. *The New Zealand Wars*, Vol. I, James Cowan, 1922 p 16
8. *When Two Cultures Meet*, John Robinson, p 126
9. Some sources report around 500
10. *Note on Maori casualties in their tribal wars 1801-1840*, James Rutherford papers MSS and Archives A-42, Box 16, Folder 6. Special Collections, the University of Auckland Library. His estimate is discussed in *When Two Cultures Meet.*
11. *From Hongi Hika to Hone Heke, a Quarter Century of Upheaval*, Ormond Wilson, 1985, p 167
12. Quoted in *When Two Cultures Meet*, John Robinson
13. Dictionary of New Zealand Biography website
14. *Te Kerikeri*, ed. Judith Binney, 2007 (Chapter 12)
15. *An account of New Zealand and the formation of the Church Missionary Society's mission in the northern island*, Willaim Yate, London, 1835.
16. Ibid
17. *When Two Cultures Meet*, John Robinson, p 87-92
18. *The Story of New Zealand*, Vol. I, A.S. Thomson, 1859, pp 312, 313 and 327
19. *When Two Cultures Meet*, P. 88
20. 18th June, 1838

21. *Narrative of a residence in various parts of New Zealand*, Charles Heaphy, London, 1842, p 66
22. *Sydney Herald*, 1 June, 1840, reporting Instructions from Lord Normanby to Captain Hobson of 14 and 15 August, 1839
23. *When Two Cultures Meet*, John Robinson

Real Treaty, False Treaty; The True Story of Waitangi
1. *No Sort of Iron*, R. Duff, Art Galleries and Museums Association of New Zealand, 1969, p 8
2. *Song of Waitaha*, B. Brailsford, p 34
3. *The Penguin History of New Zealand*, Michael King, p 41
4. *Kei Put ate Wairau*, W.J. Elvy
5. *Fatal Frontiers* (2006) and *This Horrid Practice* (2008)
6. *This Horrid Practice*, Paul Moon, p 149.
7. Ibid, P. 151
8. At Bluff School there was one half-caste in my class, Mick Anglem, a descendant of Captain Anglem, after whom the highest point on Stewart Island, Mt. Anglem, is named. I also knew the last full-blood at Karitane, Johnny Matthews, or "Hoani Matiu" as his gravestone describes him.
9. *Conversion and Civilisation of the Maories of the Far South of New Zealand*, Rev. J.F.H. Wohlers, 1881, pp 123-134
10. *Te Wiremu*, Caroline Fitzgerald, 2011
11. *Letters from the Bay of Islands*, Caroline Fitzgerald (2004)
12. *The Great Divide*, Ian Wishart (2012) Chapter 3.
13. *Fatal Frontiers*, Paul Moon, p 103
14. *A Penguin History of New Zealand*, Michael King, p 154
15. Paul Moon in New Zealand Herald, 5 October, 2010
16. Christchurch Press, 10 May, 2010
17. James Stephen, written instructions to Hobson, 14 August, 1839
18. S. Martin quoted by Martin Doutre in The Littlewood Treaty (2005) p 115
19. Ibid, p 68
20. Ibid, p 61
21. *The Life of Henry Williams*, Vol. II, H. Carleton
22. *Te Wiremu*, Caroline Fitzgerald, p 317
23. He is "Thomas" in Whyte's list Claudia Orange gives his name as Thoms.
24. There is a microfilm copy of this despatch and attachments in the library of Auckland University
25. USS Vincennes letter book copy of Despatch No. 64, microfilm 1262, University of Auckland library, pp 163-4. Original at Kansas Historical Society, Topeka, Kansas, U.S.A.
26. Martin Doutre, personal communication, May, 2007
27. R. Maunsell to Lay Secretary, 30 March, 1840 CMS Archives CN/M v 12 pp 308-9
28. E-mail from John Key's office to Bruce Moon, 23 December, 2009
29. *The Treaty of Waitangi*, Claudie Orange, p 103
30. Ibid, pp 131-2

31. *Was There a Treaty of Waitangi, and Was it a Social Contract?* B.Easton, Archifacts, April, 1997, p 21-49
32. Preserved in the Archives of the Colony; the English Drafts of the Treaty of Waitangi, P. Parkinson, Revue Juridique Polynesianne, Cahier Special Monograph, 2006
33. Private communication, 20 February, 2012
34. Proceedings of the Kohimarama Conference comprising Nos. 13-18 of the Maori Messenger, republished by Victoria University of Wellington and available online
35. A. Salmond personal communication to Bruce Moon, 24 August, 2010
36. *The Treaty of Waitangi*, T.L. Buick (1914) pp 281-2
37. *The Travesty of Waitangi*, Stuart Scott, p 113
38. Ibid, p 126
39. Ibid, p 166
40. *Penguin History of New Zealand*, Michael King, p 519
41. *The Travesty of Waitangi*, Stuart Scott, p 126

Property Rights – A Blessing for Maori New Zealand
1. *Philosophy: Who Needs It?*, Ayn Rand, 1982
2. *Migrations and Cultures*, T. Sowell, 1996
3. *Conquest and Culture*, T. Sowell, 1999
4. *The Evolution of the Polynesian Chieftains*, P.V. Kirch, 1984
5. *An Ecological Approach to the Ploynesian Settlement of New Zealand*, M.S McGlone, A.J. Anderson and R.N. Holdaway in The Origins of the First New Zealanders, ed. D.G. Sutton, Auckland University Press, 1984
6. Ibid
7. *A History of New Zealand*, Keith Sinclair, 2000, p 79
8. NewZealandHistory.net.nz Te Rauparaha Biography, Steven Oliver, 1998
9. *Maori Auckland*, David Simmons,, 1987
10. Ibid
11. *Man's Rights* and *The Virtue of Selfishness*, Ayn Rand, 1964
12. *Reflections on the Revolution in France*, Edmund Burke, 1790
13. *The Mystery of Capital*, H. De Soto
14. Ibid
15. *The Noblest Triumph; Property and Prosperity Through the Ages*, Tom Bethell, 1998
16. *Capitalism, the Unknown Ideal*, Ayn Rand, 1966

The Law Made Simple
1. *Engagement Strategy for the Consideration of Constitutional Issues*, Constitutional Advisory Panel, May 2012
2. p 157
3. All these quotations, and plenty more, appear in *Maori Sovereignty, the Maori Perspective*, ed. Hineani, Auckland, 1995
4. Section 18 (1) (i)
5. The older definition, which can be found in statutes as recent as the Maori Affairs Act 1953 and the Electoral Act 1956, was that "Maori" meant "a

person belonging to the aboriginal race of New Zealand, and includes a half-caste and a person intermediate in blood between half-castes and persons of pure descent from that race". Anyone with less Maori blood than a half-caste was therefore not entitled to call himself Maori but had to be identified with the races of his greater genetic inheritance"

6. *People Power or Ethnic Elites*, Elizabeth Rata for N.Z. Centre for Political Research, 2011
7. For a more detailed description see Judicial Activism and the Treaty: the Pendulum Returns, D.J. Round, 2000 9 Otago Law Review p 653 at 667 ff.
8. For a fuller description of the Declaration, its implications and absurdities see U.N. Declaration on the Rights of Indigenous Peoples, D.J. Round 2009 NZ Law Journal, p 392
9. The final clause of the Declaration's preamble
10. Professor Jeremy Waldron in *The Half-Life of Treaties: Waitangi Rebus Sic Stantibus*, 2005 11 Otago Law Review 161 reminds us that treaties often just decline and die from changed circumstances. And many circumstances have changed in New Zealand since 1840.
11. It follows, therefore, that British xovereignty over New Zealand was not, as a matter of law, acquired by the Treaty; and it follows also that the issue of whether or not a particular chief or tribe assented to the Treaty is completely irrelevant to the sovereignty of the Crown, which exists everywhere.
12. A useful summary of many different lists of "orinciples" may be found in *Environmental Management and the Principles of the Treaty*, Parliamentary Commissioner for the Environment, 1988
13. *Te Runanga and Wharekauri Rekohu* v *Attorney-General* [1993] 2NZLR 301
14. (1990) 14 NZULR 5
15. *Tainui Maori Trust Board* v *Attorney-General* [1989] 2NZLR 513
16. Resource Management Law Reform Working Paper No. 27, 1988
17. (1989) 19 VUWLR 335
18. *Constitutional Myths and the Treaty of Waitangi,* Paul McHugh [1991] NZLJ 316
19. Report of the Commission on Constitutional Arrangements, Proceedings of the 1998 General Synod
20. For a more detailed examination of his record in Treaty cases see *Judicial Activism and the Treaty. The Pendulum Returns*, D.J. Round 2000 9 Otago Law Review 653 and De Balaenis Noviter Inventus [1996] NZLJ 164
21. See Justice in the Firing Line, NZ Herald, 5 may, 2012
22. In re the *Ninety Mile Beach case* [1963] NZLR 461
23. [2003] 3 NZLR 643
24. For a convenient summary of the rule and its exceptions see *New Zealand's legal System, the Principles of Legal Method*, Professor Richard Scragg 2005 and *The New Zealand Legal System*, Structures and Processes, McDowell and Webb (2006)
25. An honourable semi-exception must be made in the case of Gault, P., who agreed in part with the *Ninety Mile Beach* decision; although he considered that *seabed* might still be open to Maori claims, he accepted that once the

ownership of dry land had been established by a Maori Land Court there could be no further claims to the foreshore.

26. *Sovereignty in the Twenty-First Century: Another Spin on the Merry-go-round,* Sian Elias (2003) 14 Public Law Review, 148 and in the 2011 Harkness Henry lecture, printed as *Fundamentals: A Constitutional Conversation* (2011) Waikato Law Review 1. For further commentary see Two Futures: A Reverie on Constitutional Review, D.J. Round, (2011) 12 Otago Law Review p 525
27. (2003) 14 Public Law Review 162
28. Ibid p 163
29. (2011) Waikato Law Review, Vol 19, p 8
30. *The Relationship of Parliament and the Courts,* E. Thomas (2000) 31 VUWLR 5
31. Metiria Turei, co-leader of the Green Party at a 2005 election meeting at the Christchurch Polytechnic said, "Maori want two things; they want independence and they want funding" So, they want the freedom to do what they llike with other people's money.
32. Even less politically controversial judicial activism has been so described, e.g. *Judicial Activism – Justice or Treason*, Professor Thomas Campbell (2003) 10 Otago Law Review 307
33. *Te Runanga and Muriwhenua* v *Attorney-General* [1990] 2 NZLR 641 at 651
34. Now Section 6 (4A)
35. See also *Truth or Treaty, Commonsense Questions about the Treaty of Waitangi,* D.J. Round, p 89-92
36. *Lawyers, Historians, Ethics and the Judicial Process* (1998) 28 VUWLR 87
37. Wai 776 Report
38. The editor of Capital Letter, 20 July, 1999
39. The Press, 15 February, 2011

Parihaka – The Facts
1. *Moriori*, Michael King
2. *The War in Taranaki,* W.I. Grayson
3. Poverty Bay Herald, 28 September, 1881
4. Waikato Times, 14 September, 1880
5. Grey River Argus, 14 September, 1881
6. *The New Zealand Wars*, Vol II, James Cowan, p 494
7. Manawatu Times, 12 November, 1881 and Tuapeka Times, 9 November, 1881

Twsited Morality – the Matawhero Massacre
1. *The New Zealand Wars*, Vol. II, James Cowan, p 268
2. Ibid
3. Ibid
4. p 7
5. Hawkes Bay Herald, 10 April, 1869, P. 2
6. *The New Zealand Wars*, Vol. II, James Cowan, p 328

Twisted History – Treaty Settlements Criticised

1. *Adventure in New Zealand*, E.J. Wakefield, Vol I, p 39
2. Dictionary of N.Z. Biography "Guard, Elizabeth" by Don Grady
3. Letter, 20 December, 2012
4. *A Mission of Honour; the Royal Navy in the Pacific 1769-1887*, John McLean, 2010, pp 110-113 and *The Harriet Affair – a frontier of Chaos* NZ History Online
5. The First Colonist, Samuel Deighton 1821-1900, Mike Butler
6. http://www.treasury.govt.nz/budget/2012/estiamtes/est12treneg.pdf   Vote Treaty Negotiations
7. Newest Country in the World, Paul Moon, p 155
8. http://www.teara.govt.nz/TheSettledLandscape/ClaimingTheLand//LandOwnership/1/en Maori and land ownership
9. The Taranaki Report: Kaupapa Tuatahi, Chapter 1.(Waitangi Report)
10. New Zealand – the War and what led to it, Samuel ironside, Taranaki Herald, 16 October, 1869, p 5
11. http://www.nzetc.org/tm/scholarly/tei-SmiHist-t_1-body_1-d18-d8.html The Fall of Pukerangiora Pa 1831
12. Taranaki Report, First Purchases, (Waitangi Tribunal)
13. *New Zealand – the War and what led to it*, S. Ironside, Taranaki Herald, 16 October, 1869, p 5
14. Ibid
15. First Purchases, Taranaki Report (Waitabgi Tribunal)
16. *New Zealand – the war and what led to it*, S. Ironside, Taranaki Herald, 16 October, 1869, p 5
17. http://nzetc.victoria.ac.nz/tm/scholarly/tei-TurOldPtl-front-d3.html   Maori deeds of old private land claims, 1815-40
18. First Purchases, Taranaki Report, Waitangi Tribunal
19. Ibid
20. *New Zealand – the war and what led to it*, S. Ironsode, Taranaki Herald, 16 October, 1869, p 5
21. Ibid
22. *The Realms of King Tawhiao*, Dick Craig, p 33
23. *New Zealand – the War and what led to it*, S. Ironside, Taranaki Herald, 16 October, 1869, p 5
24. Ibid
25. *The Great Divide*, Ian Wishart, p 227
26. *The New Zealand. Wars*, Vol I, James Cowan, p 447
27. N.Z. Herald, 31 August, 2000
28. http://www.tainui.co.nz/docs/1995_Deed_of_Settlement.pdf Waikato Tainui Deed of Settlement
29. *The Realms of King Tawhiao*, Dick Craig, p 35
30. Ibid, p 50
31. *The New Zealand Wars*, Vol I, James Cowan, p 234-5
32. *Wairarapa: An Historical Excursion*, A.G. Bagnall (1976), p 213
33. *The New Zealand. Wars*, Vol I, James Cowan, p 252
34. Ibid, p 241

35. http://www.nzhistory.net.nz/war/new-zealand-wars/end James Cowan, New Zealand History Online
36. http://www.nzhistory.net.nz/politics/treaty/the-treaty-in-practice/waikato-tainui Legacy of War: settling the Waikato-tainui claim, New Zealand History Online
37. *The Great Divide*, Ian Wishart, p 233
38. http:www.waitangi-tribunal.govt.nz/doclibrary/public/researchnatview/vol3/chapt14.pdf Rangahaua Whanui – National Overview, The South Island
39. http://www.ngaitahu.iwi.nz/Whakapapa-Registration/NgaiTahu1848Census.pdf
40. Ngai Tahu Land Report http://www.waitangi-tribunal.govt.nz/scripts/reports/reports/27/48D0AE4D-9734-410D-B1EE-14EB761D349.pdf
41. http://www.recreationaccess.org.nz/files/free_radical_27_ngai_tahu.pdf Alan Everton, *Ngai Tahu's Tangled Web* in Free Radical
42. Ibid
43. Ngai Tahu Report 1991 Waitangi Tribunal
44. Ibid, The History of Inquiries
45. Ibid
46. Alexander Mackay, Compendium of Official Documents relative to native affairs in the South Island, 1872, Vol. 2, p 148
47. Same as footnote 41
48. The Gilfedder and Haszard Commission of Inquiry 1914 in Ngai Tahu Report 1991, Waitangi Tribunal
49. *The Corruption of N.Z. Democracy*, John Robinson, p 7
50. *Struggle Without End*, Ranginui Walker, p 162
51. The History of Inquiries, Ngai Tahu Report, 1991. Waitangi Tribunal
52. Ibid
53. http://www.nzhistory.net.nz/culture/the-1920s/1927 Royal Commission on land confiscations
54. Settlements of major Maori Claims in the 1940s; A Preliminary Historical Investigation, Richard Hill, Dept. Of Justice, Wellington, 8th November, 1989
55. Ibid
56. Ibid
57. Same as footnote 41
58. *New Zealand's Constitution in Crisis*, Geoffrey Palmer, p 75
59. Ibid, p 76
60. Ibid, p 79
61. Ibid, p 81
62. *Struggle Without End*, Ranginui Walker, p 255
63. *New Zealand's Constitution in Crisis*, Geoffrey Palmer, p 80
64. Ngai Tahu Report 1991, Waitangi Tribunal
65. *New Zealand's Constitution in Crisis*, Geoffrey Palmer, p 81
66. http://www.waitangi-tribunal.govt.nz/doclibrary/public/researchnatview/vol1/execsum.pdf Page 2
67. *New Zealand's Constitution in Crisis*, Geoffrey Palmer, p 82-3

68. Ibid, p 85-6
69. Maori Definitions, Michael Bassett, 24th June, 2003
70. Same as footnote 66
71. Tribunal's Flawed Experiment, N.Z. Herald, 10 July, 2004
72. Ibid
73. *When Two Cultures Meet, the N.Z. Experience*, John Robinson, p 239
74. Tribunal's Flawed Experiment, N.Z. Herald, 10 July, 2004
75. The Eight Crown Purchases – An Overview, Ngai Tahu Report 1991, Waitabgi Tribunal
76. *The Treaty of Waitangi – An Explanation*, Apirana Ngata, p 37
77. Report Summary, Ngai Tahu Report 1991
78. Dominion, 26 February, 2000
79. Otago Daily Times, 9 October, 1997
80. Ngai Tahu Vesting Act 1997
81. http://www.nzherald.co.nz/nz/news/article.cfm?c_1d=1&objectid=10830869
82. http://www.nzherald.co.nz/nz/news/article.cfm?c_id=1&objectid=10849687
83. Autonomy, Chapter 1 of Taranaki report, Waitangi Tribunal
84. *The Great Divide*, Ian Wishart, p 203
85. Dominion, 2 September, 2008
86. New Zealand Herald
87. New Zealand Herald, 29 July, 2011
88. Dominion, 1 January, 2012
89. Ibid, 1 July, 2009
90. Ibid, 9 January, 2013-01-07
91. Evening Post, Wellington, 3 April, 1998
92. Sunday Star-Times, 30 May, 2010
93. Q and A, TV1, 6 June, 2010
94. Dominion, 31 December, 2012
95. N.Z. Herald, 3 November, 2012
96. Waikato Times, 20 December, 2012
97. Dominion, 14 September, 2004

Wellington Settlements and Consequences
1. "We own the water – Maori king", N.Z. Herald website, 14 September, 2012
2. Dominion, 10 September, 2012
3. Ibid, 11 September, 2012
4. Ibid, 26 June, 2008, and *The Corruption of New Zealand Democracy*, John Robinson, p 58
5. Dominion, 12 September, 2012
6. *The Maori and the Criminal Justice System – A New Perspective*, Part 2, Dept. of Justice.
7. *Robbery by Deceit*, Allan Titford, 1998
8. Translated from the Maori, Ngata, 1922
9. *The Corruption of New Zealand Democracy*, John Robinson
10. *When Two Cultures Meet*, John Robinson
11. Office of Treaty Settlements 1994. Described in When Two Cultures Meet, pp 246-7

12. *The Waitangi Tribunal and New Zealand History*, Giselle Byrnes, p 152
13. Letter from Finlayson to John Robinson, 15 March, 2012
14. Dominion, 8 April, 2011
15. www.ots.govt.nz
16. Deed of settlement 2.167
17. Deed of settlement 1.22
18. *Life and Times of Te Rauparaha*, P. Butler
19. Deed of settlement 1.39.1
20. *When Two Cultures Meet*, John Robinson, pp 93-100
21. Deed of settlement 1.39.2
22. *Life and Times of Te Rauparaha*, P. Butler, pp 40-2
23. Ibid pp 51-2
24. *Adventure in New Zealand*, Vol II, E.J. Wakefield, pp 334-5, 374-5, 378-9
25. *When Two Cultures Meet*, John Robinson, p 134, and *A Mission of Honour; The Royal Navy in the Pacific 1769-1997*, John McLean, pp 278-80
26. *The New Zealand Wars*, Vol. I, James Cowan, p 121
27. Ibid
28. *Life and Times of Te Rauparaha*, P. Butler, p 84
29. *The Treaty of Waitangi – An Explanation*, Apirana Ngata, 1922
30. *When Two Cultures Meet*, John Robinson, pp 121-3
31. Letter from Trevor Morley to Dominion, 4 September, 2012
32. Claim Wai 2235, November, 2011
33. *The stirring times of Te Rauparaha*, W.T.L. Travers, p 160
34. *The Corruption of New Zealand Democracy*, John Robinson, p 44
35. *A political economy of neo-tribal capitalism*, A. Rata, p 226-7
36. Dominion, 23 August, 2012
37. Ibid, 26 April, 2012
38. Ibid, 8 September, 2012
39. Ibid, 17 September, 2012

Stealing the Beaches
1. *Victims of Group Think*, Irving L. Janis, New York
2. *Institutes of Justinian*, Book II, c. 1, s.1.
3. *Large Earthquakes and the abandonment of pre-histooric coastal settlements in 15th century New Zealand*, James Goff and Bruce McFadgen in Geoarchaeology, Vol. 18, No. 6 (2003) www.interscience.wiley.com
4. *The Gathering Storm over the Foreshore and Seabed*, Hugh Barr, Appendix 4
5. Ibid
6. Dominion, 5 March, 2009
7. NZPA Media release 31 March, 2010
8. National Business Review, 9 April, 2010
9. Dominion, 23 November, 2009 "Smith plays down $2 billion ETS windfall for Maori"
10. National Business Review, 9 April, 2010
11. Dominion, 25 June, 2010
12. Ibid 20 July, 2010
13. Ibid 12 April, 2010

14. Ibid
15. Ibid, 15 June, 2010
16. Ibid
17. Ibid
18. *Trick or Treaty*, Douglas Graham, Wellington, 1997, p 80
19. Otago Daily Times, 18 June, 2010
20. http:www.converge.org.nz/pma/fsarev.htm#gov2
21. National Business Review, 9 April, 2010
22. Dominion, 17 July, 2012
23. NZ Centre for Political Research, 31 July, 2010
24. National Business review, 2 November, 2012
25. N.Z. Press Assn, 31 March, 2010
26. Paper for new Zealand Centre of Political Research, 31 July, 2010
27. Ngati Whatua Claims Settlement Act 2012
28. North Shore Times, 28 March, 2012, and NZ Herald of the same date
29. North Shore Times, 10 August, 2012
30. National Business Review, 28 September, 2012
31. http://www.justice.govt.nz/policy/constitutional-law-and-human-rights/marine-and-coastal-area-takutai-moana/current-marine-and-coastal-applications/

The Extortionate Claim for Plants, Animals and Maori Knowledge

1. *When Two Cultures Meet,* John Robinson, pp 24-5
2. Ibid, pp 212-5
3. Otago Daily Times, 19 June, 1997
4. *The Future Eaters*, Tim Flannery, p 55
5. *The Third Wave, Poisoning the Land*, Bill Benfield, pp 10-15

Fish

1. *Fishing in pre-European New Zealand*, Dr. Foss Leach, published by N.Z. Journal of Archaeology – Special Publication, Vol. 15 (2006)
2. Ibid P. 308
3. Ibid P. 309
4. Dominion, 25 February, 2012
5. National Business Review, 20 December, 2012
6. Sunday Star-Times, 21 October, 2012
7. National Business Review, 20 December, 2012
8. Ibid
9. Ibid
10. Dominion, 16 April, 2012
11. N.Z. Centre for Political Research, 19 September, 2012, *Maori Fishing Reserves – Bureaucratic Racism*, Roger Beattie
12. Ibid
13. Ibid

Water

1. Otago Daily Times, 9 July, 2012

2. NZ Herald, 25 September, 2012
3. Dominion, 15 September, 2012
4. Ibid, 13 March, 2010
5. Ibid
6. Dominion, 1 October, 2012
7. Evidence to Waitangi Tribunal reported in N.Z. Herald, 17 July, 2012
8. Estimate by Willie Te Aho, head of Ngai Tahu's negotiating group on the Emissions Trading Scheme in a leaked e-mail reported in the Dominion, 23 November, 2009
9. National Business review, 7 September, 2012
10. Ibid
11. Dominion, 5 September, 2011
12. Ibid
13. Dominion, 24 February, 2012
14. Ibid, 28 May, 2011

Separate and Privileged
1. Maori privilege claim, Waitangi Tribunal http://www.waitangi-tribunal.govt.nz/sce
2. Dominion, 30 May, 2012
3. Ibid, 8 February, 2012
4. Stuff, 9 February, 2012
5. Dominion, 31 May, 2012
6. Ibid, 9 April, 2012
7. Stuff, 15 November, 2012
8. Dominion, 11 May, 2012
9. Stuff, 15 November, 2012
10. http://www.ird.govt.nz/maori-organisations/eligibility/marae/ Maori organisations – Inland Revenue
11. Dominion, 2 October, 2012
12. http://www.tgh.co.nz/default.asp?sid=11&sid=13&aid= Tainui Group Holdings
13. N.Z. Herald, 29 July, 2011
14. Waikato Times, 11 June, 2011
15. The asset base, income, expenditure and GDP of the 2010 Maori economy http://berl.co.nz/assets/Economic-Insights/Economic-Development/Maori-Economy/BERL-2011-The-Asset-Base-Income-Expenditure-and-GDP-of-the-2010-Maori-Economy.pdf
16. Briefing to the incoming Minister of Maori Affairs, December, 2011
17. Maori Economic Development, Alex Sundakov, N.Z, Institute of Economic Research, 2003
18. Ministry of Social Development fact sheets hyyp://www.msd.govt.nz/about-msd-and-our-work/publications-resources/statistics/benefit/2012-national-benefit-factsheets.html
19. Prime Minister Helen Clark speaking to Michael Laws, Radio Live, 5 March, 2004

20. http://www.scoop.co.nz/stories/PA1209/S00034/new-zealanders-encouraged-to-challenge-racist-policies.htm
21. Matua Rautia: The Report on the Kohanag Reo Claim   http://www.waitangi-tribunal.govt.nz/doclibrary/public/report_pdfs/Wai2336-download-report-18102012.pdf
22. Same as 16
23. http://www.treasury.govt.nz.budget/2011/estimates/131.htm   Vote   Maori Affairs, Budget 2011
24. Qualification of Electors Act 1879
25. Maori Representation, Report of the Royal Commission into the Electoral System, 1986
26. Struggle Without End, Ranginui Walker, p 203
27. Ibid, p 247
28. N.Z. Herald, 18 October, 2012
29. Who Speaks Maori in New Zealand? Richard Benton
30. Same as 21
31. The Unintended Outcomes of Institutionalising Ethnicity, The case of Maori Education   in   New   Zealand,   Elizabeth   Rata http://www.educ.cam.ac.uk/research/academicgroups/equality/Rata1-2.pdf
32. Ibid
33. Ibid
34. http://www.maorilanguage.info/mao_lang_faq.html   Maori   Language Information
35. http://www.waitangi-tribunal.govt.nz/reports/viewchapter.asp?reportID=6113B0B0-13B5-400A-AFC7-76F76D3DDD92&chapter=8   Waitangi Tribunal Report on te Reo Maori Claim
36. http://www.educationcounts.govt.nz/statistics/schooling/ncea-attainment/participation-and-attainment-of-maori-students-in-national-certificate-of-educational-achievement 2009
37. http://edcounts.squiz.net.nz/_data/assets/pdf_file/0017/7505/else-maori-summary.pdf
38. http://tazi.net/JFriedman/IMG/pdf/RataSS_20Address12Feb05.pdf
39. http://www.ots.govt.nz/ What is a treaty settlement
40. Ibid, Mandating for negotiations
41. Ibid, Claimant funding
42. Ibid, Negotiation
43. Ibid, Governance entity
44. Ibid, Legislation
45. Briefing to the incoming Minister of Maori Affairs, Tr Puni Kokiri, December, 2011
46. Ibid, p 263-4
47. Ibid, p 265
48. http://www.teara.govt.nz/en/urban-maori/5   Urban and Tribal Authorities, Encyclopedia of New Zealand

49. http://www.kaupapamaori.com/assets//provider_success.pdf Iwi and Maori Provider Success, Te Puni Kokiri, 2002
50. http://www.ttoh.iwi.nz/ Te Taiwhenua o Heretainga
51. http://www.nzcpr.com/weekly358.htm The cure for poverty is growth, Muriel Newman
52. http://www.scoop.co.nz/stories/PA0006/S00307.html Better economics but socially racial apartheid
53. Dominion, 4 December, 2000 "Widening The Gaps"
54. Ibid, 29 February, 2000 "Pay cuts for bosses who don't aid Maori"
55. http://www.legislation.govt.nz/act/public/2000/0091/latest/DLM80051.html Public Health and Disability Act 2000
56. Evening Post, 13 September, 2000 "Bad Way To Go"
57. ChappleMaoriEconomic Disparity.pdf Maori Economic Disparity, Simon Chapple
58. http://www.msd.govt.nz/about-msd-and-our-work/publications-resources/journals-and-magazines/social-policy-journal/spj18/ethnicity-based-research-andolitics18-pages18-30.html Ethnicity based research and politics: snapshots from the U.S. and N.Z., Ministry of Social Development
59. Dominion, 14 December, 2000 "Bill favouring race"
60. Ibid, 7 December, 2000 "Race clause to stay in job bill"
61. http://en.wikipedia.org/wiki/Closing_the_gaps
62. http://www.maoriparty.org/index.php?pag=nw&id=42&p=m257ori-set-to-rise-in-nz-poll.html
63. Dominion, 8 February, 2012 "Pakeha increasingly resentful"
64. Local Government (Auckland Law Reform) Act 2009
65. http://www.maoridictionary.co.nz/index.cfm?wordID=3452
66. N.Z. Herald, 4 September, 2012 "Brewer slams Maori plan as unrealistic"
67. Ibid, 3 September, 2012 "New territory for Council"
68. http://www.hrc.co.nz/hrc_new/hrc/cms/files/documents/13-Oct-2010_11-46-09_HRC_Maori_representation.pdf
69. http://www.hrc.co.nz/newsletters/whitiwhiti-korero/english/2011/11/nelson-and-waikato-agree-to-establish-maori-seats-on-council/
70. http://breakingviewsnz.blogspot.co.nz/2012/04/mike-butler-what-maori-and-non-maori.html
71. N.Z. Herald, 3 October, 2012 "Fletcher quits gulf position"
72. http://www.aucklandcouncil.govt.nz/en/aboutcouncil/representativesbodies/haurakigulfforum/Pages/home.aspx Hauraki Gulf Forum, Auckland Council
73. N.Z. Herald, 3 October, 2012 "Fletcher quits gulf position"
74. http://www.kahungunu.iwi.nz/ Strategic Objectives, Ngati Kahungunu Iwi Incorporated
75. Radio NZ, 17 August, 2011 "Bolivia's constitution viewed as a model for Maori"
76. Dominion, 26 January, 2008 "A three ghetto church"
77. N.Z. Herald, 2 July, 2012 "Call for Maori to get half church's assets"
78. http://anglicantaonga.org.nz/News/General-Synod/landmark Landmark decision on assets

The Brownwashing of New Zealand – Treaty Indoctrinatiom
1. *The New Zealand Wars*, Vol I, James Cowan, p 3
2. pp 214
3. Ibid
4. *The Treaty of Waitangi, An Explanation*, Apirana Ngata (1922)
5. Ibid
6. E-mail of 23 July, 2012
7. Letter to Dominion, 8 March, 2012
8. Letter to Bruce Moon, 20 December, 2012
9. Ibid
10. Letter to Bruce Moon, 20 January, 2013
11. Page 87
12. Dominion, 25 Jamuary, 2013-01-07

Meet the Members of the Constitutional Advisory Panel
1. Constitutional Arrangements Committee, Inquiry to review New Zealand's existing constitutional arrangements, August, 2005, p 6
2. N.Z, Herald, 4 August, 2011
3. Cultural Survival Quarterly, Issue 24.1, Spring 2000
4. 30 April, 2008, Presentation of Settlement Proposals

Epilogue
1. Southern Cross, Auckland, 2 November, 1876
2. Ibid, 6 January, 1871
3. Wikipedia
4. Quoted on p 448 of The New Zealand Wars, Vol. I, James Cowan
5. Evening Post, 3 May, 1909
6. N.Z. Herald, 17 August, 1882
7. Dominion, 16 June, 2010
8. *South of Suez*, London, 1950, p 73
9. NBR Online, 19 January, 2013
10. N.Z. Herald, 7 February, 1940
11. Reported in Evening Post, Wellington, 13 March, 1901

INDEX